CREATING COOL™
WEB DATABASES

Joseph T. Sinclair
Carol McCullough

CREATING COOL™
WEB DATABASES

Joseph T. Sinclair
Carol McCullough

IDG Books Worldwide, Inc.
An International Data Group Company

Foster City, CA ♦ Chicago, IL ♦ Indianapolis, IN ♦ Southlake, TX

Creating Cool™ Web Databases

Published by
IDG Books Worldwide, Inc.
An International Data Group Company
919 E. Hillsdale Blvd, Suite 400
Foster City, CA 94404
www.idgbooks.com (IDG Books Worldwide Web Site)

Library of Congress Catalog Card No.: 96-77081

ISBN: 0-7645-3019-4

Printed in the United States of America

10 9 8 7 6 5 4 3 2 1

1O/SQ/QZ/ZW/FC

Distributed in the United States by IDG Books Worldwide, Inc.

Distributed by Macmillan Canada for Canada; by Contemporanea de Ediciones for Venezuela; by Distribuidora Cuspide for Argentina; by CITEC for Brazil; by Ediciones ZETA S.C.R. Ltda. for Peru; by Editorial Limusa SA for Mexico; by Transworld Publishers Limited in the United Kingdom and Europe; by Academic Bookshop for Egypt; by Levant Distributors S.A.R.L. for Lebanon; by Al Jassim for Saudi Arabia; by Simron Pty. Ltd. for South Africa; by Pustak Mahal for India; by The Computer Bookshop for India; by Toppan Company Ltd. for Japan; by Addison Wesley Publishing Company for Korea; by Longman Singapore Publishers Ltd. for Singapore, Malaysia, Thailand, and Indonesia; by Unalis Corporation for Taiwan; by WS Computer Publishing Company, Inc. for the Philippines; by WoodsLane Pty. Ltd. for Australia; by WoodsLane Enterprises Ltd. for New Zealand. Authorized Sales Agent: Anthony Rudkin Associates for the Middle East and North Africa.

For general information on IDG Books Worldwide's books in the U.S., please call our Consumer Customer Service department at 800-762-2974. For reseller information, including discounts and premium sales, please call our Reseller Customer Service department at 800-434-3422.

For information on where to purchase IDG Books Worldwide's books outside the U.S., please contact our International Sales department at 415-655-3172 or fax 415-655-3295.

For information on foreign language translations, please contact our Foreign & Subsidiary Rights department at 415-655-3021 or fax 415-655-3281.

For sales inquiries and special prices for bulk quantities, please contact our Sales department at 415-655-3200 or write to the address above.

For information on using IDG Books Worldwide's books in the classroom or for ordering examination copies, please contact our Educational Sales department at 800-434-2086 or fax 817-251-8174.

For authorization to photocopy items for corporate, personal, or educational use, please contact Copyright Clearance Center, 222 Rosewood Drive, Danvers, MA 01923, or fax 508-750-4470.

 is a trademark under exclusive license to IDG Books Worldwide, Inc., from International Data Group, Inc.

About the Authors

Joseph T. Sinclair has been Chairman of the Multimedia Internet SIG of the North Bay Multimedia Association and was formerly on the Board of Directors and Director of Education. He teaches digital multimedia at the College of Marin, conducts seminars on business on the Internet for the Digital Village, and is a contributing editor for Multimedia Reporter.

Carol McCullough is a private computer consultant specializing in database applications and internet web sites. She teaches classes in marketing on the internet and HTML programming. She has designed and taught classes on SQL programming, database tuning, and database design.

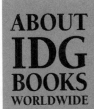

ABOUT IDG BOOKS WORLDWIDE

Welcome to the world of IDG Books Worldwide.

IDG Books Worldwide, Inc., is a subsidiary of International Data Group, the world's largest publisher of computer-related information and the leading global provider of information services on information technology. IDG was founded more than 25 years ago and now employs more than 8,500 people worldwide. IDG publishes more than 270 computer publications in over 75 countries (see listing below). More than 90 million people read one or more IDG publications each month.

Launched in 1990, IDG Books Worldwide is today the #1 publisher of best-selling computer books in the United States. We are proud to have received eight awards from the Computer Press Association in recognition of editorial excellence and three from *Computer Currents'* First Annual Readers' Choice Awards. Our best-selling *...For Dummies*® series has more than 25 million copies in print with translations in 30 languages. IDG Books Worldwide, through a joint venture with IDG's Hi-Tech Beijing, became the first U.S. publisher to publish a computer book in the People's Republic of China. In record time, IDG Books Worldwide has become the first choice for millions of readers around the world who want to learn how to better manage their businesses.

Our mission is simple: Every one of our books is designed to bring extra value and skill-building instructions to the reader. Our books are written by experts who understand and care about our readers. The knowledge base of our editorial staff comes from years of experience in publishing, education, and journalism — experience which we use to produce books for the '90s. In short, we care about books, so we attract the best people. We devote special attention to details such as audience, interior design, use of icons, and illustrations. And because we use an efficient process of authoring, editing, and desktop publishing our books electronically, we can spend more time ensuring superior content and spend less time on the technicalities of making books.

You can count on our commitment to deliver high-quality books at competitive prices on topics you want to read about. At IDG Books Worldwide, we continue in the IDG tradition of delivering quality for more than 25 years. You'll find no better book on a subject than one from IDG Books Worldwide.

John J. Kilcullen

John Kilcullen
President and CEO
IDG Books Worldwide, Inc.

WINNER
Eighth Annual
Computer Press
Awards 1992

WINNER
Ninth Annual
Computer Press
Awards 1993

IDG Books Worldwide, Inc., is a subsidiary of International Data Group, the world's largest publisher of computer-related information and the leading global provider of information services on information technology. International Data Group publishes over 276 computer publications in over 75 countries. Ninety million people read one or more International Data Group publications each month. International Data Group's publications include: **ARGENTINA:** Annuario de Informatica, Computerworld Argentina, PC World Argentina; **AUSTRALIA:** Australian Macworld, Client/Server Journal, Computer Living, Computerworld, Computerworld 100, Digital News, IT Casebook, Network World, On-line World Australia, PC World, Publishing Essentials, Reseller, WebMaster; **AUSTRIA:** Computerwelt Osterreich, Networks Austria, PC Tip; **BELARUS:** PC World Belarus; **BELGIUM:** Data News; **BRAZIL:** Annuário de Informática, Computerworld Brazil, Connections, Super Game Power, Macworld, PC Player, PC World Brazil, Publish Brazil, Reseller News; **BULGARIA:** Computerworld Bulgaria, Networkworld/Bulgaria, PC & MacWorld Bulgaria; **CANADA:** CIO Canada, Client/Server World, ComputerWorld Canada, InfoCanada, Network World Canada; **CHILE:** Computerworld Chile, PC World Chile; **COLOMBIA:** Computerworld Colombia, PC World Colombia; **COSTA RICA:** PC World Centro America; **THE CZECH AND SLOVAK REPUBLICS:** Computerworld Czechoslovakia, Elektronika Czechoslovakia, Macworld Czech Republic, PC World Czechoslovakia; **DENMARK:** Communications World, Computerworld Danmark, Macworld Danmark, PC Privat Danmark, PC World Danmark, PC World Danmark Supplements, TECH World; **DOMINICAN REPUBLIC:** PC World Republica Dominicana; **ECUADOR:** PC World Ecuador; **EGYPT:** Computerworld Middle East, PC World Middle East; **EL SALVADOR:** PC World Centro America; **FINLAND:** MikroPC, Tietoverkko, Tietoviikko; **FRANCE:** Distributique, Golden, Hebdo-Distributique, Info PC, Le Guide du Monde Informatique, Le Monde Informatique, Reseaux & Telecoms; **GERMANY:** Computer Partner, Computerwoche, Computerwoche Extra, Computerwoche Focus, I/M Information Management, Macwelt, PC Welt; **GREECE:** GamePro, Multimedia World; **GUATEMALA:** PC World Centro America; **HONDURAS:** PC World Centro America; **HONG KONG:** Computerworld Hong Kong, PCWorld Hong Kong, Publish in Asia; **HUNGARY:** ABCD CD-ROM, Computerworld Szamitastechnika, PC & Mac World Hungary, PC-X Magazine; **ICELAND:** Tolvuheimur/PC World Island; **INDIA:** Information Systems Computerworld, PC World India, Publish in Asia; **INDONESIA:** InfoKomputer PC World, Komputek Computerworld, Publish in Asia; **IRELAND:** ComputerScope, PC Live!; **ISRAEL:** People & Computers; **ITALY:** Computerworld Italia, Computerworld Italia Special Editions, Macworld Italia, Networking Italia, PC Shopping, PC World Italia, PC World/Walt Disney; **JAPAN:** DTP World, HP Open World Japan, Macworld Japan, Nikkei Personal Computing, Open World Japan, OS/2 World Japan, SunWorld Japan, Windows World Japan; **KENYA:** East African Computer News; **KOREA:** Hi-Tech Information/Computerworld, Macworld Korea, PC World Korea; **MACEDONIA:** PC World Macedonia; **MALAYSIA:** Computerworld Malaysia, PC World Malaysia, Publish in Asia; **MEXICO:** Computerworld Mexico, Macworld, PC World Mexico; **MYANMAR:** PC World Myanmar; **NETHERLANDS:** Computer! Totaal, LAN Magazine, LanWorld Buyers Guide, Macworld, MTB, Network World, PC World New Zealand; **NIGERIA:** PC World Nigeria; **NORWAY:** Computerworld Norge, Computerworld Privat (Datamagasinet), CW Rapport Norge, IDG's KURSGUIDE, Macworld Norge, Multimediaworld, PC World Ekspress, PC World Nettverk, PC World Norge, PC World's Produktguide, Windows World Spesial; **PAKISTAN:** Computerworld Pakistan, PC World Pakistan; **PANAMA:** PC World Panama; **P. R. OF CHINA:** China Computer Users, China Computerworld, China Infoworld, China Telecom World Weekly, Computer & Communication, Electronic Design China, Electronics Today, Electronics Weekly, Game Camp, Game Soft, Network World China, PC World China, Popular Computer Weekly, Software Weekly, Software World, Telecom World; **PERU:** Computerworld Peru, PC World Profesional Peru, PC World Peru; **PHILIPPINES:** Computerworld Philippines, PC World Philippines, Publish in Asia; **POLAND:** Computerworld Poland, Computerworld Special Report, Macworld, Networld, PC World Komputer; **PORTUGAL:** Cerebro/PC World, Computerworld/Correio Informático, Dealer World Portugal, MacIn/PCIn, Multimedia World Portugal; **PUERTO RICO:** PC World Puerto Rico; **ROMANIA:** Computerworld Romania, PC World Romania, Telecom Romania; **RUSSIA:** Computerworld Russia, Mir PK, Sety; **SINGAPORE:** Computerworld World, Software World Singapore, Publish in Asia; **SLOVENIA:** MONITOR; **SOUTH AFRICA:** Computing S.A., InfoWorld S.A., Network World S.A., Software World; **SPAIN:** Computerworld España, COMUNICACIONES WORLD, Dealer World, Macworld España, PC World España; **SWEDEN:** CAP&Design, Computer Sweden, Corporate Computing, MacWorld, Maxi Data, MikroDatorn, Nätverk & Kommunikation, PC/Aktiv, PC World, Windows World; **SWITZERLAND:** Computerworld Schweiz, Macworld Schweiz, PCtip; **TAIWAN:** Computerworld Taiwan, Macworld Taiwan, PC World Taiwan, Publish Taiwan, Windows World; **THAILAND:** Thai Computerworld, Publish in Asia; **TURKEY:** Computerworld Turkiye, MACWORLD Turkiye, PC WORLD Turkiye; **UKRAINE:** Computerworld Kiev, Computers & Software, Multimedia World Ukraine, PC World Ukraine; **UNITED KINGDOM:** Acorn User, Amiga Computing, Appletalk, Computing, GamePro, Macworld, Network News, Parents and Computers, PC Advisor, PC Home, PSX Pro UK, The WEB; **UNITED STATES:** Cable in the Classroom, CD Review, CIO Magazine, Computerworld, Computerworld Client/Server Journal, Digital Video Magazine, DOS World, Federal Computer Week, GamePro, InfoWorld, I-Way, JavaWorld, Macworld, Multimedia World, Netscape World Online, Network World, PC Entertainment, PC World, Publish, SunWorld Online, SWATPro Magazine, Video Event, WebMaster; **URUGUAY:** PC World Uruguay; **VENEZUELA:** Computerworld Venezuela, PC World Venezuela; and **VIETNAM:** PC World Vietnam.

7/16/96

Credits

Senior Vice President and Group Publisher
Brenda McLaughlin

Acquisitions Editor
John Osborn

Software Acquisitions Editor
Tracy Lehman Cramer

Marketing Manager
Jill Reinemann

Managing Editor
Andy Cummings

Editorial Assistant
Tim Borek

Production Director
Andrew Walker

Supervisor of Page Layout
Craig A. Harrison

Production Associate
Christopher Pimentel

Media Archive Coordination
Leslie Popplewell

Development Editors
Pat O'Brien
Greg Robertson

Copy Edit Coordinator
Barry Childs-Helton

Technical Reviewer
Sally Neuman

Project Coordinator
Katy German

Graphics & Production Specialists
Vincent F. Burns
Renée Dunn
Craig A. Harrison

Quality Control Specialist
Mick Arellano

Proofreader
Kathy McGuinnes

Indexer
Liz Cunningham

Cover Design
Three 8 Creative Group

Acknowledgments

Writing this book was difficult. The technology is moving so fast that there was never enough time to do all the research, review all the software, or cover all the ground I would have liked to cover. Without assistance from many people, many of whom are unnamed, I would not have been able to finish this book, much less a more definitive one. I would like to thank the following people for their help. Stephen Gilman, consultant and friend, San Francisco, for his clear explanations of some difficult database concepts and for his review of portions of the book. Mike Taylor and Jim Nocar of Tippecanoe, Pleasanton, California, for their review of the chapter on text search technology. Chris Hoover, programmer, Stoughton, Wisconsin, for the CGI scripts. Lee Callister and Mike Campos, colleagues in the North Bay Multimedia Association, Marin County, California, for their suggestions based on reviewing portions of the manuscript. Carol McCullough, my co-author, consultant, Kihei, Hawaii, who brought great energy and expertise to this project. Carol McClendon, my agent, Waterside Productions, Lafayette, California, for doing a great job as always. And finally the artists who agreed to place their art in the Web-database demonstration; good art is always an inspiration, even in a digital project.

Of course, the tough part of any writing project falls to the spouse and the kids, whether they like it or not. I would like to thank my wife, Lani Wallin Sinclair, and my daughter, Brook, for their support in helping me get this book done and my mother, Miriam H. Sinclair, for her support during two summers.

Joseph T. Sinclair

This book is a testimonial to the success of the internet as a means of communication. I met my co-author, Joe Sinclair, by email. We live three thousand miles and three time zones apart. Our creative efforts flew back and forth across the Pacific Ocean a thousand times as we corresponded almost exclusively by email. Thanks, Joe, for creating this project and giving me the opportunity to contribute to it. I've had quite an education along the way.

There are so many people whose faces I may never see, but whose energy and enthusiasm show up on the pages of this book. Many of you supported my research by offering advice and expertise via the internet and the telephone. Two technical support people, Bill Havlice of Dev-Com, Inc., and Pramod Gopinath of Spider Technologies, were invaluable assets toward completing this book. The artists who contributed to the art gallery demonstration project added fun and excitement to the project. Thanks to all of you.

My family has supported my work from the beginning and deserves my thanks. My lifetime partner and mate, Pat Golden Dieter, helped edit my portion of the book. My kids, Blue, Jesse, Deja, Chrystal, and Dustin, all contributed by demonstrating how to enjoy life and still get the job done. My parents, Earl and Evelyn McCullough, brought me up believing in myself. Thanks for being in my life.

Carol M. McCullough

(The Publisher would like to give special thanks to Patrick J. McGovern, without whom this book would not have been possible.)

Contents at a Glance

Table of Contents

Table of Contents

For many people, a database may be a better alternative for building a Web site on the Internet or on an intranet than creating a huge number of quasi-permanent HTML documents. Additionally, a database enables you to do things you could not do otherwise, many of which are outlined in Chapter 1. This book shows you how databases work on the Web.

This is not a book for programmers, although programmers may find some ideas here. This book is for *nonprogrammers*, such as executives, network administrators, Webmasters, and PC users who are creating Web sites. The authors, being nonprogrammers themselves, reserve the right when faced with a programming chore to say, "Hire a programmer." Fortunately, the programming chores can be minimized. A nonprogrammer can get most of the job done. In some cases, a nonprogrammer can do it all.

Executives will want to get an overall picture of how this technology works, and they get the picture here. Network administrators (nonprogrammers) will want the same and, additionally, will want to get pointed in the right direction regarding a number of issues that they need to resolve in order to incorporate a database into their Web operations; this book helps. Webmasters and PC users just want to know how to do it, or at least how to do as much of it as they can do. They get a good start on finding those answers here.

For some readers, money is an issue: the cost of a database engine, development tools, Internet service, programming labor, and the like. It is difficult to write a book for the cost-conscious and for readers on generous budgets, too. As a result, the book generally takes the point of view of the cost-conscious reader, knowing that those in more affluent businesses may be happy to save a few dollars as well. Some readers are in business for themselves. Many are likely to install a database by themselves. Other readers are working in business organizations where they assign everything to employees. The book generally takes the point of view of the person who will do everything himself or herself. Those who assign the tasks to employees at least get an idea from the book of what it is that the employees will be doing.

Examples

This book contains three major examples. The first is an example of data cataloging. It involves a flag catalog for a flag marketing company, which is discussed in Chapter 14, "Data Cataloging." Data cataloging uses a database to create HTML documents by mail merging in a word processor. Although not breakthrough technology, it's an inexpensive and time-saving technique that can be used for small Web operations.

The second example is a list (flat file) of commercial real-estate brokers together with significant information on each, which is covered in Chapter 15, "Do You Really Need a Database Program?" In this example, a custom-written program queries the list and delivers information as a result of the query. It uses no database software. This simple database application does not even require a database engine and performs perfectly adequately for many situations. It does require CGI scripting, which is "lite" programming.

The third example, although simple to create, is the most complex application of the book. It is a simple example so as not to scare anyone off, but it demonstrates the power of using a database application on the Web — a power indicated by some of the uses mentioned in Chapter 1. The example is an art gallery in Chapters 21-24. It is a relational database; it contains two tables that have a common column (field). One table contains information on the artists. The other contains information on the art. Some of the queries query both tables; that is, they obtain information from both tables in one request. This database application generates custom Web documents on the fly based on the input of a visitor at the Web site. In this example, a client-server database engine does the work.

Web-Site Location

To make things as easy as possible to understand, the book features the most probable circumstance under which you are likely to find yourself desiring to connect a Web document to a database. The first assumption is that the Web document will be on the Internet. Certainly it could be on an intranet, and intranets are not ignored, but the assumption is that it will be the Internet. The next assumption is that you will rent space on the hard disk of the Internet service provider's (ISP's) computer rather that run your own server connected to the Internet. With the two rates being approximately $50 per month (ISP) and $5,000 per month (your own server and T1 line), it is a reasonable assumption to make (see Chapter 18, "Internet Operations"). Next, because virtually all ISPs run their operations on UNIX, the assumption is that you will be using a UNIX database server. Internet providers typically use a workstation as their computer; some use 486s or Pentiums loaded with the UNIX operating system. Finally, because most people use Windows, the assumption is that all the development work will be done in Windows 95 and ported to UNIX. Because this book is written for executives, network administrators, and competent users, but not programmers, it's assumed that if and when programming is necessary, you will subcontract it to a programmer or assign it to an employee but will not do it yourself.

The assumptions made do not mean that the book does not cover other techniques and systems. The book attempts to cover adequately a variety of possibilities in UNIX and Windows. The assumptions mean merely that many of the examples illustrate the general case and that much discussion focuses on the general case. The book mentions Windows NT systems often, too.

Other fine operating systems, such as Macintosh and OS/2 Warp, are not covered, but the principles learned in this book will help you quickly ascertain what you must do and how to go about it if you do not use UNIX or Windows. Indeed, you can use Windows as discussed herein as a metaphor for other operating systems used on personal computers.

Terminology

The terminology for database technology is sometimes confusing. The following definitions are offered to enable you to follow more easily the information set forth in the book.

Client-server

Client-server technology spreads a computer's work across two or more computers that are connected together. The connection (network) helps you get the power of a big computer (server) working together with your smaller computer (client). This makes it easier for you, because you are using something familiar. For example, you may have the Netscape browser on your personal computer (PC) for looking at the Web. You have a telephone line connected to your PC. When you connect via the phone to your Internet service provider's computer, your PC is the *client*. Your ISP's computer is the *server*. As you browse from one Web site to another, you are actually using many different servers. Server computers range from PCs to monstrous mainframe computers. They use a wide variety of operating systems. You don't need to know how they work, because everything you do starts with your PC and looks the same to you, no matter which server you happen to be dealing with at the moment.

There are three main reasons that the client-server system makes life easier for you:

➡ You always work in a familiar environment This makes your work easier and more convenient. You don't have to learn a new computer system to do new things with your computer.

➡ A lot of work can be done on your PC (client) before sending any work over phone lines to the server. This potentially saves money by reducing time online.

➡ Heavy-duty computing can be done on an appropriately powerful computer. For example, you can browse through the Library of Congress archive, which requires enormous amounts of disk space, as if it were right on your desk.

The server computer is the computer of the ISP or the dedicated computer that runs a LAN (local area network) or a WAN (wide area network). You use your client computer to gain access to the network and thus to the server computer. But this book is not about hardware. For the purposes of this book, the term *client-server* should not be understood in physical terms. Because this is a book about database software, the term *server* means server software, not necessarily hardware, and the term *client* means client software.

Wherever there's an Internet protocol (standard program or programming interface), it is likely to be a client-server program. Sometimes things become confusing. Clients sometimes go by different names, such as browsers, players, viewers, or readers. Even servers sometimes go by different names, such as daemons. Regardless of what a client or server is called, you must keep the client-server paradigm in mind to understand Internet protocols.

Database terminology

Database terminology sometimes confuses people because it is often vague. The word *database* can mean many things, from data to a database-management program. This book attempts to clarify meanings by establishing the definitions that follow.

Database

A *database* is a collection of information organized in tables, rows, and columns. In this book, you see database used most often in combination with other words, such as "database application" and "database engine."

Database is also an adjective meaning "having to do with a database application or system." *Data* refers to the data that resides in a database application.

Table, row, and column

A *table* is a collector of data. It keeps similar things organized together in the database. For example, in a car dealership database application, one table might keep track of all the salespersons and another table might keep track of all the cars.

Every table, no matter what it is used for, contains columns and rows. *Columns* determine what kind of information should be gathered. *Rows* store that information. In the salesperson table, there might be columns for name, hire date, salary, commission, and total annual sales. There is one row for each salesperson. You can visualize a table and its rows and columns as a grid with rows going horizontally and columns going vertically. Data is inside each of the boxes created by the grid.

A *row* of data is also known as a *record*. A *column* is also known as a *field*. *Rows* and *columns* are now widely used terms among nonprogrammers.

SQL

Structured Query Language (SQL) is the universal language of databases (see Chapter 7, "Basic SQL and SQL*Plus"). It is sparse, and database-software developers typically use their proprietary extensions to SQL to make their software more robust. For example, Oracle provides SQL Plus for its customers. IBM originally developed SQL for mainframe database applications, but it is now incorporated into most database engines, large and small.

BLOB

Text works very well in a flat-file or relational database table. Using different rows, column names, SQL commands, and operators, you can make queries and otherwise manipulate the data. However, you cannot so easily use queries to manipulate nontext data (programs and multimedia elements also known as *binaries*). Because binary files are often large, they go by the name Binary Large Object (BLOB or Blob).

Database engine

The *database engine* is an integral set of computer programs that keep a database organized (see Chapter 17, "Choosing a Client-Server Database"). These are behind-the-scenes programs, meaning that you never deal directly with them. You always go through some kind of go-between program. When designing your database and creating the end product your visitors will use, you use *database development tools* and *Web-database development tools* as the go-between programs (see Chapter 16, "Web-Database and Database Development Tools"). When your visitors actually use what you have created, they are using the *database application*.

A database engine is also known as the *database manager*, the *RDBM* (relational database manager), the *RDBS* (relational database server), the RDMS (relational database management system), the *client-server database*, and the *database server*. For the purposes of this book, the *database engine* is a client-server relational database management program.

Database application

What you do with the programming capability of a database engine, a fourth-generation database language (4GL), a Web-database development program, CGI scripts, a daemon, or a Web-integrated database manager constitutes the data management or *database application*. This includes tables, forms, queries, reports, and the like. Most database applications are custom programmed.

Database system

The overall system of database technology, including the data, database engine, and database application, constitute the database system.

Database development tools

You can use database development programs such as Oracle PowerObjects in place of programming in a 4GL database language. These are often referred to as *development tools*.

Web-database development tools

Special tools created for developing database applications that work on the Web or on an intranet, such as Cold Fusion, are specified as *Web-database development tools*.

Internet

Although this book is for readers who are familiar with the Internet, the following definitions can help clarify Internet concepts as they are used in this book.

Web

The World Wide Web (Web) is a collection of Internet protocols, or, more specifically, a client-server program called a *Web server*. A *Web site* consists primarily of a specific series of HTML document files and graphics (GIF, for Graphics Interchange Format) files served by the Web server to Web clients (browsers). A Web server can host many separate Web sites. The added capability to deliver other types of files, such as JPEG (Joint Photographic Experts Group), animation, 3D, and Real Audio makes the Web increasingly robust. For most purposes in this book, the *Web* refers to a Web site on the Internet. The book does not always present the Web in this context, however. It also uses the term Web site to mean a Web site on an intranet, whether or not the intranet is connected to the Internet.

TCP/IP

The basic network programs that enable you to communicate over the Internet with diverse computers using diverse operating systems are Transmission Control Protocol (TCP) and Internet Protocol (IP), which, taken together, make up the basic Internet communication protocol TCP/IP. This protocol is not limited to the Internet. You can use TCP/IP on an intranet that is not connected to the Internet. For example, you can use TCP/IP on a private network such as a LAN or a WAN in addition to other network protocols; TCP/IP need not be exclusive.

As more new programs are developed and existing programs are converted to run on the IP network (Internet, intranet, or both), the importance of TCP/IP will grow.

Intranet

When referring to a TCP/IP network running on a LAN or a WAN, this book uses the term *intranet*. Many organizations now use the TCP/IP protocol for their internal networks, their intranet. TCP/IP will run with network software such as Novell's NetWare, which offers IP in the most recent versions. An internal IP network (intranet) can provide much groupware (software that helps people collaborate in getting work done) functionality as well as accommodate database applications. The TCP/IP protocol, built into Windows 95 and the latest versions of most other operating systems, enables the use of Internet programs on an individual PC. Therefore, in addition to using a database application through a Web document on the Internet, you may want to use a Web system on your intranet. You can easily use a database application through an HTML document on an intranet, just as you can on the Internet.

The term *intranet* is unfortunate. The two words *Internet* and *intranet* are pronounced so much alike that it becomes confusing to hold a conversation. (Attorneys have been struggling with these words for decades with interstate commerce, intrastate commerce, interstate offering, and intrastate offering.) Journalists have found the word *intranet* so irresistible, however, that it has already taken hold and will introduce a long epoch of confused conversation in a field that is already confusing.

The use of the TCP/IP protocol may possibly have as big an impact because it enables intranets as because it has enabled the Internet. There is little difference between a Web site on the Internet and on an intranet. Perhaps the biggest difference is that intranets are much more likely to use Windows NT as an operating system. With that in mind, this book covers using databases on intranet systems that use Windows NT as the operating system. Most readers, however, will use Windows 95 as the operating system for the CD-ROM that comes with this book. That's why the CD-ROM uses Windows 95 for the Web-database demonstrations.

Visitors

This book refers to those who go to your Web site as *visitors*. They could be called surfers, cruisers, customers, consumers, visitors, or patrons, but visitors is perhaps most generic. Remember, it's ultimately the visitors who will make your Web site successful.

The book uses the term *visitors* for intranets also. In this case, it means management and employees, faculty and students, and perhaps vendors and customers as well.

ISP

An Internet service provider (ISP) is a firm that provides connections to the Internet for consumers and businesses. Although the national online services such as CompuServe are now technically ISPs, the book refers to them as *national online services*. Large ISPs are providers such as Netcom. You can find small ISPs in many counties nationwide now, and someday soon perhaps in every county. ISPs typically provide traditional Internet services such as Telnet, File Transfer Protocol (FTP), Gopher, Web, Usenet (newsgroups), e-mail, and Internet Relay Channel (IRC), all of which are covered in Chapter 10, "Internet Programs and Protocols."

Value-added networks

Called *value-added networks* (VANs), another group of network providers will emerge that provide nontraditional as well as traditional Internet programming. Nontraditional programming includes the latest, greatest, and most expensive TCP/IP programs (including Web servers) being developed for Internet and intranet use. Because some of these programs cost a lot, they are unlikely to be offered by an ISP. VANs are a new phenomenon and are likely to become widespread as businesses require a higher level of Internet service. For example, an ISP that offers a client-server database engine as well as a Web server today might be considered a VAN. In the future when such an offering becomes commonplace, it will probably take more than that to be considered a VAN.

National communications companies such as MCI, Sprint, and the Baby Bells are likely to be VANs rather than merely ISPs when they offer business Internet services. They will justify higher monthly fees by offering a higher level of programming.

General

Some general terms useful to your understanding of the book follow.

API

Application Program Interface (API) is an important term, because many servers have an API that enables you to easily connect to another program that is to be used through the server program. The prime example for the book is connecting a database engine to a Web server. An *API* is simply a programming gateway within a program (for example, a Web server) that provides for another program (for example, a database engine) to communicate with it. The programmers of the original program set up the API as a standard way for other programs to communicate with it. The programmers of the other program must write code according to the API specifications of the original program in order for the communication to take place easily. Otherwise, the programmers of the other program would have to invent a way to connect to the original program, a more difficult and time-consuming task.

ODBC

Open Data Base Connectivity (ODBC) is Microsoft's standard cross-platform SQL API that any programmer can use to create a gateway in a program for a database engine to be connected to the program. This makes connections easier. If a programmer puts an ODBC API in a program, that program can be connected to any database engine that also has an ODBC API. Likewise, if a database engine programmer puts an ODBC API in the database engine, any program that has an ODBC API can be easily connected to that database engine. Thus, ODBC is a standard API for connecting database engines to programs that use database services (see Chapter 28, "Ideas for Using Web-Database Technology" for more on ODBC). SQL APIs other than ODBC may be more capable and more widely used for certain purposes, but it is beyond the scope of this book to comment on a variety of SQL APIs.

GUI

After you turn on your PC's power and are ready to begin using it, what do you see? If you see a blank screen with a C:\> you are in the nongraphical, or *command-line,* interface for your PC. If you see the Windows or Windows 95 boxes and icons, with nice colored backgrounds, you are in the *GUI* (graphical user interface) for your PC.

You can communicate with a computer through a command-line interface such as that used in DOS or UNIX. For many purposes, however, you can interface more easily with a computer in a graphical environment, particularly when using multimedia programming. Windows 3.1, for example, uses a GUI. Although — technically — Windows 95 and Macintosh use an *object-oriented user interface* (OOUI), for the purposes of this book, OOUIs fall under the definition GUI because an OOUI operates in a graphical environment.

Software

The North American software industry constitutes the greatest hotbed of capitalism in the world today. It is very competitive and innovative. For this book to give an endorsement for any software would be a disservice to both readers and software developers. Magazines can do a better job than books when it comes to a comparative analysis of software both because they have testing labs and because they are more current. Any use of or mention of particular software in this book or on the CD-ROM does not constitute an endorsement. No serious attempt has been made to survey definitively the software relevant to the book, although the authors have aggressively pursued all leads. When mentioned or used in an example, a particular program may have been picked more for the authors' convenience (such as a knowledgeable contact at a software company) than for the superiority of the software. On the other hand, no software has been mentioned or used that the authors perceived to be substandard or incompetent.

In the specific cases of Oracle and Microsoft software, they were picked based more on demonstrations attended by the authors or convenience than for any other specific reason. Oracle is a leader in bringing database technology to the Web, but it is not the *only* leader. Oracle publishes excellent software, but you will certainly want to survey Oracle's competitors before you make a decision. Microsoft's Access and SQL Server are widely used database engines but have plenty of capable competitors, too.

Today, you can download much software, including database software, from the Web for trial over a specified time period. Take advantage of this convenient way to evaluate software without making a financial commitment and without relying on the authors or anyone else to unduly influence your choice.

Online with Client-Server Databases

World Wide Web sites (Web sites, for short) — if they are active either on the Internet or on an internal company network (intranet) — tend to grow more complex. A manageable collection of documents soon turns into an unmanageable collection of documents, color graphics, and other multimedia items. To keep track of all these digital items conveniently, put them in a database. After you have them in a database, you can use database techniques to manage the documents and multimedia items — and to expand the functions and capability of the Web site, too.

This book makes no distinction between a Web site on the Internet and a Web site on an internal TCP/IP network (intranet) that may be connected to the Internet or that may be available only to company employees. Many companies have existing database applications, such as employee records, membership lists, statistics, parts lists, catalogs, document repositories, and so on, which constitute desired additions to the company's online resources. You can integrate these into the Web site, too, whether on an intranet or on the Internet.

Web Database Capabilities

The following sections describe more specific activities that a Web database application can enable. Some of these activities can be supported only by the use of a database.

Queries

A Web-site visitor can make normal queries to a Web database application (ask the database engine to search on key words). If, for example, you have a database that contains all the insect exterminators in the state of Louisiana, a visitor can ask the database for those located in Baton Rouge or for those specializing in cockroaches. You can facilitate this search through a Web document by using the *form* capability of HTML (HyperText Markup Language) to enable a visitor to enter the input for the query. The visitor enters the input, and a CGI (Common Gateway Interface) script sends the query to the database and returns the data requested.

Simple queries

The example of a simple query in the book is a query to a directory of commercial real estate brokers (see Figure 1-1). You can request to see a custom-generated list of brokers by geographical location, by specialty, or by name. The information returned is a multiple-paragraph professional profile of a broker with color graphics included (see Chapter 15).

Figure 1-1: Home page graphic for the commercial brokers directory.

Complex queries

Beyond simple queries to a database with one table, you can make a query to a relational database with two tables or more. This constitutes a more complex query. Although the complexity of a query is limited only by your imagination and innovation, this book uses a straightforward query addressed to two tables in a relational database as the example of a complex query. This is an art gallery presentation (see Figure 1-2). One table contains the digital art and information about the digital art. The other table contains information on the artists. For example, the input *Miller AND modern* will provide all the art by the artist Miller that is classified as modern art. The database returns a collection of digital graphic images *custom-generated* just for you based on your input.

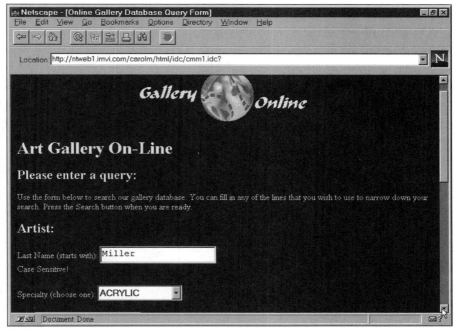

Figure 1-2: Home page graphic for the art gallery.

Delivery of multimedia

As you have read, a database can contain and return more information than just text. It can contain any type of digital multimedia files, including items such as text documents, color graphics, audio bites, video clips, and executables (computer programs). Because the Web is a digital multimedia system, using a database capable of storing more than text is a practical requirement (see Chapter 9).

Custom HTML documents on the fly

In the example mentioned previously, when the database returns the information, the database generates a report. The form of the database report on the Web is an HTML document. Because HTML documents are multimedia documents, the report can incorporate any digital media usable with HTML. Similar to normal database reports, the database application generates the HTML document on the fly. This means that the HTML document does not preexist. Only the *template* of the HTML document preexists. The database system creates the HTML document only in response to the query (see Figure 1-3).

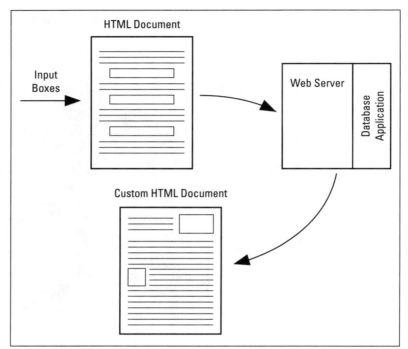

Figure 1-3: The database application uses a visitor's input to create a custom Web document.

What's the significance of documents created on the fly in response to a query? Such documents are *custom* documents; that is, they are created by one person's input, one person's query. Having a Web system that can create custom documents on the fly for Web visitors has far-reaching implications for education, entertainment, and publishing. Moreover, it has particularly far-reaching implications for marketing and customer service.

For intranets (see the following expanded definition of intranets), the *visitors* are employees or, possibly, the employees of vendors and subcontractors. The custom-generated HTML documents can help them do their work. More important, HTML forms read by a Web browser can give visitors convenient cross-platform access to existing databases without the training required to learn a database program interface.

Complex documents on the fly

It's not just a matter of creating custom text HTML documents on the fly. The documents can be multimedia documents. Beyond multimedia, they can be interactive documents too — by including hyperlinks, even custom-generated hyperlinks. In fact, the documents can be almost anything you want them to be. Thus, operating through a database is just another way of authoring HTML documents. For many purposes, authoring via a database is the most efficient and effective way to create a Web site. It is the *only* way to create documents on the fly in response to visitor input.

Transactions

What about databases that do calculation and transactions? Can they be used at a Web site? There's no reason they can't, and in fact, systems such as branch office accounting (for intranets) and retail online ordering systems (for the Internet) are natural applications of connecting a database to a Web document.

Visitation record keeping

Web server software has built-in record keeping capability. It can keep track of the number of *hits* you get on your Web site (that is, the number of visitors to your site and the number of hits on each directory). Future servers will have advanced capabilities in this regard. The record of the hits can be delivered to you by e-mail or in a special file where they accumulate as raw data. Why not have the records delivered to a database instead, where you not only can keep the raw data but can analyze the data through queries? This is particularly important to those who want to monitor their Web marketing activities by analyzing the hits. It may also be important on intranets, where you may want to monitor the volume and peculiarities of employee use.

Web-tracking database programs that assign each visitor a session ID number are available (see Chapter 25). The database application records all of a visitor's hits within a site for that session. When the visitor revisits the site, the program analyzes the hits from the previous sessions to present the Web site in a special way. Because the HTML documents are generated on the fly, an entire custom-generated Web site can be published for that visitor. Suppose that a visitor visits a general bookstore on the Web and peruses only the mystery books. When that visitor returns in the future, the Web site could appear to be a bookstore specializing in mystery books. These types of database applications are already widely used.

Multimedia asset accounting

The biggest problem in digital multimedia is keeping track of the various media files (*assets*). In a multimedia medium, the number of multimedia assets in even a small presentation gets out of hand quickly (see Chapter 9). The best way to keep track of the huge number of multimedia files used in a presentation is to keep them in a database. Not only do you have better control over them, but you can keep track of them by inputting information about each multimedia asset (*meta information*) and relating such information to the asset. Now if you want to know the digital artist who created a certain color graphic, the database can tell you.

This concept is particularly important in keeping track of copyrights. Because multimedia presentations use diverse assets, just making sure that you have the proper rights to use such assets becomes a burdensome task. Mistakes can be expensive or even lead to litigation.

Keep in mind, too, that the Web is a multimedia medium. Although most Web sites today primarily use text and color graphics, you can already use an additional diverse set of media protocols and programs, such as Real Audio. Their use will soon become widespread.

Legacy databases

There is no shortage of *Legacy* brand names, but *legacy* as used in this book means simply this: preexisting database applications, such as an old mainframe database. It could be an enterprise system for a large company or a small system for a small firm. Unless you recently created your existing database using the latest version of a Web-connected database engine, it is a legacy system. Thus, an aspect of a legacy database — for the purposes of this book — is that you did not create it to operate at a Web site.

Maybe you don't have a clever application where you need to use a database through a Web document. Perhaps you just want to conduct your routine database operations, but you want to do it over the Internet or an intranet, using a Web document (HTML form) as an interface. This book covers how to do that. The same techniques that are used to create multimedia Web documents on the fly can be used to conduct traditional, text-based database reports. Thus, many people will want to use Web database technology to install and use their legacy databases at their Web sites. Others will want to use such technology to make their legacy databases available to employees on their intranet.

Remote database access

You might use a legacy database at a Web site simply to provide access to your database for home workers, telecommuters, field workers, and traveling workers. It makes sense to use the Internet to do so.

Shared databases

Although UNIX client-server database programs have come down substantially in price in the last three years, most are not yet a consumer item (under $500). It might be more cost-effective to share a database with someone.

Many client-server databases can scale upwards, which means that they can be designed for a huge capacity. You might share through a third party. Perhaps your Internet service provider (ISP) will purchase the database and provide you and other business customers with Web database capability (see Figure 1-4). In such a case, expect your monthly fee to go up.

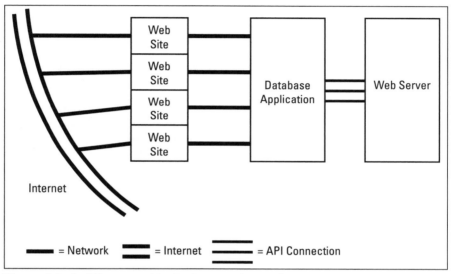

Figure 1-4: An ISP can provide database engine services.

Perhaps you can create a group of four or five small firms to license and operate a client-server database engine, using a part-time database programmer. Because these client-server database engines are heavyweights, this idea makes sense. With restricted access and security built in, these powerful programs are set up to provide multiple levels of secure access. Such security is a handy feature designed for internal security on an intranet, but it also makes sharing a client-server database engine more feasible on the Internet.

Examples of database applications

The U.S. Census Bureau (www.census.gov) has one of the largest repositories of data on the planet. The Bureau now makes much of that information available via the Internet through powerful database searching and reporting capability at the Bureau's Web site. You can now access the census data and put together a custom report. Moreover, the Bureau provides you with a special program for putting together your own custom surveys based on the census data.

If that isn't enough, the Bureau also offers the Tiger Map System (TMS) at its Web site. You can generate a digital color map of any size and anyplace. You can easily and quickly create a map of California, Alameda County, Oakland, or the subdivision where you live in Oakland by using TMS and its zoom feature. The Bureau provides this service with a combination of database and digital graphics technology. Try it; the Census Bureau provides instructions, and it's free.

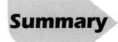

Summary

Applying database technology to the Web is a new application of an old technology — an old technology well-suited for the future. The examples and ideas of this chapter are just the beginning, not an assessment of the full scope of the art. By the time you read this book, there will be new Web-database inventions, no doubt some surprising and clever ones. The next chapter provides you with a general overview of Web-database development to set the stage for more specific details later in the book.

Databases in Web Documents

Many Web-site operators rely on an Internet service provider to connect to the Internet. Most ISPs use UNIX. That means most Webmasters will develop in Windows and port the database application to UNIX.

Develop in UNIX?

Can you develop in UNIX using Windows on a PC? Yes! You can get a program such as Hummingbird's eXceed 5 for Windows. You stay in a Windows environment while working via the Internet on the ISP's UNIX computer. These kinds of programs translate what you do into the standard UNIX GUI called X-Windows. This approach is only necessary where the development tool you need to use is not available in a Windows version.

Those Web publishers who run their own servers connected to the Internet are likely to use UNIX even on PCs, but they may choose to use Windows NT instead of UNIX. Such publishers develop in Windows and port the database application to UNIX or Windows NT.

Porting

Porting is moving a program from one operating system to another (such as from Windows to Macintosh). To be able to port a program, the program must be cross-platform; that is, it must be able to run on multiple operating systems. Specifically, the program must be able to run on the operating system to which you want to port it.

Web publishers running Web sites on intranets develop in Windows and port the database application to UNIX or Windows NT. As you can surmise, a cross-platform development approach is important. The following chart summarizes the normal choices:

Usage regarding Web-database development and operation						
	ISP Server	Private Internet Server	Intranet Server	Scripts	Development	Database Engine
UNIX	Current standard	Widely used	Common	Perl, TCL, C	Windows	scalable
Windows NT	Uncommon	Increasingly used	Widely used	Visual Basic, C++, Perl	Windows	Win NT or Win version

These various approaches may be used both for database applications set up specifically for the operation of Web sites and for legacy systems integrated into Web sites. There are, of course, exceptions to the general practices listed here. For example, some Web publishers use Windows 95 servers for Web publishing on small LANs, not Windows NT. Some develop in UNIX directly, not in Windows, in cases where the server software physically resides on the same premises (such as a private Internet server or an intranet server).

Finally, some Web servers include programming that facilitates linking HTML forms to a database. In these cases, the Web servers include the database engines, or the Web servers are easily connected to the database engines in a standard way via an API (Application Program Interface) or via ODBC (Open Data Base Connectivity). This way of integrating databases will become increasingly popular, particularly for systems set up solely to create and operate Web sites.

Create a Database Application

Before you can use a database application at a Web site, you have to create the database application. It may not be quite as simple to create a client-server database application as using Access, Approach, or Paradox (three popular Windows database engines). Because you are likely to install your database engine on a UNIX computer — most ISPs offer only UNIX systems — you must use a UNIX client-server database engine. See Chapter 28, "Ideas for Using Web-Database Technology," for an ISP-hosted alternative to UNIX.

If you are using Windows NT, however, you can use desktop database engines such as Access, because they come in versions that run under Windows NT. You can do your database application development in Windows.

Database Development Tools

After you get away from the popular Windows desktop database engines, you need a *database development tool* to create your database. By using such a development tool, you can avoid programming in a fourth-generation database language (4GL). Unfortunately, using one of the tools may be difficult itself, so you have to choose a tool carefully. A few tools, such as Oracle's Power Objects, are reasonably easy to use. Normally, you use the tool in Windows, even though you construct a database application to run on a UNIX database engine. Thus, the product of the tool must be cross-platform; that is, the tool must run in Windows, but the product created (the database application) must run in UNIX. Chapter 16, "Web-Database and Database Development Tools," covers selecting development tools.

Another way to create a database application, if done with precision, is as follows:

1. **Create database tables in Windows by using a Windows database engine.** For many database applications, creating the tables is easy, straightforward, and quick.

2. **Create the queries in Windows.**

3. **Create identical database tables in UNIX by using a UNIX database engine.**

The queries created in Windows should work with the UNIX database application too, although the CGI scripts may have to be adjusted. For this approach to work, the UNIX database tables must be exactly the same as the Windows database tables. This approach will not work well for complex database applications.

Chapters 15 and 20–24 provide detailed examples of using CGI scripts and development tools for specific demonstration projects.

HTML forms

You create Web documents by using HTML, a simple markup language that anyone can master. HTML has a set of *form* markups that make creating inputs easy. *Inputs* are required for database operations such as making queries or adding data. A *form* is a fill-in-the-blank screen for gathering information in an organized way. A database application then processes the input into the form.

CGI scripting

The HTML forms by themselves do not do anything but accept the input. You must use CGI scripting to connect the HTML input document to the database engine to make something happen (see Figure 2-1). Unfortunately, CGI scripting falls into the realm of programmers, and unless you are a programmer, it is not something you want to try yourself. Programmers usually use Perl scripting, TCL scripting, or the C programming language to write their scripts for UNIX computers. For Windows NT, Visual Basic, C++, and Perl are popular. CGI scripts are covered in Chapter 5, "HTML Forms."

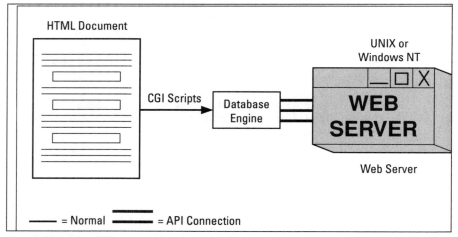

Figure 2-1: The CGI connection.

Database Reports

A database engine at a Web site generates a report in response to a query by generating an HTML document on the fly in response to input typed in an HTML form. The document might consist of one word, one sentence, a multiple-paragraph text document, or a multimedia document.

Web-database tools

Special Web-database development tools, such as WebBase by Expertelligence (http://www.expertelligence.com) — specifically designed for creating Web-database applications — are now available. Generally, they are designed to make the development of Web-database applications easier and faster. Many can be used by nonprogrammers. Many eliminate the need for CGI scripting or generate CGI scripting for the user. Thus, it is possible for a nonprogrammer to create a Web-database application. Chapter 16 reviews many of the Web-database development tools.

Database engines

The database engines used on UNIX computers connected to the Internet tend to be scalable (expandable) client-server versions; that is, they have a lot of horsepower and take up a lot of room. More than 40MB is not uncommon. Oracle 7 is an example: Its various versions are from 40MB to 120MB. Although these database engines have come down dramatically in price recently, they are not truly an easy-to-use consumer product yet. Nevertheless, they seem to be moving quickly in that direction. Many are beginning to cater to Web designers, because there is a growing demand for database engine use in Web sites. Web designers demand database engines and Web-database development tools that offer both lower cost and more ease of use.

Only a few ISPs use non-UNIX systems. Even the ones that have PCs use UNIX instead of Windows NT. With the plethora of inexpensive Windows NT Web servers now on the market, this situation may change. Until it does, however, you probably will have to use UNIX.

Another issue is whether your ISP provides the database engine you need or can accommodate economically a database engine you provide; or, if not, whether you can find an ISP that *can* provide what you need.

Alternatives

What alternative do you have to using a UNIX database engine on hard disk space you rent from an ISP? You *could* run your own computer connected to the Internet and use Windows NT or another operating system.

For more horsepower in a database engine for Windows NT, you might try using one of the scalable database engines, such as Oracle 7 or Sybase, on Windows NT. They come in competitively priced Windows NT versions but they may not be quite as easy to program as Access, Approach, or Paradox. Nonetheless, these high-end databases are becoming easier to use, as you will see in this book, and they can be scaled up to handle huge database applications and large numbers of visitors simultaneously — if the hardware has the capacity to do so as well.

Web server/database engine

Some software companies, such as NaviSoft (GNNServer), provide for connecting HTML forms to a database application in their Web server software. In other words, the Web server itself has the database capability built in and does not necessarily require CGI scripts. A database engine may be built in too, as it is in the GNNServer, or a convenient standard way to connect a database (ODBC) may be built in. Software companies offering these database-enhanced Web servers often provide built-in tools or supplementary tools to create and manage the database application. A few of these Web-server and database-engine combinations are intended for a special activity, such as retail sales or document distribution on the Web and on intranets.

Another approach is a third-party program that works with a Web server and a database engine to transform the two, in effect, into a combination Web/database server, as described in the preceding paragraph.

Web server systems must provide a convenient standard interface, an API, for connecting database engines. For example, a Web server with an API that is ODBC compliant can connect to any ODBC-compliant database engine. This means that a Web server can, in effect, incorporate a database engine and database application almost as if it were a combination Web/database server.

Specialized Alternatives

If you are relegated to using a TCP/IP network for reasons beyond your control (upper management decision, for example) but want to run database operations without using TCP/IP programs, you can do it with *middleware*. In this case, middleware is a layer of software between your programs and TCP/IP that enables non-TCP/IP programs to operate over a TCP/IP network.

Middleware used over the Internet on a 14.4 or 28.8 modem will not be the same as using such database applications on a PC, but these are viable programs for those who need them. Because such specialized uses are beyond the scope of this book, they will not be covered.

Summary

The table at the beginning of this chapter summarizes your choices for using a database application at a Web site. Web server/database combinations are becoming popular, whether they come as an integrated package or are created through the use of a standard interface such as ODBC. You may find without much research that there is a combination of Web and database software that meets your needs. On the other hand, your requirements may be so special that it may take careful studying and creative imagination to come up with the best combination of software for your purposes.

Types of Databases

In This Chapter

Flat-file database overview

Relational database overview

Object-oriented database overview

Hybrid database overview

If you have looked up a product in a Web catalog or at a retail Web site, you have used a database on the World Wide Web. Databases make it easy for you to find products, go job hunting, vote for your favorite genetic fractal art, or sign a guest book. All of these applications use databases either to gather information or to deliver it to you, or both. The type of database used varies. This chapter describes four types of databases that are being used for Web sites.

The Four Basic Database Types

Although many other types are out there, these four are the primary ones, and most off-the-shelf databases fall into one of these categories. When deciding on the type of database best for you, first review the strengths and weaknesses of each kind. What is the most important feature you need?

Of course, you also need to take into account other considerations when selecting a database, such as size, cost, and portability, which Chapter 16, "Web-Databases and Database Development Tools," and Chapter 17, "Choosing a Client-Server Database," discuss. For now, focus on the overall goal you want to accomplish with your database, or just peruse the possibilities and let your imagination take over.

Flat-file databases

Your checkbook register has horizontal *rows* for writing down each check and vertical *columns* for date, check number, description, amount, and so on. The table of contents for this book has two columns: one for chapter title, and one for page number. Each line in the table of contents is a row containing the title and page number of one chapter. These are two examples of the flat-file database. One *table* (a grid of horizontal rows and vertical columns) divides all your facts into neat, easy-to-read compartments (see Figure 3-1). Sometimes rows are called *records* and columns are called *fields*. Records and fields are terms from earlier, nondatabase computer languages. Rows and columns are truly database terms and are used consistently throughout this book.

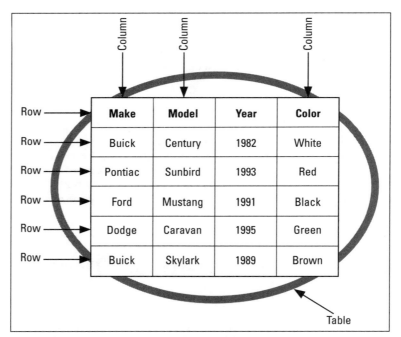

Figure 3-1: *A table arranges everything into vertical columns and horizontal rows.*

Flat-file is the oldest type of database. This type existed when computers were the size of your living room and were filled with vacuum tubes instead of silicon chips. Today, you can find dozens of variations on the flat-file database for sale at any computer store. Some specialize in bookkeeping, mailing labels, or scheduling appointments. Others are all-purpose, and you decide for yourself how to arrange the tables. Flat-file databases are often referred to as *spreadsheets*. All flat-file databases use columns and rows to collect small pieces (elements) of information into a list (table).The table stands alone and isolated from other tables.

In this type of system, one table keeps everything in the entire database. This table can be complex, such as a life insurance amortization table with complex mathematical functions applied to many rows and columns of data. On the other hand, a simple thing like a grocery list reflects a simple table structure having only one column.

Suppose that you have two departments in your agribusiness consulting company: Consulting and Billing.

The Consulting Department keeps track of the following information:

➥ The ID number, name, and address of each client.

➥ A contact name and phone number for every client.

➥ The type of business, whether the client was satisfied, and so on.

The Billing Department needs to know this information:

➥ The name and address of each client.

➥ A contact name and phone number for every client.

➥ The client's current bill, credit rating, and the total amount billed to each client.

You purchase a flat-file database and give one copy to each department. Consulting decides that it needs ten columns, as shown in Figure 3-2.

Consulting Department

Client ID	Client Name	Contact Name	Contact Phone	Address	Type Of Business	Size Of Business	Satisfied?	Last Contact	Last Proj. Desc.
345	Sunny Farms	Bob Andrews	887-8765	Box 45 Westfield, VA 97643	Dairy	Big	Yes	2/1/96	Built a shed for...
200	Happy Acres	John Miller	699-6789	RR 4 South Bend, IL	Hog	Small	No	4/1/92	Fencing
067	Best's Farms	Nancy Smith	897-5432	140 West Rd. Mill Pond, MD	Sheep	Medium	Yes	7/1/94	Out Building

Figure 3-2: Consulting creates a table for tracking clients.

Billing designs its flat-file database table with eight columns (fields) The columns are named Client Name, Contact Name, and so on. Figure 3-3 shows the Billing Department's table. Note that four columns are the same in both tables (Client Name, Contact Name, Contact Phone, and Address). They are things that both departments need. The rest of the columns are different. Consulting does not care about invoices and, likewise, Billing does not have to know about the size of the business.

Billing Department

Client Name	Contact Name	Contact Phone	Address	Current Bill	Invoice Number	Credit Rating	Total Billed
Sunny Farms	Bob Andrews	887-8765	Box 45 Westfield, VA 97643	$3,200	A9501	A	$15,503
Happy Acres	John Miller	699-6789	RR 4 South Bend, IL	$300	A0194	C	$12,356
Best's Farms	Nancy Smith	897-5432	140 West Rd. Mill Pond, MD	0	C456	A	$24,599

Figure 3-3: Billing has its own table for client information. The first four columns are the same as Consulting's second through fifth columns.

These four columns that are in both departments' tables carry identical information, which is repeated in both tables. Each department must contact the other to be sure their database tables are synchronized with the most current information. If Billing fails to inform Consulting of a change in a contact name, then Consulting may be embarrassed when attempting to make a sales call. And every time information must be recorded repeatedly gives another opportunity for an error to occur.

As your business grows and you add more clients, both databases grow larger. Each department has its own copy of the client name, address, and so forth. In addition, this approach requires twice as much room (storage space) to keep all that repeated information. Worse yet, it takes at least twice as much time to type it in.

Now that your departments are using databases, you can get quick answers to questions like these:

➥ How many clients do I have?

➥ Are most of my clients satisfied customers?

➥ What is the total amount I billed to Client A?

➥ What is the total amount I billed to everybody?

➥ Will you give me a list of all my clients arranged by the type of business?

The flat-file database's built-in features help you answer all these questions.

Strengths of flat-file databases

Flat-file databases do have some strong points, such as the following:

➥ Many specialized products are available. Prearranged tables with the right column headings are ready to go, so you can begin immediately.

➡ They have built-in sorting, averaging, summarizing, and reporting.

Weaknesses of flat-file databases

On the other hand, flat-file databases are not perfect. Following are some of their weaknesses:

➡ Two tables cannot share any information at all. Questions about information from two tables are difficult to answer.

➡ Duplicating data (because you cannot share columns) increases the risk of typing errors.

➡ Repeating lots of information takes up lots of storage space on your computer.

Common brand-name, flat-file database products

You're probably familiar with many or even most of the following flat-file database software packages:

➡ Microsoft Money, and Intuit Quicken are specialized flat-file databases for tracking personal banking.

➡ Microsoft Excel and Boreland QuattroPro are all-purpose flat-file databases. You use them for any kind of lists, designing all the columns and tables yourself.

➡ Mailing lists (mail-merge files) in word processing packages such as Microsoft Word and Corel WordPerfect act as flat-file databases.

Some questions are not so easy to answer with your flat-file database, such as when you want to see a list of the current bills for only dissatisfied clients. The Consulting department knows which clients are not satisfied (the Satisfied? column would have a No in it). The Billing department knows the amount of their current bill. Somehow, you must combine the two tables to get the final answer. This kind of work is not easy for flat-file databases. Here's what you do: Consulting puts together a list of satisfied clients and gives it to Billing. Billing then makes a copy of its entire database and deletes any client that is not on the list it received from Consulting. Finally, Billing produces your report from this database. Billing then deletes the copy of the database so that it is not confused with the original one. If you want this report every month, the whole routine has to be done all over again each month, because you cannot share information between flat-file databases. They are designed to stand alone. Take heart! There is a better way to do this: You can use a *relational database*.

Relational databases

Relational databases evolved in the 1970s and flourished in the 1980s, becoming the most popular and fully developed type of database application. Today, relational database applications remain a tried-and-true technology, well-tested and widely available. Codd and Date, the two scholars who coined the term, became famous in the computer industry. A humorous summary of their "rules of normalization" (rules that define the best way to design a relational database) rang like a mantra on the lips of computer professionals around the world: "The key, the whole key, and nothing but the key, so help me Codd!"

The relational database took the computer world by storm because it solved a big weakness of the flat-file database. Relational databases can share tables, saving repetition of information, typing time, and storage space. Suppose that you, being a modern business leader, purchase a relational database for your agribusiness. Now you have one database to share between Consulting and Billing. The software you buy costs more than the flat-file database software and it requires more power (RAM) and storage space (hard disk). But relational databases have advantages that outweigh these disadvantages.

You can now consolidate both departments' flat-file tables into one comprehensive database.

Strictly for quality control, and because Consulting is the first department to contact a client, it receives the responsibility of keeping track of client information that was formerly kept by both departments (Client name and address, Contact name and phone). Now, changes are recorded once and are accessible to both departments. Consulting adds new clients. Then, when Billing needs to send a bill, it does not need to type in the address and so on, all over again. If Billing finds out that a client has moved, it notifies Consulting, and the correction is typed into Consulting's table. Another method (if you can get them to agree) is to have both departments make these changes. That way, Billing has much less typing to do, and Consulting does not have to waste time verifying that it has the current name and address.

Now, there is still more information that only Consulting is interested in, and the same is true of Billing. To arrange all this in a relational database, you start with these three sets of information about a client:

➡ What both departments need (client name and address, contact name and phone)

➡ What only Consulting needs (type of business and so forth)

➡ What only Billing needs (bill, invoice, and so on)

Consulting is responsible for the first two sets of information, so you put all of that into one table, as shown in Figure 3-4. This table looks just like the flat-file database table! In fact, all tables in relational databases look the same as tables in flat-file databases. Both are simply a collection of columns and rows (fields and records).

Consulting Department

Client ID	Client Name	Contact Name	Contact Phone	Address	Type Of Business	Size Of Business	Satisfied?	Last Contact	Last Proj. Desc.
345	Sunny Farms	Bob Andrews	887-8765	Box 45 Westfield, VA 97643	Dairy	Big	Yes	2/1/96	Built a shed for...
200	Happy Acres	John Miller	699-6789	RR 4 South Bend, IL	Hog	Small	No	4/1/92	Fending
067	Best's Farms	Nancy Smith	897-5432	140 West Rd. Mill Pond, MD	Sheep	Medium	Yes	7/1/94	Out Building

Figure 3-4: The relational table for Consulting has the same columns as its flat-file table.

You want to eliminate duplication and have Billing share Consulting's table. To make this work, you remove the four columns (Client Name, Contact Name, Contact Phone, Address) from Billing's table.

But wait a minute! How can you tell which row belongs to which client? You need a *key!* If you take out all the client information, how will you find a bill for a client? A key is simply another column in a table. It is special because it links tables together. A key is the one column that you *do* need to repeat in both tables in order to make that link work. Each Billing row is for a client, and your Billing table is useless without the client. You also need to be able to find the address of a client in one table and the bill amount for that client in another table. How do you match up all that stuff? You simply create a key.

It turns out that Consulting already assigns a number to each client, which is used as a fast reference on all letters and memos about that client. The Consulting table has a column for this number called Client ID. The number belongs to that client no matter what happens to the client's business (new contact, new address, and so on). This number is perfect to use as a key. If Billing uses that number in its table too, you have a sure-fire method of matching up the client's name and address with the correct bill. You work with Billing, and before they remove any columns, make sure that they add this new column to their table. Consulting writes an alphabetical list of client names with their unique client numbers. Billing goes through its table and types in the correct client number in every row. Some of the clients on Consulting's list are not in Billing's table, because they have never been billed. This is all right. As soon as a bill is needed, Billing will create a row for them. Billing will look up the client's number on Consulting's table and type that number into the new Billing table row.

Ideally, your database software will be able to give Billing an easy way to select from a list of clients and will verify that only valid client numbers are used.

Now it is safe to remove the four duplicated columns from the Billing table. Look carefully at Figure 3-5. This shows the two tables together and shows their relationship to each other. Notice the one identical column in each table (key). It is called Client ID in both tables. Notice that the number of columns in the Billing table has been reduced from eight to five. By looking at Consulting's table of clients, which combines data from both tables based on the key (Client ID), Billing derives a list of clients, their addresses, and their current bills.

Consulting Department

Client ID	Client Name	Contact Name	Contact Phone	Address	Type Of Business	Size Of Business	Satisfied?	Last Contact	Last Proj. Desc.
345	Sunny Farms	Bob Andrews	887-8765	Box 45 Westfield, VA 97643	Dairy	Big	Yes	2/1/96	Built a shed for...
200	Happy Acres	John Miller	699-6789	RR 4 South Bend, IL	Hog	Small	No	4/1/92	Fending
067	Best's Farms	Nancy Smith	897-5432	140 West Rd. Mill Pond, MD	Sheep	Medium	Yes	7/1/94	Out Building

Billing Department

Client ID	Current Bill	Invoice Number	Credit Rating	Total Billed
345	$3,200	A9501	A	$15,503
200	$300	A0194	C	$12,356
067	0	C456	A	$24,599

Figure 3-5: The completed relational database contains two tables with a key (Client ID)

Now you can ask a lot more questions (queries) about your clients and get answers more quickly and easily than you can with the flat-file database.

Some relational databases such as Paradox, provide simple tools to guide you through the process of posing questions and designing a report from the resulting answers.

Questions (queries) that required painstaking steps to answer using the flat-file database become elegantly easy with a relational database. A special language was developed just for relational database queries. It is called Structured Query Language (SQL). Nearly all relational databases use SQL as their query language. It is remarkably easy to use, even for nonprogrammers.

As your business grows, you add new tables to your database and link them together with keys that are common. For example, salespersons have assigned clients, so you link the salesperson table to the client table by adding a new column (salesperson id) to the client table. This way, you can assign a salesperson to as many clients as you need. A relational database allows unlimited connections between tables and an unlimited number of tables (unless the specific product you buy limits these). So long as each table relates to at least one other table by at least one column, the tables compose a relational database.

Strengths of relational databases

Relational databases reduce duplicated information by relating tables together with keys. You can save storage space and typing time, and lower the risk of error because you type in your information (data) only once. They enable you to answer complex questions (queries) easily and quickly.

Weaknesses of relational databases

Relational database software costs more and requires more power (RAM) and more storage space (hard disk) than most flat-file databases. Most relational databases allow only numbers and text in the database.

Common brand-name, relational database products

Following are some of the relational databases that you may know:

➡ Microsoft Access

➡ Oracle

➡ Sybase

➡ Paradox

Unfortunately, most relational database software cannot accept a photo into its database. A newer kind of database, called *object-oriented,* accepts photos and other kinds of data.

Object-oriented databases

The term *object-oriented* simply means that all the data is assigned to categories (*classes*). Each piece of data is called an *object.* Thinking of data as objects may sound new, but you work with it every day! Your computer has a built-in set of instructions about what to do with each class of file. Object-oriented databases use the same kind of built-in instructions.

An object-oriented database has tables with rows and columns, just like the relational database. Each object has one class. Actually, a relational database uses this concept in a small way. All data in a relational database falls into three classes (*data types*): numbers, text, and dates. The database knows that you cannot do math on text. It has special math that can only work with dates (such as adding one month). The database knows how to sort dates or words or numbers properly. Object-oriented databases expand the concept of classifying data (objects) into many more categories (classes). Here are some of the classes you might see in an object-oriented database:

➡ Digital pictures (with built-in editors)

➡ Chemical compounds (with formulas that relate each to others)

➡ Building materials (and how they fit together)

➡ Latitude and longitude (with instructions on how to calculate distance)

All that built-in information is called *meta-information*. Object-oriented databases enable you to define any kind of built-in information you need. Specialized object-oriented databases contain meta-information that simplifies complicated jobs, such as designing an airplane or a house. For example, a CAD/CAM application may use an object-oriented database to store the schematic design for a house. The database classifies building materials by size, weight, and how they connect to other classes of objects. For example, a pipe fitting has three-dimensional proportions and attaches only to certain pipes. All the pipes that fit together are a class or a group of related classes. If the designer tries to attach the wrong two pipes, the database issues an error message.

Strengths of object-oriented databases

Object-oriented databases have expanded classifications of nontext data, such as pictures, building materials, or chemical compounds. They are capable of storing BLOBs (binary large objects) efficiently.

Weaknesses of object-oriented databases

Object-oriented databases have limited query capabilities. Software is usually specialized for engineering or scientific research.

Common brand-name, object-oriented database products

VODAK is a newer object-oriented database developed in Russia for multimedia. It is free for educational institutions.

The object-oriented database may seem like the perfect solution to your problem. Here is a database that takes care of pictures and text, plus just about any kind of data. Unfortunately, object-oriented databases favor engineers and scientists, not businesses. The technology evolved independently of the relational database technology. Object-oriented databases do not handle text well. They do not use SQL, the query language universally used by relational databases. Relational databases give you a fast and easy way to pose complex questions about your data. Object-oriented databases don't have that capability. What you are really after is something that gives you the query power of a relational database and the enhanced object classifying of an object-oriented database. This brings you to the *hybrid* database.

Hybrid databases

A *hybrid database* combines the best of relational and object-oriented databases. It handles nontext data such as pictures because it incorporates meta-information, like the object-oriented database. It also handles text well and has the capability of processing complex queries quickly by using SQL, like the relational databases.

Your idea of adding a photograph to form letters works if you use a hybrid database. Your business in this digital world grows increasingly "multimedia". Today, color graphics proliferate in documents, and Web sites buzz with pictures (graphics), video, and sound (audio). The Web is part library and part video arcade — it is ready for multimedia. Ride that wave. Imagine your visitors clicking on a picture and hearing a sample song from a new CD you sell. Or your visitor clicks on a brand of car and selects colors and accessories. With one more click, your visitor enjoys a video of his customized car cruising down the highway. Storing all this information in your database means visitors can interact with the information and view multimedia Web pages built on the fly — just for them.

A hybrid database application may work more efficiently with multimedia than a relational database. Oracle's relational database, although not considered a hybrid, does handle multimedia objects within its relational framework with efficiency and speed. Hybrid database technology is new, and very few hybrid databases are on the market now.

Strengths of hybrid databases

Some strengths of hybrid databases are the following:

➡ They have expanded classifications of nontext data, such as pictures, sound, and video.

➡ Hybrid databases can process complex queries like relational databases.

Weaknesses of hybrid databases

The following is a weak point of hybrid databases:

➡ It is a very new technology with no standards.

Common brand-name, hybrid database products

Informix Illustra is the leading example of a hybrid database. Although designed for digital multimedia in general, it is particularly well-suited for use in a Web site where you need to generate dynamic multimedia Web documents. GNNServer, by GNN combines a Web server with an Illustra hybrid database. GNNServer is an elegant example of leading-edge Web software.

The Future of Databases

Commercial and noncommercial uses for databases on the Web are endless. Searching for a Web site in Yahoo (a search engine) is just the beginning. Imagine visitors to your Web site browsing catalogs of clothing, coffee, gifts, or flowers. They select what they want to buy with a mouse click on a picture of that item. Your database keeps track of their orders, showing them what they have selected so far and how much it all costs. You tap into the same database from your warehouse and print out an order and an address label to fill the visitor's order. Your Web site verifies the credit card number and then faxes a receipt to the visitor.

In a different scenario, you've created a special map on your Web site using a database. Your visitor clicks anywhere on a map of California and sees statistics on income, industries, population, watersheds, or roads. Another click shows pictures of hotels, resorts, travel agents, real estate for sale, and so on. The world of information is at hand, and you lead the way when you combine the power of multimedia on the Web with the power of a database.

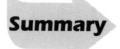

Summary

Databases are the best way to organize all kinds of data. Databases keep multimedia presentations well-organized and accessible.

Flat-file databases work best for data that stands alone. Relational databases work best for text where complex queries are needed. Object-oriented databases tend to apply best to science and engineering rather than business. Hybrid databases perform especially well when delivering multimedia information.

Basic HTML

If you are a database specialist or new to the World Wide Web, this chapter is for you. To do anything on the Web, including using a database, you must use HyperText Markup Language (HTML) programming. Programming is a heavy-duty name given to the simple markups that you apply to plain text in American Standard Code for Information Interchange (ASCII) format. ASCII text can be read by any kind of computer. HTML is simple, straightforward desktop publishing; nothing fancy, just the typesetting basics. It facilitates the inclusion of color graphics and other multimedia elements placed in the text (*in line*). It is also a *hypertext* system; that is, you can create connections (*links*) in one document to another document. The links are right in the text, and with a click of the mouse, a visitor can jump to the linked document and back again. The link, called a *hyperlink*, can be to another document you created or to any document anywhere on the Web. All this, and you can do it with simple markups.

Working in HTML

Books can teach you HTML thoroughly. Many are handy and worthwhile. With the following basic guide, however, those unfamiliar with HTML can learn to do attractive HTML documents within a few hours. What do you need? You can do the markups in your word processor. You can view the results in your Web browser. Here are the steps:

1. **Use your word processor to call up the ASCII text file you desire to convert to a Web document.** (That is, you must use your word processor to create the document and then save the document file as an ASCII text file).

2. **Type the markups in the appropriate places.**

3. **Save the ASCII file (sometimes called a *plain text* file or a *text file*).** You must then change the file extension to *.htm* (Windows) or *.html* (Windows 95 and Windows NT). This extension tells the browser that it is a Web document.

4. **Use your Web browser to access the file. To do so, you must also have the TCP/IP protocol installed on your PC.** If your Web browser works on the Internet, the TCP/IP protocol is already installed. Use the browser in *local host* mode when you look at files on your own computer. You do not need to put your document on the Web until later.

HTML editor

You may want to use a special editor made just for coding HTML (HTML editor). One of the most popular is called Hot Dog. You can download it for a 30-day trial from this Web site:

http://www.sausage.com/

When working with HTML, keep in mind that HTML markups are *not* case sensitive. The markups can be lowercase or uppercase. We suggest always using uppercase, because that makes the markups easier to see and edit.

Also keep in mind that UNIX directories and file names *are* case sensitive, just like your user ID, logon, and e-mail passwords for your Internet account. Uppercase and lowercase are different. A file named "Harry.html" is not the same as one named "harry.html". This is important for Internet addresses and internal addresses, particularly ones that you place in your document as hypertext links. The best practice is to use all lowercase letters in all your file names.

Learning HTML

Resources for learning HTML abound on the Web. You can supplement the basic HTML instructions found here with more in-depth reading. These sites are good places to find helpful information.

The following address contains lists of other links for tips on HTML, graphics, and marketing on the Web:

`http://maui.net/~mcculc/resource.htm`

The following newsgroup can help answer your questions, review your HTML documents, and provide advice and resources:

`comp.infosystems.www.authoring.html`

The Barebones Guide to HTML gives you the syntax for HTML, brief descriptions, and some good hints:

`http://werbach.com/barebones/`

Definitions

The first line and last line of your document define it as an HTML document. Next you need to create a *head* and a *title*. The head is invisible but is read by Web search engines. In other words, it contains information such as keywords, copyrights, and authors. The title appears at the space at the very top of your window in Windows or Macintosh.

`<HTML>`	This goes at the beginning of every document.
`</HTML>`	This goes at the end of every document.
`<HEAD>`	This indicates the heading information for a document.
`</HEAD>`	This indicates the end of the heading information.
`<TITLE>`	This is the title that goes at the top of the window.
`</TITLE>`	This is the end of the title name.
`<BODY>`	This marks the beginning of the body of the document.
`</BODY>`	This marks the end of the body.

Here is a standard document beginning:

```
<HTML><HEAD><TITLE>[title]</TITLE></HEAD><BODY>
```

Here is a standard document ending:

```
</BODY></HTML>
```

This is not difficult computer stuff.

Markups

Markups are formatting commands that you put into your HTML document. The browser recognizes these markups and replaces them with the desired formatting.

Headings

Headings are easy. There are six sizes, with 1 being the largest and 6 being the smallest. As a practical matter, usually only the first three (1,2,3) are a larger type size than the text. A heading adds a line of space before and after itself. Headings, like many HTML markups, have a start and an end mark:

    `<H1>`   This mark starts a heading.

    `</H1>`   This mark ends a heading.

Breaks

The Web browser ignores all carriage returns when it translates your document. Lines are wrapped to fit into the window. To cause the browser to go to the next line, you use either a line break or a paragraph break, which are two different things. No line of space follows a line break. After a paragraph break, however, a line of space is added.

    `<BR>`   Line break. No blank line.

    `<P>`   Paragraph break. Blank line between paragraphs.

Horizontal line

You can add a horizontal line with one markup:

    `<HR>`   Horizontal line (rule).

Preformatted text

With this markup, you can add ASCII text and keep it exactly as you created it — including the carriage returns. It is usually displayed with Courier monospaced type, but in any case, it is monospaced like ASCII text. In other words, it suspends all other formatting commands for the duration of the chosen section. By using this markup, HTML leaves the text alone, and you see it in its ASCII form. The only real advantage of this markup is to control line spaces, blank spaces, and carriage returns.

```
<PRE>[text]</PRE>    Preformatted text.
```

You can use this for general formatting too. No matter how many paragraph markups (<P>) you add after a paragraph, you will get only one line space (one blank line). If you use the preformat markups, you can add as many line spaces as you desire (see the two lines of space in the following example):

```
<PRE>


</PRE>
```

Emphasis

You also can use normal italics and bold characters. HTML includes an emphasize markup for text-only Web browsers that cannot display italics or bold:

```
<I></I>      Italics
<B></B>      Bold
<EM></EM>    Emphasized
```

As more and more people join the ranks of multimedia-capable users on the Web, you may want to forego the use of the emphasized markup (<EM>).The emphasized markup was created primarily for text-only Web browsers such as Lynx and normally appears as italics in Netscape. (*Note:* Text-only browsers are those that are not able to display graphics, animation, or anything other than text.)

Lists

HTML offers a variety of list markups:

```
<OL> <LI>          Ordered (numbered) lists
<UL> <LI>          Unordered (bulleted) lists
<DL> <DT> <DD>     Glossary lists
```

Numbered (ordered) lists start with `<OL>` and end with `</OL>`. Each item is prefaced by `<LI>`.

Bulleted (unordered) lists start with `<UL>` and end with `</UL>`. Each item is prefaced by `<LI>`.

Glossary lists start with `<DL>` and end with `</DL>`. Additionally, glossary lists have one of two other markups. The markup `<DT>` prefaces the glossary term. The markup `<DD>` prefaces the glossary definition.

Ordered

This is what the HTML code looks like for ordered lists:

```
Consider the following benefits:
<OL>
<LI>Lower price.
<LI>Higher quality.
<LI>Faster delivery.
</OL>
Additionally, we process your order on the day received.
```

This is what the actual resulting page looks like:

```
Consider the following benefits:

#1.   Lower price.
#2.   Higher quality.
#3.   Faster delivery.

Additionally, we process your order on the day received.
```

Unordered

This is what the HTML code looks like for unordered lists:

```
Consider the following benefits:
<UL>
<LI>Lower price.
<LI>Higher quality.
<LI>Faster delivery.
</UL>
Additionally, we process your order on the day received.
```

This is what the actual resulting page looks like:

```
Consider the following benefits:

* Lower price.
* Higher quality.
* Faster delivery.

Additionally, we process your order on the day received.
```

Glossary

This is what the HTML code looks like for a glossary:

```
Consider the following benefits:
<DL>
<DT>Lower price.
<DD>The lowest in Maine according to the Fenner survey.
<DT>Higher quality.
<DD>Triple inspection in the production process.
<DT>Faster delivery.
<DD>All orders shipped Federal Express.
</DL>
Additionally, we process your order on the day received.
```

This is what the actual resulting page looks like:

```
Consider the following benefits:

Lower price.
    The lowest in Maine according to the Fenner survey.

Higher quality.
    Triple inspection in the production process.

Faster delivery.
    All orders shipped Federal Express.

Additionally, we process your order on the day received.
```

Indented lists

Lists are normally rendered by browsers as indented. In the case of the glossary markup, the <DT> markup represents the normal amount of indentation and the <DD> markup represents an increased amount of indentation. You can use either the <DT> markup or the <DD> markup — without the other — for an unordered (unnumbered) list that does not have bullets.

Nested

Lists can also be nested. Each nested list has an increased amount of indentation. You can create an outline effect by using nested lists. In fact, you can use list markups to move text anywhere on the page. For example, the following markups will move the word *Welcome!* well toward the middle of the page:

```
<DL><DL><DL><DL><DL>
<DT>Welcome!
</DL></DL></DL></DL></DL>
```

Here is how it appears on-screen:

```
                              Welcome!
```

Beyond the preceding descriptions, lists are difficult to explain. To learn to use lists, experiment with them in a variety of browsers. The other list markups for menus (`<MENU>`) and directories (`<DIR>`) are obsolete; don't use them. If you should run across either one, they both do the same thing as an unordered (bulleted) list.

Images

You can insert images into the text by a markup that shows the address of the graphics file. The address goes between the quotation marks, as follows:

```
<A SRC="">        Inserts a graphic.
```

Here's an example:

```
<A SRC="gif/sunset.gif">
```

Note that the Web browser will find the file sunset.gif in the gif subdirectory of the current directory (folder).

Other media

Media other than graphics files must be hyperlinked as explained for images (but using `HREF=` in place of `SRC=`). Some examples of these other media are videoplayers, audioplayers, and audio- or videoconferencing programs. When you execute the hyperlink, the media will play in a special player or be seen in a special viewer. A visitor must have installed the special player, plug-in, add-on, or viewer in his or her Web browser ahead of time. Such special viewers are usually made available for free downloading off the Internet by the various software vendors. Some common examples of these are QuickTime or MPEG (for video playback), Naplayer or Raplayer (for audio playback), CU-SeeMe (for videoconferencing) and Shockwave (for audioconferencing). Frequently, one of each of these applications will be bundled together with a popular browser for your convenience.

Anchors

If you want to have a hyperlink go to someplace within a document, that place must have an address. The *anchor* is the address. The anchor has a unique name (in the document), and the name is put between the quotation marks, as follows:

```
<A NAME="[anchor name]">[text label or GIF]</A>  Anchor
```

Here's an example:

```
The first battle of <A NAME="#civilwarbattle3">Bull
Run</A> was fought with great losses for the North.
```

Elsewhere in the text, it will read:

```
To read more about Bull Run, <A HREF="#civilwarbattle3">
early major battles</A>.
```

When you execute (click on) "early major battles", the hyperlink jumps the reader to the words *Bull Run*. The # sign indicates an internal address (an internal anchor).

URLs

A Uniform Resource Locator (URL) is simply an address on the Internet. All valid addresses on the Internet are unique. A URL is prefixed by the type of server delivering the files, as follows:

ftp://	FTP
gopher://	Gopher
http://	Web
telnet://	Telnet
wais://	WAIS
mailto:	e-mail
news:	newsgroups (Usenet)
file://	local file

Next is the domain name. Often the domain name has a prefix to denote the server:

`uswars.com`	Domain name
`ftp.uswars.com`	FTP server address
`gopher.uswars.com`	Gopher server address
`www.uswars.com`	Web server address

You can drop the prefix for one of the servers and use just the domain name. If you did that for the Web server, the URL would be:

`http://uswars.com`   Web address

Using just the domain name in the address will get you to the domain's root directory. If the root directory name for the domain is *allwars* and no file is specified, the browser will look for the file *index.html* on the root directory and display that first. Neither the root directory nor the filename need be included in the address. Suppose that you have a subdirectory of the root directory named *civilwar* and you want to access a specific file on it named *battles.html,* where you expect to find some information on the Battle of Bull Run. The address of the document will be the following:

`http://uswars.com/civilwar/battles.html`

Finally, you can even go right to the anchor for the Battle of Bull Run, *civilwarbattle3,* as mentioned previously:

`http://uswars.com/civilwar/battles.html#civilwarbattle3`

Suppose, however, that you are in the document *index.html* in the root directory *allwars.* Further suppose that a hyperlink exists to the anchor *civilwarbattle3* in the document *battles.html* in the subdirectory *civilwar.* The address in the hyperlink is as follows:

`civilwar/battles.html#civilwarbattle3`

Every part of the address (URL) is unique. The address *uswars.com* (domain name) is unique on the Internet. The domain's root directory *allwars* is a unique directory at the top level on the hard disk of the computer. The subdirectory *civilwar* is unique as a subdirectory of the root directory. The file *battles.html* is a unique file on the *civilwar* directory. And the anchor *civilwarbattle3* is a unique anchor in the document *battles.html.*

Just like your PC

Note that there can be only one *uswars.com* in the entire Internet. But after you get to that place, the directories and files act just the way directories and files on your PC act. In other words, there can be a file called *civilwarbattle3* in the *civilwar* directory and an identically named file in the *spanishcivilwar* directory.

Internal hyperlinks

Within an HTML document, a *hyperlink* marks a word or phrase and states the address (between the quotation marks) to which the word or phrase is linked. The visitor simply clicks the word or phrase (or graphic) and goes directly to the anchor, wherever it might be.

This is how the basic code for a hyperlink looks:

```
<A HREF="[file name]">[text or GIF]</A>
```

In the following paragraph in the *battles.html* document, the words *early major battle* compose a hyperlink to the anchor *civilwarbattle3*:

```
In one of the <A HREF="#civilwarbattle3">early major
battles</A> of the war, Mr. Lincoln was not pleased with
the generals.
```

An *internal hyperlink* in a document refers to an anchor somewhere else in the document. The preceding text will look like the following with the link either underlined or in a different color than the other text:

```
In one of the early major battles of the war, Mr. Lincoln
was not pleased with the generals.
```

Hyperlinks

A hyperlink can go to another document in your domain. It can even go directly to a specific document at another domain. Within a Web system, you use *relative references;* that is, the address is stated relative to the directory on which you are located. Outside your Web system, you use *absolute* addresses. Here's a hyperlink used in *index.html* to *battles.html*:

```
<A HREF="civilwar/battles.html">[text or GIF]</A>
```

Here's a hyperlink to another domain, which takes you to the *index.html* file on the root directory of that domain:

```
<A HREF="http://www.hotwired.com">[text or GIF]</A>
```

References

Most UNIX books explain absolute and relative references more thoroughly, and you will need a book on UNIX to learn a few commands and to use as a reference. Included here is a summary explanation.

Relative references

Within your Web system, it is easiest to use relative references. It makes maintenance easier too, because you can do your Web-site maintenance on your PC, as explained in Chapter 12, "System Design". An example best illustrates relative references. Suppose that you have the directory *airplane* with the subdirectory *military*, which has the subdirectory *twin-engine*. *Twin-engine* has the subdirectory *fighter*, which has the subdirectory *F-14* (see Figure 4-1). In UNIX notation (almost identical to DOS), it will look like this:

```
airplane/military/twin-engine/fighter/F-14
```

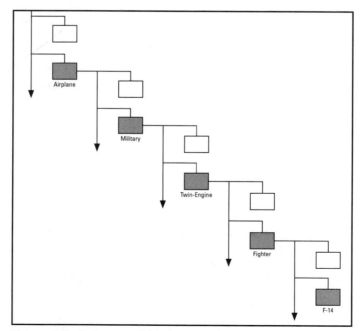

Figure 4-1: A directory (folder) tree.

If the document you are working on is in the *twin-engine* directory, to go via hyperlink to the *F-14* directory, you preface the filename with *fighter/F-14/*. For example, if the file is *wings.html*, the relative address is as follows:

```
fighter/F-14/wings.html
```

To go via a hyperlink to the airplane directory, you preface the filename with ../../. The double periods with a slash (../) represent moving up one level in the directory hierarchy. In this case, you want to move up two levels, so there are two sets of the double periods and slashes. For example, if the file is menu.html, the relative address is:

```
../../menu.html
```

Relative references work both on your PC and on the hard disk of your ISP without change — so long as you have exactly the same directory structure on both your hard disk and the hard disk of your ISP. You can and must do this yourself from home on your PC.

Absolute references

Absolute references are full Internet addresses to Web, Gopher, WAIS, Telnet, or FTP sites outside your Web site.

HTML Markups: An Example

The following example of an HTML document illustrates the markups in this chapter:

```
<HTML><HEAD><TITLE>iBOX</TITLE></HEAD><BODY>

<A NAME="top">From the Multimedia Reporter</A>

<H2>The Revolution Begins</H2>

by Joseph T. Sinclair
<P>
Think things have been moving fast for the Internet? Hold
on to your hat. You're not even in the fast lane yet. But
you will be soon. Network computers (NCs) were announced
in 1995 as essentially inexpensive limited computer devices
to access the Internet (or intranet) and nothing more.
Although greeted with skepticism, NCs will appeal to
those who do not use computers yet want to access the
Internet. They will also appeal to companies that want to
```

(continued)

(continued)

```
provide access to company intranet publishing and company
databases for employees who do not otherwise use computers.
They will be valuable in training situations too. They are
intended to be easy to use.
<P>
JCC Corp's iBOX is a device about the size of a small VCR.
It has standard connections for:
<OL>
<LI>monitor
<LI>TV
<LI>mouse
<LI>keyboard
<LI>phone line
</OL>
It includes:
<UL>
<LI>CD drive
<LI>4 MB RAM
<LI>28.8 modem
<LI>ISDN interface
</UL>
Software includes an operating system based on UNIX, a Web
browser, built-in encryption capability, and an e-mail
program. The iBOX starts by loading the operating system
and other software off a CD. It has minimal controls and
is quite easy to use.
<DL>
<DD><IMG SRC="ibox.gif">
</DL>
<P>
The iBOX evolved from American smart terminal technology,
a seasoned digital technology. It is manufactured in Japan,
where it has sold successfully at retail. According to Richard
A. Flores, President of <A HREF="HTTP://www.ibox.com">JCC
Corp</A>, the iBOX will be in the stores in April, about
five months ahead of its competitors.
<PRE>

</PRE>
<A HREF="#top">Return to Beginning</A>

</BODY></HTML>
```

Text wrapping

The key to rational HTML programming is using *text blocks*. In Web browsers, HTML always wraps text. How it wraps text is based on the size of the window that the Web browser provides.

If you think in terms of text blocks, your HTML programming will proceed more efficiently. You should see every grouping of text, large or small, as a block of text. Within that block, the browser will wrap it according to the size of the window a visitor happens to be using.

Testing

The only way to learn and use HTML is by constantly testing what you have programmed. To do so, you use your HTML editor. Then you switch to your browser to test what you have done. Every time you switch to your browser, you must "reload" or "refresh" the document to see how your revised programming looks. Different browsers render HTML differently. You may want to test your programming in several browsers. To see a list of the differences among the various browsers, look at this URL:

```
http://www.colosys.net/~rscott/barb.htm
```

Netscape

Netscape has become the de facto operating platform for the Web. Netscape has created its own markups that extend the number of HTML markups available beyond the officially sanctioned ones. Because Netscape is leading the pack, you can be confident that most of Netscape's HTML extensions are likely to be officially adopted in the next round of HTML standards. Netscape publishes its HTML extensions at the Netscape Web site (`www.netscape.com`).

You should use the Netscape extensions. They add considerable aesthetic and publishing functionality to HTML, and from 1996 on, all browsers that want to be competitive will offer the capability to view the Netscape extensions. The Netscape extension used in the demos for this book is for creating a page background:

```
<BODY BACKGROUND="sky.gif ">
```

In the example in this chapter, the document appears superimposed over a color graphic in the file *sky.gif*. You cannot use a background image without it.

The Future

HTML markups will become much more complicated. Soon, they will approach the full functionality of desktop publishing. At that time, the HTML markups will be difficult to use, because there will be so many to remember. Fortunately, HTML authoring programs will make HTML documents easy. In fact, word processing programs will become HTML authoring programs. Many word processing programs already have HTML conversion. This is the first step toward integrating more complex HTML into conventional desktop publishing packages.

Summary

Being proficient in the use of HTML is a prerequisite to building a Web-database application. Most database engines at Web sites cannot create Web documents on the fly by themselves; they need HTML templates. Good HTML templates requires a good working knowledge of HTML.

HTML Forms

In This Chapter

Overview of HTML forms
Syntax of input markups
A sample HTML form
CGI scripts and HTML forms

Overview of HTML Forms

To use a database at a Web site, a visitor must be able to tell the database what to do by providing it with information, or input. The input creates the queries or otherwise starts the actions required to make a database application work. HTML provides special commands (form markups) for getting this input. Any document that receives input from the visitor is called a form.

Think of a form as if it were a fill-in-the-blank questionnaire. It can appear anywhere within your HTML document. There can even be several forms within one document. When designing a form, you have five basic types of input to consider:

- *Text.* Use this type for small boxes where a visitor can type in a word, his or her name, or some query criteria. Use the related type, *textarea*, for large boxes where a visitor may type in a comment, message, or explanation.

- *Checkbox.* This is a simple way to provide your visitor with choices. The items appear with a small checkbox near each item. The visitor clicks the box to mark it with an *X*. A second click removes the *X*, if desired. Use this for multiple-choice replies, where your visitor can check all that apply.

- *Radio.* This is similar to a checkbox, except that it displays a round button in front of the choice and allows the visitor to select only one of the choices. A mouse click on one choice puts a dot in the round button, marking it as selected. A click on a different choice removes the dot from the first choice and places a dot in the current choice. Use this where only one answer is allowed, such as the sex of the visitor.

➡ *Password.* This gives the visitor a box to type in but displays only asterisks instead of the letters typed. Use this for passwords or any sensitive input.

➡ *Menu.* The menu type is similar to the pull-down menus you see in many Windows applications. A list of correct answers pops up when the visitor clicks in the box. The visitor scrolls through the list and clicks on the proper selection. Use this for long lists, such as the names of cities or states.

After a visitor enters the input into the HTML form, nothing happens. It just stays there. You need to add corresponding CGI programming (scripts) that tell the computer what to do with the input. CGI is a Web server API (Application Programming Interface). You create CGI scripts — actually programming — with a language such as C or a high-level scripting language such as Perl. Instruction on writing the scripts is beyond the scope of this book, but Chapter 6, "CGI Scripts," explains them more fully.

The form markups included in this chapter will provide you with an easy introduction to HTML forms. To become proficient in HTML forms programming, however, you should get an HTML programming book to use as a reference and to learn additional markups and attributes. Chapter 4, "Basic HTML," covers some basics of HTML. Chapter 22, "Linking the Oracle Database Application to the Web Site," and Chapter 24, "Connecting the Access Database Application to the Web," contain more real examples of HTML forms and other HTML documents.

What can you do with HTML forms? You can allow a visitor to send an e-mail message from an e-mail message form right in the Web document. You can provide a form (such as a survey or questionnaire) for a visitor to fill out, and the computer will accumulate the answers to the questions in a special file. You can allow a visitor to set a computing process into motion. Through the input, you can enable a visitor to use the power of the computer to do just about anything. For database use, the HTML form gives a visitor a way of providing the input for queries or for otherwise using the database application.

Normal markups

You can use normal HTML markups, such as headings, italics, graphics, and so on, inside HTML forms. A Web document can have multiple forms (form sections). Refer to Chapter 4, "Basic HTML," for a good start on these kinds of HTML markups. Using normal markups within forms gives you the same kind of formatting control as any other HTML document.

Syntax of Input Markups

It's difficult to put markups in an HTML document if you don't know what markups you can use. This section shows you the syntax of input markups.

FORM

Use the following markups to begin and end a form:

```
<FORM></FORM>
```

There are two additional parameters within the FORM markup: METHOD and ACTION.

METHOD

You can use one of two methods for submitting information (input) to the CGI script, GET or POST. With GET, the input in the form is assigned to an environmental variable on the server. The CGI script then retrieves the value of the variable. With POST, no variable is assigned, and the input is passed directly to the CGI script. Because the UNIX shell has limits on the number of characters it can handle at one time, if you use GET for a form with a high volume of input, some of the input may be lost. Therefore, using POST is safer, at least for a form with voluminous input:

```
<FORM METHOD="POST">
```

ACTION

The ACTION part of the form markup defines (between the quotation marks) what the computer will do, as follows:

```
<FORM ACTION="">
```

This requires an address for a CGI script. Such an address looks like this:

```
<FORM ACTION="../../cgi-bin/insuranceform">
```

This shows that the CGI script *insuranceform* is located two directories up the directory tree, then over to a subdirectory called cgi-bin. The complete FORM markup looks like this with the METHOD and ACTION added:

```
<FORM METHOD="POST" ACTION="../../cgi-bin/insuranceform">
```

Input

This section describes each of the variations that HTML provides for accepting visitor input.

Text

You must specify an input type. Although the default type is *text*, it is best to specify text anyway for auditing purposes, as follows:

```
<INPUT TYPE="TEXT"
```

A text input must have a unique name and specify a size. For example, in the text input, the size indicates the size of the box where text may be entered, as in the following:

```
NAME="visitorname" SIZE="30">
```

The *30* indicates that the input box appears to be 30 characters long on the form. An HTML input box has just one line for input (see Figure 5-1). The input accepts more input than 30 characters, but the box in the form appears as if it accepts only 30 characters. (You can use the additional MAXLENGTH attribute if you desire to limit the number of characters the visitor can type into the text box.) It all goes together like this:

```
<INPUT TYPE="TEXT" NAME="visitorname" SIZE="30">
```

Password

A special type of text input is the PASSWORD box. This type echoes back all the characters typed by a visitor as asterisks (*******).

```
<INPUT TYPE="PASSWORD" NAME="user password" SIZE="8"
MAXLENGTH="8">
```

Textarea

For multiple lines of text, visitors need a larger box in which to type. Use the textarea markup, which includes three attributes: name, rows, and cols. The syntax is as follows:

```
<TEXTAREA NAME="explain" ROWS="5" COLS="30">
```

The preceding markup provides a text area 5 lines long by 30 characters wide for input. If a visitor types in too much text for the text area, the text box scrolls. The text area can be used for entering comments (see Figure 5-2).

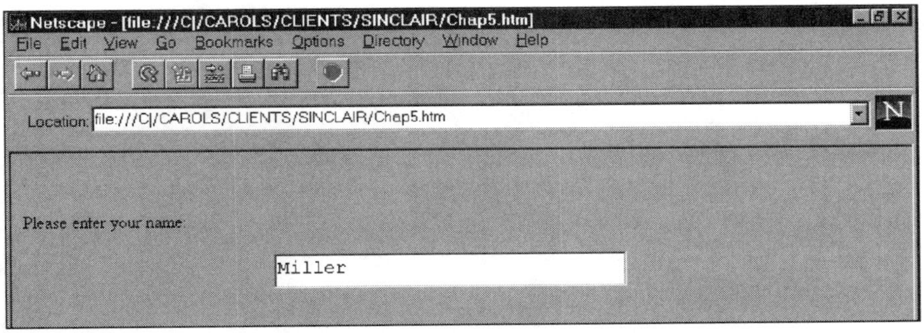

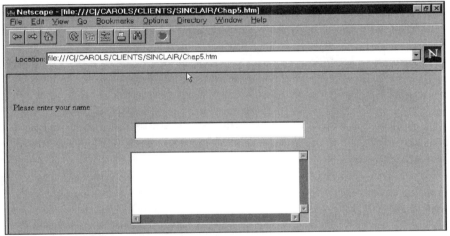

Figure 5-1: An HTML input box has one line for input.

Figure 5-2: An HTML text area input is often used for comments.

Checkbox

Checkboxes enable the visitor to make one or multiple nonexclusive choices, giving more control over the input. Figure 5-3 shows the checkboxes in the lower left corner of the screen. Each box is either on or off. The type is *checkbox*. For a checkbox, you will often use list markups (see Chapter 4) with the form markups:

```
<UL>
<LI><INPUT TYPE="CHECKBOX" NAME="life"> Life Insurance
<LI><INPUT TYPE="CHECKBOX" NAME="health"> Health Insurance
<LI><INPUT TYPE="CHECKBOX" NAME="casualty"> Home Casualty
Insurance
<LI><INPUT TYPE="CHECKBOX" NAME="auto"> Auto Insurance
</UL>
```

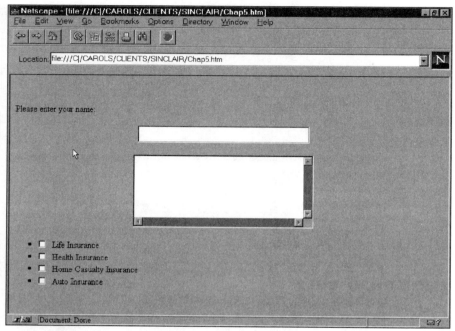

Figure 5-3: An HTML form checkbox allows more control over input than a text box.

You can also use the value attribute to place words you need in the variable. For example, if you want the variable to contain the words "Life Insurance" when the "life" box is checked, your HTML code looks like this:

```
<INPUT TYPE="CHECKBOX" NAME="life" VALUE="Life Insurance">
```

Another option enables you to put a check in the box by adding the checked attribute to your checkbox. The visitor can change the choice. The default value is set at un*checked* if the checked attribute is not used. When a checkbox input is checked, the variable contains the word "on" or the word(s) contained in the value clause. The HTML code for a checkbox that is checked when the visitor first sees the form is as follows:

```
<INPUT TYPE="CHECKBOX" NAME="life" CHECKED>
```

Radio buttons

Radio buttons provide multiple choices, only one of which a visitor can choose. The radio buttons are round and in the lower left corner of Figure 5-4. The type is *radio*. Each button must have a value attribute. The value attribute is what goes into the input variable when the visitor chooses that button. The value attribute looks like this:

```
VALUE="single"
```

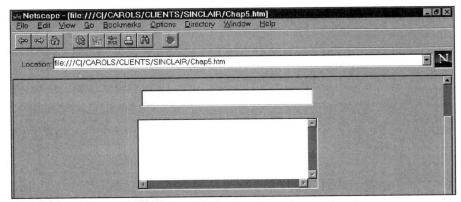

Figure 5-4: HTML form radio buttons allow only one item to be chosen.

Radio buttons are invariably used in a list. Notice that in the following example, each radio button has the same name but a different value.

```
<UL>
<LI><INPUT TYPE="RADIO" NAME="maritalstatus"
VALUE="single"> Single
<LI><INPUT TYPE="RADIO" NAME="maritalstatus"
VALUE="married"> Married
<LI><INPUT TYPE="RADIO" NAME="maritalstatus"
VALUE="divorced"> Divorced
</UL>
```

Menus

With the select and option markups, a visitor can make an exclusive or nonexclusive selection from a menu, as in the following example:

```
<SELECT Name="area">
<OPTION>Asheville
<OPTION>Chapel Hill
<OPTION>Charlotte
<OPTION>Durham
<OPTION>Fayetteville
<OPTION>Greensboro
<OPTION>Greenville
<OPTION>Raleigh
<OPTION>Wilmington
<OPTION>Winston-Salem
</SELECT>
```

Figure 5-5 shows an example of an HTML form menu.

Submit

After a visitor completes the input, he or she uses the Submit button to start the CGI script that uses the input (see Figure 5-6). The HTML form markup scheme provides only one Submit button per form:

```
<INPUT TYPE="SUBMIT" VALUE="Submit Answers">
```

The value attribute becomes the label on the Submit button. Otherwise, the default label *Submit* appears.

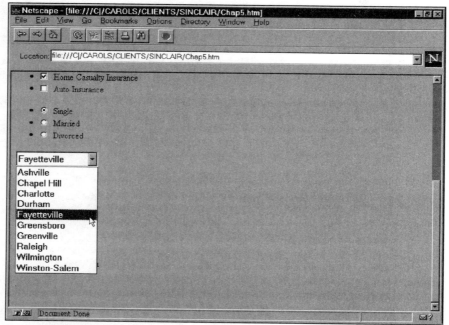

Figure 5-5: An HTML form menu.

Reset

Naturally, you will want to give visitors a chance to clear the form. Sometimes the form or the information requested confuses a visitor, who makes mistakes, and then wants to start over again. The Reset button resets all the input to their default state (see Figure 5-7):

```
<INPUT TYPE="RESET" VALUE="Reset the Form">
```

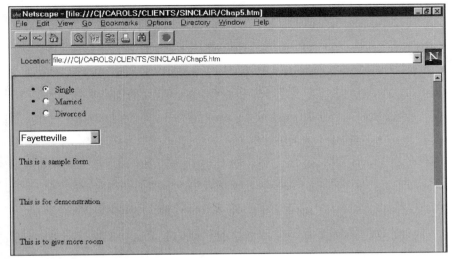

Figure 5-6: An HTML Submit button.

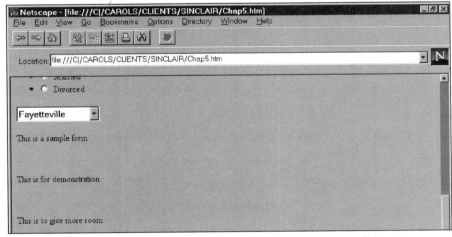

Figure 5-7: An HTML Reset button enables the visitor clear all input fields.

Sample

Here is what it looks like when you put all this information together in one form. The HTML code is as follows, followed by the actual view you see in the browser (see Figure 5-8).

```
<FORM METHOD="POST" ACTION="../../cgi-bin/insuranceform">

<H2>Insurance Application</H2>
<PRE>

</PRE>
Name: <INPUT TYPE="TEXT" NAME="visitorname" SIZE="30">
<P>
Check the types of insurance for which you desire to
receive pricing:

<UL>
<LI><INPUT TYPE="CHECKBOX" NAME="life"> Life Insurance
<LI><INPUT TYPE="CHECKBOX" NAME="health"> Health Insurance
<LI><INPUT TYPE="CHECKBOX" NAME="casualty"> Home Casualty
Insurance
<LI><INPUT TYPE="CHECKBOX" NAME="auto"> Auto Insurance
</UL>

Indicate your marital status:

<UL>
<LI><INPUT TYPE="RADIO" NAME="maritalstatus"
VALUE="single"> Single
<LI><INPUT TYPE="RADIO" NAME="maritalstatus"
VALUE="married"> Married
<LI><INPUT TYPE="RADIO" NAME="maritalstatus"
VALUE="divorced"> Divorced
</UL>

Area of the state where you reside: <SELECT NAME="area">
<OPTION>Asheville
<OPTION>Chapel Hill
<OPTION>Charlotte
<OPTION>Durham
<OPTION>Fayetteville
<OPTION>Greensboro
<OPTION>Greenville
<OPTION>Raleigh
<OPTION>Wilmington
<OPTION>Winston-Salem
</SELECT>
<P>
If you have ever had an insurance policy canceled, please
indicate the circumstances under which it was canceled and
the reasons the insurance company gave for making the
cancellation:<BR>

<TEXTAREA NAME="explain" ROWS="10" COLS="30">
```

```
<H3>Thank you for your application.</H3>

<INPUT TYPE="SUBMIT" VALUE="Submit Answers">
<INPUT TYPE="RESET" VALUE="Reset the Form">

</FORM>
```

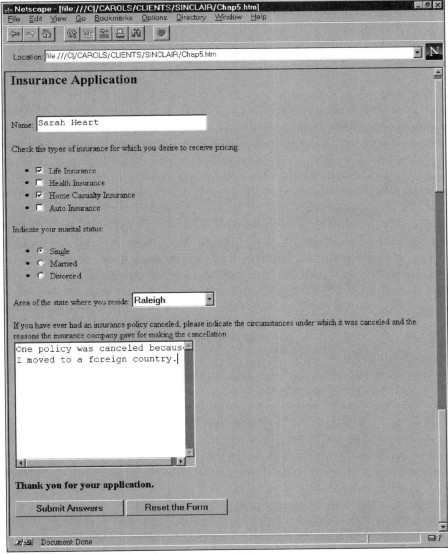

Figure 5-8: A Web browser view of the HTML form sample.

Common Gateway Interface

After the HTML form has done its work by collecting information from the visitor, that data is passed on to another program in the server. The computer requires CGI scripts to send input from the HTML form to the database or to the application software that uses the data. The CGI script reads in the input from the HTML document. In Figure 5-8, a visitor uses the sample form shown previously and fills it in with some information about herself. When she clicks the *Submit Answers* button, a CGI script starts up and does something with the information. The information is contained in the input variables that were defined in the HTML form. Following is a list of the variable names and the contents of each one:

➡ visitorname: Sarah Heart

➡ life: on

➡ health: (blank)

➡ casualty: on

➡ auto: (blank)

➡ maritalstatus: single

➡ area: Raleigh

➡ explain: One policy was canceled because I moved to a foreign country.

This information can be fed into a database and retrieved later by a salesperson, for example. The same information might be sent in an e-mail message to someone else. It all depends on the CGI script that is started by the Submit button.

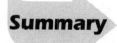

Summary

Use CGI scripts together with HTML forms to (1) enter data into a database application, or delete it, and do other maintenance tasks; (2) enter the information required for making queries; and (3) start a preprogrammed database action. Thus, CGI scripts and HTML forms are germane to using a database in a Web site.

CGI
Scripts

The Web server includes programming to let you call on the computer through the backdoor to do things the server doesn't do. Such a backdoor is called an Applications Programming Interface (API), but its name for the purposes of Web technology is Common Gateway Interface (CGI). This chapter describes some common uses of CGI and the different ways of using CGI for UNIX and Windows.

Tapping the Power of the Computer

CGI enables you to tap into the power of the computer to do processing — and calculations — not possible in the Web HTML programming environment. Naturally, this takes programming. Thus, the CGI script is a program, often a small program. The CGI script runs on the computer hosting the Web site; that is, it runs on the ISP's computer, the intranet computer, or the private Internet server computer.

What does tapping the power of the computer take besides programming? In the interactive environment of the Web, it takes *input*. The CGI script does something, usually something that HTML programming by itself cannot do. To do *anything*, a program must have some direction, even if that direction is just one command to start the program. Thus, the first thing a CGI script must do is process the input supplied by an HTML *form*. The form provides the input necessary for the CGI script (program) to run. The input in the form is placed there by a Web-site visitor. A CGI script does not absolutely require input to run, but you will use inputs with CGI scripts as a primary technique for creating a database application at a Web site (see Figure 6-1).

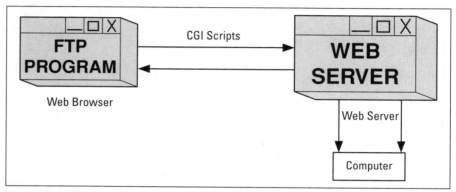

Figure 6-1: *Using the computer through an HTML form with CGI scripts.*

Sometimes the CGI script is not a program in the normal sense; it is merely a connection between an HTML form and a preexisting program, such as a database engine. Thus, for a database application, the CGI script acts as an intermediary between the HTML document and the database engine; that is, it conveys the input to the database engine.

HTML forms

HTML form programming by itself is reasonably easy, just like any other basic HTML programming (see Chapter 5, "HTML Forms"). After the forms and input formats have been programmed into a Web document, however, they must have some way to transfer the input to the computer. That's where CGI scripting comes in.

Data accumulation

A typical use for CGI scripts is in using a questionnaire (form) in an HTML document. The CGI script takes the input from the form filled in by a visitor and places it in a file, where the input accumulates. You periodically check the file to take a look at the input you've received from visitors at the Web site who have filled out the questionnaire. This type of *action* is desirable when you want to organize or tabulate the questionnaire input into a list or table.

E-mail

Another typical use for CGI scripts is to take the input and e-mail it to your e-mail address rather than accumulate it in a file. This particularly makes sense when the HTML form that you've programmed is, in fact, an e-mail message form. The form appears right in the Web document and makes it very convenient for a visitor to send you an e-mail message.

Likewise, you can have an online order form that gathers a visitor's name, mailing address, order, and credit card number (that is, gathers input). All this information passes from the form to the CGI script, which creates an e-mail message and sends it to you. When you receive the e-mail message, you can fill the order, charge it to the credit card, and ship it. E-mailing rather than accumulating is appropriate when the input is reviewed by a person reading it rather than by organizing or tabulating the input into a list or table. Most ISPs have a CGI script for sending e-mail that you can use without doing any programming yourself.

Database connection

You do not have to accumulate data into a file. You can accumulate it directly into a database. For the purposes of this book, *the CGI scripting capability to connect a database to an HTML form in a Web document is of major importance*. The CGI scripts for this purpose can be somewhat complex. They can load the data, make queries to the database application, deliver multimedia information from the database application, and maintain the data. Even a simple connection to perform one of these tasks can amount to a significant program. If you need only simple database functions, such as sorting and retrieving lines of text, a less-robust scripting application can serve the purpose.

Database application

Data can be used two ways on a Web site. The first is as a simple flat-file list. Here, the list is two-dimensional (rows and columns) and you make it in a systematic format. It is, in effect, a simple database table. You can use reasonably simple CGI scripts to query the list. A visitor fills out an HTML form (input); the CGI script uses that input to formulate the query; the CGI script retrieves the information from the list; and the CGI script formulates the output into an HTML document template and creates an HTML document on the fly (see Figure 6-2). You can get a lot of mileage out of this simple system. Nonetheless, it is difficult to administer because it does not have the features of a database engine. If you add CGI scripting to provide database maintenance functions and the like, however, you may be reinventing the wheel at considerable programming expense.

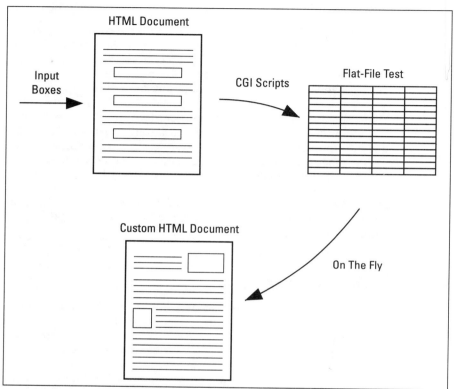

Figure 6-2: A flat-file database application.

The second way to use data at a Web site requires an actual database engine. A visitor still fills out a form (input). A CGI script formulates the query and then passes it to the database engine. The database engine executes the query and sends the results back to the CGI script. The CGI script then arranges the results into an HTML document and sends that to the visitor. The CGI script has a lot more to do compared to the flat-file example in the preceding paragraph. Along with the increased complexity, however, comes a lot more power (the database engine itself) and greater flexibility in your application.

If you are using an ISP, you need a database engine that runs on UNIX, such as Oracle, Sybase, Informix, and their competitors. Fortunately, the price of such UNIX database engines has dropped drastically in the last two years, to the point where they are no longer a major investment. The development tools for programming UNIX databases have also become easier to use, so you don't necessarily have to be a database programmer to create basic systems. Many of these traditionally UNIX database engines now run on Windows too, which provides you with convenience; you can develop in Windows and port the database application to UNIX. For the Windows environment, off-the-shelf database programs such as Access, Approach, Paradox, and their competitors also work on Windows NT.

Most database engines today are *relational* databases, which means you have the flexibility of using multiple tables that are linked by a common column. This approach enables you to create new tables by combining certain columns (fields) from separate existing tables as suits your purpose. This capability provides the infrastructure for complex queries. These databases also have built-in calculation capability. These give you considerable power with which to be creative at your Web site.

You use CGI scripting to connect the HTML form to the database engine. There are now some Web-database tools (programs) that enable you to use a database on the Web without having to write CGI scripts. Some of the tools have prewritten CGI scripts (Oracle), some work by plugging a full-fledged program (*daemon*) into the Web server (Spider Technologies), and others depend on capability programmed into a special Web server (GNNserver). Some work in UNIX, some in Windows, and some in both. This is a quickly developing technology, so you will want to thoroughly investigate the Web database tools available when you are ready to use a database.

One of the primary database activities is making legacy databases available on the Web, whether on the Internet or on an intranet. Additionally, don't overlook the potential for using databases to create custom Web documents on the fly. Keep in mind that the Web is a multimedia system, and digital multimedia systems are better and more efficiently managed with a database than with more primitive techniques. To put it more succinctly, you can use a database to do many things, including the following:

➡ Make a legacy database application available online.

➡ Keep track of visits by visitors (employees).

➡ Store and keep track of HTML documents.

➡ Create custom Web documents in response to the visitor's queries.

➡ Create Web pages based on data from prior visits to the Web site.

➡ Keep track of all the multimedia elements that make up the Web site.

➡ Deliver interactive education and training.

➡ Provide calculating capability (such as an accounting system).

➡ Create an entire Web site solely within a database application.

➡ Do all the normal things that databases do off the Web.

Scripts

Scripting means easy programming. But don't doubt that it *is* programming. When scripting is required you need a programmer. CGI scripts to carry out a major task can be very short. On the other hand, they can be very long when doing a minor task. Don't waste your time trying to do it yourself. Hire a programmer. You can hire a freelance programmer for a reasonable fee (as low as $30 per hour in some areas).

Almost any computer language will work for CGI programming. Perl scripting, C programming, and TCL scripting are popular for CGI on UNIX. Visual Basic, C++, and Perl for the PC are popular for Windows. Large CGI scripts or numerous small CGI scripts to be executed at one Web site can consume a large amount of computer power. You need to consider this possibility before deciding to use CGI technology as part of your Web system.

A CGI script can take input from an HTML form, make calculations, and return output as an HTML document. A hyperlink can activate a CGI script without any further input. For example, a screen button created by an HTML form can start a CGI action when you click on it. Although they are not the only way to tap the power of the computer in a Web system, CGI scripts are a simple, inexpensive way.

CGI scripts need not be custom written. For example, you can have a generic survey with 20 questions. To change the survey, you change the text in the HTML programming for the 20 questions. You do not have to change the CGI scripting, but you cannot increase or decrease the number of questions without requiring a programmer.

You can find a wealth of prewritten CGI scripts on the Internet. You can download them and use them free of charge. Try searching for *CGI* at Yahoo or Alta Vista to find the latest CGI offerings.

UNIX

UNIX has been the most widely used operating system in Web development. Some of the scripting languages used for UNIX are described briefly in the following sections.

Perl

When programming is called scripting, that means to programmers that the scripting is easy programming, easier than using a normal programming language. This is called a *high-level* programming language. Don't let that deceive you. Unless you are a programmer, you cannot do CGI scripting efficiently.

In UNIX, a programmer is likely to use Perl (Practical Extraction Report Language) scripting. Bookstores carry books on Perl, so it is available to any programmer. Many UNIX programmers are familiar with it. It seems to be the most popular way to do CGI scripting. Keep in mind that a Perl interpreter must be running on the computer for Perl scripting to work. Most ISPs run a Perl interpreter on their UNIX computers.

TCL

Pronounced *tickle*, TCL (Tool Command Language) is an alternative to Perl and works well on other operating systems, such as the Macintosh. It is best for small applications. It runs as much as eight times faster than Perl.

Eva

Eva is a new scripting language apparently developed solely for the Web. It is a cross-platform scripting language. It purports to be more secure than Perl. (Check out `http://www.techware.com` for more information.)

C

For UNIX, the C programming language is also a popular way to do CGI scripts, and C runs much faster than Perl because it can be compiled into machine language. C is widely used for commercial software development. C is not as popular as Perl, however, because Perl is easier and often less expensive.

Windows

Windows is also a popular operating system for Web development. Following are descriptions of some of the Windows scripting languages.

Visual Basic

In the Windows environment, you use Visual Basic for CGI scripting. It's not as easy as Perl scripting in UNIX, but it gets the job done. The latest version of Visual Basic (4.0) contains more database functions than prior versions.

C++

C++ combines C programming with object-oriented programming capability. It's not as easy as Visual Basic.

Perl

In 1995, Perl scripting for the PC became available. It promises to become popular for CGI scripting because it's easier than the other choices.

Testing

Like any other programs, CGI programs must be tested and debugged. Sometimes this is a simple, short-lived process. More often, it takes a considerable amount of time and energy. It would not be unusual for the testing to take as much time as writing the original programming. When hiring a programmer, be sure to take into account the necessary testing phase of developing workable CGI scripts.

CGI-BIN

The CGI scripts go in a directory named *cgi-bin* under the server's root directory. Providing access to this directory creates a security problem for most UNIX systems. Therefore, some ISPs do not allow access to cgi-bin. Some ISPs insist on writing and testing the CGI scripts themselves. Others allow you to write your own, but require a test and review period before they allow you to use it. This may be inefficient and more expensive than other alternatives, particularly if you have competent programmers on your staff.

Many IPSs maintain security but allow you access to cgi-bin by creating a cgi-bin subdirectory off your Web-site root directory, just for your use. With such an arrangement, you can use the programmer of your choice to write and test your CGI scripts. *Access to a cgi-bin directory is one of the features you will need from an ISP unless you use a non-CGI means of operating a database.*

Computing resources

Keep in mind that using a Web presentation through CGI scripting consumes computer resources; that is, it slows down the computer. This is especially true when you have created a large program with your scripting. Every visitor to your Web site can use such a program, and the demand on the server can add up quickly. Programming compiled in C runs up to 10 times faster than CGI scripts. Conserve computing resources. Use CGI scripts only when no reasonable alternative exists. The Web server can handle normal HTML programming faster than lengthy CGI programming.

Summary

CGI scripts provide you with a straightforward, popular, powerful, and widely understood means of tapping the power of a UNIX computer. CGI scripts can work well for incorporating a database into a Web site. This does not mean that CGI scripting is always your best alternative, but it is always a viable alternative.

Basic SQL and SQL*Plus

Overview

Structured Query Language (SQL) is a straightforward database language intended to be the common language for relational databases. It is now a part of virtually every relational database program for every computer on every operating system. A short review here of the highlights will help you better understand how you can create a database system on a Web site by using a robust database program such as Oracle 7. Some SQL*Plus commands — Oracle's brand of SQL — are included.

The example for this chapter is a simple table named *citypeople* that has four columns. This table shows the names of people, their sex, and their preferences in music and art.

The table is as follows:

Citypeople			
Name	Sex	Music	Art
Frank	male	Baroque	Postmodern
Susan	female	Jazz	Renaissance
Polly	female	Classical	Egyptian
Jack	male	Romantic	Postmodern

Data Definition Language

Data Definition Language (DDL) defines the data in a database. You use SQL commands such as *create*, *drop*, and *alter* to define data. For example, the command *drop table* removes a table from the database. These commands are covered in the following subsections.

Create

The create command gets things started. The create command for the example is as follows:

```
create table citypeople
    (name   varchar2(10) not null,
     sex    varchar2(6),
     music varchar2(20),
     art varchar2(20))
tablespace cityspace storage (initial 30k next 30k
minextents 1);
```

The preceding commands show that a table is being created that has four columns of variable-length character data, with the maximum size in parentheses. The term *not null* (on the second line) here means that data must be in the *name* column. On the sixth line, the *tablespace* command sets the parameters for the location and size (in kilobytes) of the table. The command ends with a semicolon. This signals the end of the command for all SQL commands.

Drop

You use the command *drop* to remove a table and all its data, in contrast to the command *delete*, which removes rows of data from a table. The syntax is the following:

```
drop table citypeople;
```

Alter

You use *alter* to make a change in a table, such as adding a column. You can alter many database objects, such as indexes, primary and foreign keys, the size or datatype of a column, and the space allocated to a table. The following line shows the syntax:

```
alter table citypeople add (literature varchar2 (20));
```

This adds the text column *literature* to the *citypeople* table.

Data Manipulation Language

Data Manipulation Language (DML) manipulates the data in the database. Some of the SQL commands are *insert*, *delete*, *update*, and *select*. For example, *delete* deletes rows from a table. The *from* and *where* clauses are used in all four kinds of DML commands. The *order by* clause is used in the *select* command. The following subsections cover these commands.

From

The *from* clause precedes the name of the table from which you get the data. For example, if you want to simply list every person in the city and everything you know about them, the query would look like this:

```
select * from citypeople;
```

This retrieves all the rows in the citypeople table. You can use the results in a printed report, place them on an HTML document, or use them as input into a spreadsheet. There are many other uses for the information retrieved from your database, of course.

Where

To set conditions or selection criteria, use the *where* clause in the following syntax:

```
select * from citypeople where name = 'Jack';
```

This gets one row from the citypeople table (the one where the name column is 'Jack'). Use this means to narrow down the results of your query. Instead of seeing all the people in the city in your report (or Web page, and so forth), you see only people named Jack. The where clause uses *operators*, which enables you to compare the contents of a column to a constant value (as in the preceding example), to another column , or even to another query (called a *subquery*).

Table 7-1 shows some of the most common operators that are used in the where clause.

Table 7-1: Partial list of operators

Operator	Purpose
=	equal to
< >	not equal to
<	less than
>	more than
<=	less than or equal to
>=	more than or equal to
in	equal to data in parentheses
not in	not equal to data in parentheses
between A and B	more than or equal to A and less than or equal to B
like 'xxx%'	contains text beginning with xxx (% is a wild card)

Order by

This is a sort clause. When no order is specified in the *order by* command, the sort is ascending. Following is the syntax:

```
select * from citypeople order by name desc;
```

This command lists all the rows in the citypeople table in reverse alphabetical order (from z to a) by name.

Insert

The *insert* command enables you to insert a row of data into a table. Use this syntax:

```
insert into citypeople values
   ('Jill','female','Jazz','Postmodern','Gothic');
```

This statement inserts a new row into the citypeople table. Each column is assigned the value shown in the list of values. In this case, for example, the sex column is assigned the value of female.

Update

Use *update* to change data in a table:

```
update citypeople set music = 'Modern' where name = 'Susan';
```

In contrast to the command alter, which alters a table's structure, the update command modifies the data inside the table.

Delete

To delete one or more rows, use the delete command, as follows:

```
delete from citypeople where name = 'Polly';
```

After you've made all the changes, what does the table citypeople look like? It looks like this:

Citypeople

Name	Sex	Music	Art	Literature
Frank	male	Baroque	Postmodern	
Susan	female	Modern	Renaissance	
Jack	male	Romantic	Postmodern	
Jill	female	Jazz	Postmodern	Gothic

Select

This useful *query command* enables you to retrieve data from a table. Assume that you want to find out about people who live in the city and who have selected Postmodern art as their favorite type of art. In building a query to gather this information from your database, first decide which table contains the information. In this chapter's example, the table to use is called citypeople. *Citypeople* goes in the *from* clause. Next, review all the columns that are in the citypeople table and find the ones you want to see. You decide to use them all, so you use an asterisk (*) in the *select* clause to indicate this. Finally, you know that the art column contains each person's favorite art, so you add a *where* clause to narrow down the rows you retrieve to only those who list "Postmodern" in the art column. The resulting query is:

```
select * from citypeople where art = 'Postmodern';
```

This will provide three rows from the updated *citypeople* table:

```
name     sex       music      art          literature
------   --------- ---------  -----------  ----------
Frank    male      Baroque    Postmodern
Jack     male      Romantic   Postmodern
Jill     female    Jazz       Postmodern   Gothic
```

You can use *and, or, not,* and other operators as well as *order by,* as in the following:

```
select name, art, sex
from citypeople
where art = 'Postmodern'
and sex = 'male'
order by name desc;
```

This code produces only two rows sorted on name, in descending order:

```
name           art              sex
----------     ----------------  ------
Jack           Postmodern       male
Frank          Postmodern       male
```

Note that the columns can be listed in the select command in any order.

Here are some other examples of *select* commands. This query answers the question: "Which people in my database are male and enjoy Postmodern art?"

```
select art, name, music, sex
from citypeople
where sex = 'male'
and art = 'Postmodern'
order by art, name;
```

There are two men, Frank and Jack, who fit this description:

```
art              name          music            sex
----------------  ----------   ----------------  ------
Postmodern        Frank        Baroque          male
Postmodern        Jack         Romantic         male
```

The following query asks a similar question and also tells the database to sort the results. "Which people in my database are *either* male *or* enjoy Postmodern art?"

```
select name, art
from citypeople
where sex = 'male'
or art = 'Postmodern'
order by art, name;
```

Here are the results. This time a third person, Jill, fits the query's criteria:

```
art                name          music             sex
---------------    ----------    ---------------   ------
Postmodern         Frank         Baroque           male
Postmodern         Jack          Romantic          male
Postmodern         Jill          Jazz              female
```

The following query uses the *not in* operator to eliminate certain rows from the results. In this example, you want a list of names of everyone in the city except those named Frank or Jill. The query is:

```
select name from citypeople
where name not in ('Frank','Jill');
```

There are two people (Jack and Susan) in the citypeople table that are not named Frank and are not named Jill:

```
name
----------
Jack
Susan
```

Note that the rows are not returned in any specific order when the *order by* clause is omitted.

Data types

There are three basic data types: number, text, and dates. Be careful how you use them. Databases offer a variety of additional data types, such as Boolean (for logic) and Longraw (for graphics). Not all are supported by every database.

Number

You can put numbers in a text column, but you can't do any calculations with them. In a number column, you can use them for calculations. Here's a partial list of the calculations possible using number datatype columns:

Operator	Operation
+	add
–	subtract
*	multiply
/	divide
avg	average
max	maximum
min	minimum

Sometimes, numeric information belongs in a character datatype. Telephone and Social Security numbers are this kind of data. They contain numbers, but you never add them, and their exact positions (including leading zeros) are very important. Define these as character datatypes.

Character

This is text data. The name of this datatype varies from database to database. Oracle, for example, has several different datatypes for character data: char, varchar, varchar2, and long. Each is used for a different kind of text data, ranging from very short (such as one- or two-character codes) to very long (32KB of text). Access uses text and memo datatypes for short and long text data. The characters can be either letters or numbers.

Date

You can place dates in a text column, but you will not be able to run time calculations (date functions) unless they are in a date column. Some of the date functions available in Oracle are the following:

Date Function	Definition
add_months(date,n)	Date plus n months
last_day(date)	Last day of the month for the date. For example, last_day(7/15/96) is 7/31/96.
next_day(date,weekday)	Date of the first day of the week named that is equal to or later than the date

Summary

As you can see, SQL is straightforward. This chapter covered the basics, but SQL gets much more complex. SQL is different from many programming languages, because it works with sets of data rather than with one record (row) at a time. Sometimes, SQL cannot perform complicated logic. When this happens, there is a need for a new language that contains all of SQL and adds the procedural logic to it. For example, Oracle has an extension language, PL/SQL, that provides the additional functionality to create complex database applications.

If you want to learn more about SQL, these URLs explain the history of SQL and how to code SQL effectively:

```
http://www.bf.rmit.edu.au/Oracle/
     docs.html#TinaLondon
http://waltz.ncsl.nist.gov/~len/sql_info.html
```

Designing Queries with HTML

A *query* asks questions about a database and receives answers. When you combine a database and the Web, both the queries and the answers appear like any other Web page (that is, HTML document). This chapter explores the best methods of using the HTML form for queries. These techniques show a range of queries, from the simplest to the most complex. Each variation has advantages and disadvantages that you must consider for your special circumstances. This chapter covers the design of the input forms.

What Is a Query?

A query to a database engine requires input from a visitor, and the HTML form provides the place where a visitor can enter that input. The form goes inside any HTML document. Thus, the overall design of a query requires careful coordination of the HTML form and the CGI scripts that comprise the design of the SQL query.

The primary consideration in designing queries is the level of expertise of the expected visitors to your Web site. If your Web site is on an intranet, where everyone is familiar with database technology, you can give visitors (employees) plenty of latitude to make their own queries. If your Web site caters to the general public, you should design your form to make it easy for visitors to make queries.

Suppose that you have a simple table that looks like the following:

Borrowers					
Borrower	Balance	Payoff Date	Interest Rate	Loan Officer	Loan Type
Brown	982.97	07/08/97	16.375	Shorely	L14
Cook	485.16	03/18/97	18.250	Belton	L9
Doe	313.83	09/05/97	16.875	Shorely	L14
Jones	619.24	01/15/97	18.250	Shorely	L32
Smith	814.76	11/06/97	16.000	Loren	L29

Assume that the rows here represent a database with hundreds or thousands of rows. The data includes the borrower, the amount owed, the date the loan will be paid off, the interest rate being charged, the loan officer, and the type of loan. This example is used later in this chapter to describe some types of queries visitors can create to get the information they need from the database.

Single-Input Queries

The simplest query is a *single-input* query. For example, a visitor can use a single-input query form to make an input for a single-column query. This kind of query is very simple (see Figure 8-1).

```
<FORM METHOD="POST" ACTION="">
Borrower: <INPUT TYPE="text" NAME="input1" SIZE="15">
</FORM>
```

Single-column queries

A *single-column* query is one that calls up the row of a borrower (returns a result). If you want to see Ms. Smith's loan information, you enter **Smith**. By searching on the Borrower column, the database application provides you with the Smith row of information. Another single-column query identifies all the loans at a certain interest rate. If you input **18.250** percent and search on the Interest column, you get the rows for Cook and Jones. A single-column search is easy to set up and easy for a visitor to understand.

Boolean operators

Boolean operators in regard to searching data are *OR* and *AND*. These operators apply to inputs.

Figure 8-1: A single-input query.

Within one column, you can use OR. For example, if you search the Borrower column using **Brown OR Smith**, you will receive both the Brown and the Smith rows. Were you to search using **Brown AND Smith**, however, you would receive nothing, because a Borrower column cannot have one row that is *both* Brown and Smith.

Use the AND operator in searching multiple columns. For example, if you search the Borrower and Interest Rate columns using **Jones AND 16.500**, you would get no report, because no combination of column data satisfies such a query. If you use **Jones AND 18.250**, however, the database application will report the Jones row. The OR operator doesn't work for multiple columns.

You can string together multiple individual column searches with AND to narrow the field of inquiry. For example, you can search the Borrower and Interest Rate columns using **Brown OR Cook AND 16.375 OR 18.000**. That will get you the Brown row only; there's no match for 18.000. But **Brown OR Cook AND 16.375 OR 18.250** will get you both the Brown and Cook rows.

Database operators

The prior chapter on SQL includes a table with a partial list of operators from Oracle SQL Plus. You can use such operators in performing searches. People commonly use the following operators:

$>$ more than

$<=$ less than or equal to

Suppose that you want all the loans that are over 18 percent. Using **>18.000** in a search of the Interest column gives you the rows for Cook and Jones. On the other hand, suppose that you want all the loans that are 18 percent or under. Using **<=18.000** gets you the rows for Brown, Doe, and Smith. Database operators work on one column.

Using the AND operator, moreover, gives you the capability to create complex queries by stringing together individual column searches to narrow down the field of search. For example, using **>500.00 AND <= 18.000** in searching the Amount and Interest columns results in Brown and Smith.

Multiple-Input Queries

Although not as simple as single-input queries, multiple-input queries are potentially easier for visitors than single-input complex queries.

Boolean operators

To do a Boolean search using OR in one column, you can use two inputs, as in Figure 8-2. Following is an example.

```
<FORM METHOD="POST" ACTION="">
Borrower:
<P>
<INPUT TYPE="text" NAME="input2-1" SIZE="15"> OR <INPUT
TYPE="text" NAME="input2-2" SIZE="15">
```

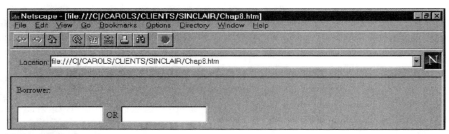

Figure 8-2: Two inputs, one operator.

Another possibility is to use three inputs or more, as shown in Figure 8-3:

```
<FORM METHOD="POST" ACTION="">
Loan Officer:
<P>
<INPUT TYPE="text" NAME="input3-1" SIZE="15"> OR <INPUT
TYPE="text" NAME="input3-2" SIZE="15"> OR <INPUT
TYPE="text" NAME="input3-3" SIZE="15">
</FORM>
```

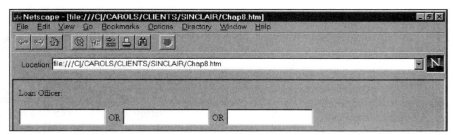

Figure 8-3: Three inputs, two operators.

If some of the inputs have no entries, it doesn't matter. By using this HTML form to do this simple Boolean search, you make it easier for visitors to do a Boolean search.

To do a Boolean search using AND with two columns, you can use two inputs, as in Figure 8-4:

```
<FORM METHOD="POST" ACTION="">
Borrower: <INPUT TYPE="text" NAME="input4-1" SIZE="15">
AND Interest Rate: <INPUT TYPE="text" NAME="input4-2"
SIZE="15">
</FORM>
```

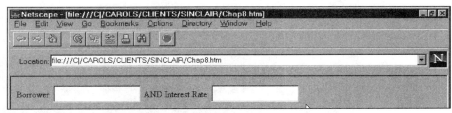

Figure 8-4: Two inputs, one operator.

You can use three inputs or more with multiple operators, as shown in Figure 8-5. Following is an example of the code:

```
<FORM METHOD="POST" ACTION="">
Loan Officer: <INPUT TYPE="text" NAME="input5-1" SIZE="15">
<P>
AND Interest Rate: <INPUT TYPE="text" NAME="input5-2"
SIZE="15">
<P>AND Loan Type: <INPUT TYPE="text" NAME="input5-3"
SIZE="15">
</FORM>
```

Figure 8-5: Three inputs, two operators.

For more complex queries, you can use four or more inputs. Figure 8-6 shows a query for this situation. Here's an example:

```
<FORM METHOD="POST" ACTION="">
Borrower: <INPUT TYPE="text" NAME="input6-1" SIZE="15"> OR
<INPUT TYPE="text" NAME="input6-2" SIZE="15">
<P>AND<P>
Interest Rate: <INPUT TYPE="text" NAME="input6-3"
SIZE="15"> OR <INPUT TYPE="text" NAME="input6-3"
SIZE="15">
</FORM>
```

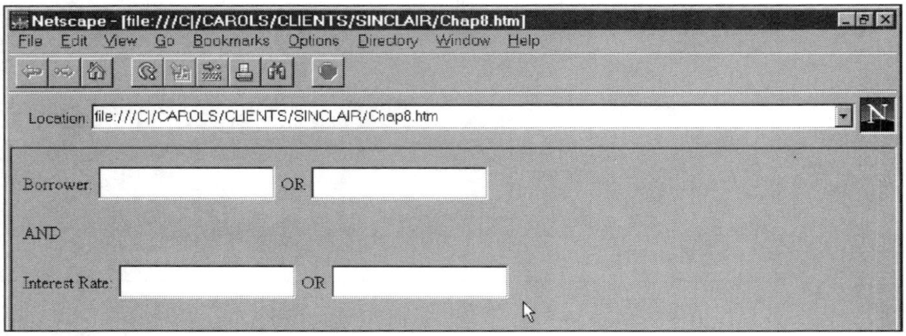

Figure 8-6: Four inputs, three operators.

The most common database query forms use this kind of logic. Usually, you do not see the word AND on the form. It is implied. Figure 8-7 is a typical example of a query using multiple AND Boolean operators:

```
<FORM METHOD="POST" ACTION="">
Fill in one or more of the search fields below and press
the search button.
<P>
Loan Officer: <INPUT TYPE="text" NAME="input7-1"
SIZE="15">
<P>
Interest Rate: <INPUT TYPE="text" NAME="input7-2"
SIZE="15">
<P>
Loan Type: <INPUT TYPE="text" NAME="input7-3" SIZE="15">
</FORM>
```

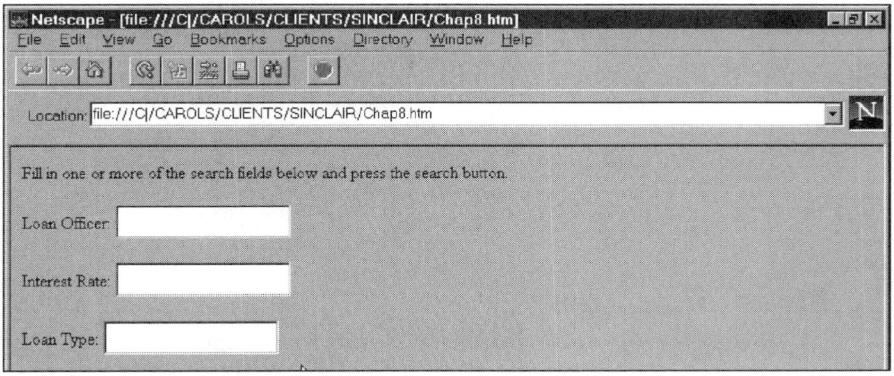

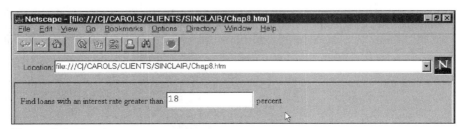

Figure 8-7: Query form using implied Boolean operators.

Before you post your new database form for the public, test it thoroughly. Sometimes the combination of logic you have designed does not work as you intended. Test your forms with low-volume tables at first (that is, tables with fewer than 100 rows). Use actual data if possible, or test data that contains examples similar to the real world. Test your form by filling in data that is good and bad, just to see what might happen. This takes valuable time, but it pays off in satisfied visitors. Nothing is more discouraging than visiting a site and getting an unexpected error message!

Database operators

You can also use database operators with a single-input or multiple-input HTML form. You do this as you do when using multiple inputs with Boolean operators; that is, you express the operators in the text. For example, to find all loans with an interest rate greater than 18 percent, use the method shown in Figure 8-8. Here is the code for the query:

```
<FORM METHOD="POST" ACTION="">
Find loans with an interest rate greater than <INPUT
TYPE="text" NAME="input8" SIZE="15"> percent.
</FORM>
```

Figure 8-8: One input, one operator.

If you want to find all the loans over $500 that are at 18 percent interest or lower, you use the following code (see Figure 8-9).

```
<FORM METHOD="POST" ACTION="">
Find balances over <INPUT TYPE="text" NAME="input9-1"
SIZE="15"> dollars that are at <INPUT TYPE="text"
NAME="input9-2" SIZE="15"> percent or less.
</FORM>
```

Fixed operators

Multiple inputs make queries easier for most visitors, particularly people who are not familiar with database and search technology. Such queries, however, are cast in concrete. They are a sort of hybrid between single-input simple and simple-input complex queries. You must hide the Boolean and database operators or embed them in the text where they cannot be changed except by you. This is appropriate for situations where visitors are not knowledgeable in using databases but does not offer much flexibility to knowledgeable visitors.

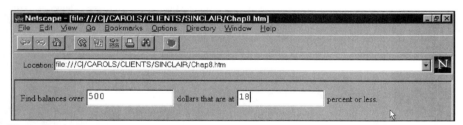

Figure 8-9: Two inputs, two operators.

Single-Input Complex Queries

If the query is so designed, a database-savvy visitor can enter any kind of a complex query command in a single-input query to manipulate the data in a variety of ways. The query form will look much the same as a simple single-input query; it will just work differently (see Figure 8-10). To do anything, however, requires the correct entry of a complex query using Boolean or database operators. Your visitors must have the ability to make such complex queries if they are to use the single-input form effectively this way. If they don't have the ability and you offer this type of input, you should provide ample instructions on how to formulate queries that will work. Following is an example of such code:

```
<FORM METHOD="POST" ACTION="">
Enter your query using Boolean and database operators:
<P>
<INPUT TYPE="text" NAME="input10" SIZE="30">
</FORM>
```

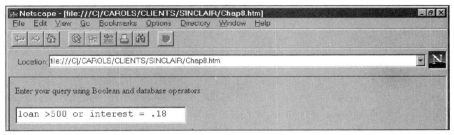

Figure 8-10: Single-input complex query.

Questionnaires and Surveys

Questionnaires and surveys are input forms too, even if visitors do not use them specifically to query a database. Essentially, they are input devices for adding data to a database. Adding data may be their only purpose. After the visitor adds data, however, the database application can be designed to take some action, such as returning an HTML document created on the fly. In such a case, the database application generates an HTML document (a report) based on a predetermined query that operates with the data that the visitor filling out the HTML form has added to the database.

The forms for questionnaires and surveys are often more self-evident than search queries. After all, most people fill out questionnaires, surveys, and other data-collection forms from time to time, even if they know nothing about database and search technology. Figure 8-11 is a questionnaire about cars. Its code is as follows:

```
<FORM METHOD="POST" ACTION="">
<B>Car Survey</B>
<P>
Name: <INPUT TYPE="text" NAME="nput11-1" SIZE="15">
<P>
What kind of car do you drive? <INPUT TYPE="text"
NAME="nput11-2" SIZE="15">
<P>
Which model? <INPUT TYPE="text" NAME="nput11-3" SIZE="15">
<P>
How many miles have you put on it? <INPUT TYPE="text"
NAME="nput11-4" SIZE="15">
<P>
Where did you buy it? <INPUT TYPE="text" NAME="nput11-5"
SIZE="15">
<P>
When do you expect to buy a new car? <INPUT TYPE="text"
NAME="nput11-6" SIZE="15">
</FORM>
```

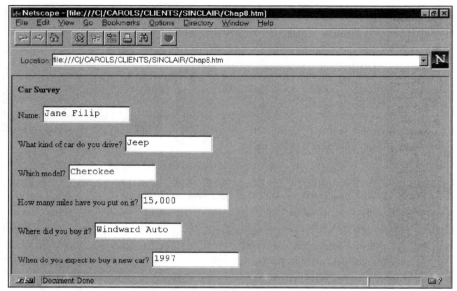

Figure 8-11: A questionnaire about cars.

Using the information provided by a visitor filling in this form, the database can generate an HTML document on the fly with a template, as covered elsewhere in this book.

Text Searches

One popular solution to getting around the complexity of queries is running a text search; that is, a database engine or a text-search engine searches for a key word or key words supplied by a visitor. This can work two ways. First, you can enable the search of an entire database (all rows, all columns). Second, you can use text documents as your database and search such documents with a text-search engine.

Many of the Web directories and search facilities are not databases as generally defined in this book. They consist of information published about Web sites. You might call such Web sites *objects*.

A text-search engine will find this Web site description (object) by searching for a word or words included in the title or description. The words a visitor might logically pick to search are *canoe*, *dugout canoe*, *Native American*, and *water transportation*. Each will find the object (Web site). The problem is that the words *canoe*, *Native American*, and *water transportation* are likely to find a long list of objects (Web sites) unrelated to dugout canoes. The words *water vehicle*, *boat*, and *pirogue* (a type of dugout canoe) will not find the object (that is, Dugout Canoe Center).

Text searches of documents, although like database searches in many ways, work well with unstructured text information and general keyword queries. They do not work as well as using structured data in database applications or with complex queries that can produce more precise reports. In any case, visitors will need help in making their queries whether using a database search or a text search.

Visitor Help

Regardless of what kind of query you create, you must assume that some-one very *un*knowledgeable will try to use it, unless you are sure that is not the case. Therefore, you need to write instructions that anyone can follow.

Procedural help

For any search scheme, you must provide visitors with guidance. In the case of a single-input, single-column search, the instructions for the general public can be minimal. In the case of an unlimited single-input search, you may have to provide the general public with a good deal of database and search instruction to enable your visitors to use your database effectively. A hybrid or middle ground, as you have seen with fixed operators, requires expressing the Boolean and database operators in the text as a specified route to a desired result. Regardless of which approach you take, make sure that you provide ample instructions.

Keep in mind that HTML documents allow you to easily and effectively supply as much help as necessary. A treatise on database and search technology, if that's what is needed, is only a hyperlink away. Don't leave your visitors to fend for themselves and guess how to use your database. Give them adequate and convenient information.

Help for input

Besides help with queries, visitors may need help with the input (information) they need to provide to fill in the query blanks.

Databases

Sometimes a visitor doesn't know the choices for searches. For example, suppose that you need a mechanic and you are able to get access to a database of mechanics on the Internet that you can search.

Suppose that you can search for mechanics by city. Is your city represented on the list? If not, is a nearby city represented on the list? Do you have to find out by trial and error, or is there another way?

If you provide only a single input without help information, you may be putting a visitor in the position of guessing what input may yield useful information. Trial and error can be time-consuming and frustrating. You will do better to provide a list of possibilities or a list of suggestions. This can take various configurations. A simple list can be built into the form itself. It's the HTML menu (the example from Chapter 5, "HTML Forms"). Figure 8-12 shows a simple list. The code is as follows:

```
<FORM METHOD="POST" ACTION="">
<SELECT Name="input12">
<OPTION>Asheville
<OPTION>Chapel Hill
<OPTION>Charlotte
<OPTION>Durham
<OPTION>Fayetteville
<OPTION>Greensboro
<OPTION>Greenville
<OPTION>Raleigh
<OPTION>Wilmington
<OPTION>Winston-Salem
</SELECT>
</FORM>
```

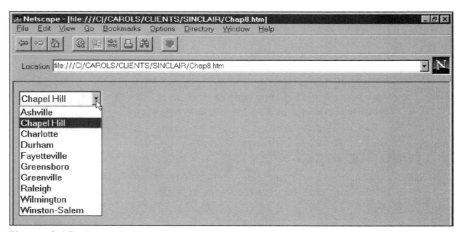

Figure 8-12: A sample Help menu.

The menu provides the choices, and the visitor simply chooses one. This suffices when the choices are limited, but you must devise another scheme where a long list will be more useful. A list published right on the page where the input form is located will provide you with room for a longer list, but even this approach is limited (see Figure 8-13). Following is the code for this approach:

```
Asheville<BR>
Chapel Hill<BR>
Charlotte<BR>
Durham<BR>
Fayetteville<BR>
Greensboro<BR>
Greenville<BR>
Raleigh<BR>
Wilmington<BR>
Winston-Salem
<P>
<FORM METHOD="POST" ACTION="">
Select a city: <INPUT TYPE="text" NAME="input13"
SIZE="15">
```

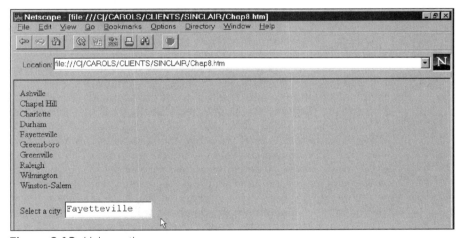

Figure 8-13: Help on the page.

How about an input embedded in text? That is one way to provide help.
Figure 8-14 shows an example. The code is as follows:

```
<FORM METHOD="POST" ACTION="">
In order to make an effective search, you must use a key
word; that is, a word that is closely associated with
topic you seek. Place that word in the input <INPUT
TYPE="text" NAME="input14" SIZE="15"> and then click on
the submit button below to start the search. The search
results will be delivered to you after a short wait.
</FORM>
```

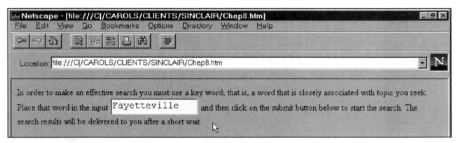

Figure 8-14: Input embedded in text.

You can use a system of static lists to help visitors. For example, suppose that a visitor is in Pushmataha County, a sparsely occupied county in Oklahoma, and she is looking for a mechanic. It might be useful to have a static list of Oklahoma counties and another static list of their cities and towns to narrow the search. In the list of counties (an HTML document), each county is a hyperlink to a list of cities and towns in that county (another HTML document). By seeing which towns are included in the database, she can make a choice that will work. In the case of Pushmataha County, there are many small towns. Only a few will have a mechanic listed in the database. The static lists will help the visitor make an input that yields useful information to her. This will work more quickly than trying to input all the towns in Pushmataha County individually on a trial-and-error basis.

In the Pushmataha County example, the static lists can become somewhat awkward. Too many static lists (HTML documents) to go through may defeat the purpose of having database access for visitors in the first place, and it will be less efficient to maintain your overall system. It might be more efficient for you to design the list generation into the database application itself. Thus, with an input of **Oklahoma**, the database will generate a list of counties (an HTML document generated on the fly). Clicking on a hyperlink to Pushmataha County will have the database generate a list of towns (another HTML document generated on the fly). Clicking on a town will have the database generate a list of mechanics (still another HTML document generated on the fly). Keep in mind that in almost every system, the end result is an HTML document generated on the fly, which is the database application's way of providing a report in a Web system. That final HTML document generated on the fly will have information from one database row or multiple rows.

You *can* use graphics instead of lists. For example, you can have a succession of maps with hot links. On the Oklahoma map, Pushmataha County will be a hot link. On the Pustmataha County map, each town will be a hot link.

Text searches

You may find text searches handy, because visitors can easily use them. Plug in any word that happens to be in the database row or the text publication of the object sought, and the object will appear in the final list (an HTML document generated on the fly). The problem here is limiting the final output to a useful size. If too many objects appear on the final list, it may not be useful for a visitor. To limit the results to a useful size may require the skillful use of keywords and Boolean operators, if permitted. If a visitor is to be skillful in using these techniques, you will need to provide some handy instructions for using keywords and learning to use Boolean operators.

Seamlessness

The goal of providing visitor help starts with the database application design itself. It also encompasses the information you provide about your system and your data that will allow a visitor to access your data easily. Whatever combination of techniques you use — and there are more than enough to be amply creative — it should build a system transparent to visitors that is easy to use.

CGI Scripts

The HTML form provides to visitors the *appearance* of what you do with their input. What you actually do with the input you do with CGI scripts written by a programmer. In addition, some Web-database development tools will allow you to create the necessary scripting or Web-database application without hiring a programmer.

Design Guidelines

The following list of questions will help you decide how to design your query form to fit your data and your visitors:

1. **Which columns will visitors most likely want to search on?** Include the columns in your query form.

2. **Will visitors know the exact values in the column?** If not, add help by using a menu, or text on the form itself, or radio buttons, or a linked help page.

3. **Will visitors want to specify ranges rather than exact values in a column?** If so, build it in (see examples under "Database operators" in this chapter).

4. **Which columns are not searchable (such as very long text columns or graphics)?** Leave these out of your search form.

5. **Which columns contain uniform or nearly uniform values in all rows?** Searching on these columns does not narrow the number of rows returned, so consider *excluding* this kind of column from your search form.

6. **Will most of your visitors have SQL knowledge and will they want to write their own queries?** If so, provide a single-input form for free-style queries. If you have a mixture of visitor types (visitors with and without SQL skills), consider providing a selection of two different forms.

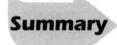

Summary

Every target group has different capabilities. Every database application is different. Legacy databases exist as they are. New databases can be specially designed for Web use. Every situation is different, so no one solution fits all. You should carefully design forms and queries to provide easy access to data for a target group with a system that enables a narrowly focused search.

Multimedia Technology

Many different elements make up the multimedia technology used today on the Web. Even simple text lends itself to new methods. Your Web site may involve one or more of these exciting features — exciting because they are a substantial improvement over text-only methods of prior electronic publishing:

- Text
- Color graphics
- Audio
- Animation
- Video
- Embedded programs

This chapter describes all these elements and goes on to discuss the following important concepts regarding the presentation of your Web site:

- Interactivity
- Authoring programs
- Electronic delivery technology
- Database considerations

The end of the chapter relates how database technology is a superior method of enabling multimedia technology.

Text

The Web is a text-based multimedia authoring environment. As such, text is an important element that should be used with intelligence.

Word processors

Text usually starts out on a word processor, and each word processor has its unique and proprietary markups that code the text for formatting and typesetting. Such markups serve much the same function as HTML. The word processor hides such markups from the user, but the markups are there. Sometimes you can see them by using a *view* command in the word processor — usually found on a menu. The word processor file, which includes the markups, will not work in another program unless that program has the proper *filters* to translate the file into something the program can use. It would take many dozens of different filters for a program to be able to use text files from all other programs.

Word processing *files,* being proprietary, are generally not very important to multimedia or to online publishing. But word processing *programs* are. Most writings originate in a word processor, and word processors can be important in multimedia authoring. Moreover, word processors also make excellent viewers for downloaded files; and if you can *view* it in a word processor, you can also *print* it. Thus, word processors can be real workhorses for visitors to your Web site. Finally, if all the visitors to your Web site use the same word processor, such as in a corporate situation, the word processor file itself becomes a useful medium with which to distribute information.

Formatted as an ASCII text file, the following sentence is plain and takes minimal storage space. As a Word for Windows file, it is about 30 percent larger because it includes all the Word markups in addition to housekeeping information:

ASCII

```
The quick reddish-brown fox jumped over the lazy tan dog
one sunny afternoon in Nunnelly, Tennessee, about 4:30 PM.
```

Word for Windows

The quick reddish-brown fox jumped over the lazy tan dog one sunny afternoon in Nunnelly, Tennessee, about 4:30 PM.

ASCII

The American Standard Code for Information Interchange (ASCII) file is a universal file with minimal formatting that every word processor, spread-sheet, database engine, and program can import or export. For example, when a word processor exports a file as an ASCII file, it first strips all the proprietary markups and then uses only simple ASCII characters and for-matting. Thus, an ASCII file provides the common denominator for text between all programs. Unfortunately, the ASCII system by itself cannot accommodate complex formatting.

ASCII files are the fodder of online information systems. E-mail is ASCII text. Gopher documents are ASCII documents. You offer ASCII text files on FTP to reach the greatest number of people. Web documents are ASCII files, albeit marked up with HTML. ASCII files can be imported into any word processor and viewed or printed. The only drawback is that ASCII documents look as if they came from an IBM Selectric typewriter. In this age of attractive desktop publishing, the typewriter look is obsolete.

Typically, 1,000 words is about 5.75KB in ASCII form, 7.5KB in word processor form, and 8KB in Rich Text Format (RTF) form. This varies with the size of the document and the complexity of the formatting.

RTF

In the late 1980s, Microsoft established the Rich Text Format as a kind of super ASCII. An RTF file is actually an ASCII text file except that it uses ASCII characters to mark up the text for more complex formatting. RTF offers a high degree of flexibility and precision in page layout and typeset-ting. It conveniently and effectively provides a common denominator that far surpasses the capability of the ASCII system. It is not limited to PCs. Macs and other operating systems can use it, too. All Windows word processors and many other programs can import or export RTF files.

Oddly enough, although it has been around for a while, it is often overlooked as a potential solution to incompatibility problems. In text-based multimedia, it plays an important role in the authoring process. More important for online use, every Windows word processor and some Macintosh word processors can import it. That means you can distribute an RTF file — a fully formatted and typeset document — and almost everyone with a word processor can view it and print it. This is clearly a system with great potential for distributing published materials intended for printing.

PostScript

PostScript, a highly sophisticated and precise page description language, creates files that carry the highest degree of formatting and typesetting for print media. It is a proprietary format owned by Adobe. PostScript has been the backbone of the commercial desktop publishing and prepress industry, an industry that primarily uses Macs. Thus, many Mac owners use Post-Script. Unfortunately, few PCs have software that can use a PostScript file. Because Macs make up only about 10 percent of the personal computer market, PostScript is not practical as a online distribution medium except for Macs. Unless all the visitors to your Web site have Macs with PostScript capability, don't use this system.

HTML

Hypertext Markup Language (HTML) is the markup system for the Web. It is a simple, straightforward system that is a sort of crude desktop publishing but with the capability to create *hypermedia* (links between different media, including text). If you publish on the Web, you use HTML to mark up the ASCII documents exported from your word processor, or you create your documents in an HTML editor or authoring program. You will find HTML quite easy to learn and apply.

HTML is on an upward path of improvement. With each release of a new HTML standard, it gains additional capability and eventually will be a sophisticated and precise desktop publishing system. Even now, it creates an attractively typeset document with embedded color graphics. It has a slick, magazine-like appearance that, together with its hypermedia capability, makes it a uniquely capable online system.

Keep in mind that because an HTML document is essentially an ASCII document, every computer can use it. Users need only a Web browser, which are available for PCs, Macs, UNIX workstations, and other computers.

In the future, HTML documents will be the information-distribution system of choice for many purposes. For example, suppose that you put an HTML file together with two graphics files (GIFs) on an FTP directory for the public to download. Someone who downloads these three files and views the HTML document in his or her browser (in local host mode) will see an attractive typeset document with two graphics in color. As a universal cross-platform system, HTML is very powerful and has great potential. HTML often proves to be the best way to share information on an intranet as well. One program, the browser, can be used to view Web documents on both an intranet and the Internet.

Hypertext

Hypertext is the technique used to link one word or phrase to another word or phrase in a digital publishing system. You can jump from hyperlink to hyperlink (that is, from word to word). For example, you can link a word to its glossary definition. The reader simply clicks on the word, which is a hypertext link, and instantly goes to the same word in the glossary. Hypertext is the mainstay of a Web document. Windows help screens provide another example of hypertext. These help screens use the same kind of linking as a Web document, except that all the links are contained within a set of help documents on your PC.

Hypermedia

Think of hypermedia as hypertext except that the media need not be text. In other words, a color graphic or a video clip can be a hyperlink to another color graphic or to a word or phrase. Thus, hypermedia provides you with the ability to jump around from one piece of information to another, and the pieces of information can be text, color graphics, or other multimedia elements.

Interactivity

The hyperlinks don't just happen. You must create them by using HTML markups. When you make hypermedia, you are creating interactivity; you are giving the reader a choice (to click or not to click?). Interactivity makes a Web site interesting and stimulating for your visitors. It gives them a sense of control.

Color Graphics

Using color graphics is a new practice for many people who are building Web sites. It's a mixture of aesthetics and high technology: complex but fun.

Digital art

Digital art (color graphics) and typesetting drive the success of the Web. You can program in HTML to provide the typesetting. Use artists to provide the digital art. Don't take the color graphics lightly. An electronic document without HTML and color graphics looks like a page created by an IBM Selectric typewriter; it's boring.

For a text-based multimedia production or for a Web site, a custom-made user interface is desirable. This means color graphics for the multimedia presentation and a graphical navigation system for the Web site (see Figure 9-1). In these multimedia presentations, the digital art gives the text an attractive, magazine-like quality that is noticeably missing without the art. In fact, without the art, the production looks like a plain printed page in black and white. The art should play a modest role and not be overwhelming or cumbersome, but to publish without color graphics is not advisable except perhaps for reference documents. For the Web, too much digital art can cause your document to load slowly on a visitor's browser, because graphics are larger than text files and require more time to download.

Figure 9-1: Opening graphic on the CD-ROM that accompanies this book.

Digital art should predominate, of course, when the Web document is art or is about art. In this case, the text, if any, plays a subordinate role, and presumably, visitors will endure the long download times because they desire to see the art.

Color graphics programs

There are two kinds of color graphics programs: paint programs and draw programs. Paint programs, such as Corel Photo Paint, use bitmaps, in which each dot of color is mapped in a matrix. Draw programs, such as Corel Draw, use mathematical descriptions of curves and vectors to create images. The types of files created by each are incompatible, but you can convert the draw files to bitmaps. Generally speaking, unless you are an artist, you will use bitmapped files.

There are many different types of color-manipulation programs that use bitmapped files. Some of them perform standard darkroom types of operations in a simulation of a photographic darkroom, whereas others take a photograph and turn it into a van Gogh painting. You will need at least a program such as Paint Shop Pro to manipulate bitmapped files (for example, digital photographs), even if you do not use it for art. For free trials of color programs, try the following Internet address:

```
http://sun1.bham.ac.uk/s.m.williams.bcm/images/viewers.html
```

Color density and resolution

Resolution for a color monitor equates to image *size* rather than density. For example, 640 x 480 pixel resolution is the minimum size for use today. Most people set their monitors at 800 x 600, and those with large monitors might choose to set theirs at 1024 x 768.

Good color monitors have a density of about 72 dpi (dots per inch), which is how resolution is normally designated. This density is independent of the image displayed by the color graphics card and the software. Thus, any good monitor, large or small, can display 640 x 480, 800 x 600, 1024 x 768, and other sizes (see Figure 9-2).

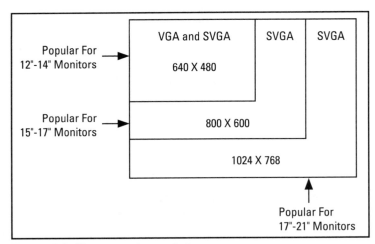

Figure 9-2: Three popular resolutions.

The number of colors used to display a graphics file is determined by the number of bits used. Thus, 4-bit color contains 16 colors, 8-bit color contains 256 colors, 16-bit color contains more than 65,000 colors, and 24-bit color contains more than 16,000,000 colors (TrueColor). Today, the standard is 8-bit color. Anything less doesn't make a photograph look good, but in 8-bit color, photographs don't look too bad. It doesn't make sense to provide graphics to your visitors in 16-bit or 24-bit color when it is likely that most will be able to view the graphics only in 8-bit color. Nonetheless, before the end of the decade, the standard will be 16-bit color.

GIF files

There are many graphic file formats. The one with the most widespread use on the Web is the Graphics Interchange Format (GIF) file. GIF is an 8-bit (256-color) image format. A GIF file compresses a graphic to about half its normal size (2:1 compression). When working with color graphics, you can work with a variety of graphic file types, such as TIF, BMP, PCX, and others. When you finish your work, however, you must convert your graphic files to GIF or JPEG files to use them in HTML documents.

Transparent GIF

Transparent GIFs appear to float on the page. You can design them to appear to be irregular shapes rather than rectangular or square. They add an attractive dimension to your art work.

The normal number for a GIF file is 87a. To create a transparent GIF, you must index the color to be transparent and change the file to a GIF 89a file. You must use a color-manipulation program for this purpose, but not all can do it. Then you must use a program that converts the GIF 89a file into a GIF file in which the indexed color will match the background color upon which it is displayed (see Figure 9-3). Again, not all color graphics programs can do this. Fortunately, this process has been integrated into the newest versions of some color graphics programs, making it very easy for you to do. This process is beyond the scope of this book, but you can find out more about it at the following Internet address:

```
http://melmac.corp.harris.com/transparent_images.html.
```

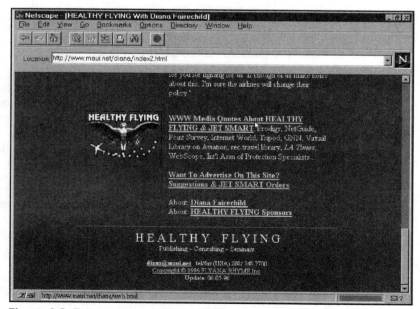

Figure 9-3: This transparent GIF image is actually as large as the thin rectangular outline indicates.

JPEG

A Joint Photographic Experts Group (JPEG) file is a compressed file format growing in popularity on the Web. This compression method, originally intended for motion pictures, has been used productively for still graphics too. As the compression goes to a higher ratio, the quality decreases. A 10:1 compression ratio, however, shows little loss of quality in 8-bit color.

Stock images

Don't overlook stock images and color clip art as an inexpensive source of color graphics. If you pay $20 for a CD-ROM, you don't have to use very many of the 100 to 6,000 color images to justify the price. Clip art CD-ROMs are a good source of such mundane but handy items as state flags, signs of all kinds, and drawings of common objects. Stock photo collections come in all configurations. If you can't get what you need in a small thematic collection, get as large a collection as you can find and wade through it. If the images you buy on a CD-ROM are not royalty-free, you will have to arrange to pay for their use. If you don't want to pay royalties, read the licensing agreement on the package carefully to ensure that you are getting the royalty-free rights you need.

Stock images are now available on the Internet. You can look through and find what you want. You might even be able to download a low color-density copy of an image to try it. When you finally decide what to buy, you pay your money and obtain access to download the high color-density version.

Kodak Photo CD

If you take a color negative or color slide into a service bureau (a firm that provides services for print and digital publishing), the bureau scans it and then color-balances it for a cost of somewhere between $20 and $60. You will get it back on a diskette or, if it's too large for a floppy, on a tape. On the other hand, if you take a roll of film (36 photos) into your local photo-finishing outlet, you can have the roll developed, color balanced, and put on a Kodak Photo CD for about $28. The process includes negatives and thumbnail color prints. You also can have existing negatives and slides placed on a Photo CD. The CD holds each photo in five different sizes in 24-bit color. A CD can hold up to 100 photos, each in five sizes. This is truly amazing technology.

You are most likely to use the smallest three sizes: Wallet (about 1/20 the size of a 800 x 600 screen); Snapshot (about 1/5 the size); and Standard (about 2/3 the size). Uncompressed in 256 colors (8-bit color), the Wallet size is about 25KB, the Snapshot size less than 100KB, and the Standard size less than 400KB. When converted to GIF files, the file size is less than one-half of the stated size. Most color-manipulation programs can import a Kodak Photo CD image from the CD-ROM quickly and easily. Thus, this system is not only inexpensive and convenient, but the CD-ROM provides you with a handy permanent-storage archive. Kodak's names indicate the rough equivalancies to actual color prints, with Wallet being small, Snapshot being about the size of normal color prints, and Standard being about the size of an 8 x 10 color print.

If you use color photos, this is an excellent system to use to integrate them into your Web presentation. You can easily crop the photos as well as make darkroom-like changes to them, such as changing contrast, with a bitmap color-manipulation program. These photos converted to a GIF format make a great enhancement for an HTML document (see Figure 9-4).

Figure 9-4: Kodak Photo CD Wallet-size digital photograph.

Digital cameras

High-quality digital cameras are still very expensive, but they do present an alternative to Kodak Photo CD. Some lower-priced digital cameras have become available recently, but you will want to evaluate their quality carefully before committing to their use. You should compare the archiving cost of using a digital camera to Kodak Photo CD before making a decision. Remember that the Kodak Photo CD provides the archive for your photographs.

Audio

Audio software is no longer dreamware for the Web. It is available, useful, and easy-to-use — now. The day is quickly coming when people will expect it at high-quality Web sites.

Sound

You can incorporate sound into multimedia presentations by using a *multimedia authoring program*. A multimedia authoring program is like a word processor, except that it manipulates multimedia elements (including text) instead of *just* text. The sound recording can be started by a button or hyperlink when the user chooses to hear it, or it can be started automatically as the presentation progresses to a section where sound is seamlessly integrated. In either case, the computer being used must have sound capability. Even in 1996, a significant portion of PCs cannot use sound. Nonetheless, sound is important in multimedia and grows in importance as an increasing percentage of PCs come equipped with audio boards.

Like everything else in the digital world, sound comes in files. The audio file formats commonly used on the Web are the following:

➡ WAV for the PC

➡ SND for the MAC

➡ AU and AIFF for UNIX

A software player plays an audio file. On the Web, you will have difficulty making sound work transparently without the use of a special protocol. An audio file must be downloaded by a visitor. After it's downloaded, the file may or may not be played automatically. And if the visitor doesn't have the proper player, the sound won't play at all. Because audio files tend to be quite large, the download times tend to be quite long. This is not conducive to seamless integration.

Fortunately, several audio protocols on the Internet, such as Real Audio (RA) and True Speech, have much promise. A visitor can play sound immediately in real time without waiting for the entire audio file to be downloaded first. This is called *streaming*. The sound begins as the audio file starts to be downloaded and continues during the download (see Figure 9-5). A Web audio protocol such as Real Audio uses heavy-duty compression, so the files are much smaller than normal audio files. Nonetheless, even compressed audio files are large. To read about how to configure your computer for sound, go to the following Internet address:

```
http://www.thesphere.com/Sphere/SoundConfig.html
```

Read about Real Audio and download free software at

http://www.realaudio.com/

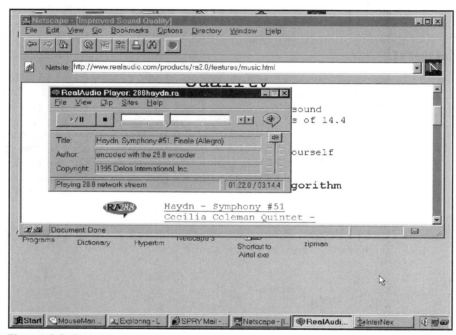

Figure 9-5: Real Audio player.

Recording

You can record directly onto your hard disk if your computer has sound capability (that is, an audio card). In many cases, this will not be convenient. If you use a normal analog tape recorder, you can convert it to digital audio, but the audio quality will not be maximized. It is better to use a digital tape recorder. A good quality digital tape recorder for voice costs about three times as much as a comparable-quality analog tape recorder (that is, about $800).

Audio-editing programs

Today, you can obtain an audio-editing program inexpensively that equals thousands of dollars of studio equipment (see Figure 9-6). To use audio editing programs efficiently, you must have a large amount of space on your hard disk *dedicated* to that purpose. Even as much as 200MB is not too much. For extensive and recurring work, it would certainly be convenient to have more than 200MB. As with audio recording, your computer must have audio capability (an audio card) to use an audio editor.

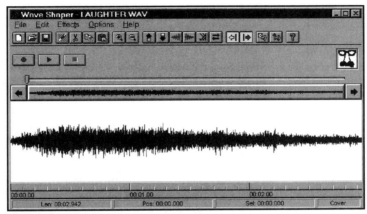

Figure 9-6: The Wave Shaper digital audio editor.

Music and voice

The quality of digital audio is determined by the sampling rate at which it is recorded and played. The higher the sampling rate, the higher the quality; and the higher the sampling rate, the more storage space required. You usually record voice and play it back at a lower sampling rate than music. The Multimedia PC Marketing Council (MPC) specifications recommend that you use 16-bit digital audio at 44.1 KHz for audio. At this rate, you will use 5.25MB per minute for storage. A 10-minute music bite will take up 52.5MB on your hard disk — or wherever else it might be stored. Double this amount for stereo.

For voice, a sampling rate of 22.05 KHz with 8-bit audio is probably adequate for most purposes. This requires 1.3MB per minute of storage, or 13MB for a 10-minute talk. You can see why audio lags behind color graphics in becoming a normal feature of the Web. Nonetheless, compression technology and the new Web audio protocols are accelerating the use of audio on the Web.

MIDI music

Musical instrument digital interface (MIDI) music is synthetic music; that is, a digital synthesizer generates it. The synthesizer is the orchestra. The composer writes the music, and the synthesizer plays it through a PC sound system. The synthesizer imitates various instruments in the orchestra. Originally, just a few instruments were imitated. Lately, the number of instruments imitated has grown substantially. MIDI music can sound very real today. Someday, perhaps, it may be impossible to tell the difference between real music and MIDI music.

The fact that MIDI music can sound real should not cloud the fact that MIDI music has become a legitimate music form itself. MIDI music can be just as delightful or just as haunting as real music. Because it is a native digital medium, it offers composers who are composing music for digital multimedia presentations the potential for complete and efficient control. Certainly the potential cost savings is considerable, too. You don't have to hire an orchestra to play it. The computer becomes the middleman between you and the composer, instead of the orchestra. Note that the word *orchestra* as used in this section could be a rock band, a quartet, a jazz combo, or an individual performer as well as a traditional orchestra.

The great advantage of MIDI music is that it takes up about 1/1000th the amount of space that a digital recording of real music uses up. In other words, MIDI files are small. Although MIDI music has not been integrated well into the Web yet, it's just a matter of time. This digital medium offers much potential.

Stock music

If you cannot supply your own music and you do not want to hire musicians to provide your music, you can purchase stock music out of a catalog. This can be an inexpensive way to acquire music, and there is plenty of good stock music available.

Animation

Animation can bring things to life, illustrate difficult concepts, and entertain. Some animation techniques are within your reach. Most require an animator. Here's a rundown on types of animation.

Sprite animation

Simple animation programs enable you to move a graphic around the screen and across a different graphic that is the background. The graphic to be moved is called a *sprite,* and it is relatively small. The background graphic is static. To use the program, you move the cursor along the path you want the sprite to take. The program then creates an animated presentation that features the sprite moving across the background graphic along the path that you specified (see Figure 9-7). The presentation is stored in an animation file. Anyone can do this simple sprite animation with an inexpensive animation program.

Figure 9-7: A sprite on a background.

Normal animation

Creating animated graphics is somewhat more complex than sprite animation. Animation consists of a series of images, often superimposed on a dynamic background, that create the illusion of movement. Animation is a great teaching tool. It can show how a part fits into a machine, how a corporate bond reacts to a decline in the Federal Reserve discount rate (animated charts), and so on. Additionally, animation can tell a story with comic characters or even more life-like characters. Full-fledged animation programs can assist digital artists in creating animation by using basic graphics and *rendering* them into an animation.

Animation is labor intensive and requires a professional animator or a graphic artist with some animation experience. This is a great technique for Web sites with big budgets, but it's not something that you're likely to do yourself or have your staff do without the big budget.

You distribute animation in an animation file. These files tend to be large, because they contain a lot of graphic information. Such files can be downloaded from an FTP site or hyperlinked in an HTML document for downloading. They require an animation player. Animations use file formats common to video technology, such as AVI and QuickTime, as well as animation formats such as FLI and FLC.

You usually do an animation of any substantial length in a multimedia authoring environment. Thus, Macromedia's Director (a multimedia authoring program) is an appropriate program to use for publishing animation on the Web. Some Web browsers now have the capability to play multimedia presentations made with Director through the Shockwave plug-in (a player program that plays automatically through a Netscape browser).

GIF animation

GIF animation is a new form of animation that is becoming popular on the Web. It is limited in its scope, so it's used for introductory banners or simple cartoons. This animation is supported in the Netscape browser and does not require any separate downloading. Essentially, it flickers through a series of images that you must create (usually about eight).

Virtual Reality

Reality for digital graphics means three-dimensional (3D). Thus, 3D graphics are becoming popular, and a variety of programs will *render* graphics to have a 3D effect. Simple 3D graphics can be normal graphics files. Ultimately, however, virtual reality means that you recreate part of the real world in a digital 3D environment that actually changes in perspective as you move through it. This is something like a combination of 3D and animation. This type of virtual reality does not go into a normal graphics file. Indeed, an enabling environment for virtual reality has become part of the Web publishing system.

Virtual Reality Markup Language (VRML) enables you to create a graphic in a Web document that is a window to a virtual world. Thus, you can create a presentation in which a visitor can see an automobile in a graphic in a Web document and have the ability to "move" around the automobile and see it from any perspective (see Figure 9-8). One needs a Web browser that will handle VRML (or that has a VRML plug-in) in order to use VRML graphics. Netscape 3.0 supports VRML.

VRML has diverse application potential. Currently, it holds particular interest for architects, engineers, designers, and scientists. If your Web site draws such people, you may be able to put VRML to good use. Additionally, VRML will become the medium of choice for online games. Still, it remains a technician's medium in the hands of digital artists and programmers and, therefore, must be considered similar to animation.

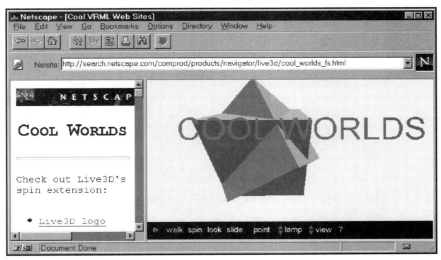

Figure 9-8: VRML graphic.

Video

Digital motion video has a way to go before it becomes a full-bodied digital publishing medium. It plays in a small window. It depends on the speed of the processor to play at a reasonable rate. It takes a huge amount of storage space. And it plays in a separate player.

Normal television operates at 30 frames per second (fps), which means that during every second, one sees 30 separate sequential pictures. New compression programs now exist that will play full-screen motion video at 30 fps on a computer. Such programs require a Pentium processor or its equivalent to work properly using only software. A lesser computer will play back the video only in a partial screen and at a lower frame rate. Thus, you may be able to use this new technology to enhance your Web site for all, but only visitors with Pentium computers or the equivalent will be able to enjoy the video fully enabled. Those with fast 486s may be able to see the video at a tolerable frame rate, but others will be stuck with the jerky movements that have characterized digital motion video in the past. By adding a motion video board to any reasonably up-to-date computer, however, you can enable full video capability. Unfortunately, few people have motion video boards for their computers.

Video clips of any substantial duration are huge files. If you include them in a Web document, they will take plenty of time to download. New Web video protocols, such as VDO and Xing, work much as Real Audio does for sound. They stream the video; that is, they start playing the video as soon as the downloading starts. The speed of the streaming depends on the bandwidth (speed and carrying capacity) of the Internet connection. With a 28.8 modem, the frame rate is well under 10, which is somewhat jerky.

When everyone uses ISDN (Integrated Services Digital Network) lines, cable, or other broadband connections, real-time video will be a more useable technology on the Internet, both for delivery of information and for teleconferencing. Until then, real-time video must be considered a protocol emerging from long experimentation (see Figure 9-9). Don't overlook the fact, however, that most *intra*nets run at a higher speed than modem connections. The new Web video protocols may run well on your intranet.

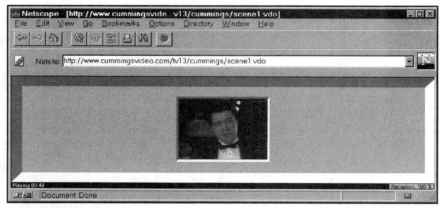

Figure 9-9: A VDO video clip.

Embedded Programs

The use of embedded programs in digital publishing is easy to enable. Why? Because the computer provides the digital publishing but can do much more. It is simply a matter of tapping into the power of the computer. A screen button or hyperlink calls up a program and runs it. Suppose that you are writing an article on currency conversion for a digital magazine on the Web. You may want to embed a currency converter into the HTML document. A visitor can input $1000, and the converter will tell him or her how many marks $1000 can buy today, or users can input 1,000 kroner and see what they're worth in dollars (see Figure 9-10). The converter can be updated every day by accessing the latest currency reports on the Internet.

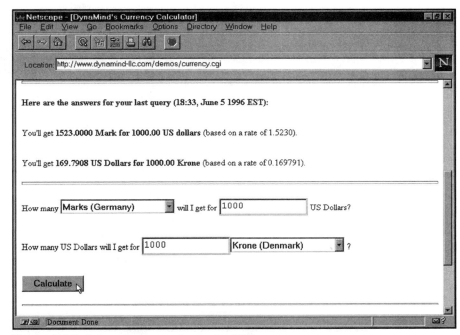

Figure 9-10: A currency converter on the Web.

You can install embedded programs in any digital publication:

➡ First, this process requires a programmer to write the program — unless you have acquired an existing one that you want use. It must be a program that runs on the computer you are using. For example, if it's for your Internet site and you use your Internet service provider's computer, it should be a UNIX program.

➡ Second, the input must be programmed into the digital publication, and the output must conform to the protocol of digital publishing. For the Web, the input will be in an HTML form. The output will be an HTML document.

➡ Third, the program must be connected to the computer by a programmer. For your Web site, the programmer will use Perl scripts or another programming language. In fact, the program itself can be done in Perl scripts in many cases. You can do almost anything you want to do in regard to using programs in a digital document.

A legacy application

Do you have a handy application that you've been using for years that you would like to make available on the Web? If it makes sense to use it via a Web browser, it might be worthwhile. Although it may be too expensive to connect the application to a Web document with CGI scripts, you won't know until you ask a programmer. If the expense is too high, you might consider reprogramming the application in Perl script or Java. Reprogramming may be less expensive than trying to connect it the way it is.

➡ Embedded programs are appropriate for the Web and will come into widespread use. Keep in mind that a database engine connected to a Web server is essentially an embedded program. It is connected to the Web documents by CGI scripts. The calculation capability of most database engines make them a competent environment for creating calculation programs as well as multimedia programs.

Java applets and applications are like embedded programs. Java programs, however, are downloaded into a visitor's Web browser, where they run on the visitor's computer instead of on the Web-site computer. The effect is exactly the same, and you can use Java to create any type of program. See Chapter 29, "Advanced Web-Database Technology," which includes information on Java.

Interactivity

Interactivity is essentially any digital procedure that requires a user to make a choice or an input. A hypertext link is interactive because it asks the user to, in effect, "Click on this link if you want additional information that's relevant to the subject matter of the document. If not, don't click." Thus, hypertext and hypermedia make possible convenient interactivity that a printed document cannot provide so easily. The Web, WAIS (Wide Area Information Server), and Gopher are unique in digital interactivity in their capability to enable a user to jump from link to link — not only within a document system but also from one document system to another (see Chapter 10, "Internet Programs"). Your visitors will be able to do more than just read individual documents. You can design documents that will draw them in and potentially provide them with a more satisfying experience that enables them to pursue their unique interests more conveniently. Web documents generated on the fly based on visitor input enhance the interactive capability of the Web considerably and can only be facilitated by a database.

Digital multimedia *online* adds a new dimension to digital interactivity: personal communication. Not only can you interact with the information as you can in a multimedia title on a CD-ROM, but you can interact with *people* too. E-mail and other Internet communications programs and protocols integrated into Web sites create a supportive environment for diverse communication interactivity. This quickly developing capability is a substantial step forward in the productive use of digital media.

Authoring Programs

A word processor is a text authoring program. A spreadsheet is a financial modeling authoring program. A multimedia authoring program is a program that makes it easy to create a multimedia presentation — or at least easier than creating a multimedia presentation by programming from scratch.

Text-based multimedia

Text-based multimedia authoring programs, such as RoboHelp, and multimedia authoring programs, such as Macromedia Director, are important for creating presentations on diskettes and CD-ROMs. Why are they important for the Internet? Text-based authoring programs can create digital hypertext multimedia documents that can be distributed by making them available for download at an anonymous FTP site or by sending them with e-mail. The productions can be as small as one document with internal hyperlinks or as large as book-like document systems in which each document might be a chapter. You can distribute such multimedia presentations via automatic FTP downloads generated out of a Web document.

Anonymous FTP

An FTP (File Transfer Protocol) site is simply a directory at an Internet domain where files are made available for downloading. Normally, access to an FTP site is controlled by a user or login name and a password. Only those authorized can have access. If you want to make the FTP site public, however, you have to provide access to everyone. You normally do this by making the login name the word *anonymous* and the password either the visitor's e-mail address or the word *guest*.

Many text based authoring programs require that run-time players be sent along with the productions to make them work. This is not significant on a CD-ROM, but on a diskette or online, the run-time player tends to take up too much storage space. Some text based authoring programs run on the Windows Help engine. In other words, the Windows Help engine acts as the run-time player. In Windows 3.1, the Help engine was not fully multimedia capable, and Dynamic Link Libraries (DLLs) were added to beef up the multimedia capabilities. In Windows 95, the Help engine is a multimedia hypermedia program, and it makes a good run-time player. Doc-to-Help, an authoring program that runs on the Windows Help engine, not only displays text and other media digitally but also prints the documents so that they look nicely typeset. A Doc-to-Help production will also run well on a local-area network (LAN), giving you another option for reaching visitors, if appropriate.

Many of the text based authoring programs actually run in Microsoft Word for Windows. Doc-to-Help and RoboHelp are examples. You create your text as you normally would using Word, but you save your work as an RTF file. Using the authoring program from within Word, you easily add the markups as needed. When you are finished, you compile all the documents in the production into one file, which runs on the Help engine. It's easy and creates a great product. Some of these text based authoring programs, such as Ntergaid's HyperWriter, will start with a finished document from almost any source (for example, Word, WordPerfect, RTF, ASCII, WordPro 96), making your multimedia authoring potentially easier.

Unlimited multimedia

Multimedia authoring programs such as Macromedia Director are important for the Internet because some of the browsers will have the capability to run the presentations created by them. A few browsers have Director run-time capability now via the Shockwave plug-in, and other run-time capability is certain to follow. This means that a multimedia production created in Director can be played through the browser. This technology still has limitations and has not reached its full potential yet, and perhaps will not do so until greater bandwidth is generally available. Nonetheless, digital multimedia is powerful technology, and its incorporation into the Web system gives you yet another option for delivery of information to your visitors.

HTML multimedia

The Web publishing mechanism itself is a powerful hypermedia multimedia system. You can do on the Internet quite adequately much of what the text based authoring programs can do offline. You simply use HTML to mark up ASCII documents. The Web browser then reads the documents, magically turning them into nicely typeset pages with color graphics.

Do you have to be on the Internet? No. You can read HTML documents just fine from a diskette, a hard disk, or a CD-ROM with the Web browser in the local host mode. Because HTML is a cross-platform system, this approach might be convenient for your distribution scheme. The finished product will not be as polished as one authored in RoboHelp, but it will work well and will run faster locally than it does on the Internet. Of course, your visitors must have Web browsers to see HTML productions, whether on the Web or off.

Conversion programs convert a word processor document into an HTML document. Moreover, the new versions of many programs include automatic converters. These programs are good for long documents but do not completely eliminate the need for custom HTML programming to create a good presentation. Because the markups themselves are ASCII characters, you can actually do your HTML programming in a word processor by typing in the markups. This might be a bit tedious, however, and an HTML authoring program, such as Microsoft Front Page, or an HTML editor, such as HTML Assistant Pro, will make things easier for you.. The authoring tools or programs make the placement of the markups easier — or even transparent.

Electronic Delivery Technology

When you're talking about digital media, focus on compression. The smaller the file, the shorter the download time. The public resists long download times. One reason for the resistance is the fact that many people are paying for their Internet service by the minute. Another is because visitors become bored sitting through long downloads, particularly those who have computers that do not multitask effectively. The possibility that a modem may disconnect in the middle of a long download causes tension and is yet another reason many people avoid long downloads. Whatever the reasons, compression reduces download times and makes people happier. Therefore, you will want to compress your files before making them available to visitors. The most common compression software for Windows is Winzip. You can download it at no cost from the following Internet site:

```
http://www.winzip.com/winzip/download.html
```

Many compression programs provide about 2:1 compression. This is okay for executables and text, but you can achieve higher compression for graphics, audio, and video, which tend to be huge files.

Assuming that you send uncompressed files, Table 9-1 shows you the download times for sending the amount of digital information indicated.

Table 9-1:	Transmission time in seconds			
Amount	14,400	28,800	ISDN	Cable (Uncompressed)
50KB	35	17	4.4	.33
100KB	69	35	8.9	.66
1MB	694	347	89	6.66
Time in seconds	11.5	5.8	1.5	.1

Compression of 2:1 prior to transmission will decrease the above transmission times by half.

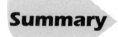

Summary

What is the relevance of this chapter to databases? It's a multimedia world! A multimedia database can deliver all the multimedia elements discussed in this chapter. Text, for example, does not have to be delivered as data in a column. It can be delivered as a Word file, an HTML document, or a Doc-to-Help executable file. Multimedia files are binary files unless they are ASCII text files. Binary files such as color graphics and executables (programs) can be stored in and delivered out of a database. Because binary files are often large, they have the name Binary Large Objects (*BLOBs*). Today, many database engines can handle BLOBs.

BLOBs are quickly becoming the routine building blocks of the information world. As more information goes online, information in general will grow richer and richer. What once would have been a 10-page report in monospaced type becomes a typeset document with 15 color graphics and two embedded executables. Keeping track of information elements has the potential of becoming a huge chore.

As discussed throughout the book, a database system is a superior way of handling and accounting for multimedia elements in most situations. Because the Web is a multimedia system, a database system is an ideal means for presenting and managing the multimedia elements that make up the Web site. Beyond just handling and accounting for multimedia elements, however, a database system provides the capability to perform programming functions easily that document systems cannot do or are able to do only with great difficulty.

Internet
Programs
and Protocols

 **In This Chapter**

Internet programs

Protocols

Web programs

All the hardware most people have to use on the Internet consists of simply a phone line, a modem, and a computer. But you can only use this hardware with the right software (computer programs). To use the Internet to do one thing, you use one program. To do something else on the Internet, you use a different program. To transmit a file, for example, you use FTP. To operate a remote computer, you use Telnet. When programs become so widely used by so many people that they set a de facto standard, they become *protocols*. Protocols can also be widely used APIs, such as ODBC. Often, standards committees develop and set protocols that become widely used.

Net Services

This chapter covers traditional Internet protocols as well as new or potential Internet protocols. The term *protocol* is used loosely in this book to include any new programs that have gained popularity or appear as though they might gain enough popularity to set a programming standard. (You'll find that technical people have a more precise definition of protocol.) In this chapter, the word protocol implies a *communication* program or, otherwise, an API.

Although this book primarily covers the Web, the other Internet protocols (programs) cannot be ignored. But virtually all of the new Internet protocols that have appeared in 1995-96 are actually Web protocols, and many have gained quick acceptance as part of the Web environment. Netscape leads in incorporating new Web protocols such as Java (a new language for network programming) and VRML (Virtual Reality Markup Language) into its browser. Many other software developers are following suit. This chapter outlines some of the Internet and Web protocols and relates them to using a database.

Telnet

With Telnet, you can access a remote computer and use the programs that reside on the remote computer. The Telnet protocol is essential for managing a Web site and a database engine on an ISP's computer. You will use a command-line interface and UNIX commands to manage the Web site (see Figure 10-1). Such commands are similar to DOS. Normally, you would have to use only a few commands for managing a Web site. Managing a database in a Web site using only a command-line interface, however, is more complex. An alternative is to use a program, such as Hummingbird's eXceed 5 for Windows, that enables you to simulate X-Windows on your PC, thereby providing you with a Windows-like graphical user interface (GUI) to manage your database on your ISP's UNIX computer.

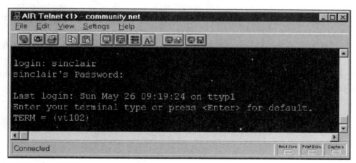

Figure 10-1: *Telnet in Windows is still a command-line interface.*

Table 10-1 lists some of the UNIX commands you need for Web-site housekeeping chores using a command-line interface.

Table 10-1: UNIX commands	
Purpose	**Command**
Change a directory	cd *or* chdir
Change modes and permissions	chmod
Display the directory files	dir
Make file links	ln
Create a new directory	mkdir
View long files	more
Move or rename files	mv
Identify the working directory	pwd
Remove files	rm
Remove directories	rmdir
Separate files and directories	/

As you can see, many of the commands are similar or identical to DOS. You will need a good basic book on UNIX to use as a reference for Web-site management. Look up *chmod* and *ln* in a UNIX book. They are useful commands that take you beyond the capability of DOS.

FTP

File Transfer Protocol (FTP) provides a means of transferring files from one computer to another. You use it for uploading or downloading files. When a file is to be used in the Web environment, the Web protocol Hypertext Transfer Protocol (HTTP) downloads it for a visitor to use (view) instantly on his or her own computer. When you download a file for future use, however, you use FTP, and the file remains outside the Web environment. A file can be delivered from a database via FTP just as it can be delivered from a database via HTTP. Because you use an FTP client to upload and download files, keep in mind that you can do so only at an Internet site that has an FTP server.

FTP provides you the means of transferring (uploading) the programming files to your ISP's computer for your database engine (see Figure 10-2). The objective is to do as much programming as possible on your computer in Windows and then upload it via FTP to your ISP's computer. If you can avoid doing any programming on your ISP's computer via Telnet, so much the better, because it will be slow to do via a modem.

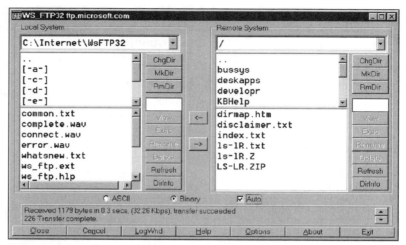

Figure 10-2: WS_FTP32 Windows FTP client. Note that your PC directory appears on the left and the directory on your ISP's hard disk appears on the right. The program enables you to transfer files back and forth (upload and download).

Gopher

Gopher is a competent Internet publishing system that predates the Web. It uses ASCII files and provides limited hyperlinking capability though special menu files. Formatting capability is limited to ASCII formatting, and there are no inline graphics (see Figure 10-3). Graphics can be downloaded automatically but cannot be viewed within a Gopher document. Because the Gopher system contains a huge amount of information internationally and because the Web system can access the Gopher system, you can routinely provide the hyperlink to a Gopher document out of a database in your Web site. Again, keep in mind that it takes a Gopher server to make Gopher documents available.

E-mail

E-mail is a useful type of program that has significance beyond just sending messages back and forth between people.

Everyday e-mail

E-mail is a separate and mature digital system outside the realm of the Web that offers many configurations and much flexibility. Providing e-mail communication capability from within a Web site, however, is useful and is already a traditional feature of prime Web sites. You can deliver the Web HTML forms and CGI scripting to accommodate an e-mail message — and even do so from a database on the fly in the form of an HTML document.

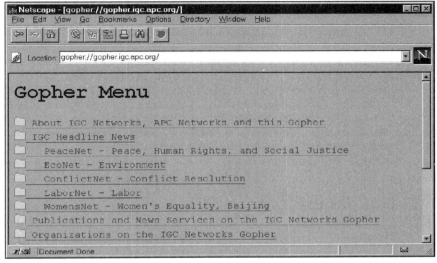

Figure 10-3: A Gopher document.

Auto-responder

You can use auto-responders (robots) effectively inside Web sites, too. An auto-responder automatically replies with an information document in e-mail form to an e-mail message sent to the auto-responder's address. For example, info@ is a traditional auto-responder address. If you sent a message to info@dogs.com, you would expect to immediately receive an e-mail document having something to do with dogs. For example, the message you receive might instruct you to send an e-mail message to dogfood@dogs.com to get information about dog food, or doghealth@dogs.com to get information on vaccinations. You can routinely deliver the addresses for auto-responders out of a database application in a Web site, and different queries can generate the delivery of different combinations of auto-responder addresses. Alternatively, the actual delivery of auto-responder documents from the auto-responder can be initiated by a database application.

Mailing lists

Mailing lists are e-mail programs that automatically send an e-mail message — which has been sent to the mailing list program — to everyone on a mailing list of people. Suppose that Jennifer, Ben, Steve, McCabe, and Brook are on the mailing list of people (named fivestrive), and Majordomo is the mailing list program. Brook sends an e-mail message to fivestrive@domain.com, where Majordomo resides. Majordomo in turn automatically sends the message to Jennifer, Ben, Steve, McCabe, and Brook. If Jennifer, Ben, Steve, or McCabe reply, the e-mail reply message is automatically sent out to everyone on the mailing list of people.

For convenience, these mailing list programs are referred to as *Listserv,* although there are mailing list programs other than Listserv (such as Majordomo). You use Listservs for direct e-mail (a marketing technique) and for online forums or conferences (discussion groups, a group communications technique). Because you actually program a Listserv via e-mail messages to the Listserv itself, a Listserv could be programmed out of a database. For example, in a database of people who had visited a gourmet food Web site, a query could determine all those who had ordered chocolate items. The list of chocolate customers and their e-mail addresses could then be sent via e-mail to program a Listserv. The Listserv could then be used for direct e-mail to the chocolate customers or to start a Chocolate Lovers Online Forum.

E-mail database systems

E-mail systems are evolving into groupware. As such, they will need more power and capability to organize and keep track of important communications, communications threads (such as found in newsgroups), and group work. Database technology has much potential for enhancing the power and capability of e-mail programs. Many capable e-mail programs and systems now exist, and it probably doesn't make much sense for you to develop your own custom e-mail system using a database application unless you do it for a sizable organization. Nevertheless, as e-mail systems evolve, they will become more reliant on database technology than they are today.

WAIS

WAIS (Wide Area Information Service) is a proprietary Internet publishing system designed for a large body of information that you can easily navigate by hyperlinks. For example, WAIS is great for a 2,000-page publication of a government agency's regulations and other such formal documents. America Online now owns this technology and provides a publishing service that uses WAIS. There is a huge amount of information in existing WAIS documents, and the number of documents (mostly for specialized uses) will grow. You can deliver a link to a WAIS document out of a database in a Web site.

Java

A object-oriented programming language similar to C++, Java is designed to provide programming capability in the Web environment while resisting viruses. One way Java is used is for the downloading of executables (programs) that run in a visitor's computer, hence the need for virus resistance.

These executables are called *applets* (miniprograms). This new language was meant to enhance multimedia presentations beyond the capability of HTML. A Java multimedia presentation (applet) can be delivered out of a database just as any BLOB can be.

Is there life beyond applets? Although the glamorous use of applets is for multimedia entertainment, Java is also appropriate for an unlimited range of practical uses (see Figure 10-4). In other words, you can use Java for database programming in Web sites with JDBC (see Chapter 29, "Advanced Web-Database Technology"). In fact, Java offers more robust programming capability and can be used for general programming too. It is already a standard for general programming on the Web and is unique in having its origin in network technology.

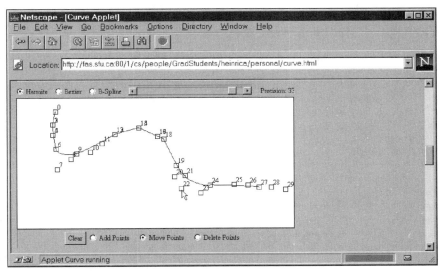

Figure 10-4: A Java applet.

VRML

Virtual Reality Markup Language (VRML) is a new language created to provide 3D programming for the Web. It works best via modem when a considerable amount of programming is already stored on a visitor's computer. You can accomplish this with a huge initial download followed by periodic update downloads. The language facilitates 3D presentations initiated from the Web site but also draws on the digital programming materials stored in the visitor's computer, whether on a hard disk or a CD-ROM. Considerable potential exists to integrate VRML and database technology for the delivery of these 3D presentations.

SGML

Standard Generalized Markup Language (SGML) is a document description language of which HTML is a subset. By virtue of the existence of special SGML browsers and because some Web browsers will read SGML, this will continue to be an important medium of text communication. Delivering documents in this format out of a database is much the same as delivering any ASCII document, including HTML documents. Because a substantial portion of the publications of the federal bureaucracy and many corporations are in SGML form, this is an important standard — which will become more important in the years ahead. SGML is an important component of a cross-platform document-management system, and many organizations that set up intranets soon after begin looking for cross-platform solutions to handling information and documents.

Director and Shockwave

Macromedia's Director multimedia authoring program is popular on both the Mac and the PC. A Director player is required to play digital multimedia presentations made with this authoring program. Some Director presentations can also be played in some Web browsers via Shockwave, a plug-in (http://www.macromedia.com). A short Shockwave presentation can provide excellent multimedia communication or entertainment (see Figure 10-5). Such a presentation can be stored in a database and delivered in response to a query.

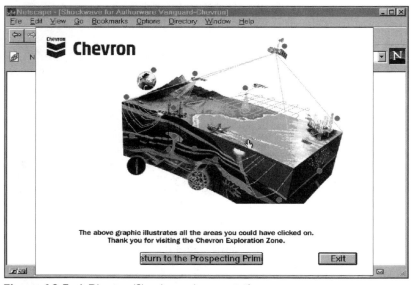

Figure 10-5: A Director (Shockwave) presentation.

Acrobat

Adobe's Acrobat is essentially paper replication programming. It is useful for organizations that handle large amounts of paperwork rather than electronic text. The files tend to be large, but they can be stored in and delivered out of a database. Some Web browsers display Acrobat files via a plug-in, although you normally view them in a separate Acrobat reader.

Newsgroups

The difference between mailing lists and *newsgroups* is that newsgroups have a central point where all e-mail (called *posts* in newsgroup) is sent and stored. You must go to this central point to read and reply to posts. Like e-mail programs, newsgroup-management programs are traditional on the Internet and highly refined. They make use of database technology. That is not to say, however, that they cannot benefit more from database technology in the future. Database engines can easily store and account for messages and, therefore, will continue to be useful in the evolution of e-mail-based communications systems.

Real Audio

To understand Real Audio, you have to understand three different versions of digital audio. The first is *not-in-real-time* audio. This is like a recording that you buy, take home, and play. On the Internet, you download audio files and play them later on a player. The quality can be excellent, but the files are very large. For that reason, you may have to wait a while to hear the file after a long download. This kind of sound is used for samples of CD recordings that are for sale and for other applications where high sound quality is important.

A second type of audio is a recording that one can listen to without downloading. A visitor can listen to it as it plays on the server in real time. This is called *streaming*. A visitor needs a Web browser plug-in or a separate player. The quality of the sound is not as good — it's like an AM radio broadcast — but this will improve as the technology advances. With streaming, the visitor does not wait for a download.

A third type of audio is not a recording, but a live broadcast. It's essentially the same as the second type of audio except that it's a live performance that streams. You listen to it in real time.

Real Audio is a Web protocol that offers all three types of audio mentioned here. To hear these audio files play, a visitor needs the Real Audio player or a browser that incorporates a Real Audio plug-in. You can store these Real Audio files in a database and deliver them.

Real Audio is not without competition. True Speech and Voxware offer similar capability (see Figure 10-6). All of these programs use heavy-duty compression for audio files, which substantially reduces the huge size of such files. Nonetheless, the files are still large and are indisputably BLOBs. All these programs are designed to run at low bandwidth (14.4 and 28.8). These programs make up a technology that provides an attractive and practical dimension to the Web.

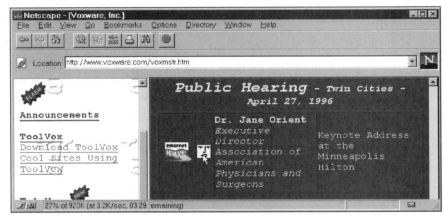

Figure 10-6: A Voxware audio bite.

Video

Cornell University has provided a teleconferencing (videoconferencing) protocol that you can use over the Internet. It runs at 14.4 or 28.8, albeit slowly, and is in black and white. You can use a $80 cam (video camera) that plugs into a serial port on a PC to provide your teleconferencing image. Up to six people can be on the screen at the same time. The screen sizes are small and the frame rate is very low, but it works.

Two relatively new video protocols are VDO and Xing. Each provides a reasonable size screen (not a full screen) in color that streams video somewhere between 5 and 15 fps with a 28.8 modem and a Pentium. These real-time programs work well over an ISDN line. Clearly, video is now a viable Web protocol for high-performance PCs (Pentiums) with high-bandwidth connections (ISDN). For lesser equipment, it is marginal. These files (streaming files) can be delivered by a database just like any other BLOB.

Secure Server

The *secure* Web server will continue an ascent to eventually dominate the market. A secure server provides some form of encryption for some or all e-mail or other communications transmissions. Soon, security will be taken for granted. It is important in stimulating commerce on the Web by providing for secure transactions. Large businesses, such as banks, that have a lot to lose through unsecure communications practices find security germane to their online operations. A database application presents an appropriate programming environment in which to enable secure transactions and to keep track of the details. The calculation capability of database engines provides a well-proved development technique for transaction accounting.

TruDoc

Bitstream's Web protocol provides for using the fonts of your choice for creating your Web documents, thus giving you control over the typesetting. The TruDoc document is a special text file, and TruDoc capability in the HTML editor, browser, and server is required to make it work. Bitstream licenses its protocol to other Web software developers. The advantage of TruDoc is that the file sizes are small. The files are not graphics files, even though they provide the appearance of a page.

TruDoc may never achieve universal usage but may provide necessary functionality for a certain market. Many protocols will fit this profile. Only by keeping your eyes and ears open on the Web and elsewhere will you find protocols that you or your company can use to your benefit.

Netscape

A protocol? A bamboozle? A curse? A blessing? In setting new open standards for Web publishing, Netscape is, in effect, establishing an open development platform for Web-software development. Think of TCP/IP as the operating system for the Internet, albeit an invisible operating system. Think of HTML and Java as the programming languages for the Web. By creating the market-leading browser, keeping open development standards, providing an API for third-party plug-in programs, and incorporating some of the new protocols into its browsers and servers, Netscape creates a development environment from which all can profit: software developers, content developers, and consumers alike. This open environment has stimulated one of the most entrepreneurial periods in computer history.

Although Netscape sells only one of dozens of browsers available in the market and only several of the many dozens of servers available in the market, it has proven to be a strong leader not only in establishing new standards and validating useful new protocols but also in keeping the Web-development platform open. This does not necessarily mean that you have to buy Netscape software products to have an up-to-date system. Capable competition abounds. Rather, it means that you should keep on eye on what Netscape is doing and offering if you want a glimpse of the future.

Stretching the Protocols

The VRML requirements mentioned earlier in the chapter present an interesting programming situation. Effective use of VRML requires that information be stored on both the Web server and the visitor's hard disk (or a CD-ROM). Conceivably, you might use databases to store graphics and other digital multimedia materials both on the Web server and on the visitor's hard disk. In this instance, the queries might address two different database engines (or flat files), which adds programming complexity but improves performance. This approach seems to have much potential, particularly for intranets. You can take this idea and apply it to GIFs, Real Audio, video, or other media to improve performance, particularly over narrow bandwidths.

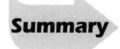

Summary

For readers not familiar with the growing number of diverse protocols becoming available on the Internet and, particularly, on the Web, consider this chapter an imagination expander rather than a definitive list. Some of the protocols not mentioned may be appropriate for database treatment; those mentioned may be appropriate for additional database treatment that has not been covered; and new protocols will be announced by the time you read this book.

The protocols are the building blocks of Web-site systems. The better you know them, the more creative you can be. The list of protocols used in this chapter and in the book provide an especially wide range of Internet and Web programs as building blocks. Virtually every type of communication or information is delivered via a computer file. If it's in a file, it can potentially be stored and managed in a database. As the Web becomes a more complex development environment, which is certainly happening, database systems will become more and more valuable for efficient and effective management of Web sites.

Other Web-Publishing Tools

HTML Editing and Authoring Programs

Editors and authoring programs make applying HTML markup proceed more quickly and easily for most people — except the fastest typists. For novices, these programs are essential

HTML editors

Markups are the simple characters you add to ASCII text to transform it into an HTML document. HTML is a simple markup language that a fast typist can use with just a word processor. Many people, however, will find it easier to use a simple markup editing tool. Typically, these HTML editors have a series of buttons on a toolbar across the top of the screen. Each button is for a particular markup. Some of these editors use menus instead of buttons. Markups can consist of anywhere from three characters to a dozen or more characters. The buttons provide some efficiency, particularly for those persons who have marginal typing skills. They also allow unlimited creativity. These editors require a knowledge of HTML, and without such knowledge they are useless. Brooklyn North's HTML Assistant Pro (`fox.nsta.ca/~harawitz`), shown in Figure 11-1, is a leading representative of these handy tools, as is Sausage Software's Hot Dog Professional (`www.sausage.com`).

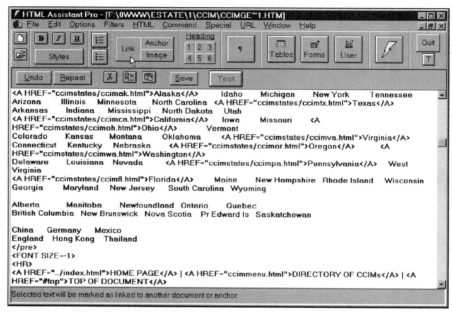

Figure 11-1: Brooklyn North HTML Assistant Pro.

When you do your HTML editing, use a Web browser to check your work at the same time. In general, the process goes like this:

1. Activate your HTML editor and a browser.

2. Work with the editor and then switch to the browser (one keystroke in Windows — Alt+Tab).

By going back and forth this way, you can work quickly and accurately. Some HTML programs enable you to do this switching internally rather than through Windows. Incredibly, it sometimes takes more keystrokes to do this internally than to do it in Windows.

If you do creative work using HTML, you will find an HTML editor indispensable. Even if you use other Web-publishing tools, you will need an editor to tune up the documents so that they perform exactly the way you desire. In fact, it is difficult to imagine a well-functioning Web site that hasn't seen the touch of an HTML editor.

Because an HTML document is ASCII text, you will have no trouble transferring an HTML document between a word processor, an HTML editor, and a database application. Thus, in many cases, an editor may come in handy in creating well-tuned templates for your database work (refer to Chapter 14.) Even where templates must be programmed in an SQL extension language such as Oracle's PL/SQL, you may find an HTML editor handy for some phases of the programming process. For example, it may be easier to transform, tune, and test an HTML document, or form, by making an HTML prototype before you program such a document with a database development tool. If you take this approach, the time-honored *copy and paste* technique will come in handy, too.

An HTML editor gets into the guts of the matter. An HTML program that purports to do it all for you so that you do not have to know HTML usually makes a poor HTML editor. If you are planning to connect the Web to a database application, it's going to be difficult to do so without learning HTML reasonably well. Fortunately, you can learn HTML easily. An HTML editor is a must-have addition to your tool box. More than anything else, personal preference provides the basis for choosing one editor over another, because the top three or four editors are somewhat similar.

HTML authoring tools

Another type of HTML program is more user friendly than HTML editors. This type of program attempts to provide an *authoring* environment in which you need not even know HTML. These programs seem to have much promise, yet they do not seem to work well for fine-tuning except perhaps for novices who do simple and straightforward documents. For those knowledgeable of HTML, these tools are often more trouble to use than the HTML editors and do not provide as much control or flexibility. Creativity is curtailed. On the other hand, where you do repetitive work, these authoring tools may provide you with some efficiency that an HTML editor will not. Some of these tools give you WYSIWYG ("what you see is what you get") capability, which means that you can work on the HTML document while the browser displays it, rather work on it in its ASCII source form.

These HTML authoring programs are popular and, with careful consideration, you may find one useful to you. Netscape's Navigator Gold (http://www.netscape.com), Quarterdeck's WebAuthor (http://www.qdeck.com), NaviSoft's GNNpress (http://www.gnn.com), SoftQuad's Hot Metal Pro (http://www.sq.com), InContext Systems' Spider (http://www.incontext.com), and Adobe's PageMill for the Mac (http://www.adobe.com) are examples of this type of software.

HTML site managers

These advanced tools offer the capability of managing more than one document at a time. They purport to manage your entire Web site. Some even provide a diagram of all the documents and hyperlinks in your Web system. Although some offer an excellent variety of useful features, these tools still cannot improve on the basic utility of an HTML editor for creating documents. You may find these tools best for managing large or complex Web sites and other tools more appropriate for detail work and fine-tuning.

When a Web site becomes so large or so complex that you feel you need to create a chart to keep track of it, a Web-site management tool may come in handy or even prove indispensable. Besides making management of the site easier, these tools usually provide template capability for creating large document systems easily. Microsoft's FrontPage (www.microsoft.com) is an example of a Web-site manager (see Figure 11-2), as are GNNpress and Oracle PowerBrowser (http://www.oracle.com).

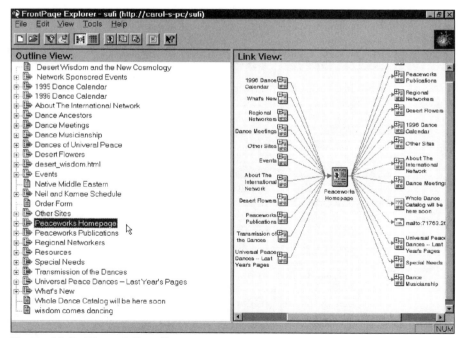

Figure 11-2: Microsoft FrontPage.

HTML document-management systems

Specialized Web-site managers create, convert, and manage large text-publishing systems on the Web, such as 2,000-page maintenance manuals,

5,000-page volumes of governmental regulations, and so on. These programs organize and maintain text documents effectively, and many include a powerful text-search capability that can search the entire document system quickly on keywords. InfoAccess' HTML Transit (`http://www.infoaccess.com`) is an inexpensive example of this type of program without the text search (see Figure 11-3). Fulcrum Technologies offers a variety of more expensive examples of the types of programs that include text search.

Figure 11-3: InfoAccess' HTML Transit.

Specialized HTML tools

A variety of specialized authoring tools now find a place in the market. They do a certain kind of Web development. Oracle's PowerBrowser is one example. PowerBrowser specifically creates a database application in a Web site — but in a specific environment. First, this is a desktop system for a limited number of users on an intranet, not an Internet system. PowerBrowser includes a Web browser, a Web-database development tool, a database engine, and a Web server (see Figure 11-4). It runs in Windows 95 and is intended to be used on a small LAN. To do the Web-database development, you use a set of Wizards, which are preprogrammed tools, to create simple applications. To do any customized work, you must use the Oracle BASIC programming language, with HTML extensions. Although easy programming, it is still programming. You do all development work through the browser.

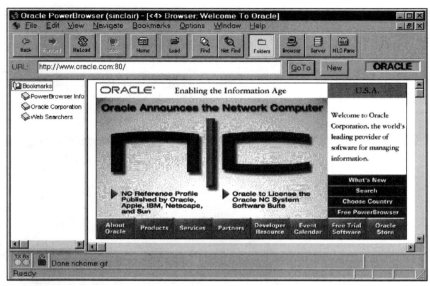

Figure 11-4: Oracle PowerBrowser.

You can see that this system will be handy for a variety of situations for small-scale operations, because it constitutes an entire client-server system. If Oracle eventually provides easy-to-use functions for the PowerBrowser that do not require programming, like those in PowerObjects (Oracle's easy-to-use database development tool), this specialized Web-database development tool might become very popular for small businesses and other small organizational efforts.

Overview

After you become a capable Webmaster, you will probably do creative work with an HTML editor, database work with a Web-database development tool, and site management with a Web-site manager. You might even find one tool that does more than one of these tasks well. To become a competent Webmaster today — or even to work on Web projects — there is no substitute for learning HTML.

Conversion Programs

The latest versions of WordPerfect, Microsoft Word, and other word processors have HTML converters built in or supply converter programs free of charge. Whatever word processor or other text program you use, you can get a conversion utility for it now. These converters automatically transform a word processor document into an HTML document. They translate standard documents created with word processor templates well but offer minimal capability for creative Web document design. To use these converters effectively, you must customize a special template to facilitate your conversions. Otherwise, considerable touch up after conversion may be required to give your documents a professional look. Microsoft Word's converter is free to download at the following Internet address:

```
http://www.microsoft.com
```

Your existing word processor templates may not work well with these converters. For example, a template heading markup with the name *Heading 1* is almost certain to translate into the HTML markup *H1* with a converter. The *Heading 1* markup in your word processor template may set 13-point type, and a Web browser's *H1* may set 18-point type. Thus, the conversion won't achieve the desired typesetting effect. It will take some coordination to make converters work well, and if you don't know much regarding word processor document templates, you will have to investigate how they work (read the word processor manual).

These conversion utilities do well for lengthy documents that are primarily text, for first drafts, or for preexisting text documents. Certainly the use of a conversion tool makes a rational first step in handling long text documents. But these conversion tools do not necessarily get the job done completely, and additional HTML editing may be necessary.

Database Applications

The example that follows illustrates how database technology can be considered a relatively simple Web-publishing tool in a specific situation. In this example, you can create a simple text-document management system that constitutes a Web text-publishing system. Here's the scenario: You operate a Web site that is an online magazine, and you publish ten articles each month. Each article is one HTML document. Additionally, you publish four books a year online, averaging 20 chapters each and with each chapter being a separate HTML document. That's a total of 200 documents each year. To digitally garnish the documents, you use an average of three unique graphics per article or chapter, for a total of 600 GIFs each year. What's the best way to handle your workload?

Store and deliver

This is just a store-and-deliver mechanism. You merely create an HTML document. You copy and paste it into the desktop database table (that is, into a column). You then export the data and upload it to the Web site as a flat-file list. To update at any time, you simply export the data again and upload it to the Web site to replace the existing (outdated) flat-file.

All you need is a desktop database engine. Store all the articles in a desktop database application. Then transfer the data to your Web site. Here's how to do it, step by step:

1. **Use a desktop database engine (such as Access, Approach, Paradox).**

2. **Create each HTML text document manually to maximize its uniqueness and attractiveness, and then store it in the desktop database application by following the remaining steps.**

3. **Create a row for each article and each graphic.**

4. **Create columns for the articles and graphics.** Use a memo column (field) for the articles. Note that the graphics will be filenames only, not the actual graphics file (see Figure 11-5). Make sure that each row has an ID column with a unique number.

5. **Export and upload the data to your Web site in the form of a flat-file list.**

6. **Upload the graphics files to your Web site.**

7. **Create a CGI script (query) to retrieve a single document (see Chapter 15).**

8. **Instead of using a relative address for a document, use the CGI script.** Substitute the name of the document to make the CGI script work for each article and chapter to be retrieved from the database.

TABLE				
ID	Document	Graphic 1	Graphic 2	Graphic 3

Figure 11-5: Table for a store-and-deliver system.

This system is crude but inexpensive and effective. You eliminate the directory (folder) structure and the HTML documents that would be stored in the directories. You can have a programmer write the one CGI script inexpensively. You can use a flat-file list on the Web site, thus avoiding the cost of a database engine, although you store the data off-site in a desktop database application. Nothing complex is involved, such as creating HTML pages on the fly.

On the fly

If this example is too simple, you can make it more robust with more CGI scripts. With minimal additional CGI programming, you can use HTML templates for articles and chapters and thereby create HTML documents on the fly, which saves considerable HTML programming (see Chapter 12).

Meta information

In this system, it is easy to add meta information (such as authorship, copyright ownership, royalties paid, and so on). You simply expand the table in the desktop database application. Such meta information doesn't have to be exported and uploaded unless you have a need to access it from the Internet.

Web-publishing tool

Based on the previous example, you can consider an ordinary desktop database engine, such as Microsoft Access, a simple Web-publishing tool. Such database engines are powerful and easy to use. You can export and upload an entire table as a flat-file list to a Web site. You can use a store-and-deliver approach, or you can use templates for creating HTML documents on the fly. You can do some very useful things without a Web-site database engine, without extensive CGI scripting, and without making your Web site into a large, complex, and expensive database application project.

Web-site development tool selection

If you want a large and complex Web site database technology creates it in the most efficient and economical manner. Indeed, other chapters dwell on the techniques. A capable database application installed in a Web site can perform incredible feats of publishing and management, create custom documents on the fly, track visitors, administer transactions, multimedia assets and more. The question is when is it better to use other software than it is to reinvent (to program) the functionality of such software by using database technology? After all, many Web-publishing and site-management tools have internal database applications as an integral part of their programming.

Although database technology can do it all — or most of it — the rational approach is to consider a useful mix of Web tools that, combined, can help you build a Web site that suits your purposes. With this approach, each program will do what it does best.

Data-Publishing Tools

If all you want to do is publish your database tables or reports in HTML form, many new tools can make that easy for you to do. Most future versions of database engines will enable automatic conversion of database tables, queries, and reports to HTML documents — if they don't already include such a feature. In the meanwhile, the tools to enable such publishing are widely available.

You can download the Internet Assistant free (`http://www.microsoft.com`). It installs as a part of Access 7.0, and you can find it in the Tools menu at the Add-Ins option. The Internet Assistant is easy to use and does a straightforward job of publishing data. These kinds of tools are great for an intranet where all you want to do is to make data (alphanumeric text) available to employees — and you're not interested in fancy looks.

Like automatic text-conversion programs, these tools do not necessarily produce attractive, fancy, multimedia Web documents suitable for commercial publishing. You will want to use a database application that dynamically delivers HTML documents, if commercial publishing is your objective.

Combinations

You can combine tools such as Access Internet Assistant with other techniques covered in this book to make publishing on the Internet or on an intranet easier. For example, in the last paragraph of Chapter 14, where using the reporting capability of a database engine is suggested as a shortcut to data cataloging, using a tool such as Access Internet Assistant may make a lot of sense. In effect, it does your data cataloging for you.

Likewise, you can effortlessly publish documents stored in database memo columns (fields) with one of these tools. These tools can make an effective Web-document publishing system like HTML Transit, albeit with less capability.

CGI Scripting Development Programs

CGI scripting is custom work. Nonetheless, a few Web-development tools store prewritten CGI scripts to be called up for the right situation. net:Genesis (`http://www.netgen.com`), consists entirely of CGI scripting capability for all occasions.

Color Graphics Programs

Programs that manipulate bitmapped images are called paint programs, imagers, photo programs, and graphic-manipulation programs. Because color GIF files and JPEG files are the spice of the Web, you may have to use one of these programs. Corel Photo Paint, Microsoft's Imager, Adobe's Photoshop, and Hijaak Pro are good examples. You will find some of these programs easy to use. Many have advanced capability that probably only a digital artist or photographer will use. Printshop Pro is a powerful shareware paint program. LviewPro is a popular shareware program because it can create transparent GIF formats (as can Paintshop Pro) and can read and write a variety of graphics file formats. The following site lists graphics software for downloading:

```
http://sun1.bham.ac.uk/s.m.williams.bcm/images/viewers.html
```

Look for basic capability to change contrast, brightness, and gamma. You can use such capability to tune up digital photographs even if you aren't an expert. A convenient means of cropping, filling, rotating, resizing, zooming, color reducing (reducing the number of colors) and converting files is also desirable.

Some color graphics programs go beyond traditional color manipulation. They are for artists. You may find them useful, and easy to use. For example, Altamira Composer converts a digital photograph into a van Gogh automatically. With a program like Composer, you can create enough thematic art from photographs to nicely enhance a large Web site.

Don't confuse paint programs with draw programs. Paint programs use bitmapped images. Every pixel in the matrix of the monitor is specified. In draw programs, the images (vector images) are created by lines and curves through mathematical formulas. The two types of images are incompatible without a conversion utility. Thus far, you cannot use draw files on the Web. You can use bitmapped images in GIF files and JPEG files.

Other Multimedia Programs

Programs to edit and manipulate audio files, motion video files, animation files, and 3D files are readily available if you need them. There are programs for professionals only, and ordinary PC users. As the Web uses more multimedia elements, these programs will become more important.

For Web protocols — loosely defined — such as Real Audio, TrueSpeech, and Adobe Acrobat, the authoring program is proprietary and a part of the protocol system. For example, Macromedia's Director multimedia authoring system is a Web protocol by virtue of offering a plug-in (Shockwave) for the Netscape system and the GNN system.

Browser/Development Tools

Because you can switch so easily between an open browser and an open development tool, it's unclear what advantage there is to a combined browser/tool design if you are developing on a desktop computer. After all, as a prudent developer, you will still test your work in a Netscape browser and other browsers as well. Most of your visitors probably will use the Netscape browser, which has set the browser standard. Thus, the browser/development type of development tool may be overrated for developing on a desktop computer.

If you develop on an ISP's computer (or an intranet server) from your desktop computer, the browser/development tool makes sense. The browser provides an easy way for you to connect to the Web site to do your development work. The GNNserver and GNNpress system is a good example of where the browser is essential to developing a database application remotely.

Summary

The number of Web-development tools grows rapidly in every category. It appears that the trend for many segments of the software industry is to put an Internet patina on their software products. Web-programming capability will be in most software products soon.

The number of markups in HTML is increasing quickly. The standards committee cannot keep up with the new markups being invented and widely adopted. Although HTML is a crude sort of desktop publishing today, within a few years, it will be a sophisticated system providing Webmasters with more functionality and more control for creating their online publishing products. By that time, there should be HTML authoring programs that work as efficiently and as transparently as word processors and with all the precision of word processors.

System Design

In This Chapter

Static Web sites

Database Web sites

Ideas for advanced Web sites

Well-functioning systems do not just happen; you plan them. Plan. Build a small prototype. If it doesn't work, go back to planning. If it works, build the entire system. This chapter makes no provision for the enormous creativity using a database application at a Web site will enable. Whatever you want to do at a Web site, you can achieve such capability only by carefully building a supportive system. The digital art might be great, the HTML documents might be great literature, and the interactivity might be exemplary, but good multimedia presentations are ultimately good media *systems*. A *static* Web-site system features HTML files that you upload to create and maintain the Web site. The HTML documents change only when you upload new or updated documents. In contrast, a *dynamic* system operates out of a database application and creates HTML pages on the fly by using data stored in it. A dynamic system has the capability to tailor its HTML documents based on new data put into the database application by a visitor. However, you may not be able to do easily with a database application everything you need to get done. Static system design elements can help you round out your dynamic system. Additionally, static design techniques can help you better plan a dynamic Web system enabled by a database. This chapters covers both static and dynamic Web system design.

Static System Design

Static systems consist of Web documents organized by placement in directories (folders) and interconnecting hyperlinks. The document files are uploaded to a Web server to propagate the Web site.

Directory system

You design your system based on HTML documents and the hyperlinks that connect them. From one point of view, the system looks like a hierarchical structure, as shown in Figure 12-1.

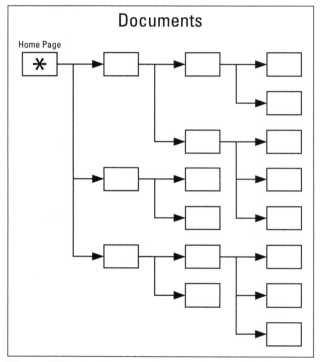

Figure 12-1: A hierarchical link structure of HTML documents at a Web site.

Nonetheless, you're sure to have hyperlinks that are not hierarchical; they're simply convenient. From another point of view, then, the hierarchical structure may get lost in the chaos of links, as illustrated in Figure 12-2.

You have several options for structuring your Web site. You can use one directory (folder), a directory for each Web document, or a hybrid approach.

One directory

You can put all the HTML documents (files) in one directory on the hard disk. For small systems — say, fewer than 20 documents — that may be the best technique. The hierarchical hyperlink structure will determine the organization. At some point, however, all those files on one hard disk directory may become cumbersome and confusing.

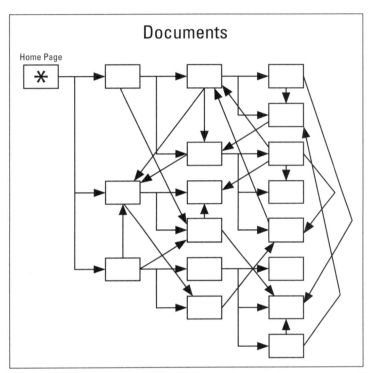

Figure 12-2: The complete link structure of HTML documents at a Web site.

Multiple directories

At the other extreme, you can have a hard disk directory (folder) for every HTML document in the hierarchical hyperlink structure. For a large system, this will turn into a huge, unwieldy system of hard disk directories, subdirectories, and sub-subdirectories. Even this system does not reflect all the links. Although there is only one hierarchical link between a directory and a subdirectory, any document may have several hyperlinks to other documents. Thus, such a hard disk directory structure does not represent the actual structure of the Web system.

Hybrid

The answer to this conundrum seems to be some sort of compromise in which the hard disk directories attempt to match the hierarchical hyperlink structure but consolidate them wherever possible. In other words, you might use the hard disk directory structure to organize the files by subject matter or file types, which may have little to do with how the documents are linked (see Figure 12-3).

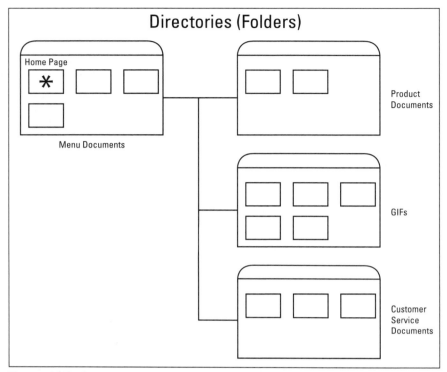

Figure 12-3: The directory and link structure of HTML documents at a Web site.

Don't cast your Web site's structure in concrete; cast it in lead (well, graphite) — using a pencil and paper. Look at it as an evolving structure that will change regularly. Indeed, it *will* change regularly. Make sure that the pencil has an eraser.

Maintenance system

Whatever Web system you design and establish, you can test it on your PC with your Web browser in localhost mode. Make sure that it works perfectly on your PC before you upload it to your Web site via FTP. Your Web site should consist of a structure of hard disk directories and subdirectories on your Internet provider's hard disk *identical* to the one on your PC — a precisely parallel system (see Figure 12-4). This parallel system makes your Web site (on your ISP's hard disk) an exact replica of the Web system on your PC's hard disk. If these two get out of sync, it will drive you nuts.

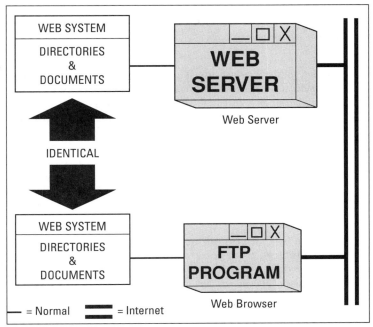

Figure 12-4: Precisely parallel systems.

Using references

Doing references properly is unavoidably important. Extra-Web-site addresses must be absolute references. Intra-Web-site addresses must be relative references to make the maintenance system previously described work properly.

An *absolute reference* states the full Web address of a Web document. A *relative reference* states the address of a Web document *relative* to the document containing the reference. Make the addresses *relative* references for the hyperlinks, images, and other multimedia elements inside the Web site on your PC. They reference the hypermedia relative to where the current document is located. For example, suppose that at the domain topdogs.com you are in a document in the root directory. You want to link to the document file hound.html, which is in a subdirectory named packdogs. The absolute address of the file is the following:

```
http://topdogs.com/packdogs/hound.html
```

The *absolute* reference is simply the full Internet address of the file. If you try to use this absolute reference on your PC, it won't work. The browser will try to dial up the Internet to find the topdogs.com domain.

Use a relative reference instead of an absolute reference, as follows:

```
packdogs/hound.html
```

The preceding relative reference is the address to be used in the hyperlink (remember, you are in a document in the root directory for topdogs.com). If you use this relative reference on your PC, it will work just fine. It will also work fine at the Web site when you upload the file onto your Web site.

Now, suppose that you're in the document hound.html and you create a hyperlink to a document named dogmenu.html in the root directory. Using a relative reference, the address will be

```
../dogmenu.html
```

The two dots show that you are going back up the directory tree. When you go down the directory tree, you must name the next subdirectory and subsequent sub-subdirectories. When you go up the directory tree, you show ../ for every directory level that you go up.

Uploading files

Now, to upload your files in an organized fashion, either initially or later for maintenance, you simply copy a file from its directory on your PC to the identical directory on the UNIX computer. This dual hard-disk directory system will keep you from losing track of how the system is organized, and the relative references will work the same on each computer.

If the UNIX computer's hard disk crashes, don't worry. You have an identical backup Web site on your PC. If *your* hard disk crashes, the Web site still resides on the hard disk of the UNIX computer, where you can use it as a backup.

Keep in mind that you may want use this dual system even if you run your own server. You might do your design and development work on your own PC and then upload it to another PC (the server PC) that has the Web server.

Self-directing catalog

A self-directing catalog presents a good example of a static system. A smart way to organize a catalog (or a personnel directory) is with a self-directing series of documents. For example, on the root directory, the home page file (first document) usually serves as an index to the Web site. In that index document, the word *Footwear* is a hyperlink to another document, which is also a menu. The second menu has the words *Boots*, *Shoes*, and

Sandals, all of which are hyperlinks to three more documents that are also menus. On the *Boots* document are more hyperlinks, with names such as *Mexican, Western, European, Argentine,* and so on. This series of documents makes up a self-directing catalog that ultimately leads you to the boots that interest you. You can conveniently find what you're looking for. The more menus you have to travel through, however, the more tedious this kind of system becomes (see Figure 12-5).

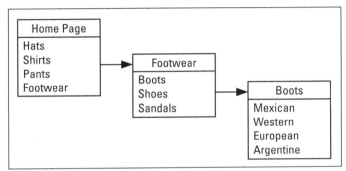

Figure 12-5: A self-directing catalog.

Why static?

One of the reasons this chapter covers the static system for a Web site is that many people need to design a static system before they can envision how a dynamic site will work. Learning to plan a normal HTML document system is a good starting place for Web site design. This gives you an interim step that you may want to take until you become accustomed to designing exclusively dynamic Web sites. After you have mastered the basics, you will be better able to plan a database application for a Web site that operates entirely out of a database.

Dynamic System Design

A *dynamic* Web system has the capability to respond to a visitor by creating Web documents on the fly.

Database system

By putting your catalog in a database, you can keep better organized with less effort while providing better convenience to your visitors. For example, in the input for the database (a Web form), a visitor might put the words

Boots AND Mexican. The database would find the information on the Mexican boots, format it into an HTML document on the fly, and deliver it to the visitor.

This is great! A database system presents a couple of drawbacks, however. First, someone who just wants to browse through the catalog may find it inconvenient to browse via the database. Second, some people may not like to browse — they know what they want — but, nonetheless, they feel more comfortable going through a self-directing catalog than they do creating a Boolean or database search (query) in a database mechanism.

You can solve this conundrum by using both static and dynamic systems. You keep the self-directing catalog and use the database search system, too. You give people a choice of how they're going to find Mexican boots. The dual system is not quite as much extra work as it might seem. When a visitor gets to the end of the last document in the self-directing catalog, the document for Mexican boots is not waiting there. It does not exist. The last hyperlink activates a CGI script or another programming device that creates the Mexican boots document on the fly from a database application and delivers it to the visitor.

You can also simulate the static document system with a dynamic database application. Each hyperlink in a document is a CGI script or another programming device that creates the hyperlinked document on the fly and presents it to the visitor. Thus, a database application is not relegated to a strictly dynamic Web system. You can use a database application to create both the static and dynamic characters of a dual system; that is, you can use a database to simulate a static system but also include the dynamic delivery of some of the Web documents.

Remote database link for Web sites on the Internet

Regarding a Web site on the Internet, there is no reason that your Web site must be limited to one domain. Through the magic of hyperlinking, you can easily span two Web locations or more and make them seem as if they are one. You can do this by having your home page (first HTML document) at the domain address you want to promote as your permanent Web location. Your system can thereafter span to another domain address, which hosts another portion of your Web site, and few visitors will notice the change in domains. All the hyperlinks at the second domain will work to eventually return the visitor to the first domain, if desired, as if both domains were one Web site (see Figure 12-6).

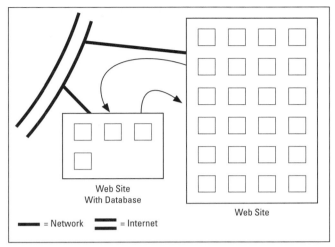

Figure 12-6: A Web site spanning two domains.

Therefore, your database does not need to be at your main Web site. The database can be at another domain. Certain ISPs and VANs will specialize in database services. You may elect to have your Web site with one ISP and your Web database with another. Through the wizardry of hyperlinks, you can make it appear as if the database application is located at your Web site. With the number of Web servers that do a multitude of different things coming on the market, it seems likely that many Web sites will consist of a number of Web domains artfully arranged by hyperlinking. Few ISPs will be able to provide you with everything you need.

For a business organization with database and publishing resources spread around among multiple computers, you can use Web technology to make it appear as if multiple resources are in one convenient location (that is, one convenient intranet address).

Database maintenance

It isn't enough to design a database application that serves some desirable function. You also must maintain it. The HTML form provides the interface to the database application in many, if not most, situations. Thus, you must maintain the data and the database application through that interface. You must load and delete and even change information, tune performance, and change the database application itself to accommodate the circumstances. As much as practical, all this must be done through HTML forms. For maintenance, however, HTML forms may not be enough. The primary alternative is to use Telnet and the command-line interface, although an X-Windows simulator such as Hummingbird's eXceed 5 offers you an alternative.

Keeping track of multimedia assets

One of the prime advantages of using a database on a Web site is that the Web is a multimedia environment. Many database engines today have multimedia capacity; that is, they can store any kind of digital information. Such a database engine can accommodate text, graphics, audio bites, video clips, and the like. Additionally, such database engines are powerful and scalable. Multimedia producers must keep track of multimedia assets for legal as well as other purposes. When all the assets already reside in the database application, the capability to easily add the columns necessary to accommodate the administrative (meta) information (for example, copyrights, technical specifications, use categorizations, and so forth) can generate an administrative cost savings. In this way, the database application serves a dual purpose. Because client-server database engines have a lot of capacity, it makes sense to put that capacity to work.

Advanced Design Considerations

New uses of the Web bring new considerations in Web-site design. This section briefly mentions some new uses that you may have to consider in designing your Web site.

Portable visitor link

Although well beyond the scope of this book, remote access from portable computing devices should be a consideration in planning your Web site and your data access, if they are to be used in your system. Whatever limitations the portable devices have, if any, must be accommodated by your database application.

Network Computer (NC)

In 1996, inexpensive RISC (reduced instruction set computer) computers, called network computers (NC) — manufactured solely for accessing the Web — began appearing on the market. Many, such as the NCD Xplora, are made strictly for intranets. Some, such as WebTV set-top boxes, can use a TV for a monitor and are consumer devices. They seem certain to become popular with the noncomputer crowd, who want to use the new Internet medium. The NCs have limitations that normal PCs do not have. You must assess their features, capabilities, and the markets they represent and take them into account in your Web-site planning. Oracle's specifications for the NC (http://www.oracle.com) and WebTV's specifications for WebTV set-top devices (http://www.webtv.com) should be helpful to your planning.

For business organizations, the NCs may present an opportunity to enable employees who otherwise would be left off the company intranet. At one-third the cost of competent multimedia PCs, the NCs make it financially feasible to spread access to databases and other information resources more broadly across your labor force (see Figure 12-7).

The NCs have custom-programmed operating systems. Some use custom-programmed Internet programs and Web browsers. Others use familiar Internet programs and Web browsers adapted for their custom operating systems. All have limitations compared to multimedia PCs. For example, they have limited internal memory and no hard disk. On the other hand, they are easy to set up and easy to use.

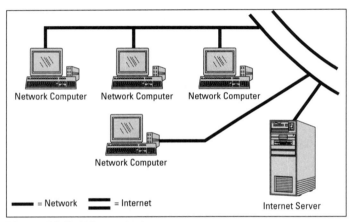

Figure 12-7: NCs on the Internet.

More than half a dozen NCs will come on the market in the first year and their capabilities will vary widely, so assessing the various NCs may not be a simple chore. Because NC capabilities will vary, you will have to design a Web site to accommodate the lowest common denominator. The significance of new NCs to your Web-database application is that you will need to keep most of the digital processing at your server rather than attempt to shift it to the browser. That limits your use of CD-ROMs and other local programming resources, which the NCs don't have. The NCs are a fact of life. Don't neglect them in your planning.

NCs, set-tops, Internet appliances?

Because they are new, there is some confusion as to what they are to be called. Oracle has trademarked both *Network Computer* and *NC*. Those companies meeting the NC standards set by Oracle (in conjunction with other companies, such as IBM, Netscape, and Apple) and paying a licensing fee can use the N/C logo on their network computer products. In this book, *network computer* and *NC* are used in their generic sense. For use by consumers with a TV instead of a monitor, network computers have been called set-top boxes. It remains to be seen what the general public will call them. Many set-top makers, following the lead of Sony and Philips, will license the *WebTV* technology. Perhaps the set-tops will become known as WebTVs. Another term that some commentators have used is *Internet appliance*. Because these devices will not be widely used until 1997, it's not certain which names will stick or what new names will emerge to describe these devices in their various applications.

Using CD-ROMs

Most dial-up users find the Internet slow. In 1996, the 33.6 Kbps modem, still relatively slow, emerged as the latest standard. It will be a few years before ISDN or cable achieve widespread use. In the meanwhile, CD-ROMs, with their 650MB capacity, provide a potential source of convenient storage to supplement the Internet.

For example, you can create a Web site with substantial graphics that can load quickly. You store the graphics on a CD-ROM, which you provide to your visitors via the Postal Service or another means of distribution. When they access your Web site, your Web system pulls the latest information from the Web site on the Internet and the graphics from the CD-ROM. The graphics load much more quickly, of course, because they do not travel via the modem. Ventana Publishing (http://www.ventana.com) has used this technique since early 1995.

The next advance in CD-ROMs, the DVD (Digital Video Disk), will feature four storage volume choices, as follows:

Type	Storage Capacity
Single-sided, single-layer	4.7GB
Single-sided, double-layer	9GB
Double-sided, single-layer	13.7GB
Double-sided, double-layer	18GB

The single-sided, single-layer DVD can hold a 130-minute Hollywood movie, which gives you an idea of its multimedia potential. The double-sided, double-layer CD-ROM holds more than 27 times as much information as the current 650MB CD-ROM. This huge additional capacity may be useful even after online connections with greater bandwidth become available.

Keep in mind that although most CD-ROMs are mass produced, you can also record CD-ROMs reasonably inexpensively one at a time. CD-ROM recorders have become inexpensive (under $800), and the blank CD-ROMs also have become inexpensive (under $5). This makes a CD-ROM a viable storage medium for a small organization to use with a Web system.

Nonetheless, visitors will find it inconvenient to insert a CD-ROM when they visit your Web site. This system will work best where the visitors (consumers) are very dedicated to using what you are providing on your Web site. It will work well in business organizations where the visitors (employees) will need the CD-ROM while on the Internet or intranet to do their work efficiently. It will also work well in associations where visitors (members) will need the CD-ROM while on the Web to get the full benefit of their membership.

Any digital multimedia information can reside on the CD-ROM. A database system can span the Web server, the database engine, the browser, and the CD-ROM. The database engine residing on the ISP's computer can hold updated enterprise data, whereas static data can be stored on the CD-ROM. The database application can manage both data resources.

Hard Disks

Do you need a CD-ROM to store information locally? No. You can use a visitor's hard disk. This is not something you can reasonably do without a special relationship with the visitor, but it works well. For example, America Online (AOL) downloads new color graphics occasionally into a subscriber's AOL program. The color graphics go on the subscriber's hard disk and never have to be downloaded a second time. The AOL program stays up to date without relying on redundant transmissions. With larger and larger hard disks, this type of system may become more acceptable to your Web visitors. In fact, VRML (Virtual Reality Markup Language) requires this type of system in order to work well.

For a business organization, this technique can work well if you can ensure that all the employees working on the Internet or intranet have adequate hard disk capacity to store the amount of multimedia information you desire to store locally. A database system incorporating local hard disks might work much the same as one incorporating local CD-ROMs.

Perhaps the best place to begin your consideration of system design is on the Internet itself. Surf around. Follow your interests. When you find something that works well, take notes on its organization. If you want to learn more, download the HTML documents (using Save in your Web browser) and look at the markups (that is, the source code). If you find strange references or coding, you'll know that the Web site uses CGI scripting or database access.

Intranets

LANs

WANs

Database interface

Perhaps your company links its employees' PCs with its mainframe using an internal network. Your employees need ready access to the company database, or perhaps they need to share data between the databases on minicomputers or PCs in different departments. If you are a small partnership, possibly you and your business partner both use e-mail and Web browsers and want a familiar way to connect your PCs together to better share your business duties. This chapter is dedicated to those of you who are interested in using the powerful TCP/IP software and networking technology developed for the Internet on a *local* network, which is called an *intranet*.

As stated elsewhere in the book, many readers will create a database application on an ISP's UNIX computer. Nonetheless, many will use databases on an intranet, perhaps using Windows NT or another familiar operating system. This use of intranets reflects a substantial grass roots movement and is seldom mandated from the top down.

An Overview of Intranets

Why do local TCP/IP networks (intranets) make sense? Here are some reasons:

➡ TCP/IP is cross-platform. It will run on any operating system or computer.

➡ TCP/IP is not exclusive. It will run simultaneously alongside other network protocols. You can have two network operating systems at the same time.

➡ TCP/IP has a long history of proven effectiveness (the Internet).

➡ TCP/IP has a substantial stable of protocols and programs.

➡ TCP/IP is becoming a rich development and operating platform and has spawned a dynamic new software industry.

➡ TCP/IP offers a multimedia online publishing system (the Web) that is easy to develop for and easy to use.

➡ TCP/IP offers universal multimedia e-mail both within the company and beyond the confines of the company (that is, the Internet).

➡ TCP/IP offers high-quality free or inexpensive programming as well as commercial programming.

➡ TCP/IP is compatible with the Internet, which is a TCP/IP network.

➡ TCP/IP offers programs that can be used easily and effectively both on a local network and on the Internet. A Web browser is quite easy to use. An e-mail program is almost as easy to use. Between the two, one can do 80 percent of the computing work one needs to do on a network.

➡ TCP/IP programs make excellent and easy-to-use groupware.

➡ TCP/IP provides a means of publishing (the Web) that is considerably less expensive than printing on paper.

➡ TCP/IP via the Web provides cross-platform access to company databases.

Because this is a book about databases, focus on this last reason. The Web furnishes a means to provide every employee with access to all company databases without considering which computers or operating systems the databases use, which computers or operating systems the employees use, or what the employees' level of computer expertise is. HTML forms programming together with CGI scripting (or other Web-database techniques) make access to all company databases possible through a Web server and browser. Web browsers are quite easy to use and require little training. Using Web browsers as the doorway into company databases is an ideal way to take advantage of the popularity of Web browsers. Companies will find that more and more of their employees already use Web browsers or are eager to learn.

The Web sites of many companies are voluminous publishing mechanisms. Companies now routinely publish on the Web — instead of on paper — maintenance manuals, software documentation, rules and regulations, and other documents many hundreds or thousands of pages long. Sheer volume tends to create complex Web sites. Complex Web sites are best managed by using database applications. Databases help any visitor (employee) find his or her way directly to the information needed. For example, Oracle (http://www.oracle.com) and Spider Technologies (http://www.w3spider.com) allow a visitor to search for keywords in the text of all their Web pages.

Thus, there are two primary reasons for using database applications on intranets: (1) universal, easy access to new and legacy databases, and (2) organizing complex Web sites. It all starts with a LAN.

Span a local area

A local area network (LAN) enables employees to share files by interconnecting their hard drives (see Figure 13-1). With a Web browser and a LAN, employees can view HTML documents stored on each other's PCs. The LAN does not, however, necessarily allow two people to simultaneously view one HTML document. For a LAN with numerous computers, therefore, a Web server is desirable. This way, employees can use the LAN just like the Internet, with multiple employees sharing access to the same HTML document at the same time regardless of its location. A Web server efficiently serves the Web documents to all comers. Other client-server software is desirable, too (such as a mailing list program or online conferencing program). A LAN provides a client-server medium.

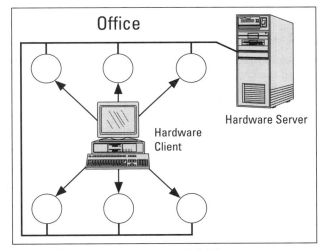

Figure 13-1: A local area network (LAN).

Today, most LAN vendors and software publishers offer a TCP/IP option. Because TCP/IP can coexist with other network protocols, you may not necessarily have to choose between TCP/IP and what you already have installed. Each computer (client) on the LAN must also have TCP/IP software installed in order to connect to the TCP/IP network. Windows 95 and other operating systems now include TCP/IP software.

TCP/IP features infinite expandability. A TCP/IP network that starts on a Novell LAN in one department can easily span (extend) to a non-Novell LAN in another department. This practice grows until the company links all its computers together on one enterprise-wide TCP/IP network. From there, the enterprise intranet can connect to the Internet, which covers the rest of the world. Branch offices in other countries can be tied together using this powerful combination of intranet and Internet. The significance for databases is that a Web server in one department that acts as a front-end for a department database application can now, through the intranet, serve the entire enterprise. Information flows more freely through the company to those who need it *when* they need it. The flow of information need not stop at employees. Preferred clients can receive special passwords to access certain company information via the Internet, saving time for both the clients and the company's customer service department. The general public can step into a Web-site *storefront* to drop in, look around, and perhaps place an order.

Security, of course, is an issue. Some employees need not have access to certain information. Connecting two physically distant branch offices via the Internet also becomes a security issue. TCP/IP is competent to provide such security, and the security capability of TCP/IP is growing more robust with the TCP/IP software boom.

Span the organiztion

A wide area network (WAN) is typically an enterprise network that spans a company, covering multiple locations — sometimes in multiple cities or countries (see Figure 13-2). The Internet itself being a WAN shows that TCP/IP is well suited for WANs, and that TCP/IP delivers to the enterprise the benefits discussed.

WANs, in one sense, are different from LANs. They are larger, more complex, and require more administration. The larger the organization, the more complex the WAN. A WAN that connects three offices in the Detroit metro area will probably be relatively simple. A WAN that connects the offices of a large global corporation may be more complex than the telecommunications system of a small country. From a user's point of view, however, TCP/IP WANs are no different than TCP/IP LANs.

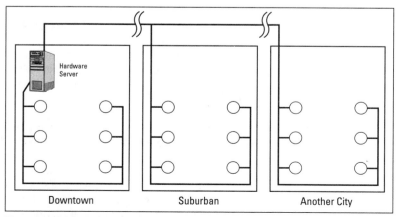

Figure 13-2: A Wide Area Network (WAN).

Firewalls

As the name implies, *firewalls* are strong and resistant to all but the most determined efforts to break through. How do you provide security to your intranet when you connect it to the Internet? You connect it through a firewall (see Figure 13-3). The firewall keeps nasty people from coming in and doing funny things on your intranet. Firewall technology provides a variety of ways to establish security for a variety of situations. Security is a complex topic involving a variety of technologies and techniques. Firewalls are just one technology used in the specific case of connecting an intranet to the Internet.

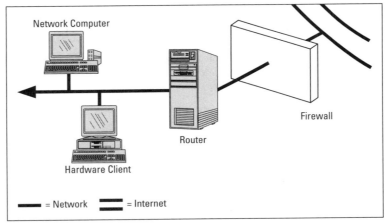

Figure 13-3: A LAN with a firewall.

Small LANs

LANs and WANs sound large. Small LANs, however, may benefit from a TCP/IP network, too. Even LANs as small as one server and one client may benefit. Before dismissing TCP/IP as overkill, give the power of a TCP/IP network serious consideration. Between Web publishing and e-mail, you have covered 80 percent of most people's groupware needs. Even two people on their own two-person intranet can make TCP/IP networking worthwhile. They can use familiar tools and take advantage of the explosion of new software designed for TCP/IP networks. In fact, database access through the Web may be just as desirable for small groups as for large groups. And software ease of use constitutes an issue in a group of almost any size. TCP/IP has the potential to accommodate small business efforts just as well as large ones.

Browser

The Web browser is at once the great equalizer, the lowest common denominator, and the salvation of the computer-illiterate. It is easy to use. In most cases, it is a GUI and potentially fun to use. And it works the same for all Web presentations. Currently, the Web browser does the following:

➥ Brings vast network computing power via the network computer (NC) to those who have not had it before

➥ Forces all developers to filter their software offerings through a format that is easy to use

➥ Runs via TCP/IP on every computer and every network, including the Internet

➥ Lets anyone easily make queries to database applications

What it boils down to is that all the gyrations covered in this book (such as CGI scripting) are ultimately invisible to the employee using the browser. The browser always works the same.

Network computers

Network computers, or NCs, are another great equalizer. These easy-to-use and inexpensive computers put network computing power into the hands of those who otherwise would not use a computer (see more on NCs in Chapter 12, "System Design"). One of the most important uses is database access. With NCs and an intranet, you can economically expand access to databases to every employee.

NCs will likely replace the millions of dumb computer terminals based on ancient digital technology that many corporate employees still use.

The database interface

The Web browser thus becomes the database interface, or the database front end. Any employee who can use a browser can access any data that he or she has the authorization to access. If the database application is a Sybase application, users have no need to know a Sybase interface or to have a custom-made interface. The Web browser is the interface.

Some employees, however, have the responsibility to maintain, load, unload, or intensely use the database application. Currently, they cannot do everything they need to do through an HTML form. Likewise, it is difficult for them to work via a standard Telnet terminal-emulation program featuring a command-line interface. It makes sense to furnish these employees with the normal program interface used with a specific database application that provides them with the functionality and ease of use needed to do their jobs efficiently. This, however, may be a temporary anomaly. As HTML and Web software grow more robust, they will take on more functionality that may someday eliminate the need for a separate database interface for expert database employees.

Any difference between a LAN and the Internet?

So long as the network and each networked computer have the proper TCP/IP protocol software, the entire system functions just like the Internet. Because the operating system for many intranet server computers (such as Windows NT and OS/2) is likely to be something other than UNIX, the choices in database engines are more familiar to PC users (for example, Access, Paradox, and Approach). Cross-platform scalable databases such as Oracle work well too, however. Likewise, your Web-database development tool choices may be different. Otherwise, everything is remarkably the same.

The database software market

The Internet has the glamour. Every TCP/IP software publisher touts the Web. The volume sales, however, are to the intranets. Much software that seems designed for the Internet is actually designed for intranets. Regardless, Internet software works well on both the Internet and intranets because both are TCP/IP networks. Virtually every database software publisher now has Web middleware or Web development tools. (*Middleware* is a layer of software that exists between a specific application and the control program. For example, in the context of database technology, it refers to software that is between the database application and the database engine.) Some Web servers incorporate databases. Many Web servers offer ODBC compliance or some other database API. Whether you have a small LAN or a large WAN, you have many options for Web-database connectivity. Most of these options were designed for the intranet market.

Don't feel alone

Using local TCP/IP networking is a grass roots movement in that it has come from the employees rather than from the top down (see Figure 13-4). If you find it obvious that TCP/IP networking, including accessing data via the Web, makes sense, give it a try. Many other people have come to the same conclusion, have taken action, and have made it work. The benefits are there, and, in most cases, the price is right.

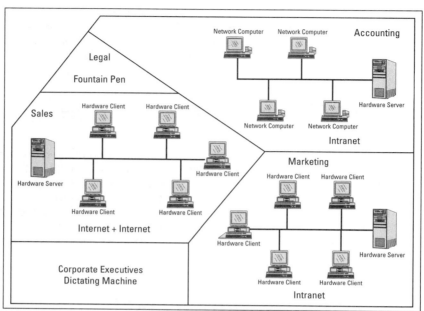

Figure 13-4: Intranets from the grassroots.

Computer service

If your company has internal computer support service available, you can have the service provide you with the CGI scripting and the other program-ming you need to take your database application online. This book will help you understand how much of the Web-database development you can do yourself, and how much you will want your computer support service to do.

Summary

TCP/IP works as well on an internal network as it does on the Internet. The Web browser through the HTML form makes an easy-to-use interface for accessing company databases. The new, low-cost NCs give employees who do not need PCs access to the intranet and to database applications, as well as access to the Internet.

Data Cataloging

In This Chapter

Mail-merge basics

HTML template

Data exporting

Mail merging

Mail-merge publishing

Shortcut

If you use a PC database engine and a word processor, you can perform *data cataloging,* which is simply mail merging data into an HTML template in a word processor to create catalog-like documents. You do it completely on your own PC and subsequently upload the files you have created to your Web site. This technique is not offered as a preferred technique but as an *alternative* when using a database engine or a flat-file database at a Web site is not feasible. Here are some reasons to use the data cataloging technique described in this chapter:

➡ You do not have access to a UNIX database engine that is connected to the Internet.

➡ You do not have access to a Windows NT server that is connected to the Internet.

➡ You cannot get access to cgi-bin on your Internet server.

➡ You do not want to incur the expense of having a programmer code CGI scripts.

Additionally, this chapter sets the stage for better understanding how database technology works with the other techniques that follow in later chapters. *Pay particular attention to the use of templates.*

Can you have the best of both technologies — a database presentation without the cost of a UNIX database engine or CGI scripting *and* a nicely published data report on the Web? Yes, in fact, there *is* a way. By creating a database application and mail merging data into a word processor template, you can create catalogs, personnel directories, and other data formats almost automatically. (If you are a database expert, the Shortcut section at the end of this chapter shows you how to bypass the mail merging and use a database technique to accomplish the same thing.)

Database Application

Creating a database application with data cataloging requires only a few simple steps that anyone who has a desktop database engine can do. Following are the basic steps:

1. Create your database application using a PC database engine such as Paradox, Approach, Access, or a comparable Mac database engine. Such database engines have development tools built in and are easy to use. You can learn to use them by reading the program documentation.

2. Export the data in such a form that your word processing can use it for mail merging. This is usually an ASCII comma-delimited file, which any database engine can export.

3. Mail merge the data into an HTML template (word processing document) to create the Web documents that make up your catalog. Your word processor documentation explains mail merging.

4. Mail merge parts of the data into HTML hyperlinks that serve as an index.

5. Combine the index and the catalog into one HTML document and upload it to your Web site. You do this by copying and pasting.

Example: Flag Vendor

For an illustration of the data-cataloging method, imagine that you are the Web-site designer for a mail-order catalog company that sells flags from around the world. The flags are colorful and come in a variety of sizes for all occasions. You want to design an interesting Web site offering your flags for sale. You'll provide an online order form, although visitors can also call the 800 number for ordering. You have only your desktop database (Microsoft Access) and your desktop word processor (Microsoft Word for Windows). You have a modest Web site space at the local ISP, who does not allow any CGI scripts by its customers.

The Flag Database Application

In this chapter, the Microsoft Access 1.0 database engine is used, although 2.0 and 7.0 work almost identically. Each row (record) will hold the data for a catalog entry. Because you will use columns (fields) for paragraphs of text as well as for words and numbers, you will create *memo* columns for the larger blocks of words. A database application for a flag catalog might have the following columns:

Column	Description
name	name of flag (country, state, or city)
size	size in inches
price	price
origin	country of origin if imported (blank if not imported)
special	special characteristic (such as "disposable")
ordercode	product number
shipping	shipping method
marketpara	marketing paragraph*
para1	additional paragraph*
para2	second additional paragraph*
image1	digital image filename (flag image)
image2	second digital image filename (flag image or blank)

Of these columns, the marketing paragraph and the additional paragraphs (indicated by *) will be memo columns; that is, they will be able to accommodate a substantial amount of text. An example of a catalog entry follows:

France 25 x 40 $1.49 Imported from: India

Special feature: disposable

Order Code: 00341 Shipping: UPS

These disposable flags made out of light-weight cotton are great for the one-day occasion where flags are required in numbers. And at this price, you can afford to buy as many as you need.

Take these inexpensive flags seriously. The colors are beautiful, and they are made to last for several days just to insure that they will certainly last for your one-day event. This French flag is great for Bastille Day.

Minimum order is one dozen. Contact us for special pricing on quantities over five dozen. On quantities over ten dozen, you can save the shipping cost too. We can also save you additional money on our five-year annual event contract.

To order dial 1-800-123-4567 or fill in order form.

You can create this catalog entry with a mail merge into a template by using the database table described previously.

Word processor mail-merge statement

The mail-merge statement for your flag catalog entry looks like this:

```
<<image1>>
<<name>> <<size>> $<<price>> Imported from: <<origin>>
Special feature: <<special>>
Order Code: <<ordercode>> Shipping: <<shipping>>
<<image2>>
<<marketpara>>
<<para1>>
<<para2>>
To order dial 800-123-4567 or fill in order form.
```

You create a word processor document (as shown) using your word processor. The document is a template into which you will mail-merge data. The words between the << >> indicate mail-merge fields in Word for Windows.

Adding HTML markups

Next you add the HTML markups, which turn the word processing file into a Web document after you save it as an ASCII (text) file. The markups are as follows:

```
<<image1>>
<P>
<B><<name>></B> <<size>> $<<price>> Imported from:
<<origin>><BR>
Special feature: <<special>><BR>
Order Code: <<ordercode>> Shipping: <<shipping>>
<P>
<<image2>>
<P>
<<marketpara>>
<P>
<<para1>>
<P>
<<para2>>
<P>
To order dial 800-123-4567 or fill in <A HREF="order.html">
order</A> form.
```

Adding variety with IF...THEN statements

To create some interest in the flag catalog entries, you use whatever techniques you can devise to prevent all the entries from looking exactly the same. You can do this one way by using the mail-merge scripting capability in a word processor to do simple IF...THEN statements. For example, the *origin* column prints only for an imported flag, and the *special* column prints only for a flag with special characteristics. Normally, a column will not print if it does not have an entry. In some situations, however, a column without an entry may leave a gap and will require an IF...THEN statement to eliminate the gap. Or the column may be used in combination with other nondata words that must be eliminated by an IF...THEN statement when the data is not present.

For example, here's how the images in the flag catalog can be handled:

➡ If the *image1* column contains an image, the image appears first. If not, the line with the image disappears.

➡ If, instead, the *image 2* column has the image, it appears after the three heading lines and just before the marketing paragraph. If not, the line with the image disappears.

➡ For different catalog entries, you can use your choice of one color graphic in *image1,* one graphic in *image2,* no graphics, or two graphics, with one in *image1* and one in *image2.*

These options give a different look to each catalog entry.

For imported flags, you use the words Imported from: with the *origin* column. If the flag is not imported, you want these words to disappear. For one-day disposable flags, you want a line that reads Special feature:, followed by the word disposable from the *special* column. For nylon flags, you want to have the *special* column print the word heavy-duty. If there is no special feature, you want the line to disappear.

For each catalog entry, you will create a marketing paragraph and at least one additional paragraph. For some entries, you will create a third paragraph. When there is no third paragraph, you want the blank line before the third paragraph to disappear so that there are not two blank lines before the last line of text. Because HTML reads two <P> markups as if they were one, you do not need to do anything more for the third paragraph.

To add IF...THEN statements, you must put the Word document into *Field Codes* view. (Each word processor will offer its own techniques for using mail merging and will look similar to the following Fields Code view.) In the Fields Codes view, the document now looks like this:

```
{MERGEFIELD image1}
<P>
<B>{MERGEFIELD name}</B> {MERGEFIELD size} ${MERGEFIELD
price} Imported from: {MERGEFIELD origin}<BR>
Special feature: {MERGEFIELD special}<BR>
Order Code: {MERGEFIELD ordercode} Shipping: {
MERGEFIELD shipping}
<P>
{MERGEFIELD image2}
<P>
{MERGEFIELD marketpara}
<P>
{MERGEFIELD para1}
<P>
{MERGEFIELD para2}
<P>
To order dial 800-123-4567 or fill in <A HREF="order.html">
order</A> form.
```

Now you add the IF...THEN statements, so that it appears like the following:

```
{IF{MERGEFIELD image1}<>"" "<IMG SRC="}{MERGEFIELD
image1}{IF{MERGEFIELD image1}<>"" ">"
}{IF{MERGEFIELD image1}<>"" "<P>"}
<B>{MERGEFIELD name}</B> {MERGEFIELD size} ${MERGEFIELD
price} {IF{MERGEFIELD origin}<>"" "Imported from:"}
{MERGEFIELD origin}<BR>
{IF{MERGEFIELD special}<>"" "Special feature:"
} {MERGEFIELD special}{IF{MERGEFIELD special}<>"" "<BR>"}
Order Code: {MERGEFIELD ordercode} Shipping: {MERGEFIELD
shipping}
<P>
{IF{MERGEFIELD image2}<>"" "<IMG SRC="}{MERGEFIELD image2}
{IF{MERGEFIELD image2}<>"" ">"}
<P>
{MERGEFIELD marketpara}
<P>
{MERGEFIELD para1}
<P>
{MERGEFIELD para2}
<P>
To order dial 800-123-4567 or fill in <A HREF="order.html">
order</A> form.
```

Note that if *image1* doesn't exist, the first line will cease to exist. The IF...
THEN statements remove `<IMG SRC=` and `>` if there is nothing in the
image1 column.

If the flag is imported, the *origin* column contains a country. The IF...THEN statement will then print Imported from:. Otherwise, Imported from: is not printed.

If the flag has a special feature such as *disposable*, the IF...THEN statement prints Special Feature: followed by disposable. Otherwise, the entire line disappears, in which case an IF...THEN statement removes the <BR>.

The *image2* line is the same as the first line (image1) and disappears if there is nothing in the *image2* column.

The *para2* column may not have anything in it. If not, the line for it disappears. Web browsers interpret the two <P> codes as if there were only one <P> markup.

IF...THEN confusing?

If this seems confusing, forget about the IF...THEN statements. Try doing just a normal mail merge without any IF...THEN statements. Your word processor manual explains mail merging thoroughly (common 1970s software technology). It is more busy work than it is difficult work.

After you have mastered normal mail merging, you can progress to adding IF...THEN mail merge statements, if you need them. Certainly much useful data cataloging can be done without IF...THEN statements. Eventually, however, you will want to try some IF...THEN statements to provide some format variations in the HTML documents you generate by using data cataloging.

Extracting the database

Now take three rows from a database and mail merge them. The following rows are in *comma-delimited* form. The columns are inside quotation marks, and the columns are separated by commas. Where double commas appear, the column contains nothing. The first of the following paragraphs is the header, with the column names required by Word for Windows:

```
"name","size","price","origin","special","ordercode",
"shipping","marketpara","para1","para2","image1","image2"
"France","25 x 40","1.49","India","disposable", "00341",
"UPS","These disposable flags made out of light-weight
cotton are great for the one-day occasion where flags are
required in numbers. And at this price, you can afford to
buy as many as you need.","Take these inexpensive flags
seriously. The colors are beautiful, and they are made to
```

(continued)

(continued)

```
last for several days just to insure that they will certainly
last for your one-day event. This French flag is great
for Bastille Day.","Minimum order is one dozen. Contact us
for special pricing on quantities over five dozen. On
quantities over ten dozen, you can save the shipping cost
too. We can also save you additional money on our five-year
annual event contract.","fr.gif",,
"USA States","42 x 60","39.95",,"heavy-duty", "00917","UPS",
"These heavy-duty nylon flags will last about as long as
anything you can buy. Great for corporations, institutions,
and governmental agencies. Money-back guarantee if you are
not satisfied with the quality.","We have these in stock for
every state. The colors are bright and guaranteed to be
authentic. Used by governmental agencies in all 50 states
and used by the National Guard in 43 states. You can fly
these flags proudly for a long time.","Don't forget to
specify the state when you order. There may be some slight
variation in size to comply with state statutes regulating
size increments.","co.gif", "mi.gif"
"Jamaica","39 x 57","21.95","Jamaica",,"00112","Parcel Post",
"This is our standard flag made to our specifications in the
country of origin. It is a middleweight Dacron that will
provide you with durability at a reasonable price.","By
importing these flags from Jamaica, we can provide you a
good price by avoiding the small and expensive local
manufacturing run that the US market for these flags would
necessitate. Compare our prices.","",,"jamaica.gif"
```

The mail merge

When you mail-merge the preceding three rows, you get the following Web documents after saving them as ASCII (text) files:

```
<HR>
<P>
<IMG SRC=fr.gif>
<P>
<B>France</B> 25 x 40 $1.49 Imported from: India<BR>
Special feature: disposable<BR>
Order Code: 00341 Shipping: UPS
<P>
<P>
These disposable flags made out of light-weight cotton are
great for the one-day occasion where flags are required in
numbers. And at this price, you can afford to buy as many as
you need.
<P>
```

Take these inexpensive flags seriously. The colors are beautiful, and they are made to last for several days just to insure that they will certainly last for your one-day event. This French flag is great for Bastille Day.
<P>
Minimum order is one dozen. Contact us for special pricing on quantities over a five dozen. On quantities over ten dozen, you can save the shipping cost too. We can also save you additional money on our five-year annual event contract.
<P>
To order dial 800-123-4567 or fill in <A
HREF="order.html">order</A> form.
<P>

<HR>
<P>
<IMG SRC=co.gif>
<P>
<B>USA States</B> 42 x 60 $39.95
Special feature: heavy-duty
Order Code: 00917 Shipping: UPS
<P>
<IMG SRC=mi.gif>
<P>
These heavy-duty nylon flags will last about as long as anything you can buy. Great for corporations, institutions, and governmental agencies. Money-back guarantee if you are not satisfied with the quality.
<P>
We have these in stock for every state. The colors are bright and guaranteed to be authentic. Used by governmental agencies in all 50 states and used by the National Guard in 43 states. You can fly these flags proudly for a long time.
<P>
Don't forget to specify the state when you order. There may be some slight variation in size to comply with state statutes regulating size increments.
<P>
To order dial 800-123-4567 or fill in <A
HREF="order.html">order</A> form.
<P>
<HR>
<P>
<B>Jamaica</B> 39 x 57 $21.95 Imported from: Jamaica
Order Code: 00112 Shipping: Parcel Post
<P>
<IMG SRC=jamaica.gif>
<P>

(continued)

(continued)

```
This is our standard flag made to our specifications in the
country of origin. It is a middleweight Dacron that will provide
you with durability at a reasonable price.
<P>
By importing these flags from Jamaica, we can provide you a
good price by avoiding the small and expensive local
manufacturing run that the thin US market for these flags would
necessitate. Compare our prices.
<P>
<P>
To order dial 800-123-4567 or fill in <A
HREF="order.html">order</A> form.
<P>
```

You might note that the image markups have no quotation marks as required by HTML programming. It doesn't matter; they work anyway (see Figure 14-1 for a diagram of the mail-merge process).

As you can see in the following example, each catalog entry looks a little different, but you automatically generate them with a template using this mail-merge system. Here's how they would look in a Web document online:

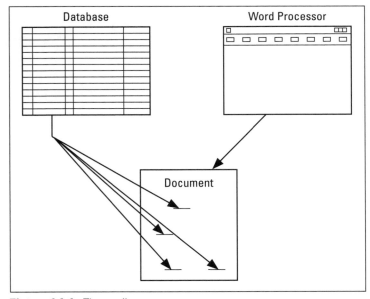

Figure 14-1: The mail-merge process.

France 25 x 40 $1.49 Imported from: India

Special feature: disposable

Order Code: 00341 Shipping: UPS

These disposable flags made out of light-weight cotton are great for the one-day occasion where flags are required in numbers. And at this price, you can afford to buy as many as you need.

Take these inexpensive flags seriously. The colors are beautiful, and they are made to last for several days just to insure that they will certainly last for your one-day event. This French flag is great for Bastille Day.

Minimum order is one dozen. Contact us for special pricing on quantities over five dozen. On quantities over ten dozen, you can save the shipping cost too. We can also save you additional money on our five-year annual event contract.

To order dial 800-123-4567 or fill in order form.

USA States 42 x 60 $39.95

Special feature: heavy-duty

Order Code: 00917 Shipping:

These heavy-duty nylon flags will last about as long as anything you can buy. Great for corporations, institutions, and governmental agencies. Money-back guarantee if you are not satisfied with the quality.

We have these in stock for every state. The colors are bright and guaranteed to be authentic. Used by governmental agencies in all 50 states and used by the National Guard in 43 states. You can fly these flags proudly for a long time.

Don't forget to specify the state when you order. There may be some slight variation in size to comply with state statutes regulating size increments.

To order dial 800-123-4567 or fill in order form.

Jamaica 39 x 57 $21.95 Imported from: Jamaica

Order Code: 00112 Shipping: Parcel Post

This is our standard flag made to our specifications in the country of origin. It is a middleweight Dacron that will provide you with durability at a reasonable price.

By importing these flags from Jamaica, we can provide you a good price by avoiding the small and expensive local manufacturing run that the thin US market for these flags would necessitate. Compare our prices.

To order dial 800-123-4567 or fill in order form.

Adding an index

Although these catalog entries are attractive and readable, you cannot expect a reader to wade through long documents filled with such entries to find what he or she is looking for. You can create an index to the catalog entries in each document by using HTML interdocument hyperlinks and anchors. The mail-merge statement for the index entry looks like this:

```
<<ordercode>> <<name>>
```

Add the HTML markups, and it looks like this:

```
<A HREF="#<<ordercode>>"><<name>></A>
```

Link

This establishes a link from the word *name* to the anchor *ordercode*. It makes sense to use *ordercode* as the anchor name, because it is unique. Here's what the entry for the French flag looks like after the mail merge:

```
<A HREF="#00341">France</A>
```

The index entry looks like this typeset in a Web document:

France

Revising the mail merge to add the anchor

Now you have to add the anchor to the original catalog entry mail-merge template. The anchor will be the first line after <HR>. Here's how it looks:

```
<HR>
<A NAME=<<ordercode>>>
```

Here's what the anchor for the French flag looks like after the mail merge:

```
<HR>
<A NAME=00341>
```

When a visitor clicks the hyperlink "France" in the index, the link takes the visitor to the anchor "00341" somewhere below in the document.

Mail merge

You can mail merge the flag catalog database into the one-line mail-merge template:

```
<A HREF="#<<ordercode>>"><<name>></A>
```

The resulting index will look like this:

```
<A HREF="#00341">France</A><BR>
<A HREF="#00112">Jamaica</A><BR>
<A HREF="#00917">USA States</A><BR>
```

As displayed typeset in a Web document, the index looks like this, with the underlines indicating that the words are hyperlinks:

France

Jamaica

USA States

The final document

How do you put all this together? First, you create a shell HTML template document that will hold both the index and the catalog entries. Put a blank space near the top to paste in the index entries after you mail-merge them. The index must come before the catalog entries. Second, put another blank space lower in the document to paste in the catalog entries after you mail-merge them.

After you have mail-merged the index, you place it into the shell (copy and paste) on the blank space near the top of the document (see Figure 14-2). After you generate the catalog entries by the mail merge, you place them into the shell (copy and paste) on the blank space lower in the document. You now have an HTML document with an index at the top, and catalog entries lower in the document, in which the index entries are hyperlinked to the catalog entries.

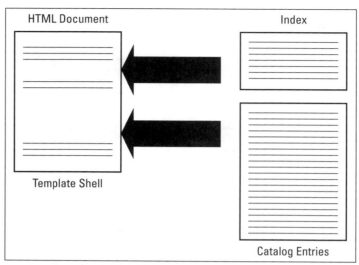

Figure 14-2: Fitting the two mail-merge results into the final HTML document.

Example: A Web Magazine Article

Data cataloging is not limited to making catalogs and directories. Use your imagination to devise other uses. Look at the following template for a Web magazine article. In this example, a database stores Web magazine articles. Each row in the database contains a complete article. Every article has up to 25 paragraphs, stored in 25 columns (p1 through p25). If a paragraph is the beginning of a new section of the article, text for the section heading goes in the heading column. For example, if paragraph three starts a section, then column h3 contains the section heading. The mail-merge code shown here illustrates how this database can be mail merged into the complete magazine article. When a column contains no data, it does not appear. Thus, you could have several sequential paragraphs without a headline. Or you could have several sequential headlines without a paragraph. The combinations are almost infinite.

In addition to the 50 columns for the article, more columns accommodate information for the title and byline. (You could create supplementary columns to show copyright owner, date of first publication, subject matter categorization, author's e-mail address, and so on. Thus, the articles could be queried on a variety of useful administrative data as well as on subject matter.)

```
<H2><B>{MERGEFIELD title}</B></H2>
by {MERGEFIELD byline}
<P>
{IF{MERGEFIELD h1}<>"" "<H3><B>"
}{IF{MERGEFIELD h1}<>"" "{MERGEFIELD h1}"
```

```
}{IF{MERGEFIELD h1}<>"" "</B></H3"}
{MERGEFIELD p1}{IF{MERGEFIELD p1}<>"" "<P>"}
{IF{MERGEFIELD h2}<>"" "<H3><B>"
}{IF{MERGEFIELD h2}<>"" "{MERGEFIELD h2}"
}{IF{MERGEFIELD h2}<>"" "</B></H3"}
{MERGEFIELD p2}{IF{MERGEFIELD p2}<>"" "<P>"}.
    .
    .
    .
{IF{MERGEFIELD h25}<>"" "<H3><B>"
}{IF{MERGEFIELD h25}<>"" "{MERGEFIELD h25}"
}{IF{MERGEFIELD h25}<>"" "</B></H3"}
{MERGEFIELD p25}{IF{MERGEFIELD p25}<>"" "<P>"}
```

With the preceding template, you can show the following article at a Web site generated out of a database (only the first four paragraphs of the article are shown here):

Giant Snake on Coyote Creek

by José Santa Clara

Bill Wolverton, a ranger for the Glen Canyon Recreation Area, has dinner with us at the Utah state campgrounds just outside the town of Escalante. We are using Michael Kelsey's guide book, *Canyon Hiking Guide to the Colorado Plateau*, for information on tomorrow's hike. Bill advises us to do the hike the opposite way of that suggested in Kelsey's book (good advice for this particular hike) and shows us the way into the canyon on a topo map. In spite of the intermittent light rain, Bill indicates a flash flood seems unlikely without a thunderstorm but it is always difficult to predict.

Dave Swinehart, my hiking companion, and I met in the Colorado Mountain Club Basic Mountaineering Course, and now in mid-summer we are applying the skills in a week of wilderness wet canyon exploration. Why July? The cold water in the wet canyons makes hiking too risky in all but the hottest months. Tomorrow we will hike into Coyote Gulch.

Coyote Gulch

It has rained lightly off and on all night. We drive out of the rain in Escalante south down the Hole-In-The-Rock Road about an hour to the trailhead, the last two miles across soft sand. The weather is cloudy but not rainy. The gravel road is excellent, and there's little evidence of excess rain. We find the route into the canyon through a hidden crack in the face of a cliff and down a huge sand dune to a place near the confluence of Coyote Creek and the Escalante River. The scenery is dazzling. The small stream is slightly murky, showing evidence of rain runoff. The contrast between the stark sandstone canyon and the rich green of the Coyote Creek ecosystem is beautiful beyond the reach of simple literary skills.

We stop for lunch about a mile and a half up Coyote Gulch at an over-
hanging spring situated on the bank of the stream bed. A few minutes
after we stop, without any warning or noise, a flash flood comes down
just like a giant snake cruising along a game trail. The stream goes
from a half-foot deep and six feet wide to seven feet deep and forty
feet wide in less than two minutes. The water is dark chocolate and full
of debris. The flow creates raging and dangerous rapids.

You could just as easily add 25 photo columns (photo1...photo25) to go
with the headlines and paragraphs. If there was a data entry for a photo
column, the address of the digital photograph (GIF file) would appear
together with its inline markups. If not, nothing would appear.

Doing an individual article this way seems cumbersome, but doing it this
way as part of a multiple-article system where the authors submit the articles by e-mail, for example, makes sense. You can cut and paste from the
e-mail into the database application, alleviating the need for manually typing in the data. The preceding partial article shows that data cataloging
applies to a variety of purposes, and the simple examples provided in this
book are just to get your imagination revved up.

Another design?

The database for the magazine article example could be designed several different ways, and the design presented in the book is not necessarily the best design.
Nonetheless, it is a design that readers will easily understand.

An Alternative

You can do partial or complete HTML documents and enter them into
memo columns in a database. Then mail merge such documents into an
aggregate HTML document. In certain situations, you might enjoy an efficiency gain. The resulting document becomes more varied in appearance
as well. With this technique, you must do the HTML markups for the text
prior to entering it into the database. Make sure when you do the markups
that you do not include any special characters reserved by your database
engine, because using such reserved characters will cause a garbled final
document. For some database engines, quotation marks are reserved characters, and you cannot place them in a column that will be exported in a
comma-delimited database.

Reserved characters

When you can't use certain characters (such as quotation marks) because they are reserved by your database engine, use alphanumeric characters as a code that will be replaced in the final document. For example, you can use the code *q1* in place of a quotation mark in the text. Then, after doing the mail merge, use a global replace command to replace all occurrences of *q1* with ".

Choosing Data Cataloging

As you evaluate your cataloging strategy, you will decide whether to apply data cataloging. There are powerful advantages, but you must weigh them against the drawbacks.

Advantages

What are the advantages of using a database for your catalog entries instead of just creating individual documents?

First, you save time creating the documents. You do it automatically by the mail merge. You simply fill in the columns in the database application.

Second, you can create a one-document catalog with multiple entries by mail merging into one template that repeats itself, each time with a different row (catalog entry).

Third, you can manipulate the data prior to the mail merge. For example, if you want to put all US state flags from the catalog in the same section, you can sort on the *name* column. The sort will create a special database table (to be exported in comma-delimited format) to generate a catalog section for the flags of the states.

Fourth, if you receive data for your database by e-mail, you can highlight it, copy it to the Clipboard, and paste it into the database. You will find this technique handy where the data routinely comes in from online sources.

The alternative to data cataloging is to use a database engine, database development tools, and Web-database development tools to create a database application accessed by a form in a Web document. For UNIX, such database engines can be moderately expensive, take much hard disk space at your Web site, and perhaps require some programming. Alternatively, data cataloging requires only a word processor, a PC database engine, and HTML programming. Anyone can do data cataloging without assistance from a programmer.

Disadvantages

First, as the number of rows increases beyond a certain point, data cataloging becomes burdensome. That point is different for every project, but you can efficiently use at least a few hundred rows (that is, a few hundred catalog entries) for most scenarios.

Second, at some point, the organization of HTML documents becomes too complex for visitors, and a database engine providing a search function will prove quicker and more convenient to visitors.

How to Proceed

Start by reading the mail merge section of your word processor manual. Try a simple mail merge using examples from your manual.

Next, make a simple mail-merge statement for a simple document using data in an existing database application. First, export the data from your PC database application in a format the word processor can use (such as comma delimited). Then do the HTML markups. Next, do the mail merge. Save the result as an ASCII (text) file. Change the file extension to *htm*. Finally, look at the result with your Web browser in local host mode. It's a lot of busy work, but it's not difficult.

Shortcut

Those readers who feel comfortable using a PC database application are wondering *Why go to the trouble of mail merging into an HTML template in a word processor? Why not use a database report for the template and crank out finished HTML catalog documents right out of the database application?* If you feel as competent using a database program as you do using a word processor, this technique may prove to be a worthwhile shortcut for data cataloging. Creating HTML templates with a database program is not much different from creating them with a word processor.

Summary

Not everyone *must* have a database search engine and spend lots of money to hire programmers to create their applications. For some readers, data cataloging may be all that is required. A word processor, a PC database engine, and HTML programming just may do the trick.

Do You Really Need a Database Program?

In This Chapter

Flat-file databases

Queries

Templates

CGI scripts

Chapter 3's discussion of different types of databases outlined the strengths and weaknesses of a flat-file database. They work well for smaller applications with simple query requirements, but they are restricted to data in a single table, which limits the application to a low level of complexity. For a simple table of data where only basic queries are needed, a flat file can be a Web database solution.

This chapter shows you how to combine the data from a flat-file database with a set of Web documents by using CGI scripts and HTML templates. The result creates a simple Web site where the visitor poses queries and the database application provides information displayed in a standard format. There is no provision to add, remove, or change information in the database application via the Web. This chapter uses the scenario of a commercial real-estate broker's professional directory.

How a Flat-File Database Works

A flat-file database simulates a spreadsheet: one table with rows and columns (see Figure 15-1). Rather than being separated by visible lines, as in a spreadsheet, commas usually separate the columns, and line breaks separate the rows. The rows are the *records* and the columns are the *fields*. For a large amount of data, you need a spreadsheet program or database engine to manage such a flat-file conveniently and efficiently. For a small amount of data, you may be able to manage the data without the use of such a program. After all, for a small amount of data you are simply keeping a *list*. The flat-file database can be an ASCII text file. When using a spreadsheet or database engine, you export the data into the flat-file format to use it as described in this chapter.

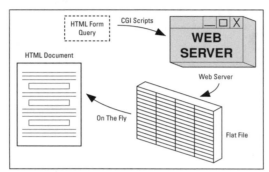

Figure 15-1: A flat-file Web database system.

Example: Commercial Real-Estate Brokers List

Imagine that you sell security systems to owners of commercial buildings worldwide, and you receive many referrals from commercial real-estate brokers. As a service to such brokers and to get more name recognition on the Internet, you have decided to create a Web site where visitors can look up commercial real-estate brokers. Visitors request a list of brokers by name, city, state (or country), designation, or specialty. You currently keep a list of all the brokers in a simple spreadsheet on your PC. You have 600 brokers on your list — too many to consider for one HTML document (too much scrolling). You want to provide a single document featuring each broker, as well as index documents listing all the brokers in a single state, city, or specialty. This example illustrates the steps you need to take to create a professional directory driven by a database engine. It includes all the HTML markups and CGI scripts. You can easily translate this example to your own use by renaming the columns in the example and using your own data.

Loading data

For very small amounts of information, an ASCII text file or *list* may be all you need. You add or change the data by using a text editor or a word processor on your PC. In the list itself, rows and column entries are separated so that they can be read correctly by the CGI script that queries the data. Sometimes tabs or spaces are used to separate the columns. More often, commas separate the columns. Line breaks usually separate the rows. For example, following is a simple flat-file list of household possessions. Each line is one household item (database row). Each household item has information about four categories (database columns): Item Name, Brand/Model, Year Purchased, and Cost. The file appears like this:

```
HOMEASSETS.TXT

camera,Nikonos-V,1986,585
4dr file cabinet,Hon,1989,137
oak table,custom made,1989,550
mattress,Simmons,1985,872
```

Data grows quickly and soon becomes too difficult to maintain in the simple list format. The next step gives better organization to larger amounts of data by arranging it in rows and columns in a spreadsheet or database application. In the primary example for the chapter, the commercial real-estate broker list, the spreadsheet or database application contains a table with 26 columns set up as follows:

- Columns 1 – 19   Text
- Columns 20 – 24   Memo (text blocks)
- Columns 25 and 26   Graphics

Column 1 must contain unique data, such as an ID number. You can select a single row only if at least one column has unique data in it. The table for our example looks like this:

```
TABLE
column    description              # of characters
1         ID #                     8
2         first name               10
3         middle name              10
4         last name                16
5         jr                       3
6         salutation               4
7         designation              9
8         firm name                50
9         address                  50
10        city                     18
11        state                    18
12        zip                      12
13        phone                    16
14        fax                      16
15        email                    33
```

(continued)

```
(continued)
16        specialty 1           33
17        specialty 2           33
18        specialty 3           33
19        specialty 4           33
20        marketing para        memo
21        resume para 1         memo
22        resume para 2         memo
23        resume para 3         memo
24        resume para 4         memo
25        page head graphic     GIF
26        person's photo        GIF
```

Any new brokers become additional rows in the spreadsheet or database application. When you export the data to the Web site, export it as a flat-file database with commas separating each column (comma delimited) and line feeds (carriage returns) separating each row.

HTML query form

Now you have a file full of data about the brokers ready to be used on the Web site. You provide several different ways to access the data. Four of them search on the data in a single column, and the fifth searches for data in any of four columns. The columns used for searching are the following:

```
Last name      Column 4
Designation    Column 7
City           Column 10
State          Column 11
Specialties    Columns 16, 17, 18, & 19
```

In addition, to facilitate a quick retrieval of one row, Column 1 (Broker ID#) is also designated as searchable.

Your Web flat file

The columns in this example have generic names simply so that this example can more easily be translated to your use. You can use this flat-file Web-database system for your own use with nominal change. Simply substitute your own data. You have five single-column queries and one four-column query. That gives you enough flexibility to be modestly creative without making any changes to the CGI scripts.

An HTML form allows your visitors to fill in specific choices in one of the six search fields. You allow only one of the search fields to be used at a time, so that the CGI script is simpler. When the form is submitted, it starts a CGI script (discussed later in this chapter) that looks up information in the flat-file database. For the broker listing example, the HTML form looks like this:

```
<HTML><HEAD><TITLE>Commercial Real Estate Brokers Request
Form</TITLE></HEAD><BODY>
<FORM METHOD="POST"
    ACTION="/cgi-bin/first.cgi">
Make selection and type in a keyword to search.
<P>
<DL>
<DD><INPUT TYPE=radio NAME="selection" VALUE="Column 1">
Last Name<BR>
<DD><INPUT TYPE=radio NAME="selection" VALUE="Column 7">
Designation<BR>
<DD><INPUT TYPE=radio NAME="selection" VALUE="Column 10">
City<BR>
<DD><INPUT TYPE=radio NAME="selection" VALUE="Column 11">
State<BR>
<DD><INPUT TYPE=radio NAME="selection" VALUE="Column 16">
Specialty
</DL>
<P>
Keyword <INPUT NAME="keyword" TYPE="text" SIZE="30">
<P>
<INPUT NAME="name" TYPE="submit" VALUE="Submit">
<INPUT NAME="name" TYPE="reset" VALUE="Reset"><BR>
</FORM>
</BODY></HTML>
```

The finished product facilitates easy input for your visitors (see Figure 15-2).

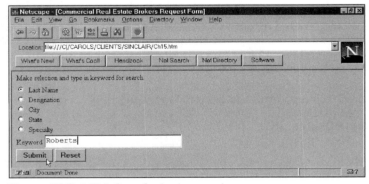

Figure 15-2: HTML form for broker queries.

If you select the City button, enter the word **Hong Kong**, and click the Submit button, you initiate a query resulting in a report (an HTML document) showing information from the rows where the brokers' city is Hong Kong. The HTML form receives the data for the queries.

HTML template

Now you have a way for visitors to select from any one of a number of query options and submit the query. The CGI script makes the queries against the flat file, identifies the rows to be used, pulls out data from such rows to fill the first template (multiple copies in many cases), and publishes the completed templates on the fly. The templates make up a list of choices, each of which is a hyperlink.

This section shows how to create the HTML template. The template is an HTML document with mail-merge-like fields into which certain data from the flat file is placed. After the CGI scripts place the data in the template, the computer delivers (*publishes*) the resulting HTML document. The delivered document did not exist before a query was made. The query determined the data to be placed in the template merge fields.

List template

In the broker example, the query returns a list of brokers that match the criteria the visitor entered. Each broker is listed on a separate line, with the broker's name, designation, city, and state. Here's what the template looks like:

```
<INPUT TYPE="RADIO" NAME="thename" value="[column1]">
[column2] [column3] [column4] [column5] [column7],
[column10], [column11]<BR>
```

In this list, each name will be a *hyperlink,* in effect, that contains a call to a CGI script and passes the unique Broker ID# (column1) to the CGI script. When the visitor selects the name, it actually starts another query to the database, looking for the record with the corresponding Broker ID#. The text of the list consists of the broker's First Name (column2), Middle Name (column3), Last Name (column4), Jr (column5), and Designation (column7). The rest of the line shows the broker's City (column10) and State (column11).

Here's what a return for the city of Hong Kong might look like:

```
[radio] William Chen, Hong Kong, China
[radio] John Li, Hong Kong, China
[radio] George G. Reed, Hong Kong, China
```

The next step is to create the template for the full-page HTML document that is created when the visitor selects one of the names shown on the list, triggering the CGI script to go get more data from the database. This second template contains two graphics, the broker's name, address, phone number, specialties, and four paragraphs of descriptions about the broker.

The final template

In the broker example, you use the final HTML template to display a single broker's information. This template contains a special page header (column25) for the broker and a photo of the broker (column26). The file names for these graphics are stored in the database. Looking at the preceding HTML list template, note that each line has a hyperlink. Executing a hyperlink for one of the names makes a query on the Broker ID# (column1), which returns a Professional Profile for the named commercial broker. Because Column 1 contains unique data, exactly one row returns for the Professional Profile template. Here's the template for the Professional Profile:

```
<HTML><HEAD><TITLE>Commercial Real Estate Brokers</TITLE>
</HEAD><BODY>


<A NAME="top"><IMG SRC="[column25]"></A>
<P>
<DL><DL><DL><DL><DL><DL><DL>
<DD><IMG SRC="[column26]">
</DL></DL></DL></DL></DL></DL>
<DD><H2><B>[column2] [column3] [column4] [column5]
[column7]</B></H2>
</DL>
<IMG SRC="line.gif">
<P>
<DL><DL><DL>
<DD>[column8]
<DD>[column9]
<DD>[column10], [column11] [column12]
<DD>Tel: [column13]
<DD>Fax: [col14]
<DD>Email: [column15]
</DL></DL></DL>
<P>
[column20]
<P>
<HR>
<P>
<H2><B>Professional Profile</B></H2>
[column2] [column3] [column4] [column5] [column7]
<P>
```

(continued)

```
(continued)
[column21]
<P>
[column22]
<P>
[column23]
<P>
[column24]
<PRE>

</PRE>
<DL><DL><DL>
<DD><B>[column2] [column3] [column4] [column5] [column7]</B>
<DD>[column8]
<DD>[column9]
<DD>[column10], [column11] [column12]
<DD>Tel: [column13]
<DD>Fax: [column14]
<DD>Email: [column15]
</DL></DL>
```

When published, the Professional Profile for an Omaha commercial broker named George Y. Smith looks like the following:

George Y. Smith

Corn Country Commercial
1234 Platte Ave., Ste. 567
Omaha, NE 33221
Tel: 123-456-7890
Fax: 123-456-7891
Email: ysmith@midwestern.com

This is a short marketing paragraph promoting Mr. Smith's professional services regarding commercial real estate.

Professional Profile

This is paragraph 1 of Mr. Smith's resume written in narrative form and referred to as a professional profile.

This is paragraph 2 of Mr. Smith's resume written in narrative form and referred to as a professional profile.

This is paragraph 3 of Mr. Smith's resume written in narrative form and referred to as a professional profile.

This is paragraph 4 of Mr. Smith's resume written in narrative form and referred to as a professional profile.

George Y. Smith

Corn Country Commercial
1234 Platte Ave., Ste. 567
Omaha, NE 33221
Tel: 123-456-7890
Fax: 123-456-7891
Email: ysmith@midwestern.com

Graphics in an HTML template

A graphics file on the Web is usually a GIF file, although most browsers can now read JPEG files *inline* (in the page). In any case, you cannot store a graphics file in the flat-file database used as the example for this chapter. You handle graphics files by placing them all in a convenient directory. Store the filename along with the relative reference path in the appropriate column in the flat-file database. Thus, the actual graphics file is not delivered with the HTML document. The HTML template contains a variable (merge field), which receives the filename of the graphics file from the flat-file database. The HTML document generated on the fly contains the link to the graphics file, which works to display the graphic in its proper place in the document.

CGI Scripting

CGI scripts provide you with a means of tapping the power of the computer for something that a Web server will not do. A Web server has no capability to perform database functions. Therefore, if you desire to use a database in some way at a Web site, you have to look elsewhere for the computing power. One place to look for such computing power is directly to the computer. In order to use computing power directly, you must write a program. Typically, you use Perl scripts to do this.

For the preceding example, the program (CGI scripts) makes queries to a preexisting simple data list (flat-file database), pulls out data, fills preexisting templates, and publishes the completed templates on the fly. Although this is simple and straightforward, you can see that the CGI scripts, which are shown in this section, seem complex.

The program could do much more. In fact, you can use CGI scripting to create almost any kind of a program you want to use in conjunction with a Web site. For example, you can create a program that enables easy data loading for the flat-file database in the example. That would be a database-management feature. Why not do that instead of having to replace the entire flat file every time you entered or changed data? The answer is, simply, Why reinvent the wheel? If you want database-management features, use a database engine such as Oracle 7 in your Web site; use CGI scripts to connect the database engine to the Web documents. Practicality limits the CGI scripting perhaps more than inherent limitations on capability.

This chapter shows you a simple way to use a simple data list at a Web site to create Web documents on the fly. This very powerful idea shows that even a system without a database engine is powerful technology. Without a database engine, however, the limitations are practical ones. How many rows can you have before the management of the data will become a heavy burden? How much programming will you have to do for each little convenience you want to add? What are the hidden costs of working without the functionality you need? At some point, you will wisely give up this simple idea and install a database engine. In fact, in most cases, it is probably advisable to forgo the method explained in this chapter and use a database engine from the start.

UNIX CGI scripts

The CGI scripting for the example in this chapter goes beyond the scope of this book, because this is not a book for programmers. Nonetheless, this section includes the CGI scripts for this example for your review and as an example for your programmer. The book provides the CGI scripts for a UNIX computer. The CGI script for Windows 95 and NT is almost identical and is on the CD-ROM.

UNIX CGI scripts to generate a list of brokers and a professional profile are as follows:

```
#! /usr/bin/perl

$/ = "";    # Enable paragraph mode
$# = 0;

# A first strike at HTML with perl.
# Copyright 1996 Chris Hoover, CCH Creative Services

# A variable to hold the size of each record. This may change.
$numcols = 26;

# And one to hold the failure string.
```

```
$fail = "The Search Engine could find <B>No Record</B> to
match your query.";


################################################################
##############
###################### Main program begins here.
##########################
#

# Read the Database into the @columns array.
&ReadData;


# Parse the INPUT and set up the %query array.
($browse, %query) = &parse_query;


# Search
if(!$browse) { # Must be a search.
    local($i, @fields, $test, $testr, $success);
    $success = 0;
I:
    foreach $i ( 0 .. $numrecs ) {
        @fields = @sfield;
            while(@fields) {
                $search = shift(@fields);
                ($test = $columns[$i * $numcols + $search])
=~ tr/A-Z/a-z/;
                ($testr = $query{'thename'}) =~ tr/A-Z/a-z/;
                if($test =~ $testr) {
                    if(!$success) {
                        &Header;
                        print "<FORM METHOD=\"POST\"
ACTION=\"first.cgi\">\n";
                        print "<p><font SIZE=+1>You may
select from this ";
                        print "menu. Then select <B>More
Info</B>.</font>";
                        print "<dl>\n";
                        &radio($i, 1);
                    }
                    else {
                        &radio($i);
                    }
                    $success++;
                    next I;
```

(continued)

(continued)

```
                }
            }
        }
    if($success) {
        if($success > 1) {
            print "<BR><FONT SIZE=+1>You can select only
one.</FONT>";
        }
        print "<INPUT TYPE=\"hidden\" NAME=\"istype\"
VALUE=\"prec\">";
        print "<br><br>\n";
        print "<INPUT TYPE=\"submit\" VALUE=\"More
Info\">\n";
        print "</dl></FORM>\n";
        &Trailer;
    }
    else { &Fail($fail); }
}


# Now browse is easy to implement
if($browse) {
    &Header;
    print "<FORM METHOD=\"POST\" ACTION=\"first.cgi\">\n";
    print "<P><FONT SIZE=+1>You may select one entry from
the ";
    print "following list. Then select <B>More
Info</B>.</FONT>";
    print "<DL>\n";
    foreach $i (0 .. $numrecs - 1) {
        if($i == 0) {
            &radio($i, 1);
        }
        else {
            &radio($i);
        }
    }
    print "<INPUT TYPE=\"hidden\" NAME=\"istype\"
VALUE=\"prec\">\n";
    print "<BR><FONT SIZE=+1>You can select only
one.</FONT>";
    print "<BR><BR><INPUT TYPE=\"submit\" VALUE=\"More
Info\">\n";
    print "</DL></FORM>\n";
    &Trailer;
}
```

```
###########################################################
######
# End of main{}
exit;


###########################################################
#########
# SUBROUTINE: ReadData{} Read the database into the
@columns array.
#
sub ReadData {
    local(@records, $record, @fields, $field, $numfields);

#    Open the database.
    open(AGENTS, "htdocs/artgal/real/mydb.txt") ||
&Fail("Error: Can't open AGENTS file.");

    while(<AGENTS>) {
        @records = split(/\n\n/);
        foreach $record (@records) {
            @fields = split(/"\,|\,"|\,\,/, $record);
            foreach $field (@fields) {
                $field =~ s/"|\,//g;
                $field =~ s/"//g;
                $field =~ s/\+/ /g;
                push(@columns, $field);
                $numfields += 1;
            }

#           Create NULL fields for any missing ones. We
need 26 columns.
            while($numfields < $numcols) {
                if($numfields == 24) {
                    push(@columns, "crc1.gif");
                }
                elsif($numfields == 25) {
                    push(@columns, "littleme.gif");
                }
                else {
                    push(@columns, "");
                }
                $numfields++;
            }
            $numfields = 0;
        }
        $numrecs++;
```

(continued)

```
(continued)
        }
    close(AGENTS);
}


###################################################################
######
# SUBROUTINE: printrec{} Print the record whose index you
passed.
#
sub printrec {
    local($i) = @_;
    local($tmp, @words, $text, $pre, $col, $post, $num,
@array, @TARGET);
    $tmp = $/;
    $/ = "]";

    open(TARGET, "template") || &Fail("Error: Can't open
template html.");
    @words = <TARGET>;
    while(@words) {
        $text = shift(@words);
        if($text =~ /\[column\d+/) {
            ($pre, $col, $post) = split(/\[|\]/, $text, 3);
            ($waste, $num) = split(/column/, $col);
            push(@array, $pre.$columns[$num - 1 + $i *
$numcols].$post);
        }
        else {
            push(@array, $text);
        }
    }
    close(TARGET);
    print "@array";
    $/ = $tmp;
}


###################################################################
#############
# SUBROUTINE: fix_state{} This will replace the state name
with it's two
# character designation.
#
sub fix_state {
    if(!defined(%states)) {
        %states = (
                'al', 'alabama',     'ak', 'alaska',
```

```
'az', 'arizona',
                'ar', 'arkansas',    'ca', 'california',
'co', 'colorado',
                'ct', 'connecticut', 'de', 'delaware',
'dc','district of columbia',
                'fl', 'florida',     'ga', 'georgia',
'hi', 'hawaii',
                'id', 'idaho',       'il', 'illinois',
'in', 'indiana',
                'ia', 'iowa',        'ks', 'kansas',
'ky', 'kentucky',
                'la', 'louisiana',   'me', 'maine',
'md', 'maryland',
                'ma', 'massachusetts','mi','michigan',
'mn', 'minnesota',
                'ms', 'mississippi','mt', 'montana',
'ne', 'nebraska',
                'nv', 'nevada',      'nh', 'new hampshire',
'nj','new jersey',
                'nm', 'new mexico', 'ny', 'new york',
'nc', 'north carolina',
                'nd', 'north dakota','oh','ohio',
'ok', 'oklahoma',
                'or', 'oregon',      'pa', 'pennsylvania',
'ri','rhode island',
                'sc', 'south carolina','sd','south dakota',
'tn','tennessee',
                'tx', 'texas',       'ut', 'utah',
'vt', 'vermont',
                'va', 'virginia',    'wa', 'washington',
'wv', 'west virginia',
                'wi', 'wisconsin',  'wy', 'wyoming');
    }
    local($state, $name);
    foreach $state (sort keys(%states)) {
        ($name = $query{'thename'}) =~ tr/A-Z/a-z/;
        if($name eq $states{$state}) {
            $query{'thename'} = $state;
            last;
        }
    }
}


##################################################################
# SUBROUTINE: Fail{} Pass this sub the error string
# you want to be part of the response html.
#
```

(continued)

```
(continued)
sub Fail {
    local($msg) = @_;
    &Header;
    print "<BR><FONT SIZE=+2>$msg</FONT><BR><HR>\n";
    print "<BR>Please feel free to try again.<BR>\n";
    &Form;
    &Trailer;
}


################################################################
# SUBROUTINE: Header{} This prints our HTML Header.
#
sub Header {
    print <<"EOL";
Content type: text/HTML

<HTML><HEAD>
<TITLE>Commercial Real Estate Center</TITLE></HEAD>
<BODY BACKGROUND="background.gif">
<H1>Commercial Real Estate Center</H1>
<img src="crc1.gif">
<p><font SIZE=+1>Welcome to the Commercial Real Estate Center
</font><hr>
EOL
}



################################################################
# SUBROUTINE: Trailer{} This prints our HTML Trailer.
#
sub Trailer {
    print <<"EOL";
<HR>
Commercial Real Estate Center <A HREF="cr.html">Copyright</A>
1996 Joseph T. Sinclair All rights reserved.</BODY></HTML>
EOL
}



######################################################################
#####
# SUBROUTINE: Form{} This prints the initial HTML <SELECT>
FORM.
#
sub Form {
    print <<"EOL";
<form method="POST" action="first.cgi">
<center>You may <input type="submit" value="Browse" >
```

```
our data base.</center>
</form></font><center><font SIZE=+3>OR</font><br>
<font SIZE=+1>
Search our data base on <b><em>one</b></em> of these criteria.
</font></center>
<form method="POST" action="first.cgi">
<center>
<input type="radio" name="istype" value="lname" checked >
Last Name.
<input type="radio" name="istype" value="desig" > Designation.
<input type="radio" name="istype" value="speci" > Specialty.
<input type="radio" name="istype" value="cname" > City Name.
<input type="radio" name="istype" value="sname" > State Name.
<input type="radio" name="istype" value="zcode" > Zip Code.
<br><br><font SIZE=+1>
<input type="text" name="thename" value="Enter Search String" >
<br>and <input type="submit" value="Search" > our data base.
</font></center></form>
EOL
}


################################################################
####
# SUBROUTINE: radio{} This produces a RADIO BUTTON <INPUT>
FORM
# for the record whose index you pass it. Pass a 1 as
$checked
# to get a preselected radio button.
#
sub radio {
    local($i, $checked) = @_;
    local($indx) = $i * $numcols;
    print "<DT><INPUT TYPE=\"RADIO\" NAME=\"thename\"
value=\"$i\"";
    if($checked) {
        print" CHECKED ";
    }
    print ">";
    print " <B> $columns[$indx + 6] :</B>";
    print " <I>$columns[$indx + 5] $columns[$indx + 1]";
    print " $columns[$indx + 2] $columns[$indx + 3] .\n";
    print " <a HREF=\"mailto:$columns[$indx + 14]\"></I>";
    print " $columns[$indx + 14]</A>\n";
    print " <dd>$columns[$indx + 7]: $columns[$indx + 15],";
    print " $columns[$indx + 16], $columns[$indx + 17],";
    print " $columns[$indx + 18]. <BR>\n";
}
```

(continued)

```
(continued)
################################################################
# SUBROUTINE: parse_query{} This is the handler for the
# GET and POST METHODs of the FORM tag. This function
# returns the %query array. Parse the query string array
# and set the switches for the search.
#
sub parse_query {
    local(@qs, $item, $name, $value, $browse, %query);
    if($ENV{'REQUEST_METHOD'} eq "GET") {
        @qs = split(/&/, $ENV{'QUERY_STRING'});
    }
    elsif($ENV{'REQUEST_METHOD'} eq "POST") {
        read(STDIN, local($input), $ENV{'CONTENT_LENGTH'});
        @qs = split(/&/, $input);
    }
    if(@qs) {
        while(@qs) {
            $item = shift(@qs);
            ($name, $value) = split(/=/, $item);
            $value =~ s/\+/ /g;
            $query{$name} = $value;
        }
        $browse = 0;

  print "@qs\n";

    }
    else { $browse = 1; }

#   Check for the other browse condition.
    if($query{'thename'} eq 'Enter Search String') {
        $browse = 1;
    }

#   What type fo search string is it
SW: {
            if($query{'istype'} eq 'lname') { @sfield = (3)
; last SW;}
        elsif($query{'istype'} eq 'desig') { @sfield = (7)
; last SW;}
        elsif($query{'istype'} eq 'speci') { @sfield =
(15,16,17,18); last SW;}
        elsif($query{'istype'} eq 'cname') { @sfield = (9)
; last SW;}
        elsif($query{'istype'} eq 'zcode') { @sfield = (11)
; last SW;}
```

```
        elsif($query{'istype'} eq 'sname') {
            @sfield = (10);
            &fix_state;
            last SW;
        }
        elsif($query{'istype'} eq 'prec' ) {
            &printrec($query{'thename'});
            exit;
        }

    }

#   The return values.
    ($browse, %query);
}
```

Win 95 CGI scripts

The CD-ROM includes the CGI scripts, too. Such scripting is done in Perl
for Win 32. You must have a Perl for Win 32 interpreter running on
Windows 95 to make these scripts work. An *interpreter* is a program that
translates the scripts on the fly into machine language that the computer
can understand. You can also do the scripts in Visual Basic.

These scripts work for the example on the CD-ROM accompanying the
book. Although the amount of data that comes with the example on the
CD-ROM is small, you have enough data to play with to discover the power
of using a flat-file database system in a Web site.

Maintaining Data

You don't have to store or maintain your data in a list using an ASCII editor
or a word processor, although that is an alternative. Why not keep the list in
a spreadsheet or database application on your PC? When you are ready to
update the flat-file list on your ISP's computer, you simply export the data in
ASCII form from your PC spreadsheet or database application and upload it
to the Web site. This provides you with extra convenience without purchasing, installing, and operating a database engine on your ISP's computer.

If you maintain a flat file directly on the ISP's computer, your Web site is
automatically current when you make changes to the file. On the other hand,
if you maintain the flat file on your PC, you must upload the data file to the
ISP's computer after every maintenance session to replace the old data file.

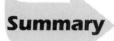

Summary

Use these steps to create a flat-file database for the Web:

1. Create the flat-file data in a word processor (for very small lists), spreadsheet, or database application.

2. Export the data in flat-file format.

3. Upload the flat file to the ISP's computer.

4. Create an HTML form document for receiving the input for a query.

5. Create an HTML template for displaying query results (a list of rows satisfying the query).

6. Create another HTML template for displaying more details, including graphics (a final document displaying information for one row).

7. Have a programmer write CGI scripts to retrieve data, combine the data with the templates, and display the results.

8. Maintain changes to the data by using the program with which you created the data.

9. Repeat the export and upload steps after you complete data maintenance.

Web-Database and Database Development Tools

In This Chapter

Web-database tool capabilities

Product evaluations

Most readers of this book will be using a database engine on an ISP's computer. ISPs use UNIX for an operating system. Traditionally, the database engines used on UNIX have been large-system database engines; that is, they have been used for large networked systems in businesses and corporations. These large businesses have had programming staff to handle any kind of programming needed to run the database engines, so, naturally, the database vendors focused on developing the best and fastest, most powerful database engine and paid little attention to the *front end*. Such database engines were designed to be programmed by database programmers. That means they are bare-bones database engines. They come without a development interface. They are designed to be programmed using a command-line interface.

Today, however, not all large system database personnel are programmers, and even programmers can work more efficiently with sophisticated development tools. Thus, a software industry that makes database development tools has enjoyed growing success for a long time. In other words, for large-system database engines, the database engine and the database development software are separate programs, often sold by different software companies. This has been inconvenient for programmers but accepted as the status quo — until now.

What's the Difference?

What's the difference in these large-system database engines, such as Oracle, Sybase, Informix, IBM, and others?

➡ They are *scalable*. They can be expanded infinitely to accommodate more users, more data, and more complexity.

➡ They are optimized as client-server programs, which means they are made strictly to run on a network providing access to many users.

➡ These engines are powerful in that they can provide a wide range of database functions.

➡ They are not priced like PC consumer software. You can't buy them shrink-wrapped off the shelf. You buy them through a company sales representative or through a value-added reseller. Until recently, such engines were generally quite expensive by consumer standards. In contrast, today they are reasonably priced, and some versions are low-priced and within the price range of PC consumer software. Indeed, with the sudden development of the Internet market, these engines are now competing with PC database software.

Yet another difference concerning these scalable database engines is important: As a nonprogrammer, you have to acquire a database development tool to use them. You may have to buy two programs: the database engine and the database development tool.

Database development tools

Originally, database development tools were designed to help database programmers. Today, many still are. Sybase PowerBuilder has been a popular program of this type. Database development tools are also available for nonprogrammers to use. Oracle PowerObjects is a program that nonprogrammers can use efficiently. Because this is not a book for programmers, however, some of the easier tools are covered here, and the apparently more difficult ones are left for the programmers.

Keep in mind that you cannot use Access, no matter how simple it is, unless you learn something about database design and technology. Likewise, database development tools will not be of much use to you as a nonprogrammer without a reasonable knowledge of databases. These database development tools can handle the design of a complex database application, but they are also useful for simple applications. The alternative to using such a tool yourself is hiring a database programmer.

These tools cover a wide price spectrum. Some are expensive, perhaps out of reach. Others are reasonably priced. The pricing trend is downward, however, because these tools enjoy an increasingly large market.

What development tools do

Development tools provide you with the means to do straightforward things, such as create tables by defining columns (fields), create queries, create complex queries, design input forms, and lay out reports. This view is simplistic, because client-server databases tend to be more complex than PC databases. Questions of access, security, cross-platform capability, and other issues not normally crucial considerations for PC programs are also of concern.

Remember, when connected to a Web document, the HTML form will be the form for the database. CGI scripts will constitute the queries. An HTML document will be the report for the database. It would be nice to have a tool that ignores the normal way of making forms, queries, and reports and makes them instead in the HTML-CGI format.

Web-Database Development Tools

When you want to develop your database application within the Web system (HTML-CGI), the traditional database tools are not adequate for doing a complete job. You can use them to create tables and other devices, but cannot provide workable forms, queries, and reports, the meat of a database application. A new genre of Web-database development tools is arriving on the market, almost all of which have been developed since early 1995. Like their traditional sisters, some of these Web-database development tools are for programmers, and some can be used by nonprogrammers. Some require supplemental CGI scripting. Others do the entire job of creating the database application. Obviously, as a nonprogrammer, you want to make sure that you acquire a program that does the entire job for you. Some of these tools are cross-platform; some are specialized.

Considerations

What are the issues you should consider in choosing and using a Web-database development tool?

➡ Is it cross-platform in regard to database engines? If it's an Oracle program, can you use it for a Sybase database engine? You certainly want a tool that works for your database engine.

➡ Is it cross-platform in regard to operating systems? Ideal is a Web-database development tool that runs in Windows, and whose finished application you can easily port to UNIX.

➡ Can a nonprogrammer use it? Does it do a complete job, or does it require supplemental scripting?

➠ Do you need a database development tool as well as a Web-database development tool, or will one tool do it all?

➠ How will it run at the Web site? Does it require a special Web server, daemon, or another program? Or is it just a file to be loaded?

➠ How much space does it take on a hard disk? Scalable database engines tend to be quite large. Will the database application require a great deal more space in addition to the large space requirement for the database engine?

➠ Is it difficult to install?

➠ How much does it cost?

➠ Is there a 90-day trial version you can try before committing to a purchase?

For most PC users, this is new software territory, and a careful evaluation of exactly what you need will be time well spent.

Types of database development tools

A typical tool, for the purpose of this book, is one that has a graphical user interface (GUI), such as Windows, and is realistically usable by a nonprogrammer. Oracle PowerObjects is a good example. It offers drag-and-drop capability, which is a powerful and easy-to-use feature.

Another approach is Asymetrix InfoModeler. This program uses sentences in English to design a database application. The logic of the language defines the logic of the application. The idea is that this is an easier way to design. After you have designed the application in English, InfoModeler automatically writes the database application code for you. For some users, this will prove an easier and more efficient approach. For others, it may be confusing, and a more traditional tool may be more suitable.

Types of Web-database development tools

A Web-database development tool can enable five functions. First is the structure for the data and other devices (tables). Second is the HTML form necessary for visitor input. Third is the CGI scripting necessary to convey the input (query) to the database engine. Fourth is the spontaneous generation of the Web document (the report). Fifth are maintenance chores that someone must perform, such as loading and deleting raw data. You must know how you will enable each of these functions.

There may be some capability built into the database engine for creating tables reasonably easily. Even so, however, because the database is on a UNIX computer, you may have trouble using such capability. You therefore need a Web-database development tool to provide such capability.

You can design and create the HTML form yourself. You don't need a Web-database development tool to do that. Review the HTML chapter in this book, which focuses on creating HTML forms. If that's not enough, buy an HTML book that covers forms thoroughly.

A Web-database development tool is essential for creating the queries. A tool may perform this task a number of ways. It may include some generic CGI scripting, which it uses to create the connection between the HTML form and the database engine. The tool may generate CGI scripts. It may include a daemon that runs along with the Web server and performs the functions of CGI scripting. The capability to do this is what distinguishes a Web-database development tool from a traditional database development tool.

Spontaneously generating an HTML document, although enabled by a Web-database development tool, nonetheless requires a template. For attractive HTML documents, the best way to do this is to create the template in HTML. Then translate it by using your Web-database development tool. When you are finished, it should look much the same as the HTML version. In other words, when it comes to doing the template, you may have to do some database markups, but it won't be difficult. It's best to get an example of an HTML template that includes database markups and then use that as a guide. HTML extensions have been created for languages such as BASIC and PL/SQL (Oracles's extension of SQL). The only way to change the HTML document created on the fly is to tweak the template.

If all you want to do is publish the database tables in a table format, Web-database engines and development tools do that automatically.

You should use a Web-database development tool to handle maintenance functions. There may be limitations, however, to the maintenance you can do through an HTML form. You may have to handle some maintenance functions by accessing the database engine directly. That means that your ISP may have to do it for you.

Keep in mind that one elegant solution to Web-database development is an integrated Web server and database engine, such as the GNNserver. An integrated approach will provide you with everything you need.

Web-database development tools are all different. No functions are standard. Certain choices may require that you use both a traditional database development tool and a Web-database development tool.

Remote use

A key problem in operating a Web site on an ISP's computer is that you're a remote user of a UNIX system. If you can program with a command-line interface, you can access the UNIX computer by Telnet and use the computer with UNIX commands and program commands. Readers with Windows will look for a different solution for a remote location.

One solution is to become a remote user of X-Windows, the UNIX equivalent of Windows. X-Windows is similar to other GUI operating systems, such as Windows and Macintosh. Via X-Windows, you can use a Web-database development tool that comes only in a UNIX version. How do you use X-Windows remotely? You need an X-Windows emulator, such as Hummingbird's eXceed. You run the emulator on your PC, connect to the remote UNIX computer by Telnet, and use X-Windows as if it were running on your PC.

A better solution is to use a Web-database development tool cross-platform. You develop your Web-database application in Windows. Then you port it to the UNIX computer, where it should work just fine. This solution has two potential drawbacks. First, to test the application on your PC, you need to have two versions of the database engine: one for your PC and one for UNIX. You could develop on your PC and port and test on UNIX. That's more awkward for testing. Second, if the Web-database development tool must reside on the UNIX computer for the Web-database application, you need *two* versions of the tool, one for developing on your PC and the other to run the application on the UNIX computer.

An elegant solution is to use a special Web browser as the development agent. The GNNserver system is a good example. This is an integrated Web server and database engine. You use the low-cost GNNpress Web browser, a Windows program, to do your database development work remotely.

If the Web site computer is a Windows NT computer, some problems may go away, but don't count on that until you do a careful analysis.

Windows NT

Readers will want to use database technology on an intranet that uses a Windows NT server connected to the Internet. For them, the problem of UNIX does not exist. Still, the problems of cross-platform compatibility, remoteness, and licensing may exist. First, the cross-platform consideration is between Windows 95 and Windows NT. Versions of the database engine and the Web-database development tool for these operating systems may be different or nonexistent. Second, the server computer is likely to be remote, and you may need two copies of the requisite software. Third, if two copies of the software are required, you may have to pay an additional licensing fee.

Desktop databases

Windows desktop database engines create something of a problem for nonprogrammers. These desktop database engines typically have integrated database development tools, so the market for external database development tools is less than scalable database engines. Because sometime in the near future these database engines will likely include integrated Web-database development tools, there is not as much incentive for software companies to create separate Web-database tools. This situation is temporary, and eventually you will have plenty of choices to make for creating desktop Web-database applications without the use of programming.

Specific Tools

The remainder of this chapter is devoted to a sampling of tools at this writing. You should do your own survey of the tools available when you are ready to take action on creating a Web-database application. By the end of 1996, practically all software companies will have a Web site and will offer a 30-day or 90-day free trial download.

Specific database development tools

Database development tools provide fast and simple applications.

Oracle PowerObjects

This tool has a slick GUI, drag-and-drop design tool. You see your tables, indexes, and other database objects as icons that you can open with a double-click. The design tool enables you to drag and drop master-detail connections and object properties. You can assign styles and insert graphics, video clips, audio clips, and other features on data-entry forms.

PowerObjects comes with a built-in SQL database called Blaze, which you can use for small database applications. It includes many good example applications and documentation. It also connects seamlessly with Oracle 7, Microsoft SQL Server, and Sybase SQL Server databases.

PowerObjects also uses a drag-and-drop interface for modifying, creating, and removing tables, indexes, and other database objects. This feature makes it more of a combination tool for both database design and Web-application design.

NetDynamics uses object-oriented concepts to help you define and design your applications. *Data sources* are sets of database tables. *Data objects* are subsets of the data source, defining the columns to be used in an HTML document. *Pages* are HTML documents. A project is the entire set of data sources, data objects, and pages. A project can be ported from one platform to another as a complete set.

InfoModeler

As previously mentioned, Asymetrix InfoModeler relies on the use of English statements to design a database application. After the application is finished and tuned, InfoModeler generates the code automatically. This is an approach that appeals to many — but leaves others cold.

Microsoft Query

Access does not generate accurate SQL code. Microsoft supplies all Windows 95 users with MS Query. You can also get it bundled with other Microsoft programs. Microsoft Query is very similar to Access; it even looks similar. Using it, you can construct SQL queries graphically, and it will generate accurate SQL code. Because SQL code is the key to a Web-database application, MS Query is an important database development tool, even though it does nothing but construct queries. By itself, this tool cannot do database applications, but it's a welcome supplement to Web-database development tools that require SQL queries.

Specific Web-database development tools

Several leaders provide powerful capabilities for custom Web databases.

Spider Technologies' NetDynamics

The Wizards included in this package are smart. You can design and test Web-database applications on your Windows 95 computer. You need 32MB of RAM for this tool, and 20MB on your hard drive. It is one of the more robust Web-database tools on the market and has features that go far beyond the basics. NetDynamics runs with SQL databases. Later in this book, the authors use NetDynamics to generate the Gallery Online, a searchable art gallery.

GNNserver and GNNpress

In many ways, this is the ideal Web-database package. It has everything: Web server, database engine, text-search engine, Web-database development capability, Web-development tool browser combination for remote developing, and special features to accommodate additional programming with high performance. It is covered more thoroughly in a later chapter.

Corel Web.Data

Almost anyone can use this tool to quickly create a simply structured presentation of data in HTML format. It is like a combination HTML authoring program and Web-database development tool. Unfortunately, as simple as Corel tries to make it, you must still know something about HTML to use it efficiently. For complex Web presentations, it may not be as useful as for simple ones. For HTML and SQL novices, it's worth a look.

Cold Fusion

Because this tool is used with Access for the Art Gallery demonstration in a later chapter of this book, you can learn about it there. It's powerful but easy-to-use. Currently, Cold Fusion comes bundled with the O'Reilly WebSite Web server at an attractive price. It is limited to Windows NT and Windows 95. Nonprogrammers who use HTML will find this tool easy.

Net Scheme

This tool is more for using legacy database applications on an intranet, but it also has potential for new database applications and for Web-database applications. It's for nonprogrammers and programmers alike and has some unusual features. A later chapter covers it in more depth.

Web Galaxy

Web Galaxy is a new design tool for Web applications and Web-database applications. It uses a *knowledge map* (a graphical representation of the flow of logic in an application) to create a C code program. The program Web Galaxy creates runs on the Web server. Web Galaxy can also create and run a Java applet and can include multimedia, such as audio or video. You do not need to know C or Java, because this is a nonprogramming tool. If, on the other hand, you prefer to modify the HTML or the Java, all the code is available to you without going outside the Web Galaxy design tool. All changes you make to the code are automatically reflected in the knowledge map. Web Galaxy runs on NT, Sun OS, Solaris, and Linux Web servers.

Web Galaxy employs a standard set of Java applets for all applications. These are downloaded once to the client computer. Thereafter, they are available for use with any Web Galaxy applications, which speeds up the performance time during subsequent visits to a Web Galaxy site.

Part of a Web Galaxy application runs on the Web server in parallel with the server. This part is called the *inference engine*. It acts like another server, sending data to and receiving data from the client on a separate port. This approach means that Web Galaxy does not compete with the primary server, and more data is transmitted at one time across two ports. In addition, the inference engine is a powerful logic machine you can use to do calculations, track visitors, debug code, and access databases. A future release will be enhanced to use fuzzy logic to interpret English words in search strings and to read e-mail.

Web Galaxy can be used by novice database developers, nonprogrammers, and advanced programmers. As your skills grow, there are more features that you can use.

Quest

Quest, by Level 5, is an easy-to-use tool for using existing database applications on an intranet or the Internet. It requires no programming. Quest enables you to create special Web-database applications that enhance existing database applications. Visitors enjoy easy, productive searches by using fuzzy logic. For easy Web publication with special enhancements for existing database tables, this program is a good choice.

Jamba

This is a Java authoring tool. Nonprogrammers can use it, but must have a reasonable overview of object-oriented programming. Jamba supports JDBC, which means that you can create Web-database applications. A nonprogrammer who wants to be on the leading edge should consider Jamba.

Summary

This chapter made no attempt to cover the field of Web-database development tools for nonprogrammers. Plenty of choices are available today. By the time you read this, almost all database development tools will have Web-development capability. The questions raised by this chapter are helpful ones, because you won't want to choose a tool blindly.

Choosing a Client-Server Database

You have seen how the tools you choose help you to set up the best environment for your visitors. You must also decide which database engine to employ. Perhaps you use Microsoft Access on your PC and you want to coordinate data among several databases spread accross several Web sites. You need a database engine that resides on your *server*, not on your PC.

The server is connected to the Internet and displays all your Web pages. It contains the database engine and the database application. Most servers used by ISPs use the UNIX operating system. PC software, such as Microsoft Access, doesn't run in UNIX. Therefore, you need new software you never dreamed would have any application in your digital activities. The ascendancy of client-server technology, especially the Internet, has forced everything to change. You find yourself among the many Web-site developers and managers who must consider the use of a *scalable database engine* in a Web site.

Companies perhaps unfamiliar to you, such as Oracle, Sybase, and Informix — as well as IBM — *own* this market. These companies are unfamiliar with the new potential mass market of consumers too. Companies such as Oracle, however, have begun to pursue the consumer market, and you can expect selling practices to change. Oracle, for example, sells aggressively over the Internet.

This chapter reviews the requirements and criteria you should consider when selecting a database engine for your Web site. A database engine must meet some basic requirements to be used in a Web site. The first section outlines these requirements. The second section discusses additional features that make one database engine more desirable for your purposes than another. At the end of the chapter you will find a brief review of several database engines.

Basic Requirements

The database engine you select must meet the basic requirements listed here. If it does not, you probably cannot implement it as a Web-site database.

➡ **Client-Server.** This is the basic technology that enables the server and the database to pass data and requests back and forth. Virtually all powerful database engines are client-server programs. Smaller desktop databases often are not fully client-server capable — and therefore are not appropriate choices for a Web-site database.

➡ **Multiple Concurrent Users.** Your Web site may have dozens or even hundreds of visitors querying the database at any given time. Low-volume sites need perhaps three concurrent database users. High-volume sites need many more. Review your plans and verify that the database engine you choose supports the traffic you anticipate.

➡ **Relational or UDB.** Relational databases and their new offspring, the hybrid databases — or universal databases (UDB) — are the only types that have the versatility you need to create a flexible and robust database application.

Intranets are the exception to the rule

You can use a desktop database such as Microsoft Access on your intranet. For example, you can use Access with Windows NT on a LAN to create a database application or to access a legacy desktop database application through a Web server. This approach enables the sharing of a database application among many coworkers by using a Web interface.

Selection Criteria

Your special business requirements are as unique as your fingerprints. The criteria discussed in this section can help you determine which features will best implement your success and help you choose among the many database engines available.

Scalable size

If a database engine provides scalability, a database application can adapt from a small size to a very large size, as your needs change. This means that your database can be used on your desktop by a single user (small) or can be used by hundreds of different users simultaneously. In addition, scalable databases allow for small or large volumes of data in a single database. This feature separates desktop databases, such as Access, from large system databases, such as Oracle, Sybase, Informix, and IBM. You may want to first implement a small part of your business with a Web-site database. As your expertise advances, so will the size and complexity of your database applications. A scalable database engine means that you don't have to upgrade to a new and unfamiliar product when your business grows or becomes more complex.

Size of software and database application

If you have limited hard disk space for your database, software size is an important consideration. The database engine and its accompanying programs take up disk space. The tables you create for storing information take up disk space. The more information you store, the more disk space you need. Scalable databases tend to be larger than desktop databases. Personal Oracle (a desktop version of Oracle), for example, requires more than 40MB. Versions for UNIX or other platforms are even larger. It is often difficult to get a good estimate of the size of your proposed database application. Ask the software vendor to provide you with some rough estimates, or ask for the name of one of their clients using a similar database application.

Cost of database engine

Not so long ago, scalable databases were much more expensive than desktop databases. Today, the market has changed. You can purchase Personal Oracle for under $500. Personal Oracle for Windows is essentially the same Oracle database engine that runs on minicomputers and mainframe computers. You can purchase other versions of Oracle at very reasonable prices, which your ISP can run. The competition between scalable database companies is intense. Oracle offers a free 90-day trial version of its software for several platforms on its Web site, which is at the following address:

```
http://www.oracle.com/products/trial/
```

One does not usually purchase a scalable database shrink-wrapped off the shelf. You purchase it from a company sales representative or through a value-added reseller (VAR). VARs combine their own products with the database engine to make a more attractive package for sale. Prices are often tied to the number of users on the network. This practice may change as these vendors become more familiar with marketing strategies for consumer markets.

Availability of development tools

You must ask two questions at this point. Does the database engine include some development tools? If not, are tools available from the vendor or from other vendors? Good development tools make or break your project.

Look for tools for these functions:

➥ Creating tables, views, and indexes

➥ Importing and exporting data

➥ Viewing and changing data

➥ Managing user IDs and security

These types of tools enable you to create tables and modify data without resorting to programming in SQL. These tools are often separate from the Web database tools described in an earlier chapter.

ODBC

Microsoft developed a standard for databases to ensure that tools and databases from different vendors can communicate with one another. Open Database Connectivity (ODBC) defines standard ways for database engines to communicate with database tools. To read more about Open Database Connectivity, see Chapter 28, "Ideas for Using Web-Database Technology."

Using an ODBC-compliant database engine enables you to mix and match development tools from multiple vendors. You may prefer to use development tools by Expertelligence and a Sybase database engine. Because both are ODBC-compliant, they fit together.

Cost of development tools

Save time and money by finding freeware or shareware to enhance your database application. Vendors offer freeware and shareware to demonstrate their products and to attract buyers. Some are time-limited trial offers, some are shareware, and others are truly free. Look into the freeware your prospective vendor offers.

Cross-platform portability

Most scalable databases are *cross-platform*. That means there are versions for almost all operating systems. A database application for the PC using Personal Oracle runs on a mainframe version of Oracle. You can expect most major database companies to offer more cross-platform products.

Connectivity

Connectivity is the capability of a database to get data from a different database (usually a requirement of intranet applications). Connectivity becomes an issue when you have several legacy databases with which to share information.

ODBC compliance is the first part of connecting two databases together. The second part is identifying and connecting to outside databases within the database engine. Oracle, for example, allows this kind of connectivity with other Oracle-compliant databases and is ODBC compliant as well.

Compatibility with Web servers

Some database engines require special servers, whereas others are compatible with virtually all Web servers. All Web servers support the CGI communications protocol. Some databases support CGI DLL. Dynamic Linked Library (DLL) is a method of storing and running routines. This method is used in some Windows and UNIX operating systems. Make sure that the Web server is compatible with your database engine. Again, ODBC is useful for compatibility.

Replication methods

As demand grows for your Web site, your Web-database application must serve many visitors at once. You may choose to replicate your database with a mirror site to distribute the load between two computers. By doing so, you solve the traffic problem — but how do you keep two databases identical?

The simplest method of replication keeps one database as the primary one where all changes are made. The other database is simply a static copy of the primary database. You can easily maintain any number of duplicate databases this way. The data does not change very often, and you can allow a great number of visitors to view the data at one time. The disadvantage of this method is timeliness. The moment you change the primary database, your duplicate databases are out of date.

Other, more complex methods of replication are available. For example, transaction logs keep records of all changes to all the databases and apply them later to update each version of the database. The word *later* may mean every hour, every four hours, or every day. Another method uses fully functioning updates that synchronize all the replicate databases *immediately*.

Backup and recovery

Imagine that your computer is running your database application and lightning strikes the building. When your computer goes back on line, what recovery steps restore the database to its previous state? Most database engines have built-in recovery processes so that your database is restored without any problems. Occasionally, a damaged disk or other physical problem requires your ISP to restore your database from a *backup* copy of the database. You lose all changes made after the backup date and time. Ask your ISP how often your database is backed up.

Security

When you see a pop-up window on a Web page asking for a user name and password, the Web server's security scheme is being used. You must verify that the security scheme that your ISP uses is compatible with your database. Primarily, database security protects your data from unauthorized access and from unauthorized changes.

A second aspect of security is inside the database application itself. Most client-server database engines allow many individual users with distinct security schemes and passwords. A few smaller databases do not make this distinction.

A Survey of Database Engines

Oracle, Sybase, Informix, and IBM (among many others) sell client-server relational database engines. All of them can be installed on a wide range of platforms, from PCs to mainframes. They can handle hundreds of concurrent users. Databases developed on one platform are fully portable to any other platform. They offer suites of tools to assist in design, development, and implementation of your application. Some freeware is available from the Web sites. A large number of VARs offer software catering to specialized areas, such as accounting and inventory. Any of these databases can connect to remote databases and are fully ODBC compliant. Security schemes can be structured by groups of users, making the schemes easier to manage. Cost of the database with tools ranges from less than $1,000 for PC versions to hundreds of thousands of dollars for the industrial-strength parallel processor versions.

A free, 90-day trial version of Personal Oracle 7 is available for downloading at this address:

```
http://www.oracle.com/products/oracle7/personal/html/
oracle7Choice.html
```

Sybase has a Web-development package called web.sql. It uses CGI scripts to pass commands from an HTML document to the Sybase database and to retrieve information to create dynamic Web pages. A free beta version has been available at:

```
http://www.sybase.com/products/internet/websql
```

Informix provides freeware to connect your Informix database to the Web. Visit the following Web site for more information:

```
http://www.informix.com/informix/dbweb/grail/freeware.htm
```

IBM offers a Web interface for its DB2 database. This is described at:

```
http://as400.rochester.ibm.com/QDLS/400home/ncc/webconn/
db2www.htm
```

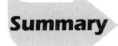

Summary

You need to decide which of these factors is the most important for your Web-site idea. If you are a new business with a tight budget, cost and size may be very important to you. If your business needs to coordinate data among several databases and ISPs, then compatibility, portability, and connectivity are probably your biggest concerns. Availability of good tools is usually important unless you have a staff of experts who love to program. As with any business decision, let common sense and careful planning guide you in selecting the right database engine for your Web site.

Internet Operations

You must perform many tasks to get your operations up and running on the Web. This chapter attempts to outline the various tasks, together with the personnel and resources currently needed. Keep in mind that as Internet technology advances, you will need to add tasks to the list.

Server Services

Putting a Web site with a database on the Internet doesn't have to be expensive, but it consumes your money, your time, or the time of your employees.

Running your own server

In 1994, a Santa Cruz, California, Web entrepreneur used a 486 PC with 16MB, Windows NT, freeware Web server software obtained from the Internet, a 28.8 Kbps modem, and a normal residential phone line to run his Web site. He connected to the Internet through a local ISP. His total cost in dollars was the price of the computer (under $2,000), the price of the operating system (about $500), the cost of his phone line ($20 monthly), and the cost of his Internet connection ($80 monthly). What did Pacific Bell think of that very long, never-ending residential phone call? Unknown.

The entrepreneur claimed he could handle eight simultaneous Web visitors, albeit at a slow speed. Although ambitious to do other things, he found himself spending much of his time maintaining his Windows NT Web server, which provided only Web and FTP capability.

If you want to get serious about running a Web site on a Pentium, for about $11,000 you can acquire a professional UNIX system, including the Pentium computer, the operating system, and the ancillary equipment. Of course, this investment justifies a hefty phone line (ISDN minimum), which will cost a minimum of a few hundred dollars each month. This system also requires a UNIX programmer to run it.

A workstation (for example, a Sun Netra) runs faster and is more powerful than a Pentium computer, and the minimum Internet configuration — including the workstation, the operating system, and the ancillary equipment — will cost about $20,000. As with the Pentium, because the operating system is UNIX, you will be able to use most of the freeware servers available for downloading from the Internet. Unfortunately, you or a UNIX programmer on your staff will spend a good deal of time using UNIX to maintain your servers.

These two examples are just entry-level examples. Internet equipment that's more robust goes up steeply in price and operating costs.

To operate a computer at normal Internet speed (1.5MB per second), you need a dedicated T1 line from the phone company. The distance between you, the phone company switching station, or the Internet provider is a significant determinant of the charge for such a line. You can use a normal phone line, but the high cost of UNIX systems does not justify using such an anemic connection. You can use a dedicated ISDN line at 128 Kbps per second (about 1/11th the capacity of a T1 line), but that will not be enough for heavy traffic. Additionally, you will need a connection to the Internet (at the end of the phone line), which you will get through an ISP. That connection is costly. For a complete package (T1 connection to your ISP, and via a T1 a connection from the ISP to the Internet), expect to pay well over $1,000 per month.

T1s and other lines

A T1 line consists of 24 twisted pairs (24 individual phone lines), providing a 1.5 Mbps per second transfer rate. A T1 line is the minimum for an ISP, but by itself does not guarantee adequate throughput. Throughput depends on the number of computers using the line simultaneously and the volume of data being transmitted by the computers simultaneously. Many ISPs use multiple T1s.

A T3 line is a fiber optic cable the equivalent of 672 twisted pairs. It has a transfer rate of 44.7 Mbps per second. A T3 is used as an Internet backbone between cities and around metropolitan areas.

There is a large surplus of fiber optic lines available. Enough T3 capacity exists now in and between cities to accommodate anticipated increases in communications consumption for the next quarter of a century. Supplying fiber optic cable is a very competitive business. Unfortunately, the bandwidth bottleneck is in the lines connecting homes and businesses to the local trunk lines. Such consumer and business lines are twisted pairs.

A twisted pair can transfer analog data at 33.6 Kbps per second, although the maximum performance over many phone lines amounts to only about 22 Kbps per second when using an analog modem without a compression protocol. With an Integrated Service Digital Network (ISDN) modem the transfer rate runs 128 Kbps. With ISDN, a twisted pair provides two 64 Kbps per second B channels, each of which can transmit separately and simultaneously (for example, separate phone lines).

Coaxial cable used by the cable TV companies has a potential transfer rate of about 1.5 Mbps per second, about 11 times faster than a twisted pair using ISDN, and is a promising potential carrier for Internet access.

Even though there are Web servers for OS/2, Windows 3.1, Windows 95, Windows NT, DOS, and Macintosh, you can seldom run an in-house Web server for the Internet cost-effectively for a small or medium-size business unless the computer also provides other services, such as an internal network (for example, an intranet on a LAN) or a networked database application, or unless you have programming capability in-house (see Figure 18-1).

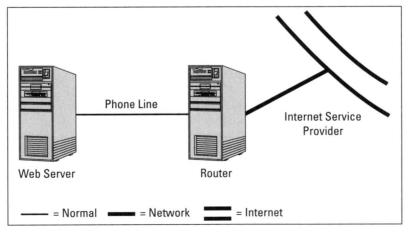

Figure 18-1: Your own Internet server system.

Windows NT is growing in popularity as an operating system for Internet servers. To some extent, many of the Windows NT Web servers on the market now may prove easier to operate than most UNIX servers, but they are not carefree.

Using other people's servers

This is something like using other people's money when you leverage an investment. You can rent space on an ISP's hard disk. Table 18-1 shows the rates from four different ISPs for hard disk space and the combined operation of Web, Gopher, and FTP servers.

Table 18-1: ISP business rates		
	MB	$/Month
ISP A	5	20
	10	40
	20	75
ISP B	10	50 + 2/extra MB
ISP C	—	50 + .50/MB
ISP D	—	45 + .18/MB + .01/hit

All the ISPs in the table supply Internet accounts to consumers as well as to businesses. They all have T1 lines and operate at the full speed of the Internet. By putting your business on their computers, you get the advantage of a full-fledged fast system for a small fraction of the cost of running your own computer and you can use your own domain name (see Figure 18-2). The ISPs can do this because not everyone uses the system at the same time. The equipment will presumably handle the largest statistically likely traffic for any one traffic period. This may be a good deal for you.

This arrangement won't work well for you in two situations. The first is where the ISP has an inadequate system for the number of consumers who have dial-up accounts. Slowdowns result on such an overloaded system until the ISP expands the system. The second situation is where the number of people visiting your Web site becomes so great that it overburdens your ISP's system. In this case, your ISP will want you to pay a higher monthly fee, and justifiably so. Your ISP has to incur the cost of expanding the system (both hardware and phone line capacity) to accommodate your business.

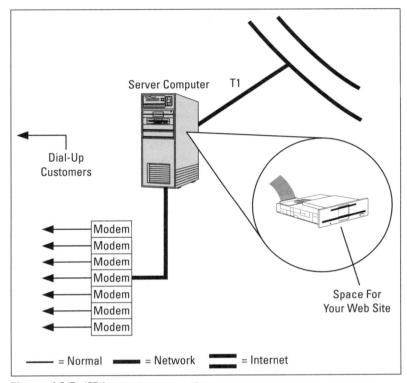

Figure 18-2: ISP Internet server system

Renting space on someone else's computer takes the burden off you to buy and maintain the computer, the servers, and the connections. You simply upload the files that make up your Web business presentation to the ISP's computer and maintain that presentation online thereafter. That is an easy task requiring only a competent FTP client.

Getting back to Santa Cruz, the Web entrepreneur (mentioned earlier) finally decided, with a little urging from one of the authors, to put his Web site on the hard disk of an ISP (in another state). His new cost was $50 per month for a UNIX computer with the requisite Web, Gopher, and FTP servers and a T1 line.

Some Internet providers offer connections only to businesses and have no consumer dial-up accounts. They are likely to be considerably more expensive. Because they service only business accounts, however, they may be more reliable in maintaining full-power service and may offer a wider range of services.

Many businesses, particularly medium and large corporations, may elect to take their Web business to one of the large providers, such as MCI or a

Where?

Does it matter where your ISP is physically located? In most cases, no. Web service is provided at the speed of light. For people in Boston, a Web site in London is the same as one in New York. When you upload your Web files via FTP to your Web site on your ISP's hard disk, you do so via the Internet at no additional cost over and above your monthly flat fee for Internet access service. Thus, it doesn't matter whether your ISP is in Chicago, Caracas, Copenhagen, Canton, Cairo, Calcutta or Canberra.

regional Bell. The cost is likely to be considerably higher for essentially the same service, but the quality and reliability of service from such a large organization is perceived as superior — whether justified or not.

You can choose from thousands of ISPs around the world. For a list of ISPs (by country, and in the U.S. by state and county), see The List at the following URL:

```
http://www.thelist.com/
```

Running an intranet

If you run an internal TCP/IP network, or intranet, you have many of the same considerations as you do when running your own server on the Internet. You provide Internet services, such as a Web site, inside your organization rather than on the Internet (see Figure 18-3).

In this case, the focus is apt to be different. For example, you probably will provide e-mail as the primary service. Or you may provide both intranet and Internet services on the same system, using a firewall for security to protect your internal network operations against unauthorized outside penetration. Or your primary service may be to provide access to a database application.

Firewalls

A **firewall** is a complex digital arrangement (often including special hardware) set up to prevent penetration by an outsider into your internal network. Sertting up a firewall is tricky business. Don't do it yourself; have an expert do it. If it's worth going to the trouble of setting up a firewall, then it's worth doing it right.

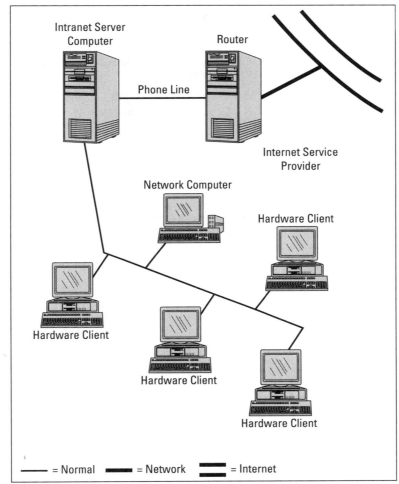

Figure 18-3: An internal TCP/IP network (intranet).

Running a database engine

The question of the hour is, What are the considerations in operating a database application on an Internet or intranet Web system?

➡ First is the hardware. Does the computer provide enough horsepower to run a database engine in addition to providing the infrastructure and horsepower for other services?

➡ Second is the software. What database engine, database development tools, Web-database development tools, and supplemental programming do you need to build a workable database application? Where can you use those programs? On a desktop PC? On the ISP's computer? On both?

➦ Third is the programming and maintenance. How difficult is the database application to install, program, and operate?

➦ Fourth is the space requirement. For your database application, do you need 5MB, 50MB, 500MB, or 5GB?

➦ Fifth is access. If you use an ISP, can you get the requisite access to the ISP's computer to install CGI scripts and to maintain the database application?

➦ Sixth is cost. Who buys and maintains the necessary software? You? The ISP? A user group?

For the integration of a database application in a Web site, most of the considerations in operating a database application are the same for intranets and the Internet (see Figures 18-4 through 18-6). The question is when to use an ISP for part or all of your Web operations, and if you do use an ISP, who is going to do what tasks and cover what costs?

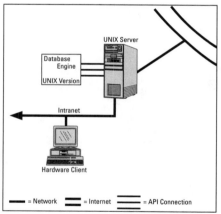

Figure 18-4: A UNIX Web database.

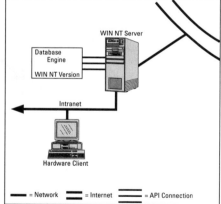

Figure 18-5: A Windows NT Web-database application.

Using a VAN

A Value Added Network (VAN) is an ISP that offers more than most of its competitors. For example, if an ISP offers the use of a powerful database engine today, it may qualify as a VAN simply because few ISPs offer the use of a database engine. If an ISP offers a broad range of servers, such as a database engine, a secure Web server, a Real Audio server, and the like, such an ISP is most certainly a VAN and will have a comparatively high cost. The large ISPs will operate as VANs to justify their high relative cost.

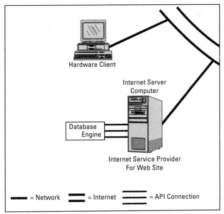

Figure 18-6: A remote Web-database application.

ISP + VAN?

Can you use both an ISP and a VAN? Sure. Set up your traditional Web site as you normally would. For the part of your Web site that requires database access, hyperlink to another Web site at a VAN that provides database service. Because you control the Web site at your VAN as well as at your ISP, you can shuttle visitors back and forth via hyperlinks, and most visitors will not even notice the change in domain addresses. Why would you use two providers for one site? As an example, the VAN might have an expensive charge for storage but an attractively priced database service. You store the major portion of your Web site at an ISP with a low storage cost and use the VAN for database capability.

In the future, you may choose an ISP for the software it offers. If you are looking for something special, such as a particular server, you will seek an ISP that provides that software, and you will require the necessary arrangements to use such software effectively (for example, access to cgi-bin to store CGI scripts). A VAN that provides a database engine will be especially appropriate for consideration if you want to use a database application in a Web site (see Figure 18-7).

Software

At one time, much of the software for use on the Internet was free or inexpensive. Today, the commercial software vendors dominate the Internet software industry, and most software is no longer free (except for temporary promotions). In fact, many of the good deals and free deals notwith-

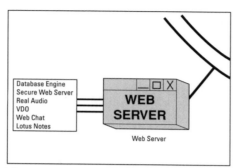

| Database Engine |
| Secure Web Server |
| Real Audio |
| VDO |
| Web Chat |
| Lotus Notes |

WEB SERVER

Web Server

Figure 18-7: A VAN.

standing, you can expect to pay substantially more each year in the future for Internet software. Such software will grow in capability and will be desirable, and you need to consider such additional software expenses in your planning. For example, Netscape offers a commerce Web server that handles secure financial transactions.

If you plan to use a database at your Web site, you will need a UNIX database engine in most cases. Most ISPs run their systems on some variation of UNIX. On intranets that use Windows NT, the Windows NT versions of database engines are also choices. As the new commercial Web servers and database engines become available, business users will demand that such software be purchased and adopted by their ISPs. Then ISPs will have to recoup the purchase cost and make a profit. That means that business-user monthly fees are likely to go up.

Installation

Installation charges for equipment, phone lines, and Internet connections can add up to a significant capital investment. Likewise, initial programming can constitute a significant up-front cost. Don't underestimate these inaugural expenses.

Server programming

UNIX programmers usually are paid well. A UNIX programmer runs a UNIX computer, the various Internet servers, and the ancillary devices. Unless you already can program in UNIX, you do not want to try this chore yourself. Even if you can do UNIX programming, this activity will take a significant amount of your time.

A Windows NT system offers the advantage of being simpler to program. Even with Windows NT, however, it takes an experienced user or a programmer to maintain the servers. As with UNIX, Windows NT programming will take a significant amount of your time. It should also be pointed out that the monthly cost of a programmer's or network manager's employment, even part-time, can exceed all the other costs of operating a server combined.

Of course, if you don't run a server, you don't have to worry about UNIX or Windows NT programming. That's why you will find using an ISP's computer your best choice in many cases.

ISP checklist

ISPs usually offer a package of services to those who operate a domain on the Internet. Here is a checklist of essential services to get when choosing an ISP:

- **Web:** A Web server is the essential requirement.

- **FTP:** If you expect to provide visitors with the capability to download files, make sure that this service is provided for use by visitors. Invariably, this service is part of a Web-site package, because you need to upload your HTML files and other files onto your Web site.

- **Telnet:** This is usually part of a *shell* account, and you should get a shell account with your Web-site package. If you don't get a shell account, make sure that you otherwise get Telnet capability. Telnet provides you a way to control the ISP's computer system remotely (within the perimeters allowed by your ISP), an essential capability needed to operate a Web site that includes a database application.

- **CGI-BIN access:** Increasingly, you will need to do some CGI scripting to operate a Web site. For some database applications, CGI scripting is often a necessity. Make sure that you have access to a cgi-bin directory.

- **T1:** If your ISP is not using at least one T1 line, that raises the question of whether your ISP is serious about providing good Web-site service. Unfortunately, the presence of a T1 does not solely determine throughput capability. Traffic load, more difficult to evaluate, is a prime determinant too.

- **UNIX:** Windows NT is not as flexible as UNIX in providing Web-site service. An ISP running UNIX can probably give you better service in most cases. Most ISPs run UNIX.

- **Storage space:** The amount of hard disk storage space included in the package and the cost of additional storage space are important considerations.

- **Gopher:** If you need Gopher, make sure that the service package offered includes it.

- **Listserv:** If you plan to use a mailing list, often a basic Web-site package will include one Listserv with additional Listservs costing extra.

In addition to essential services, some ISPs offer extras that you may need. If the ISP offers enough extras, an ISP may be considered a Value Added Network, in effect. Extras might include the following:

➡ **Database systems:** Database engines are essential for creating a Web-database application.

➡ **Specialized Web servers:** Secure Web servers and other Web servers with specialized capability may be desirable.

➡ **Internet protocols:** Both traditional (that is, WAIS) and nontraditional (that is, Real Audio) Internet protocols *not* provided in a standard ISP package may be needed.

➡ **Windows NT:** Some server software, database engines, or database middleware may run only on Windows NT, and a service offering both UNIX and Windows NT services is desirable.

Also look for ISPs that are well organized. For example, can the ISP provide you with a comprehensive FAQ (Frequently Asked Questions) regarding its business services? A well-written business user's manual? Other aids?

Timeliness

If you use an ISP or a VAN, you may be disappointed when you rely on them to do work for you. Generally, they do a good job of keeping their networks up and running. If they did not, they would not be in business long. On the other hand, they seem to do a poor job of taking care of their customer's special needs *in a timely manner*. The solution for you is to rely upon ISPs as little as possible. Do everything possible yourself, or contract it to a third-party vendor.

Unfortunately, there are certain things that only your ISP can do for you. Fortunately, most of those things have to do with setting up your service or changing the infrastructure regarding your service. Most are one-time tasks, such as establishing your domain names and installing your database engine. Nonetheless, make a conscious and continual effort to keep all tasks possible out of the hands of your ISP. This is one reason that having access to cgi-bin is so important. You don't have to rely on your ISP to do your CGI scripts and test them. Because using a database engine in a Web site requires tasks that cannot be done through HTML forms and can only be done via Telnet or locally at the server site, you will have be *insistent* to keep maintenance tasks out of the hands of your ISPs and *creative* to find ways to do such tasks yourself. Naturally, exceptions to the rule exist, and some ISPs may provide quick service — but don't count on it without ample evidence.

Sharing

This chapter shows you that running a server on the Internet requires money, time, and skill. Perhaps the best and least expensive way to put a high-powered Web site on the Internet is to share. When you use an ISP, you share. You share the ISP's hard disk, computer, software, and T1 lines; and you share the cost of maintenance. However, you do not necessarily have to buy an ISP's package of services in order to share. Most ISP are small enough that you can negotiate with them to share the desired digital assets that you need to obtain.

For example, if you reach the conclusion that you need your own Web server, you might negotiate to have an ISP run it on the ISP's computer for you. In some circumstances, more than one Web server can efficiently run simultaneously on a computer. Or suppose that you need to run your own server on your own computer to maintain an adequate Web site for your situation. Why not install your computer on the ISP's premises and share the ISP's T1 lines? This is called a *co-host*. There are many possibilities. One of the authors sent a hard disk to be installed on an ISP's computer to provide a half gigabyte of storage space at no additional cost over the normal monthly service fee. Look upon ISPs as an opportunity to share at a reasonable cost whatever you need, and you will come up with some creative proposals.

Co-hosting

When you put your computer on an ISP's premises with an Ethernet card to connect to your ISP's network, you are connected to your ISP's T1 line at a comparatively low cost (less than $200 per month in some places). To keep the cost low, you must retain the responsibility for managing the software (servers), which you can do remotely. Occasionally, you may have to call your ISP on the phone and ask someone to physically reboot the computer. Otherwise, remote management works well. Co-hosting a Windows NT or OS/2 computer can be a cost effective system. Keep in mind, however, that remote management does take time and effort.

Other Services

Of course, you'll need content for your site and pages to present it. Let's look at some of these services.

HTML programming

HTML programming does not necessarily cost as much as UNIX programming. Nonetheless, the typical ISP may charge you for HTML programming at the same high rate. Why? Because the UNIX programmers will do the work. Ironically, UNIX programmers do not necessarily make adequate desktop publishers or Web-site designers. It's probably better to take your business elsewhere. Basic HTML programming should cost somewhat more than desktop publishing work, but not too much more. Advanced HTML programming will cost more. You can find specialized Web-development firms or Web-service bureaus offering such services. Freelancers will charge less than firms. As mentioned elsewhere in this book, HTML programming is not difficult, and you can do it yourself if you want to spend the time. You can learn HTML as quickly and as easily as desktop publishing. HTML programming, however, is not the only skill you need.

Web-site design

You also need someone to design your Web system. This skill varies widely in price. Imaginative Web-site design costs a premium over routine HTML programming. If you pay a premium, make sure that you are getting the quality that justifies the premium price. If you have an active Web site where the presentation format as well as the content change constantly, then Web-system design becomes an ongoing task rather than a one-time, up-front task.

Programming

General Web work, as well as running servers, requires general UNIX programming. Your activities online will be limited without such programming. A programmer must be able to write CGI scripts. Almost certainly you will use a few CGI scripts in your Web site. For an elaborate Web site, you will undoubtedly use many CGI scripts as well as Java applications. Some of them may be complex. For example, you can embed a loan amortization calculator in a Web document with CGI scripting or Java. Such industry-specific programming enhances a Web site considerably. CGI scripts cost from $50 to thousands of dollars. After they are written, you must test and tune them. In many cases, it will take the programmer as much time, or more, to test them as to write them.

Web sites running on Windows NT may require programming almost as much as sites running on UNIX. The languages used for CGI scripting may be different in some cases, but the purpose is the same. It often takes programming to customize a major Web site to fit a particular use.

Database programming

If you plan to use a database application in your Web site, you will need a database programmer to create the database application. Such programmers cost about the same as general UNIX programmers, and many general UNIX programmers are capable of programming a UNIX database application. In any event, a database programmer working on Web-database applications must be able to write CGI scripts. There are, of course, many database applications that can only be programmed by an expert database programmer or a team of such expert programmers.

Nonetheless, if you have the time, you can do much yourself without programming by using certain Web-database development tools, assuming that your database application is not complex. Alternatively, one of your nonprogrammer but computer-expert employees can do useful Web-database applications by using nonprogrammer tools. A few of the Web-database development tools for nonprogrammers have already evolved substantially; if you can create a database application yourself with a PC desktop database engine, you can probably make it work on the Web, too.

Copywriting

For any marketing information, the writing is crucial and takes a special skill provided by copywriters. If you already have marketing materials, you may be able to use them online with little or no alteration. If you don't have existing materials, you may need a copywriter. You can do it yourself if you are a knowledgeable copywriter. Otherwise, it's well worth it to hire someone.

Color graphics

Color graphics, such as digital art and photographs, are the spice of the Web. You should not take their quality lightly. You will want to hire a digital artist to handle your color work. Today, many artists specialize in doing work for Web presentations.

It's amazing what you can do yourself with the graphics programs available today if you have any artistic talent. Unfortunately, graphics work is terribly time-consuming — and when done by the untalented, terribly unappealing.

Creating content

For marketing purposes, most businesses must publish some kind of information or entertainment to lure potential customers to a Web site. This may simply require professional writing. On the other hand, it may require the talents and services of a range of skilled people, such as graphic artists, audio engineers, videographers, and interactivity consultants. It is very difficult to put a price on this kind of work. If you hire Danielle Steel to create content, you will pay a lot; in contrast, you can hire the authors of this book for a small fraction of Ms. Steel's fee. You can also license content that someone else has already created. This may be the least expensive means of acquiring content of good quality. All writing and art must measure up to standards of commercial quality. Quality standards have proven to be just as appropriate for the Internet as they are for any other medium.

Repurposing content

Many businesses will recycle (*repurpose*) content that they already have. In some cases, this means publishing materials on the Web that are already in digital form. In other cases, it means digitizing materials in order to publish them on the Web. Whatever the case, do not overlook the potential use of existing information on a Web site to create marketing appeal. Such existing content often provides a viable alternative to creating new content and is less expensive, too.

Beyond marketing, many business will have reasons to repurpose information on the Web to cut expenses or to make the information more widely available to customers — or even employees. Whatever the reasons for repurposing, consider carefully the cost and process of repurposing in planning your Web site.

Project management

A digital multimedia producer best fits the role of managing the production of a Web site. A person with such experience can hire and oversee the other skilled people needed to create a high-quality Web presentation. After all, a Web presentation is simply a multimedia presentation placed online. After the presentation has been created, in many cases, you can turn it over to someone else for ongoing management. Although the experience of Webmasters today is measured in months rather than years, you can find experienced professionals.

Operations management

Someone has to manage your computer and server programs. As mentioned earlier, that's a UNIX programmer. Managing the computer and the servers is, in most cases, a day-to-day job.

In addition, however, someone also has to manage the presentation in the Web site and the database application day to day. This task falls to the Webmaster. The requirement for managing the these depends on how often you change documents and how often you input data. It could be an hourly, daily, weekly, or monthly job.

Marketing your site

Publicizing a Web site involves announcing your site in the usual ways, such as issuing press releases to publications. In addition, there are great opportunities to tell the Internet community about your site by using directory listings such as Yahoo. Many of these are free. Submit-It! (`www.submit-it.com`) helps you speed up the process by using an HTML form to collect data from you about your Web site and then sending it to 20 of the most popular directories/search engines with a just a few clicks of your mouse. Promote-it! lists Submit-it! and another hundred or so lists, broken down by category. See the following URL:

```
http://www.iTools.com/promote-it/promote-it.html.
```

Marketing on the Web is beyond the scope of this book. Be advised, however, that effective marketing on the Web takes time, energy, and money, just as any type of marketing does. Setting up your Web site and just waiting for the masses to come is not likely to be effective.

New business tasks

If making your database available in a Web site will generate new business for you, you will have to be ready to handle such business. For example, who will process the additional orders? Who will answer the e-mail? Who will market in the newsgroups? Because ultimately the Web is just another medium, existing personnel handling other media may be able to take on these tasks. In many cases, however, new employees may be required, or you may need to contract new services.

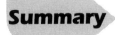

Summary

Estimate equipment costs and software costs. Get quotes for phone-line alternatives. Check on the costs of Internet connections. Estimate UNIX programmer personnel costs or other programming costs. Finally, add up your installation charges. This process gives you an idea of what it costs to run your own server. If you don't run your own server, however, you need not calculate this figure, because your alternative is to rent space on the hard disk of an ISP.

In addition to running your own server or obtaining Internet service from an ISP, evaluate the tasks needed for your Web project as outlined in this chapter and anticipate the services required to perform such tasks. Estimate the time you have to devote to these tasks. Get cost estimates from local firms or freelancers on what it will cost you to get these tasks done if you do not do them yourself. Assess the capability and availability of your employees to do the tasks and the cost of extra employees that may be needed. Don't forget the cost of additional in-house computer equipment that you may need to get the job done efficiently. And, finally, make a careful evaluation of your software requirements.

Case Studies

19

Any of thousands of great ways are suitable for using a database on the Web. This chapter explores some success stories. These stories are about people who have taken their ideas and made them real on the Web — using databases. This is a small sampling of the growing number of live Web sites using this new technology. The authors chose these case studies for their interesting applications. Nonprogrammers using the new Web-database development tools for nonprogrammers may be able to emulate or duplicate these examples.

Yellow Pages and White

URL: http://www.wyp.net

Edwin Rutsch has undertaken a huge project, which he first envisioned in December of 1994. He put the 12 million entries for the North American Yellow Pages on the Internet in 1995. Then he put the 90 million entries for the North American white pages on the Internet in 1996. In other words, you now have, at your fingertips, essentially all the phone books for the U.S. and Canada at no cost to you other than an Internet connection. Mr. Rutsch is providing this resource to promote his company, World Wide Web Virtual Office Design, a full-service Web developer in El Cerrito, California.

The Web site World Yellow Pages (wyp.net) requires 36GB of hard disk space and resides on two Pentiums using Windows NT. A Macintosh Quadra 800 also provides services to the system. The site is connected to the Internet via a fractional T1 (128 bps), which can be increased in bandwidth as needed. WebSite (O'Reilly & Associates) is the Web server. Oracle is the database engine.

About 20 people, from digital artists to Oracle programmers, have contributed to getting the site online, none of them full time. The Oracle database application was created new for the project. The requisite Web-database engine connection was created in Oraperl (an Oracle variation of Perl), and the database application was created in SQL Plus, Oracle's version of SQL. A number of Web-database development tools were considered, but developers felt that a development tool might encumber the system with too much overhead for the amount of data to be processed. The amount of data is so massive that the process took seven days of computer cranking to *index* the white pages. The data is text, and BLOBs are not used.

In addition to listing names and phone numbers, World Yellow Pages provides you with the opportunity to plug in your own Web page. You can input the database, place up to 300 words of text, and exit to see your work. If you don't like what you've done, you can go back and edit your entry at any time. This service is free.

The public seems to love the site, according to Mr. Rutsch, who receives e-mail from site visitors. He has responded to visitor suggestions by changing the system to make it easier. Currently, he and his colleagues are working on a keyword search mechanism that will add substantial search power. He also wants to expand the capability of the system eventually, in order to provide anyone who wants it with the opportunity to have a full-fledged Web site within the database system. Of course, he will charge for the additional capability.

Clearly, this is not the type of Web-database system a nonprogrammer can run out and create on the Web without any programming help. Nonetheless, World Yellow Pages shows what a massive project a few dedicated people can do with readily available, reasonably priced hardware and software.

Microsoft Access on the Web

URL: http://www.shenwebworks.com/

Mark Seder works from his rural home in the beautiful Shenandoah Valley in Virginia. He hosts Web sites with databases on his Pentium Pro 200. The Pentium runs on Windows NT. His business, Shenandoah Web Works, is featured on Microsoft's Web site as one of the first sites to bring Microsoft Access to the Web. One of the more entertaining features he hosts is the Clark County Fair. Here, a map of the fairgrounds becomes the entrance to the schedule of events database. The image map shows a bird's eye view of the fairgrounds. If a visitor clicks on the *Grand Stands/Stage* area (see the mouse pointer in Figure 19-1), the Web server goes to the database and builds a look-up document for the Grand Stand schedule of events. A visitor can click again to select a day of the week and view that day's schedule (Figure 19-2).

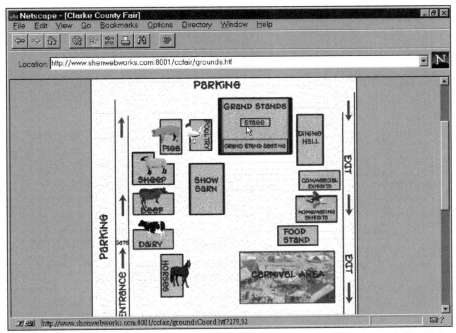

Figure 19-1: Clicking on the Grand Stands shows you a schedule of events that is in an Access database.

The architecture used for this and many of the Shenandoah Web sites includes the Microsoft Access database and WebBase by Expertelligence (www.expertelligence.com). WebBase sits on the Web server and uses Microsoft's Internet Information Server (IIS) utility to communicate with the Access database. WebBase formats the query documents and the results documents on the fly from templates you design in WebBase. No scripts and no programming are required.

The best feature, in Mr. Seder's eyes, is the speed and ease of implementing new applications with this architecture. For example, he created a small application for an HTML course he taught recently. Students filled in an online questionnaire. The answers went directly to the Access database. After completing the questionnaire, WebBase generated a Certificate of Completion for the course that the students could print out as their proof that they completed the course. All this took "half a day!"

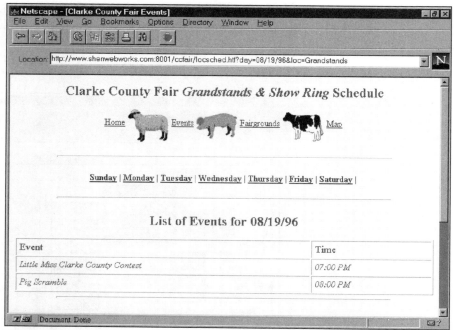

Figure 19-2: The schedule document generated by WebBase.

The applications sometimes run slowly, however, and Mr. Seder is tracking down the causes. He suspects it's some combination of WebBase, a 28.8 Kbps modem, and phone lines. Overall, though, visitors to his sites approve of the response time and the ease of use. Besides the County Fair, Shenandoah Web Works hosts:

- **Market Place.** A listing of local businesses.
- **Real Estate.** Two searchable databases of local real estate.
- **Chamber of Commerce.** A listing of events, members.

WebBase may not be the optimal Web-database development tool for nonprogrammers. It is easy to see, however, how nonprogrammers might use a more appropriate tool to emulate Mr. Seder's good work.

Fido the Shopping Doggie

URL: http://www.shopfido.com/

This innovative service enables a shopper to search for any item in its database, view a short description of items that match the search criteria, and then go to the vendor's site to make purchases. In other words, this is like a shopping mall, but the vendors all have their own Web sites independent of Fido. Fido is just a shopping doggie, and he does not get involved in purchasing or in maintaining or hosting Web sites for the vendors. The vendors set up their Web site as they want, and then get their products listed in Fido's database. Fido started in July, 1995, and was originally a free service for both shoppers and vendors. Now that Fido has 140,000 products from 100 vendors, it is charging vendors to join the database. Shopping is still free. Figure 19-3 shows the beginning of a listing as a visitor searches for shoes. The list begins with the lowest-priced items and goes to the highest-priced ones.

Figure 19-3: A search for shoes over $100 turns up five items from three different vendors.

Search by any word you want, and also specify a price range (from 0 to $100,000) to find items. Fido is beginning to categorize all its items so that you now can narrow your search to within categories, such as Food, Games, or Clothing.

Fido uses a typical interface for the query and the resulting HTML documents on the Web server. Fido uses the freeware server software called NCSA HTTP-D for UNIX. The search executes CGI scripts written in C. The query results are formatted into an HTML document with tables (if you want) or as a simple list. Each item in the list contains a hyperlink that goes directly to the correct product page in the vendor's Web site.

Fido is smart — he uses a unique and powerful set of tools to take information from a vendor's Web site and place it into his own database. It took two person-months to create the original Fido, and several person-years to perfect it. Behind the scenes, here's how it works:

➡ The Continuum staff briefly reviews a vendor's site. There are certain restrictions on the kind of Web site that Fido can process because an automated program does most of the work. For example, Fido needs to have every item's price and description on the same page. In other words, if you have one page for the description, and another for the price, Fido cannot process it. If the site passes the restrictions test, the Continuum staff takes a small sample of typical Web pages for use as example pages for the entire vendor site. Special identifiers placed in the pages mark item names, prices, descriptions, and categories.

➡ A spider crawls through the vendor's site, collecting all the pages from the site. Continuum uses the Harvest Gatherer, which is freeware. The pages are copied into files on an Alpha WMP parallel processor, a very speedy and powerful computer.

➡ A custom-written, machine-learning facility converts the vendor's Web pages into records for the database. This facility takes the sample pages and applies complex logic to each page's content, reading it and picking out the item name, price, description, and category. It uses an English language lexical pattern matcher called FLEX to help in the task.

➡ The database receives the new records. There are no graphics in the database or on the Fido site. Continuum, Inc. custom-wrote the database, which resides on a UNIX computer.

➡ A C program then extracts three text files for use by the Web server when performing searches. The first is a complete product list with all the details. The second is a keyword index file for quick searches by keywords. The third is an index of products by price to speed up the sorting of selected products.

➡ If a vendor's site changes, the process is repeated for the new or changed pages.

Fido caught the attention of the Wall Street journal recently and has received several awards for excellence and innovation.

It's not likely that a nonprogrammer would have participated in the construction of this Web site. Still, this site shows you the power of database technology on the Web. There's no reason that a nonprogrammer can't play a significant role in constructing a similar site today by using one of the new Web-database development tools for nonprogrammers.

A Mall for a Crystal Ball

URL: http://www.markvar.com

Glen Benson, in Phoenix, Arizona, created the Crystal Mall for a client. Although Mr. Benson is a programmer, he used simple Web technology to develop this Web site — where almost every Web document is generated by an Access database application. Mr. Benson used Visual Basic 3.0 and Access 2.0. O'Reilly's WebSite is the server. He runs the site on a Pentium, using Windows NT, a 28.8 Kbps modem, and a dedicated phone line. He also has other unrelated Web sites set up for other clients, using identical hardware and software.

This Web site offers free daily astrological readings. The information changes each day and is stored in the Access database application. A visitor registers by providing a set of information, including time and date of birth (see Figure 19-4). Thereafter, a visitor need only provide a user name and password to get a precise daily horoscope. The daily readings are generated by the Web-database application in the form of HTML documents, and each reading is custom-made for the visitor requesting it (see Figure 19-5). How does he keep track of visitors? He uses Access and the authentication function in the WebSite server.

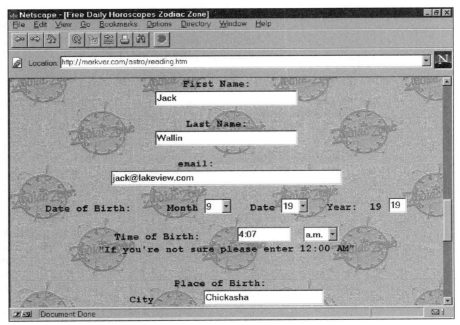

Figure 19-4: Input for daily horoscope.

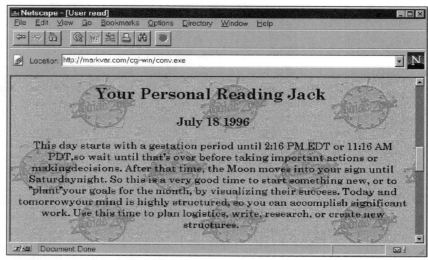

Figure 19-5: A daily horoscope.

Then you have the Stargate Romance Connection. This provides a visitor with an opportunity to put a personal profile into the Web-database application without charge. For a $10 fee, a visitor can add a digital photograph, too. Currently, the database holds more than 17,000 profiles. After a visitor has submitted a profile, he or she can browse the existing profiles, looking for a potential mate, or submit queries based on certain criteria. The Web-database application can even match you up automatically. Naturally, the profiles include personal astrological information.

This interesting Web site has a book catalog and things for sale, as well as other features. Mr. Benson indicates that the daily astrological readings are very popular, as is the Stargate Romance Connection. He believes that dynamic, useful information that changes often is the key to a successful Web site, and he uses the Web-database application to enable that concept at the Crystal Mall. The biggest limitation, he indicates, is the bandwidth. He is in the process of moving the server computer to his ISP's premises in order to get connected to a T1 line and eliminate the cost of the dedicated phone line.

Mr. Benson likes Windows NT and finds his Web-database application adequate. Nonetheless, he plans to upgrade the entire system soon with later versions of the software he has been using. Additionally, he is interested in the possibility of substituting Cold Fusion for Visual Basic to develop the Web-database application further.

A nonprogrammer is not going to use Visual Basic to create a Web-database application. This Web site demonstrates, however, that Access is a practical choice for some Web-database applications.

Listings, Texas Style

URL: http://www.texnet.com

Anthony Perkins, in Arlington, Texas, has created a public Web site for the Metroplex Region Multiple Listing Service (MLS) serving the Fort Worth area (www.texnet.com). It includes the listing information for about 10,000 properties. The system runs on a Pentium using Windows NT. The Web site connects to an ISP via a dedicated ISDN line. Microsoft SQL Server 6.0 provides the database horsepower. Mr. Perkins uses a developer's tool — WebBase (www.expertelligence.com) — to do all programming, including the database programming.

The listings include text and photographs; occasionally, audio files are used, too. Mr. Perkins created the database application from the ground up, and he now manages the Web site. An HTML form offers about 20 inputs (see Figure 19-6), and each visitor's choices are preserved for one hour, even if the visitor leaves the Web site and returns. This is accomplished with cookies (see Chapter 28, "Ideas for using Web-Database Technology"). In response to a visitors's choices, the Web-database application delivers Web documents on the fly. The first document is a list of properties that match the criteria entered by the visitor in the input document (see Figure 19-7). A visitor may elect to get more comprehensive information on a specific property by clicking on the thumbnail photo of the property, which is a hyperlink to the property's own Web document (see Figure 19-8).

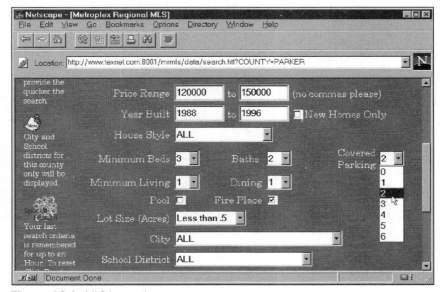

Figure 19-6: MLS input document.

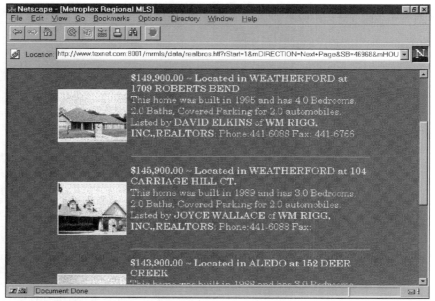

Figure 19-7: MLS property list generated by visitor's input.

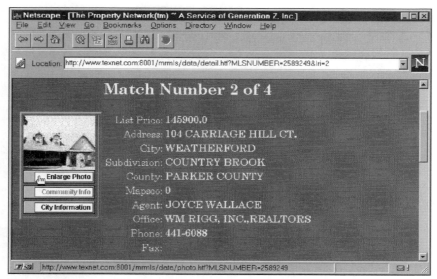

Figure 19-8: A specific property.

Mr. Perkins found learning WebBase to be difficult. After learnng it, however, he saved huge amounts of development time, he says. Mr. Perkins
has also constructed other Web-database applications, some using Access.

He has used WebBase with all of them, and they all run on his Pentium simultaneously.

Currently, Mr. Perkins is looking for a new connection, having outgrown the ISDN line. He is also switching from a Netscape Commerce Server to a Netscape Enterprise Server, which will enable him to use Java and external programming. He hopes to be able to offer interactive mapping to the real-estate public after the switch.

The Web-database application that Mr. Perkins has devised is not something that a nonprogrammer might construct. Still, it illustrates that SQL Server, which includes easy-to-use Web-database development tools in version 6.5, is suited to enabling a high-performance Web site.

ETI Sales — Private Internet

URL: Private

Here's a Web site created by InterID, Inc. (http://www.interid.com) for use by ETI Sales. InterID hosts many Oracle Web-database applications for its clients. The ETI Sales application is an excellent example of using the power of the Internet for distributed computer applications. In this case, ETI Sales has salespeople around the country who must know all the facts about the customers or potential customers they are to see that day. There may have been prior sales calls by other salespeople. Customers may have bought items in the past. A single central Oracle database in New York holds all the information for the ETI Sales customers and leads.

A salesperson in Dallas needs to know about calls and meetings scheduled for the day. She sits down with her laptop computer and telephone and connects to the Internet to find out her schedule. She logs into a secure site on the Internet, using a user name and password. At the Web site, she uses a query form to find her leads for the day. She can query by category, location, company name, dates, and a host of other criteria. All the data she needs is at her fingertips. Everything is up to date and accessible by all the salespeople. This is a great advantage to the sales force, because they can share their information very efficiently. She has a better chance of earning commissions when she's armed with good, current data about her prospects.

The query form is an HTML document that resides on an Oracle Web Server on a Windows NT computer. The server uses Microsoft's Internet Information Server (IIS) to send the query criteria to the Oracle database (see Figure 19-9). This starts up a stored procedure — written in PL/SQL — in the database. The procedure takes the query criteria, plugs them into the SQL query, and executes the query. The results are formatted into an HTML document, which is returned to IIS. PL/SQL creates the entire HTML document within the database.

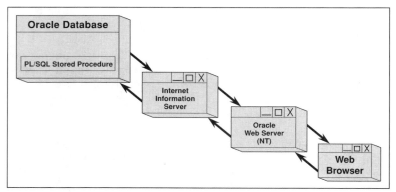

Figure 19-9: *All HTML documents are created on the fly inside the Oracle database with PL/SQL.*

The sales staff received this new application with much excitement. They say the best feature is that it's so easy to get all the client history you need. Critical data is available to you no matter where you are. For the programmers and analysts who maintain the system, their favorite feature is the fact that it uses PL/SQL, with which they are familiar. It also performs well, giving respectable response time to queries from the Web.

This application has no graphics, because graphics are not really needed for sales data. One of InterID's demonstration applications uses graphics, however, as shown in Figure 19-10.

The next enhancement planned for the system incorporates remote updates to the database by sales staff in the field. This improvement is in the pilot-project stage now. Today, all the updates happen centrally, using data called in or faxed in from around the country.

Although this is a substantial Web-database application supported by programmers, it shows how Web database applications can be used internally, whether on an intranet or on the Internet, for an organization's own personnel.

Job Bank

URL: http://www.isgjobs.com/

This Web site was created by Informatics Search Group, an employment search service in Ontario, Canada. The online job search (Figure 19-11) uses a Sun Sparc 10 computer. The database where the job data is actually stored does not reside on the Web at all. It is on a Windows NT computer in an Access database. BestWebPro, by Bestseller, Inc. (www.bestseller.com), enables developing this two-stage application.

Figure 19-10: An Oracle database with graphics retrieved into an HTML document created on the fly.

BestWebPro lives in the Windows NT PC where the database resides. The HTML documents are designed in BestWebPro without any programming. BestWebPro pulls data out of the database into a set of flat files, which are the following:

- **Search file.** This file is a flat text-only file of all data needed for the queries.

- **Template file.** This file contains the HTML template used to format the results documents. For example, headers and footers and information on how to display the results go in this file.

- **Index file.** An index file facilitates quicker retrieval of data from the search file.

Finally, BestWebPro generates a set of CGI scripts that connect the application to the Web server. The files and the CGI scripts are moved onto the Web server. This entire application was designed and implemented in about two weeks — with no programming. Three times a week, BestWebPro extracts a new set of files for the Web server. The process requires only a few minutes.

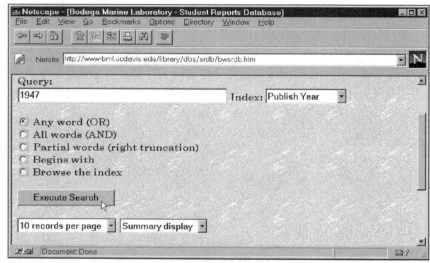

Figure 19-11: The search screen for this BestWebPro-generated database site.

The advantage of using CGI scripts and text files is their speed. The application has been online for two months, listing about 150 jobs. There have been no crashes and no complaints. The support staff is also very happy with this solution because it is so easy to use and it can search on multiple fields. The old system that it replaced was not nearly as flexible and tended to be unstable.

A future enhancement to this site involves putting the Access database on the Web and using BestWebPro to search it directly. No graphics are stored in the database, although BestWebPro supports this feature.

Tide Tables

http://www-bml.ucdavis.edu

Paul Heinrich is the computer resource specialist for the Bodega Marine Laboratory at Bodega Bay, California, an organized research unit of the University of California at Davis. Being a scientist, he also helps with various research projects on a volunteer basis, but the Web site occupies him full-time. He has put the tide tables for Bodega Bay on the Lab's Web site, and you can query the tide tables to get local tide information (see Figure 19-12).

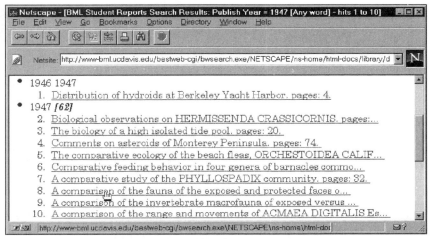

Figure 19-12: Tide information resulting from a query.

The Web site, which is used mostly by local researchers, students, faculty, and other marine laboratories, also offers two libraries via Web-database applications. One publishes student reports going back to 1920. This library is very popular with Web-site visitors, because this information was unavailable except locally before the Web site was constructed (see Figures 19-13 through 19-15). The other library offers the publications of researchers and is similar.

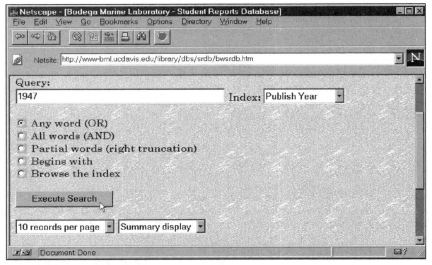

Figure 19-13: Input for a student report query.

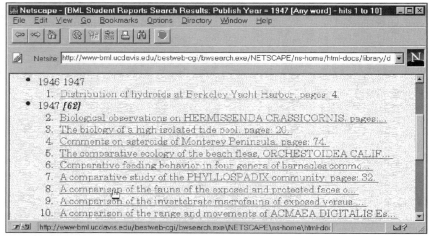

Figure 19-14: Results of the student report query.

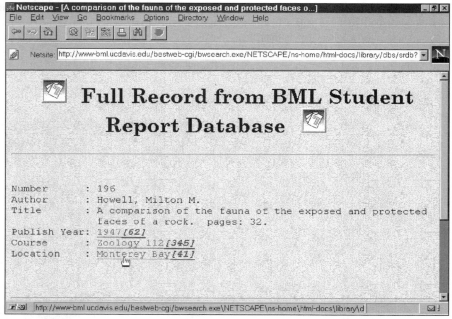

Figure 19-15: A student report description.

Mr. Heinrich is currently working on putting the Lab's library card catalog online, as well as a system of taxonomic keys, which will lead to research information. Both will be Web-database applications.

The Lab uses a Pentium running Windows NT and connects to the University of California network via a T1 line. Netscape Enterprise Server provides the HTTP horsepower.

For the tide tables, Mr. Heinrich used a flat-file that he imported into Excel and subsequently exported into Access. He then used BestWebPro to create a Web-database application with simple queries. Mr. Heinrich is not a programmer, so he used no scripting, SQL, or other programming. For the student reports and research publications, he used an InMagic database application and then used BestWebPro to create the Web-database application. Both of these library applications provide convenient search capabilities and hyperlinking, and they generate all Web documents on the fly. This site shows that a nonprogrammer can do some interesting and useful Web-site construction using Web-database applications.

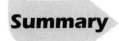

Summary

As you can see, the authors were not able to come up with many examples created by nonprogrammers. Perhaps this book will help change that situation. Nonetheless, the case studies show that it doesn't take a large organization to employ Web-database technology. They also show a surprising number of people using Access in one way or another to provide database horsepower for the Web.

Art Gallery Database Project

An art gallery on the Web can be tedious to visit. By nature, graphics of good quality are large files. Visitors may find themselves waiting several minutes to see just a few images. Imagine a gallery where the visitors can first screen the art they want to see by categories. After that, they see small—that is, fast loading—thumbnail versions of the artworks they selected. After scrolling through these miniature pictures, the visitors click on one to see the entire image. In this example, our visitor knows it is worth the extra minute to see the larger, more detailed picture. Gallery Online, this book's art gallery project, has just that kind of feature.

Project Overview

This database project shows you the basics of how to take a visitor's input and deliver a custom-made HTML document to him or her based on his or her input; that is, a custom-made document created on the fly.

This database project is an art gallery with two tables. One table contains information on the artists. The other table contains the art and details on the art. The key column, artist_id, relates the two tables. A visitor can make a query requesting any of the following items (see Figure 20-1):

➦ Artist's works by artist's last name

➦ Artist's works by artist's specialty

➦ Artist's works by artist's city

➦ Artist's works by artist's state

➡ Art works by media

➡ Art works by school of art

➡ Art works by subject matter

➡ Art works by colors

A query returns a custom-made HTML document generated on the fly especially for the visitor, based on the visitor's input (see Figure 20-2). The document contains all works of art in the art gallery that match the query. Thus, it gives the visitor just the artworks he or she asks for and nothing more.

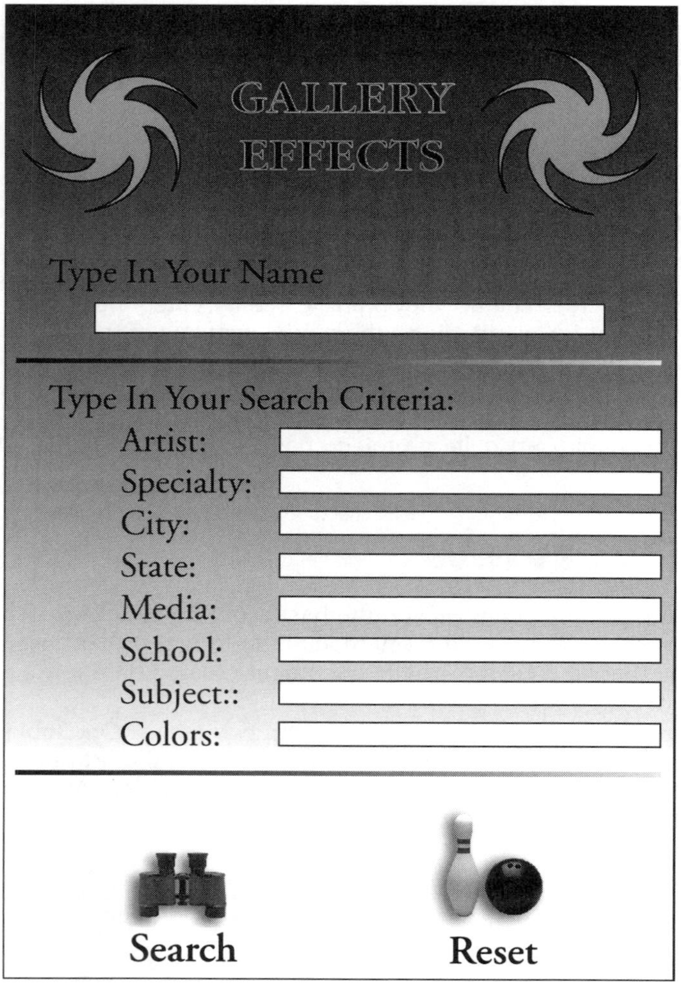

Figure 20-1: Art Gallery Online.

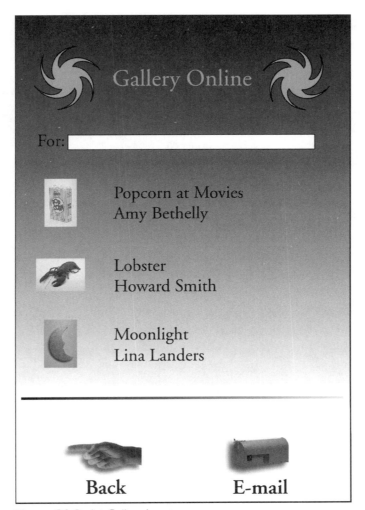

Figure 20-2: Art Gallery input.

Project Details

The Web document (Web page) generated on the fly actually contains thumbnail representations of the artworks returned by the query. If a visitor desires to see a larger version of a particular artwork, the thumbnail is a hyperlink to the full-size version. Additionally, each thumbnail connects the artist's name and a link to the information on the artist. Thus, the query uses data from both tables to create the Web document on the fly.

The Art Gallery tables

Following are the Art Gallery Online database tables:

```
Table 1: ARTIST
col                  name              datatype       comment
-----------------    --------------    ----------     ------------
artist_id            number(3)         ID number      PRIMARY KEY
first_name           varchar2(10)
middle_name          varchar2(10)
last_name            varchar2(16)
jr_suffix            varchar2(3)
salutation           varchar2(4)
firm_name            varchar2(50)
address              varchar2(50)
city                 varchar2(18)
state                varchar2(18)
zip                  varchar2(12)
phone                varchar2(16)
fax                  varchar2(16)
email                varchar2(33)
specialty            varchar2(33)                     primary media
marketing_text       varchar2(200)              marketing paragraph
resume_text          varchar2(1000)               narrative resume
artist_photo_logo    GIF                            photo or logo

Table 2: ARTWORK
col                  name              datatype       comment
-----------------    --------------    ----------     ----------------
work_id              number(3)         catalog ID     PRIMARY KEY
artist_id            number(3)         ID number      FOREIGN KEY
title                varchar2(60)                     name of work
creation_date        date                        date work created
media                varchar2(30)                 media of original
school               varchar2(30)                 school/style of art
subject              varchar2(30)                 subject matter of art
art_desc             varchar2(200)                description of art
colors               varchar2(80)                  describes colors
price                money                           price in dollars
width_inches         number(3,2)                     width in inches
height_inches        number(3,2)                    height in inches
depth_inches         number(3,2)                     depth in inches
pixel_width          number(4,0)          width of digital graphic
pixel_height         number(4,0)         height of digital graphic
filename             varchar2(30)             name of graphic file
thumbname            varchar2(30)           name of thumbnail file
copyright_year       number(4,0)                  year of copyright
copyright_owner      varchar2(40)            name of copyright owner
```

The middle variables in the preceding lists are the datatypes for each column. The datatypes shown are Oracle datatypes. Varchar2 is a datatype for text. The number denotes the maximum length of data in the column.

By looking at the column names, you can determine the contents of most of the columns. The columns in the artwork table called pixel_width and pixel_height are used to program the pixel width and height into the HTML image markup in the document template. This programming enables the graphics file containing the artwork GIF to download more quickly.

As you can see, this example is not complex. It is simple and straightforward, but it demonstrates the power of using a database in a Web site. You can easily do this yourself as the first step toward learning to create a more intricate Web-database system.

Database engine

This database application uses a database engine (Oracle in one example and Access in the other) to handle the queries. Although it is not impossible to create relational queries against multiple tables by using CGI scripts, why reinvent the database engine by using CGI programming? It might be very expensive, particularly for a complex or extensive database application.

Graphics

This example handles graphics two ways: inside the database itself and outside the database with the filename stored in the database. If the database application cannot store graphics (BLOBs), the filenames of the graphics can be stored in the database application as text. The graphics themselves can be stored in an appropriate directory (folder) and hyperlinked to the HTML document by the filename and path. In this example, the ARTIST table contains graphics in the artist_photo_logo column. However, the ARTWORK table does not contain graphics. Instead, it stores the filenames of the graphics (the filename column) and the thumbnails (the thumbname column).

Text

Note that some columns in the tables are large (for example, resume_text, 1000 characters). That means they contain a number of sentences or paragraphs rather than just words or phrases. This observation brings up two important questions: First, how do you get the text into the database tables? If you can obtain the text in digital form, you can simply copy and paste (no typing required). One easy way to obtain text in electronic form is to require the information to be submitted by e-mail. For example, some of the artists submitted information by answering a questionnaire by e-mail. If you can't get it in digital form, someone must type it in.

Second, does your database engine allow you to create columns that hold many characters? Most do, but you may want to verify the maximum column sizes for text datatypes before you begin to gather information from the artists or other sources.

HTML Documents

The Art Gallery uses four HTML documents. First is the query document, where visitors enter their names and their query input (see Figure 20-3). It contains the following:

- Web-site header GIF
- Visitor's name (data entry box)
- Horizontal line
- Query Box: Artist's last name
- Query Box: Artist's Specialty
- Query Box: Artist's City
- Query Box: Artist's State
- Query Box: Artwork Media
- Query Box: Artwork's School of Art
- Query Box: Artwork's Subject Matter
- Query Box: Artwork's Colors
- Horizontal line
- Web-site buttons

The second HTML document is the catalog of artworks, a document generated on the fly in response to a visitor's query (such as a custom-made page for the visitor). It contains the following:

- Web-site header GIF
- Visitor's name
- Thumbnail GIFs (as generated by the query)

- Title of artwork (for each GIF)
- Artist's name (for each GIF)
- Horizontal line
- Web-site buttons

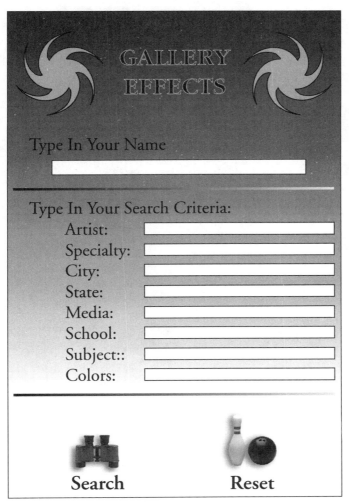

Figure 20-3: The query document contains a graphic banner and query form boxes.

Figure 20-4: The catalog of artworks is the first document generated by a visitor's query.

The third HTML document is for an individual work of art (see Figure 20-5). The thumbnail GIF in the second document is a hyperlink to this document. This document contains the following:

➥ Web-site small header GIF

➥ Full-size GIF of artwork

- Title of artwork
- Artist's name
- Original media
- Creation date
- Dimensions
- School
- Subject
- Colors
- Description
- Price
- E-mail order form
- Horizontal line
- Web-site buttons

The fourth HTML document is for the artist's professional profile (narrative resume, see Figure 20-6). The artist's name in both the second and third documents is a hyperlink to this document. This document contains the following items:

- Web-site small header GIF
- Artist's photo or logo
- Artist's name
- Artist's specialty
- Marketing paragraph
- Professional profile (multiple paragraphs)
- Address, phone, fax
- Horizontal line
- E-mail form
- Horizontal line
- Web-site buttons

Figure 20-7 shows the document system used in the Art Gallery project.

Figure 20-5: The document for an individual work of art shows only one artwork.

As you can see, this section sets the specifications for the documents in the Art Gallery Web site. The documents are manifested in HTML templates into which the Web-database application places data on the fly (that is, like mail merging) to generate the custom Web documents on the fly.

You will do well to create document (template) specifications like those given earlier. It helps you plan the tables in the database application and coordinate the documents with the data. In addition, a quick sketch of the appearance of your documents (see Figures 20-1 through 20-4) can help you convey your ideas to coworkers and HTML programmers as clearly as possible, even though the final documents may look different.

Figure 20-6: The professional profile document tells about one artist.

Custom document

Keep in mind that the second document generated (the catalog of artworks document with the thumbnails of the artworks) is indeed a custom document. It depends directly on a visitor's input for its content. The database application will return only those thumbnails requested by the visitor's query, based on the visitor's input in the first document. If a visitor makes a unique query that no other visitor ever makes, that will be the only time the database application ever generates the resulting Web document.

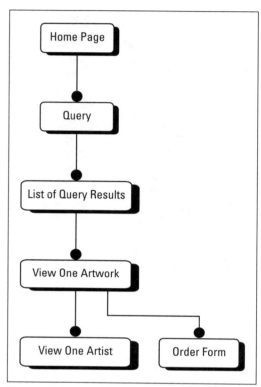

Figure 20-7: The Art Gallery document system.

Summary

When you know what you want to create, what it will look like (roughly), and the features you want to include, you are ready to dive in and create the application.

This database project comes to life in the following four chapters: Chapter 21 "Creating the Oracle Database"; Chapter 22 "Linking the Oracle Database Application to the Web Site"; Chapter 33, "Creating the Access Database Tables"; and Chapter 24 "Connecting the Access Database Application to the Web." These chapters lay the groundwork for your own Web-database applications.

Creating the Oracle Database

In This Chapter

Review of software selected for the project

Establishing a User ID

Creating the tables, indexes, and relationships

Loading data into the tables

Creating graphics files for artwork

In the preceding chapter, you saw the plans for the Art Gallery demonstration. Next, you decide what software you need to implement the plan (see Chapter 16, "Web Database and Database Development Tools"). Now construction can begin. This chapter and the following one lead you through the entire construction and installation process for the Art Gallery. Your final product is a fully functional Web database system.

This chapter covers how to create the tables and load the data into them. The chapter describes, step by step, two different ways to accomplish this task, both with and without Wizards. Don't worry about the Web documents yet.

The next chapter (Chapter 22, "Linking the Oracle Database Application to the Web Site") covers how to create the Web documents and how to use them. It goes through the entire process using two different software products.

Software Selection

The authors have selected Oracle for the database engine because it is one of the most versatile and robust relational database engines available on both the PC and UNIX platforms. The specific database is Personal Oracle 7 (version 7.2) for Windows 95. Keep in mind that Oracle is cross-platform, and presumably a Web-database application developed with this version of Oracle 7 will run on all platforms that have Oracle 7, version 7.2 or later.

The software world offers many tools for Oracle (and other database engines). The following database development tools were used for the Art Gallery project:

➡ **Oracle's Personal Oracle 7 Navigator.** This is a very useful and easy-to-use tool that gives you a graphical method of viewing your database. It contains a Table Wizard for creating tables in a simple step-by-step manner. This software enables you to do nearly all of your administrative tasks without resorting to programming at all. It has good online help screens. You can use it for tasks such as creating new users; adding or removing tables; working with indexes, views and synonyms; and performing database backups and restores. You will see two methods of building the tables (with and without the Wizard).

➡ **Oracle's SQL*Plus.** This is the basic access to the database engine using the SQL programming language. Because the SQL language is so universal, the examples that use this tool translate to many other database products.

Tables Need an Owner — That's You!

First of all, no matter which method of table creation you ultimately choose, you must get connected to your database using a fresh *user ID* created especially for you. You need to create a new user ID only once. After that, you reconnect to that user ID every time you work on your tables, whether it is to add data or to modify the table structures.

Follow these steps:

1. **Start the Personal Oracle 7 Navigator.** Double-click on the Local Database label in the left window. Then double-click on the USER label in the left window. A list of users appears in the right window. You need to create a new user ID for the Art Gallery.

2. **Create a new user.** Right-click on the USER label. This opens a little pop-up menu, as shown in Figure 21-1. Click on New. You'll see a window where you define your new user ID. For the Name, type **GALLERY** (uppercase). In the Password area, type **gallery** (lowercase) in the New box (it appears as a row of asterisks). Type **gallery** again in the Confirm box. Click the OK button.

3. **Authorize GALLERY to create database objects.** Double-click on GALLERY in the right window. A window appears with two tabs near the top. Click on the Role/Privilege tab. Click on the Role button. Here, select the word RESOURCE on the right side of the window. Click on the left arrow button in the center of the window to move it to the left (see Figure 21-2). Click OK.

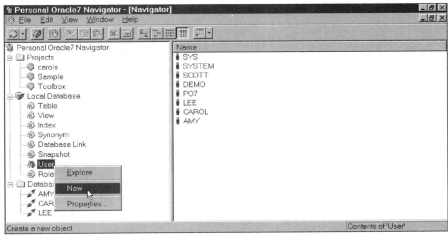

Figure 21-1: Establish a new database user ID in the New User window.

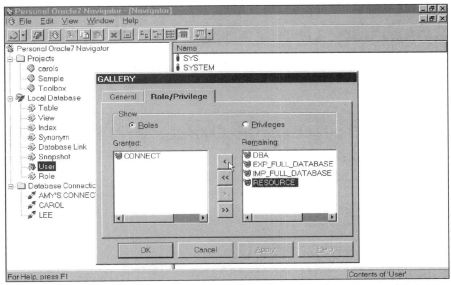

Figure 21-2: Assign the RESOURCE role to GALLERY to allow this user to create tables.

4. **Create a reusable database connection for GALLERY.** Highlight the Database Connection label in the left window. Right-click and select New (as you did to create a new user). Then fill in the boxes as shown in Figure 21-3. The Password box contains the word *gallery* (in lowercase), even though the display shows only asterisks. Hereafter, you double-click on this new database connection whenever you return to the Navigator to work on the Art Gallery.

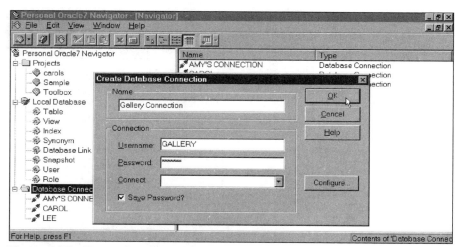

Figure 21-3: After establishing this connection, it is easy to sign on as the GALLERY user ID.

Creating the Tables

The Table Wizard and SQL incorporate powerful tools for designing tables. Let's look at how they do it.

Method 1: Personal Oracle 7 Navigator's Table Wizard

If you are already familiar with Oracle, you may opt for the manual method of creating tables. On the other hand, if you are new to Oracle or new to relational databases, you should use the Table Wizard, as described here.

Here's a tip for selecting good user IDs and passwords

Use a single word or acronym for your new user ID. If you work with a team, you may want to select a user ID that is not personal, such as a project acronym. Choose a password that you can easily remember, such as your middle name, then modify it by changing one letter to a number. A password that contains both numbers and letters is hundreds of times more difficult for a hacker to crack! Write down the name and password you make up here. Put it in a secure place; do not tape it to your monitor!

Create the ARTIST and Artworks tables now

Follow these steps to create the ARTIST table:

1. **Start the Table Wizard.** Double-click on the Gallery Connection in the left window. Then double-click on the Table item that appears just below it. A list of tables appears in the right window. These are sample tables that come with the Oracle database. You need to create a new table, so right-click on Table and select New. This brings up a small window, where you select the Wizard, as you see in Figure 21-4. Click OK to continue.

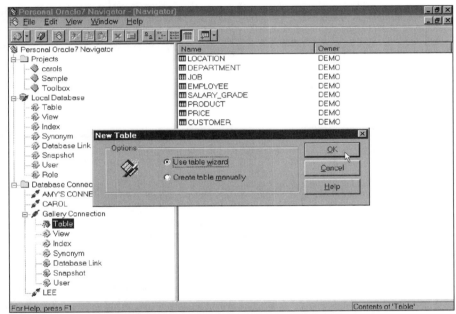

Figure 21-4: Select the Table Wizard to step you through the creation of your first table.

2. **Name the new table.** Type **ARTIST** in the Name box. Click on Next (Figure 21-5.)

3. **Create the first column.** Type **ARTIST_ID** in the Column Name box. Select Number from the Column Type drop-down menu. Either type or select **4** in the Size box. Leave the Scale box at 0 (zero). Click on Next (see Figure 21-6.)

4. **Complete the first column.** This column is the primary key. Therefore, it should never be null. Click on No, It Cannot Be Null. Now, even though it should always be unique, click on No, It Does Not Have To Be Unique. (This appears to be a bug in the Wizard.) The final specifications for this column should look like Figure 21-7. Click the Back button (*not* the Next button).

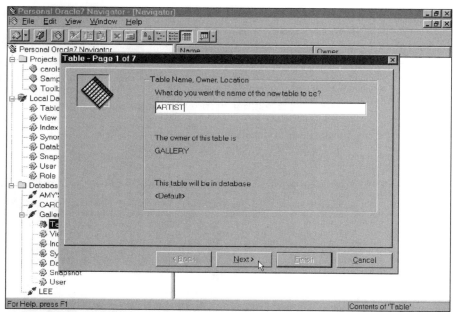

Figure 21-5: Create the ARTIST table first.

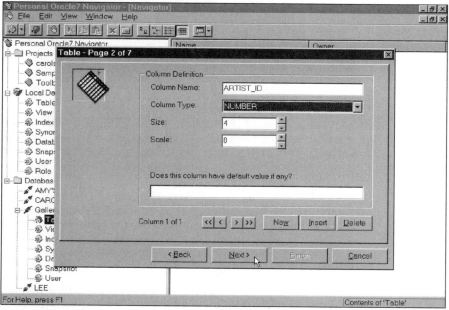

Figure 21-6: The first column in the ARTIST table is named ARTIST_ID.

Navigator's Manual Table window is the in-between method of creating tables

Personal Oracle 7's Navigator not only has the Table Wizard, it also has the Manual Table Creation window. This window enables you to create columns, select their datatypes, name the primary key, assign default values, and so on. The main difference between this and the Wizard is that it is all in a single spreadsheet-type of window rather than guiding you through all the selections for each column. After doing a table or two with the Wizard, you may want to switch to the Manual Table window for the next table. You'll find it faster after you are familiar with your choices. It's an in-between method, because it is not as difficult as writing the actual SQL.

5. **Create the rest of the columns.** Now that you have defined one column, you can go through these two windows to define all the others. Here's how:

    ➥ Get to the first column window by clicking the Back button.

    ➥ In the first column window (Figure 21-6), click on the New button to get a fresh window for your next column. Fill in all the information.

    ➥ Click the Next button to go to the second column window (Figure 21-7). Fill in all the information.

    ➥ Repeat these steps until all your columns are defined.

Here are Oracle's naming standards for tables and columns in a nutshell

* Use numbers and letters and underscores.

* *Do not use* symbols, such as ampersands (&), dollar signs ($), plus signs (+), a vertical bar (|), forward or backslashes (/ \), single quotes (') or double quotes (").

* Avoid blank spaces, but if you must use them, surround the entire column name with single quotation marks.

*The maximum number of characters for a name is 30.

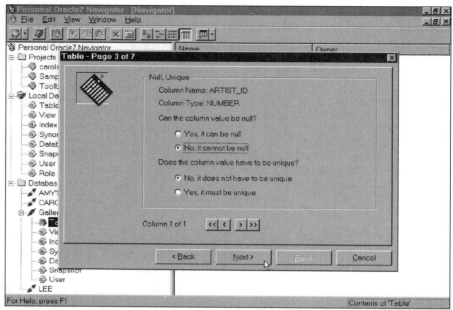

Figure 21-7: The second half of specifying a column uses the Wizard's Page 3 of 7.

6. **Define the Primary Key.** Moving right along, click the Next button until you get to Page 5 of 7. You may be asked to enter the GALLERY password again. If so, type **gallery** and press OK. Skip the Foreign Key page for now. This will be covered later, when you create the ARTWORK table and relate it to the ARTIST table. The Primary Key page creates the basic roadmap to your table (see Figure 21-8). Here you simply click the mouse in the Primary Key column next to the appropriate column name. GALLERY's ARTIST table has a primary key: the ARTIST_ID column. The numeral *1* appears in this box, indicating that ARTIST_ID is the first column in the primary key. In this case, it is also the *only* column in the primary key.

7. **Review the order and type of all the columns.** Use the Up and Down buttons, shown in Figure 21-9, to arrange the columns the way you want them to appear in the final table. If the type is incorrect, click the Back button until you get to Page 2 of 7 (see Figure 21-6) and use the small arrow buttons to get to the column that is in error. Fix it, and then use the Next button to return here. Use the Delete button to remove a column that you do not want in the table.

8. **Complete the table.** Click on the No, I Don't Want To Enter Data Now button. Then click on the Finish button to complete the table-creation process and return to the Navigator home window (see Figure 21-10).

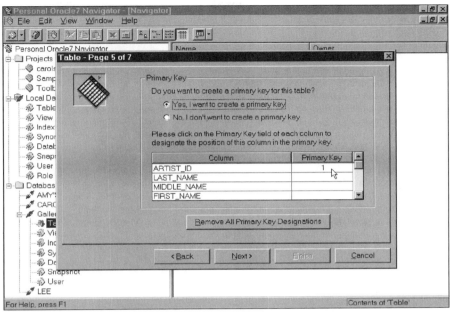

Figure 21-8: Click on the column(s) that make up the primary key.

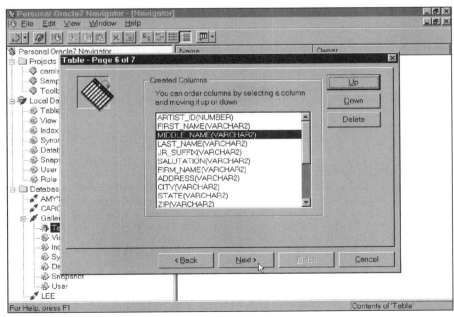

Figure 21-9: This window lets you review your columns.

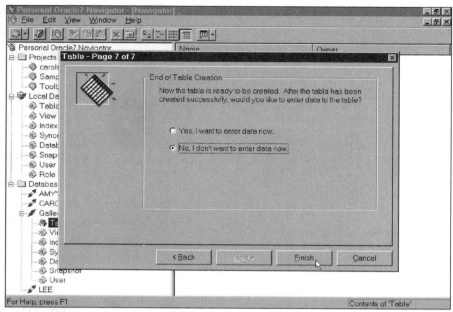

Figure 21-10: Finishing the table-creation process is just a button away.

9. **Create the ARTWORK table.** Go through the same steps for the ARTWORK table as you just did for the ARTIST table. The only exception is when you get to Page 4 of 7 (the Foreign Key page), you must select the foreign key. This foreign key associates the ARTIST_ID column in the ARTIST table with the ARTIST_ID column in the ARTWORK table, as shown in Figure 21-11. Be sure that you make the ARTIST_ID column current when you define the foreign key. Click on Next and continue with the other steps to complete this table-creation process.

Defining additional indexes

Envision your online art gallery growing into thousands of pictures and hundreds of artists. Plan ahead by adding indexes on the search columns. In the ARTIST table, there are four columns where the visitor specifies query criteria. Each one needs an index. Using the Personal Oracle 7 Navigator, it is easy to create an index. Follow these steps:

1. **Highlight INDEX on the left side and then right-click on it.** Select New to create a new index. You now have a window that leads you through the index process(see Figure 21-12).

2. **Name the index.** Follow the same naming conventions listed for Oracle tables and columns. For your first index, type **ARTIST_BY_LAST_NAME.**

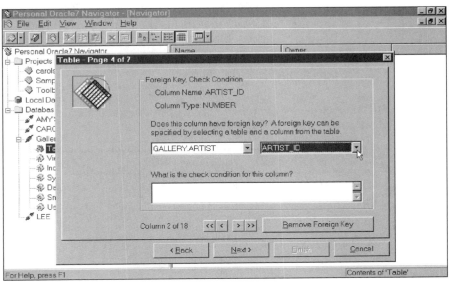

Figure 21-11: Define a foreign key for the ARTWORK table.

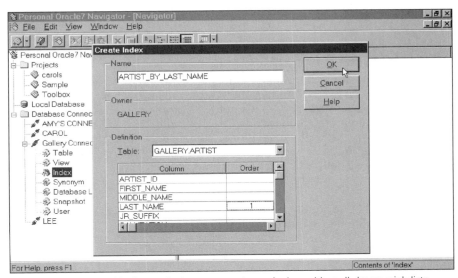

Figure 21-12: The Navigator helps you create an index with pull-down pick lists.

3. **Select the table.** Use the pull-down menu for Table to select the GALLERY.ARTIST table. GALLERY, the owner name, appears in front of the table name. This is an Oracle and SQL standard method of identifying a table with its owner.

4. **Click in the Order box of the LAST_NAME column.** A number *1* appears, indicating that this is the first column in this index. Because it is also the only column in the index, you are finished.

5. **Click on <u>O</u>K to create it.** This creates the index and returns you to the Navigator's main screen.

Use this same set of steps to create the other indexes for the tables. Table 21-1 shows a list of the indexes created:

Table 21-1: Indexes for the Art Gallery		
Table Name	**Index Name**	**Column Indexed**
ARTIST	ARTIST_BY_LAST_NAME	LAST_NAME
ARTIST	ARTIST_BY_CITY	CITY
ARTIST	ARTIST_BY_STATE	STATE
ARTWORK	ARTWORK_BY_MEDIA	MEDIA
ARTWORK	ARTWORK_BY_SUBJECT	SUBJECT
ARTWORK	ARTWORK_BY_COLORS	COLORS
ARTWORK	ARTWORK_BY_SCHOOL	SCHOOL

Method 2: Straight-up SQL

SQL is a programming language. Although this book's intent is not to turn you into a programmer, there are occasions when it's useful to be exposed to the bare SQL code. It's not too complex. SQL is one of the easier programming languages to learn. Being the standard method of communicating with virtually all relational databases, it is worth a little time to become somewhat familiar with the way it looks. In any event, you can create SQL code visually with Microsoft Query (which comes with Windows 95) and then generate the SQL code.

For your art gallery, use SQL*Plus (Oracle's SQL command processor) to execute the SQL statements shown here.

Start up SQL*Plus as follows:

1. **Start Personal Oracle Navigator, if not already there.**

2. **Double-click on Toolbox in the left window.** Your tool selections appear on the right.

3. **Double-click on Plus32.exe.** As shown in Figure 21-13, this opens a security window. Type **GALLERY** in the User Name box. Type **gallery** in the Password box. Click OK.

4. The **SQL*Plus Window** enables you to type and run SQL statements (see Figure 21-14). Pressing Enter after typing the command immediately executes it.

5. **When you're finished, close SQL*Plus.** To leave the SQL*Plus window, close it like any other Windows 95 window by clicking on the X in the upper-right corner.

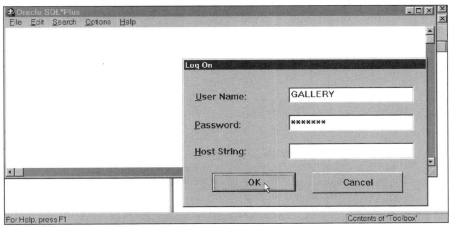

Figure 21-13: The SQL*Plus security window requires a password.

```
Oracle SQL*Plus
File  Edit  Search  Options  Help

SQL*Plus: Release 3.2.2.0.1 - Production on Wed May 15 14:34:16 1996

Copyright (c) Oracle Corporation 1979, 1994.  All rights reserved.

Connected to:
Personal Oracle7 Release 7.2.2.3.1 - 90 day trial license
To purchase a production license, call 1-800-633-0586 (U.S. only)

With the distributed and replication options
PL/SQL Release 2.2.2.3.1 - Production

SQL> create table ARTIST
  2  (ARTIST_ID        NOT NULL NUMBER(3),
  3   FIRST_NAME               VARCHAR2(10),
  4   MIDDLE_NAME              VARCHAR2(10),
  5   LAST_NAME                VARCHAR2(16),
  6   JR_SUFFIX                VARCHAR2(3),
  7   SALUTATION               VARCHAR2(4),
  8   FIRM_NAME                VARCHAR2(50),
  9   ADDRESS                  VARCHAR2(50),
 10   CITY                     VARCHAR2(18),
 11   STATE                    VARCHAR2(18),
 12   ZIP                      VARCHAR2(12),
 13   PHONE                    VARCHAR2(16),
 14   FAX                      VARCHAR2(16),
```

Figure 21-14: The SQL*Plus window accesses the Oracle database engine.

Create the tables

Here is the SQL code for creating the ARTIST table. The SQL*Plus window of the Navigator processes SQL statements.

```
create table ARTIST
(ARTIST_ID              NOT NULL NUMBER(3),
 FIRST_NAME             VARCHAR2(10),
 MIDDLE_NAME            VARCHAR2(10),
 LAST_NAME              VARCHAR2(16),
 JR_SUFFIX              VARCHAR2(3),
 SALUTATION             VARCHAR2(4),
 FIRM_NAME              VARCHAR2(50),
 ADDRESS                VARCHAR2(50),
 CITY                   VARCHAR2(18),
 STATE                  VARCHAR2(18),
 ZIP                    VARCHAR2(12),
 PHONE                  VARCHAR2(16),
 FAX                    VARCHAR2(16),
 EMAIL                  VARCHAR2(33),
 SPECIALTY              VARCHAR2(33),
 MARKETING_TEXT         VARCHAR2(200),
 RESUME_TEXT            VARCHAR2(1000),
 ARTIST_PHOTO_GIF       VARCHAR2(30),
PRIMARY KEY (ARTIST_ID)
);
```

The ARTWORK table comes into being in a most similar way. This table contains a primary key (the WORK_ID column) and a foreign key (the ARTIST_ID column). Here is the code for the ARTWORK table:

```
create table ARTWORK
WORK_ID                NOT NULL NUMBER(3),
 ARTIST_ID             NOT NULL NUMBER(3),
 TITLE                 VARCHAR2(60),
 CREATION_DATE         DATE,
 MEDIA                 VARCHAR2(30),
 SCHOOL                VARCHAR2(30),
 SUBJECT               VARCHAR2(30),
 ART_DESC              VARCHAR2(200),
 COLORS                VARCHAR2(80),
 PRICE                 NUMBER(8,2),
 WIDTH_INCHES          NUMBER(5,2),
 HEIGHT_INCHES         NUMBER(5,2),
 DEPTH_INCHES          NUMBER(5,2),
 PIXEL_WIDTH           NUMBER(4),
 PIXEL_HEIGHT          NUMBER(4),
```

```
   FILENAME                    VARCHAR2(30),
   THUMBNAME                   VARCHAR2(30),
   COPYRIGHT_YEAR              NUMBER(4),
   COPYRIGHT_OWNER             VARCHAR2(40),
 PRIMARY KEY (ARTWORK_ID),
        FOREIGN KEY  (ARTIST_ID)
                  REFERENCES ARTIST
 );
```

Create the indexes

After the ARTIST table exists, the other indexes enable faster database queries. Each search criterion translates into one index. This way, an index speeds up the query no matter which one of the criteria is used. The search criteria for an artist are the following:

- LAST_NAME
- SPECIALTY
- CITY
- STATE

There is one index created for each of them, as follows:

```
CREATE INDEX ARTIST_BY_LAST_NAME
   ON ARTIST
(
        LAST_NAME                      ASC
);
CREATE INDEX ARTIST_BY_SPECIALTY
   ON ARTIST
(
        SPECIALTY                      ASC
);
CREATE INDEX ARTIST_BY_CITY
   ON ARTIST
(
        CITY                           ASC
);
CREATE INDEX ARTIST_BY_STATE
   ON ARTIST
(
        STATE                          ASC
);
```

Next, like the ARTIST table, several indexes on the ARTWORK table help speed up queries. Your art gallery allows for searching for artwork based on the following four database columns:

➡ MEDIA

➡ SCHOOL

➡ SUBJECT

➡ COLORS

Therefore, four indexes (one for each search criterion) provide quicker access to the data for the search functions. The following code creates these four indexes. The first is for MEDIA, the next one is for SCHOOL, then SUBJECT, and finally, COLORS.

```
CREATE INDEX ARTWORK_BY_MEDIA
   ON ARTWORK
(
        MEDIA                              ASC
);
CREATE INDEX ARTWORK_BY_SCHOOL
   ON ARTWORK
(
        SCHOOL                             ASC
);

CREATE INDEX ARTWORK_BY_SUBJECT
   ON ARTWORK
(
        SUBJECT                            ASC
);

CREATE INDEX ARTWORK_BY_COLORS
   ON ARTWORK
(
        COLORS                             ASC
);
```

Indexing the columns to be queried increases the performance (speed) of the query, is little extra trouble, and is well worth doing.

Loading Data into the Tables

Loading data involves creating either actual or test entries (rows) in both tables.

Method 1: Personal Oracle 7 Navigator's Table Editor

The Navigator gives you a spreadsheet to edit data in your tables. It does not provide for validation of the data as you type it. Instead, the Navigator validates when you save the data (commit) to the database. This is inconvenient, but workable. Follow these steps:

1. **Start up the Table Editor.** In Personal Oracle 7 Navigator, double-click on Gallery Connection in the left window. Then double-click on Table in either the right or left window; and then double-click on ARTIST in the right window. This opens the table editor. Click on the first column to begin typing (see Figure 21-15). Type in the data, using the Tab key or your mouse to navigate through the columns. The draw bar at the bottom moves from the first columns through the last columns.

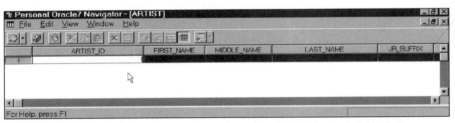

Figure 21-15: Begin inserting a new row by using the Navigator's Table Editor.

2. **Insert the row.** After typing in all the data for a row, press Enter or left-click to end the current column's editing. Then right-click the mouse to pop up the menu shown in Figure 21-16. Select Commit Insert. This adds your first row to the ARTIST table.

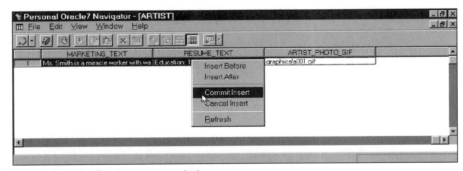

Figure 21-16: Caption text needed

3. **Insert more rows.** Now, right-click again to pop up the menu. This time, select Insert Below. This opens a new row for you to add to the table. Edit as before. Commit as before. Continue editing until all your rows are added.

4. **Change data in existing rows if needed.** If you made a mistake or want to modify some data, simply left-click on the row and column you want to change and then type in the changes. Press Enter to complete the edit. Then right-click and select Commit Changes from the pop-up menu. Delete rows here as well.

5. **Exit from the Table Editor.** Simply close the window by left-clicking on the X in the upper right corner. If you have made changes, you may see a window asking you to either commit the changes or cancel them.

Method 2: SQL code

To add and change data in SQL, start the SQL*Plus window, as described earlier. (To start the SQL*Plus window, start Personal Oracle 7 Navigator, select Toolbox, and then select plus32.exe.)

In SQL, insert rows one at a time by using an insert statement that contains specific data. Here's an example of one insert statement for the ARTIST table. Each column has a value or the word NULL as a placeholder. In this example, the fifth column (JR_SUFFIX) contains no value, so the term NULL holds the fifth column position. Each column's value resides between single quotation marks. Commas separate each value from the next. For ease of reading, this example contains relatively short statements for the MARKETING_TEXT and RESUME_TEXT columns:

```
INSERT INTO ARTIST VALUES
('1', 'Helen', 'K.', 'Keller', NULL,
'MS.', 'Keller Arts and Crafts',
'100 West Broadway', 'Lincoln',
'NE', '99887', '(808) 555-2345', NULL, 'kellerh@muses.com',
'WATERCOLOR',
'Helen works watercolors in a unique way.',
'Education: 1944, Master of Fine Art, Boston MA. Shows:
Smithsonian Institute, 1950.')
;
```

Modify any row later by using the update statement. Notice that the portion of the statement that comes after the word WHERE (*WHERE* clause) determines which row is updated.

```
UPDATE ARTWORK SET JR_SUFFIX = 'SR.'
WHERE LAST_NAME = 'Johnson'
;
```

Delete a row by specifying which row in the WHERE clause. To ensure that you are deleting the correct row, it's best to specify the value of the primary key in the WHERE clause. For example, suppose that one of the artists has sold one of the artworks and asks you to remove it from the database. The piece was entered into the database as a row with the primary key (WORK_ID) equal to 22. You delete this row with the following SQL statement.

```
DELETE FROM ARTWORK
WHERE WORK_ID = 22
;
```

Creating Graphics Files

There are many photos that need to be scanned for the art gallery. Each artist mails you these photographs:

➡ One photograph of himself or herself

➡ One photograph of each work of art

A few of the artists use computers and e-mail you electronic files instead of sending actual photos. This saves you a lot of work. Be sure to specify the size and resolution and file type that these artists should use when creating files for you. For all the others, you must now scan all the photos and produce your own electronic files that are in a consistent size and color resolution for the gallery.

After completing all the scanning, the graphics files go in a common graphics directory. Record the filenames in your ARTIST and ARTWORK tables. Naturally, each file must have a unique filename. This filename, plus the directory name, pixel width, and pixel height, must all go into the database. Each work of art corresponds to one filename. For example, Jane Smith has sent a photo of her painting called *Watchdogs*. You have logged this work of art with WORK_ID 100. After scanning the photo, you place the image into a file called w100.gif, which is 400 pixels wide and 300 pixels high. You also create a thumbnail graphic file called t100.gif. Both files are located in the directory named graphics. Here are the column values for this work of art in the ARTWORK table:

➡ WORK_ID: 100

➡ PIXEL_WIDTH: 400

➡ PIXEL_HEIGHT: 300

➡ FILENAME: graphics/w100.gif

➡ THUMBNAME: graphics/t100.gif

Summary

The creation of tables, their associated relationships, and indexes is a basic component of any database work. Whether you use a Wizard or plain SQL code, be consistent in your style of naming these items so that it is easier to go back later and analyze what you have done. This is especially important if you work on a team. This chapter sets the stage for creating an exciting and versatile Web-database application.

After you fill in your data, scan your photos, and identify the photos in the database, you are ready to proceed with the creation of the Web documents. You will use all the information stored in the database, plus some additional details, such as a gallery logo for the documents, to create an attractive, useful Web site.

Linking the Oracle Database Application to the Web Site

In This Chapter

Overview of software used for the demonstration project

Creating the HTML documents

In the preceding chapter, you built your tables. To complete the project, you connect the tables to a series of Web documents. This chapter covers how to create the Web documents and run them on the Web. It describes, step by step, *two different ways to accomplish this goal.*

Software Selection

The first approach requires some SQL and HTML coding. It uses the Windows NT Server's built-in connections to any ODBC database, called the Internet Information Server (IIS). IIS comes with Windows NT version 4, and can be installed on earlier versions as an upgrade. The documents and related scripts used in this approach were developed on a Windows 95 PC. For testing and running the documents, a developer's account on the Developers Community (Dev-Com) Web site (http://dev-com.com) was set up. The Art Gallery database application was loaded into Dev-Com's Oracle database on its NT Server (see Figure 22-1). (Thanks go to Bill Havlice at Dev-Com for his help in developing the Web documents and sample scripts that you see here.)

The following tool was used in developing this application:

➡ **Microsoft's Internet Information Server (IIS).** This tool comes standard with the Windows NT server package, version 4. If you have an earlier version on Windows NT, you can download IIS free from `http://www.microsoft.com/InfoServ`. Although the IIS does require some programming, the programming is simple. IIS comes with a method of communicating with a database — called the Internet Database Connection (IDC) — that accesses any ODBC-compliant database engine, including Microsoft's SQL Server. In this test site, the Windows NT server connects with a UNIX Web server.

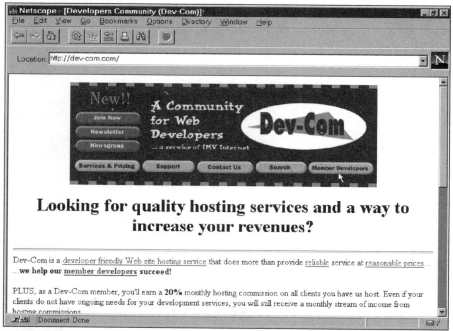

Figure 22-1: Dev-Com provides an environment for Web developers.

The second approach uses a Web-database development tool. The authors selected Spider Technology's NetDynamics to demonstrate how developers can use a Web-database tool. This requires no CGI scripts and very little HTML programming.

We selected the following Web-database software tools:

➥ **Spider Technology's NetDynamics.** This tool is very powerful and versatile in creating "on the fly" Web documents. You can develop in Windows 95 and port the application to UNIX. It features lots of extras to jazz up your documents. This tool is rather complex to use, however, because it requires several other software products to work in unison. Those products are listed following this paragraph. When the author installed this product, it was a beta release for the Windows 95 platform. Even so, it was a stable product. In addition to NetDynamics, the author installed the following software products, which are needed to complete the infrastructure for Web-database development:

➥ **INTERSOLV** DataDirect ODBC Pack for Microsoft Windows 95 or Microsoft Windows NT, Version 2.12. This is the ODBC driver that sends communications between the Web server and Oracle.

➥ **Microsoft FrontPage** for Windows 95. This is a combination HTML editor and personal Web server. Both features are needed for use with NetDynamics.

➥ **The Java Developers Kit**, release 1.0.2, from Sun. This software drives the NetDynamics project.

Creating the Documents

The two methods described in this section are very different. The first method requires hands-on HTML coding and SQL coding. Even so, this method is straightforward and easy to learn. The second method uses Wizards and a WYSIWYG HTML editor to create the documents and the database communications. The software is designed to do much more than this kind of simple example. It does require a little time to become oriented and learn its many features. Once mastered, however, it offers both efficiency and versatility.

Method 1: Internet Information Server (IIS)

You can go to the Dev-Com site to see this server in action on the Internet at http://ntweb1.imvi.com/carolm/home.htm. In addition, all the files — including the graphics — are included on the CD-ROM accompanying this book. This method uses Microsoft Internet Information Server to send queries to the database, to put the results together with an HTML template, and to send the completed HTML document to the Web server. Figure 22-2 shows the flow of events when the visitor clicks on the Search button in the query form. IIS takes the information that the visitor enters on the query form and plugs it into the query stored in the IDC file (catalog.idc).

IIS sends this query to the database and retrieves the results. Next, IIS combines the results of the query with a template file (catalog.htx) to create a complete HTML document. The final step: IIS sends this complete HTML document to the Web server.

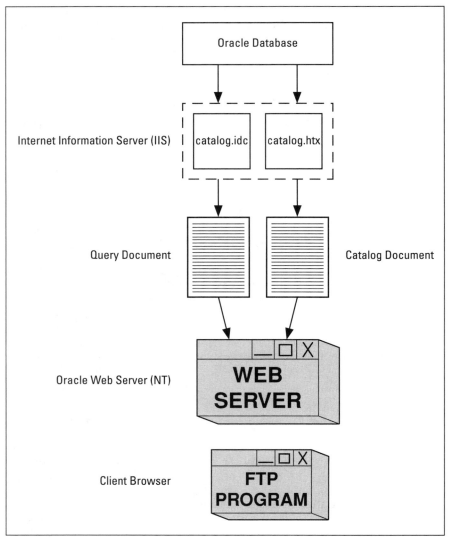

Figure 22-2: IIS controls the communication between the Web server and the database.

File suffixes identify the type of file when working with IIS

File suffixes help you keep track of the two different kinds of files that IIS process-es. The file suffix of *.htx* is used for the HTML template documents. These docu-ments contain variable names where data from the database is plugged in. The variable names match the column names in the query that retrieves data. For example, **<%title%>** is the variable where data in the column named **title** is placed on the HTML document.

The file suffix of *.idc* indicates a file that contains the query in the format required by IIS. The file format is Internet Database Connector (IDC) format. The query statement contains variables that are replaced by fields from the query form. For example, **'%specialty%'** is the variable for data in an input field named **spe-cialty** on the query form.

Gallery Online Home document

This is a standard HTML document. The only special thing is that button on the bottom, which executes the first of a series of IDC scripts. Figure 22-3 shows the document as seen on Netscape. Following that is the HTML markups for the document. Notice the Query the Gallery button. This but-ton executes an IDC script to start the query form. Listing 22-1 shows the code for the Home document.

The file called up by clicking on the Query the Gallery button is named home.idc. It is an SQL query that starts the connection to the database and brings up the first of the series of Web documents that query the database and display data. Following is the SQL code that is in the file:

```
Datasource: fubar
Username: developer
Password: developer1
Template: query.htx
SQLStatement:
+Select * from dual
```

This SQL statement, `select * from dual`, is simply a way to start the query form, which is contained in the file query.htx. The table called dual is a single row table with a single column that is a standard one in Oracle. You use it when you need to access the database, but do not really need any information out of the database. This statement executes and calls the query form file, query.htx, as a template.

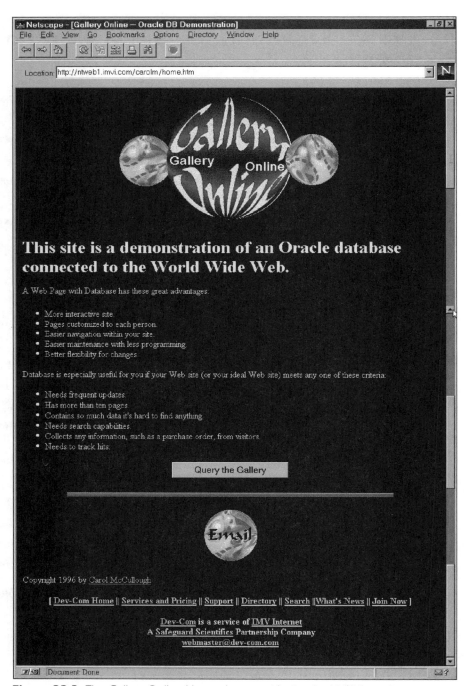

Figure 22-3: The Gallery Online Home document is standard HTML markups.

Listing 22-1 HTML markups for the Home document (home.htm)

```
<HTML>
<HEAD>
<TITLE>Gallery Online — Oracle DB Demonstration</TITLE>
</HEAD>
<! Background is Black, text is yellow Link is neon blue,
Visited link is Green,
Active link is light blue>
<A NAME="TopOfForm">
<BODY BGCOLOR="000000" TEXT="#FFFF00" LINK="#3399FF"
     VLINK="#00FF00" ALINK="#33FFFF">
<CENTER>
<IMG SRC =
"http://ntweb1.imvi.com/carolm/images/head_lg.gif"
  ALT="[gallery online logo]" WIDTH=442 HEIGHT=238 >
</CENTER>
 <H1>This site is a demonstration of an Oracle database
connected to the
World Wide Web.</H1>
<H2>
<p align=left>As featured in the book, </p>
<p align=left><em><strong>Creating Cool Web Sites With
Oracle and Access Databases</strong></em></p>
<p align=left>by Joe Sinclair and <a
href="http://www.maui.net/~mcculc">Carol McCullough</a></p>
<p align=left>Publishing this fall, 1996, by <a
href="http://www.idgbooks.com/">IDG Books</a>.</p>
<p align=left>This site uses <a
href="http://www.microsoft.com/">Microsoft's</A> Internet
Information Server (IIS), Microsoft's
Internet Database Connection (IDC) and an <a
href="http://www.oracle.com">Oracle 7 Database</a>. </p>
</H2>
A Web Page with Database has these great advantages:
<UL>
<LI>More interactive site.
<LI>Pages customized to each person.
<LI>Easier navigation within your site.
<LI>Easier maintenance with less programming.
<LI>Better flexibility for changes.
</UL>
Database is especially useful for you if your Web site (or
your ideal Web site)  meets any one of these criteria:
<UL>
<LI>Needs frequent updates.
<LI>Has more than ten pages.
```

(continued)

Listing 22-1 *(continued)*

```
<LI>Contains so much data it's hard to find anything.
<LI>Needs search capabilities.
<LI>Collects any information, such as a purchase order,
from visitors.
<LI>Needs to track hits.
</UL>
<CENTER>
<FORM ACTION="http://ntweb1.imvi.com/carolm/query.idc">
<INPUT TYPE="SUBMIT" VALUE="Query the Gallery">
</FORM>
<P>
<IMG SRC =
"http://ntweb1.imvi.com/carolm/images/lineredb.gif"
ALT="[lline]" WIDTH=587 HEIGHT=7 >
<P>
<A HREF="mailto:mcculc@maui.net"><IMG SRC =
"http://ntweb1.imvi.com/carolm/images/btn_mail.gif"
  ALT="e-mail button" WIDTH=100 HEIGHT=100 BORDER=0 ></A>
<P>
</CENTER>
<P>Copyright 1996 by <A
HREF="http://www.maui.net/~mcculc">Carol McCullough</A>
<P ALIGN="CENTER">
<STRONG>
<A HREF="http://dev-com.com/">Dev-Com Home</A>
<A HREF="http://dev-com.com/services/">Services and
Pricing</A>
<A HREF="http://dev-com.com/support.shtml">Support</A>
<A HREF="contact.htm">Directory</A>
<A HREF="http://dev-com.com/search.shtml">Search</A>
<A HREF="http://dev-
com.com/newsletter/whatsnew.shtml">What's News</A>
<strong><A HREF="http://dev-com.com/joinow.shtml">Join
Now</A></strong>
<br><br>
<a href="http://dev-com.com/">Dev-Com</a> is a service of
<a href="http://www.imvi.com/">IMV Internet</a><br>
A <a href="http://www.safeguard.com/">Safeguard
Scientifics</a>
Partnership Company<br>
<a href="mailto:webmaster@dev-com.com">webmaster@dev-
com.com</a>
</STRONG>
<br><br>
</P>
</HTML>
```

The query form

This query form is written in standard HTML, as described in a previous chapter. This form is long, because it collects all the criteria in a single document, which you can use to query the Art Gallery (see Figure 22-4). Inputs left blank do not defeat the query. Listing 22-2 is the code for the query form.

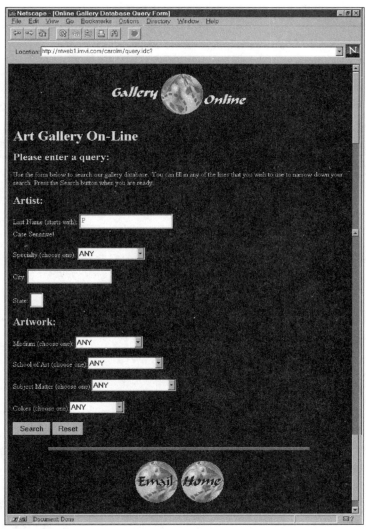

Figure 22-4: The query form includes many criteria that can be used separately or in combination with one another.

Listing 22-2   HTML mark-ups for the query form (query.htx).

```
<HTML>
<HEAD><TITLE>Online Gallery Database Query Form</TITLE>
</HEAD>
<BODY>
<! Background is Black, text is yellow Link is neon blue,
Visited link is Green,
Active link is light blue>
<BODY BGCOLOR="000000" TEXT="#FFFF00" LINK="#3399FF"
    VLINK="#00FF00" ALINK="#33FFFF">
<CENTER>
<IMG SRC =
"http://ntweb1.imvi.com/carolm/images/head_sm.gif"
  ALT="[gallery online logo]" WIDTH=323 HEIGHT=110 >
</CENTER>
<h1>Art Gallery On-Line</h1>
<h2>Please enter a query:</h2>
<p>Use the form below to search our gallery database.
You can fill in any of the lines that you wish to use to
narrow down your search. Press the Search button
when you are ready.</p>
<FORM METHOD="POST"
ACTION="http://ntweb1.imvi.com/carolm/catalog.idc">
<h2>Artist:</h2>
Last Name (starts with):
<INPUT NAME = "last_name"><BR>
Case Sensitive!<P>
<p>Specialty (choose one):
<select name="specialty" size=1>
<OPTION VALUE=ANY>ANY</option>
<OPTION VALUE=ACRYLIC>ACRYLIC</option>
<OPTION VALUE=CHARCOAL>CHARCOAL</option>
<OPTION VALUE=DIGITAL>DIGITAL</option>
<OPTION VALUE=PENCIL>PENCIL</option>
<OPTION VALUE=OIL>OIL</option>
<OPTION VALUE=WATERCOLOR>WATERCOLOR</option>
<OPTION VALUE=WOOD>WOOD</option>
</select></p>
<p>City: <input type=text size=18 maxlength=18
name="city"></p>
<p>State: <input type=text size=2 maxlength=2
name="state"></p>
<h2>Artwork:</h2>
<p>Medium (choose one): <select name="media" size=1>
<OPTION VALUE=ANY>ANY</option>
```

Listing 22-2 *(continued)*

```
<OPTION VALUE=ACRYLIC>ACRYLIC</option>
<OPTION VALUE=DIGITAL>DIGITAL</option>
<OPTION VALUE=PASTEL>PASTEL</option>
<OPTION VALUE=PENCIL>PENCIL</option>
<OPTION VALUE=OIL>OIL</option>
<OPTION VALUE=WATERCOLOR>WATERCOLOR</option>
</select></p>
<p>School of Art (choose one):<select name="school"
size=1>
<OPTION VALUE=ANY>ANY</option>
<OPTION VALUE=EXPRESSIONISM>EXPRESSIONISM</option>
<OPTION VALUE=IMPRESSIONISM>IMPRESSIONISM</option>
<OPTION VALUE=MODERN>MODERN</option>
<OPTION VALUE=POST-MODERN>POST-MODERN</option>
<OPTION VALUE=REALISM>REALISM</option>
<OPTION VALUE=SURREALISM>SURREALISM</option>
<OPTION VALUE=WHIMSY>WHIMSY</option>
</select></p>
<p>Subject Matter (choose one):<select name="subject"
size=1>
<OPTION VALUE=ANY>ANY</option>
<OPTION VALUE=ANIMALS/WILDLIFE>ANIMALS/WILDLIFE</option>
<OPTION VALUE=FANTASY>FANTASY</option>
<OPTION VALUE=FLORAL>FLORAL</option>
<OPTION VALUE=LANDSCAPE>LANDSCAPE</option>
<OPTION VALUE=PORTRAIT/PEOPLE>PORTRAIT/PEOPLE</option>
</select></p>
<p>Colors (choose one):<select name="colors" size=1>
<OPTION VALUE=ANY>ANY</option>
<OPTION VALUE=AMBER>AMBER</option>
<OPTION VALUE=BLACK>BLACK</option>
<OPTION VALUE=BLUE>BLUE</option>
<OPTION VALUE=GRAY>GRAY</option>
<OPTION VALUE=GREEN>GREEN</option>
<OPTION VALUE=LAVENDER>LAVENDER</option>
<OPTION VALUE=NAVY>NAVY</option>
<OPTION VALUE=OLIVE>OLIVE</option>
<OPTION VALUE=ORANGE>ORANGE</option>
<OPTION VALUE=PINK>PINK</option>
<OPTION VALUE=PURPLE>PURPLE</option>
<OPTION VALUE=RED>RED</option>
<OPTION VALUE=TAN>TAN</option>
<OPTION VALUE=WHITE>WHITE</option>
<OPTION VALUE=YELLOW>YELLOW</option>
</select></p>
```

(continued)

Listing 22-2 *(continued)*

```
<INPUT TYPE="SUBMIT" VALUE="Search">
<INPUT TYPE="RESET" VALUE="Reset">
</FORM>
<CENTER>
<IMG SRC =
"http://ntweb1.imvi.com/carolm/images/lineredb.gif"
ALT="[line]" WIDTH=587 HEIGHT=7>
<P>
<A HREF="mailto:mcculc@maui.net"><IMG SRC =
"http://ntweb1.imvi.com/carolm/images/btn_mail.gif"
  ALT="e-mail button" WIDTH=100 HEIGHT=100 BORDER=0 ></A>
<A HREF="http://ntweb1.imvi.com/carolm/home.htm"><IMG SRC =
"http://ntweb1.imvi.com/carolm/images/btn_home.gif"
  ALT="home button" WIDTH=100 HEIGHT=100 BORDER=0 ></A>
<P>
</CENTER>
<P>Copyright 1996 by Carol McCullough
</body>
</HTML>
```

In this example, the letter **P** has been typed into the Artist Last Name criteria, and OIL has been selected from the pull-down menu of Medium. By clicking on the Search button, the form executes the next SQL statement, passing the values from all the form's input fields to the SQL statement. Here is the SQL statement that is executed. It is in a file named catalog.idc.

```
Datasource: fubar
Username: system
Password: manager1
Template: catalog.htx
SQLStatement:
+ select
+ b.thumbname, b.title, b.work_id,
+ a.first_name, a.middle_name, a.last_name
+ from artist a, artwork b
+ where a.artist_id = b.artist_id
+ and (a.last_name like '%last_name%%' or '%last_name%'
is null)
+ and (a.specialty = '%specialty%' or '%specialty%' =
'ANY')
+ and (a.city like '%city%%' or '%city%' is null)
+ and (a.state like '%state%%' or '%state%' is null)
+ and (b.media = '%media%' or '%media%' = 'ANY')
+ and (b.school = '%school%' or '%school%' = 'ANY')
+ and (b.subject = '%subject%' or '%subject%' = 'ANY')
+ and (b.colors like '%%%colors%%%' or '%colors%' = 'ANY')
```

In the SQL statement, the words with percent signs around them are the variables from the query form. Several of the variables have additional percent signs near them, such as '%last_name%%%'. The three percent signs are translated by Oracle's SQL engine as a trailing percent sign. Following the example, the visitor typed in the letter **P** in the Last Name box, so the '%last_name%%%' becomes 'P%'. The percent (%) is a wild card, so any artist whose last name begins with the letter P is selected. In the case of the colors criterion, the column contains a list of colors in no specific order. Placing three percent signs before *and* after the colors variable tells Oracle to go find the selected color anywhere within that column. The template that is used to format the results of this query is contained in the file named catalog.htx.

The query results document

This document contains some static information on the top and bottom, as well as a repeating section in the middle. The repeating section is automatically repeated once for each row returned from the query. Figure 22-5 shows the Web page, and Listing 22-3 shows the HTML that creates it.

Listing 22-3 HTML markups for the results document (catalog.htx)

```
<HTML>
<HEAD>
<TITLE>Gallery Online — Query Results Summary List</TITLE>
</HEAD>
<body>
<! Background is Black, text is yellow Link is neon blue,
Visited link is Green,
Active link is light blue>
<BODY BGCOLOR="000000" TEXT="#FFFF00" LINK="#3399FF"
    VLINK="#00FF00" ALINK="#33FFFF">
<CENTER>
<IMG SRC =
"http://ntweb1.imvi.com/carolm/images/head_sm.gif"
  ALT="[gallery online logo]" WIDTH=323 HEIGHT=110 >
</CENTER>
<CENTER>
<H2>Here is the result of your query.</H2>
<IMG SRC =
"http://ntweb1.imvi.com/carolm/images/lineredb.gif"
ALT="[line]" WIDTH=587 HEIGHT=7>
<FORM METHOD="POST"
ACTION="http://ntweb1.imvi.com/carolm/artwork.idc">
```

(continued)

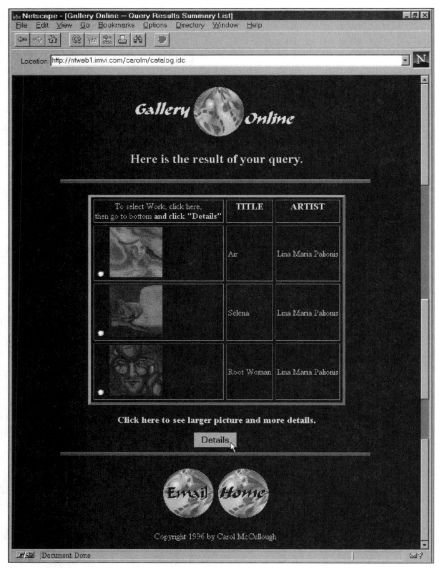

Figure 22-5: The query results document is built on the fly, based on the specific rows returned from the query.

Listing 22-3 *(continued)*

```
<B>
<table border=5 cellpadding=2 cellspacing=5>
<TR>
```

```
  <TD><CENTER>To select Work, click here,<BR>
          then go to bottom<B>
          and click "Details"</CENTER></TD>
  <TD><CENTER><H3>TITLE</H3></CENTER></TD>
  <TD><CENTER><H3>ARTIST</H3></CENTER></TD>
</TR>
<%begindetail%>
<TR>
  <TD><INPUT TYPE="radio" NAME="work_id" VALUE=<%work_id%>
>
      <IMG
SRC="http://ntweb1.imvi.com/carolm/images/<%thumbname%>"
ALT="picture of art"
             HEIGHT=100 WIDTH=100></TD>
  <TD><%title%></TD>
  <TD><%first_name%> <%middle_name%> <%last_name%></TD>
</TR>
<%enddetail%>
</TABLE>
</B>
<P>
<%if CurrentRecord EQ 0 %>
<I><B>Sorry, no Works Available for this criteria.</B>
<P>
<%else%>
<CENTER>
<H3>Click here to see larger picture and more
details.</H3>
<INPUT TYPE="SUBMIT" VALUE="Details">
</CENTER>
<%endif%>
<CENTER>
<IMG SRC =
"http://ntweb1.imvi.com/carolm/images/lineredb.gif"
ALT="[lline]" WIDTH=587 HEIGHT=7>
<P>
<A HREF="mailto:mcculc@maui.net"><IMG SRC =
"http://ntweb1.imvi.com/carolm/images/btn_mail.gif"
  ALT="e-mail button" WIDTH=100 HEIGHT=100 BORDER=0 ></A>
<A HREF=" http://ntweb1.imvi.com/carolm/home.htm"><IMG SRC
= "http://ntweb1.imvi.com/carolm/images/btn_home.gif"
  ALT="home button" WIDTH=100 HEIGHT=100 BORDER=0 ></A>
</CENTER>
<P>
<P>
<P>Copyright 1996 by Carol McCullough
</B>
</body>
</HTML>
```

These markups show how the body of the table is repeated for each row. The section that is repeated starts with `<%begindetail%>` and ends with `<%enddetail%>`.

Also note the section of markups starting with `<%if CurrentRecord EQ 0 %>` and ending with `<%endif%>`. This section is used if no rows are returned from the query.

A click of the Details button starts up the next query, passing the WORK_ID of the selected artwork (from the radio button) to the SQL code. Following is the SQL code that gets the details about the selected artwork. The file containing it is called artwork.idc.

```
Datasource: fubar
Username: system
Password: manager1
Template: artwork.htx
SQLStatement:
+ select
+ b.filename, b.pixel_height, b.pixel_width,
+ b.title, b.work_id, nvl(to_char(b.price,'$9990.00'),'Not
For Sale') price,
+ a.first_name, a.middle_name, a.last_name,
+ b.media, to_char(b.creation_date,'MM/YYYY')
creation_date,
+ b.height_inches, b.width_inches,
+ decode(b.depth_inches,0,' ',NULL,' ',' x
'||b.depth_inches) depth_inches,
+ b.school, b.subject, b.colors, b.art_desc, a.artist_id
+ from artist a, artwork b
+ where a.artist_id = b.artist_id
+ and b.work_id = '%work_id%'
```

Notice that there is only one variable, `'%work_id%'`. Because WORK_ID is the unique key to the ARTWORK table, you can be sure that this query retrieves only one row

The Artwork Details Document

Figure 22-6 shows the document that is built for the selected artwork. The height and width of the graphic come from the database, as do the other details about the artwork. The graphic for the artwork resides in a subdirectory along with all the other graphics for the gallery. The graphics themselves are not stored in the database. The filename of the graphic is stored there and is used to include the graphic in this document. Listing 22-4 shows the actual HTML code for the document.

Listing 22-4 HTML markups for the Artwork Details document

```
<HTML>
<HEAD>
<TITLE>Online Gallery Artwork Detail</TITLE>
</HEAD>
<BODY>
<! Background is Black, text is yellow Link is neon blue,
Visited link is Green,
Active link is light blue>
<BODY BGCOLOR="000000" TEXT="#FFFF00" LINK="#3399FF"
     VLINK="#00FF00" ALINK="#33FFFF">
<CENTER>
<IMG SRC =
"http://ntweb1.imvi.com/carolm/images/head_sm.gif"
  ALT="[gallery online logo]" WIDTH=323 HEIGHT=110 >
<h2>Artwork Details</H2>
<IMG SRC =
"http://ntweb1.imvi.com/carolm/images/lineredb.gif"
ALT="[line]" WIDTH=587 HEIGHT=7>
<P>
<%begindetail%>
<IMG SRC="http://ntweb1.imvi.com/carolm/images/<%file
name%>" ALT="picture of art" HEIGHT=<%pixel_height%>
WIDTH=<%pixel_width%> ALIGN="TOP" ><P>
<FORM METHOD="POST"
ACTION="http://ntweb1.imvi.com/carolm/profile.idc">
<INPUT TYPE=HIDDEN NAME="work_id" VALUE=<%work_id%>>
<H2><%title%></H2>
<H3><%art_desc%></H3>
<table border=5 cellpadding=2 cellspacing=5>
<TR>
  <TD><H2>Artist: <%first_name%> <%middle_name%>
<%last_name%></H2></TD>
  <TD><H2>Price: <%price%></H2></TD>
</TR>
<TR>
  <TD><H2>Media: <%media%></H2></TD>
  <TD><H2>Creation: <%creation_date%></H2></TD>
</TR>
<TR>
  <TD><H2>Size (inches): <%height_inches%> x <%width_inch
es%><%depth_inches%></H2></TD>
  <TD><H2>School: <%school%></H2></TD>
</TR>
<TR>
  <TD><H2>Subject: <%subject%></H2></TD>
  <TD><H2>Colors: <%colors%></H2></TD>
```

(continued)

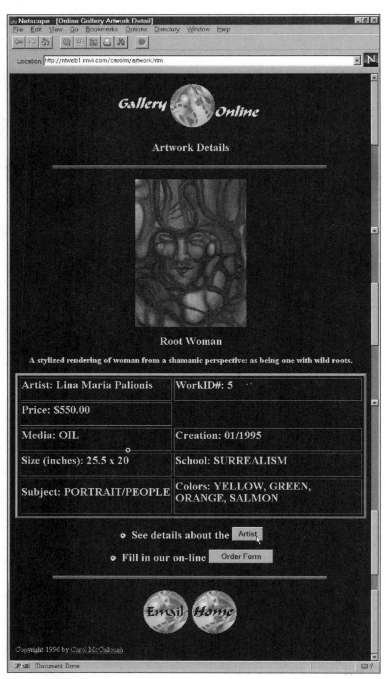

Figure 22-6: The Artwork Details document uses data from both the ARTIST and the ARTWORK tables.

Listing 22-4 *(continued)*

```
</TR>
</TABLE>
<P>
<h2><INPUT TYPE=HIDDEN NAME="artist_id"
VALUE=<%artist_id%>>
See details about the <INPUT TYPE="SUBMIT"
VALUE="Artist"></h2>
</FORM>
<FORM METHOD="POST"
ACTION="http://ntweb1.imvi.com/carolm/order.idc">
<H2><INPUT TYPE=HIDDEN NAME="work_id" VALUE=<%work_id%>>
      See how to <INPUT TYPE="SUBMIT" VALUE="Order"></H2>
</FORM>
<P>
<%enddetail%>
<%if CurrentRecord EQ 0 %>
<I><B>Sorry, no Works Available for this criteria.
<P>
<%else%>
<%endif%>
<IMG SRC =
"http://ntweb1.imvi.com/carolm/images/lineredb.gif"
ALT="[lline]" WIDTH=587 HEIGHT=7 >
<P>
<A HREF="mailto:mcculc@maui.net"><IMG SRC =
"http://ntweb1.imvi.com/carolm/images/btn_mail.gif"
  ALT="e-mail button" WIDTH=100 HEIGHT=100 BORDER=0 ></A>
<A HREF="http://ntweb1.imvi.com/carolm/home.htm"><IMG SRC =
"http://ntweb1.imvi.com/carolm/images/btn_home.gif"
  ALT="home button" WIDTH=100 HEIGHT=100 BORDER=0 ></A>
<P>
</CENTER>
<P>Copyright 1996 by <A
HREF="http://www.maui.net/~mcculc">Carol McCullough</A>
</html>
```

This document has two buttons that can be used to start either of two more documents created on the fly. In the case of the Artist button, the server sends the ARTIST_ID code to the SQL statement in profile.idc and the Oracle database executes that statement. The ARTIST_ID value goes into the radio button next to the Artist button. The radio button is preselected, using the INPUT CHECKED parameter in the HTML markups for the button. Without this parameter, the visitor would be required to click on the radio button first, and then click on the Artist button.

The second button, for the online Order Form, uses a similar technique. Notice that this button is in a new FORM. You start a new form by first marking the end of the first form with `</FORM>` and then beginning a new form with `<FORM>`. You need this second form to allow for two distinct Submit buttons.

Here's the SQL code, in the file named profile.idc, that is executed when a user clicks the Artist button:

```
Datasource: fubar
Username: system
Password: manager1
Template: profile.htx
SQLStatement:
+ select
+ a.first_name, a.middle_name, a.last_name,
a.artist_photo_gif,
+ a.firm_name, a.address, a.city, a.state, a.zip, a.spe
cialty,
+ a.phone, a.fax, a.email, a.marketing_text, a.resume_text
+ from artist a
+ where a.artist_id = '%artist_id%'
```

This query needs only information from the ARTIST table and uses the ARTIST_ID to find a single row in the table. This row is formatted into a document using the HTML markups in the file profile.htx. This is the Artist Profile document.

Artist Profile document

This document shows details about a single artist, formatted according to the HTML in the profile.htx file. The information about the artist is retrieved from the database using the SQL code in the profile.idc file.

Like the two documents before this one, the Artist document has a top and bottom section that are always the same, a details section that is used to format the data from the database, and a small section for the case where no rows are retrieved from the database. Figure 22-7 shows the final product of merging the query with the template. Listing 22-5 shows the HTML code used as the template.

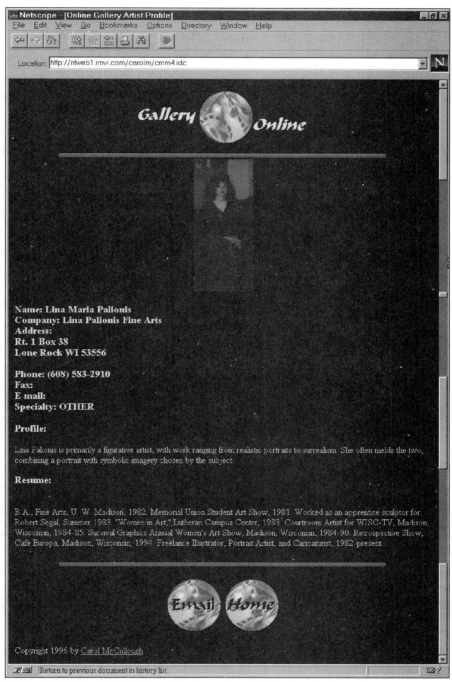

Figure 22-7: The Artist Profile tells about the artist's background.

Listing 22-5   HTML markups for the Artist Profile document

```
<HTML>
<HEAD>
<TITLE>Online Gallery Artist Profile</TITLE>
</HEAD>
<BODY>
<! Background is Black, text is yellow Link is neon blue,
Visited link is Green,
Active link is light blue>
<BODY BGCOLOR="000000" TEXT="#FFFF00" LINK="#3399FF"
     VLINK="#00FF00" ALINK="#33FFFF">
<TITLE>Online Gallery Artist Profile</TITLE>
<CENTER>
<IMG SRC =
"http://ntweb1.imvi.com/carolm/images/head_sm.gif"
  ALT="[gallery online logo]" WIDTH=323 HEIGHT=110 >
<IMG SRC =
"http://ntweb1.imvi.com/carolm/images/lineredb.gif"
ALT="[line]" WIDTH=587 HEIGHT=7>
</CENTER>
<%begindetail%>
<CENTER>
<IMG
SRC="http://ntweb1.imvi.com/carolm/images/<%artist_photo_gi
f%>"
     ALT="picture of artist" ALIGN="TOP" ><P>
</CENTER>
<H3>
Name: <%first_name%> <%middle_name%> <%last_name%><BR>
Company: <%firm_name%><BR>
Address: <BR>
<%address%><BR>
<%city%> <%state%> <%zip%><P>
Phone: <%phone%><BR>
Fax: <%fax%><BR>
E-mail: <%email%><BR>
Specialty: <%specialty%> <P>
<B>Profile:</B><BR>
</H3>
<%marketing_text%><P>
<H3><B>Resume:</B></H3><BR>
<%resume_text%><P>
<P>
<CENTER>
<%enddetail%>
<%if CurrentRecord EQ 0 %>
<I><B>Sorry, no Details Available for this Artist.
```

Listing 22-5 *(continued)*

```
<P>
<%else%>
<%endif%>
<IMG SRC =
"http://ntweb1.imvi.com/carolm/images/lineredb.gif"
ALT="[line]" WIDTH=587 HEIGHT=7 >
<P>
<A HREF="mailto:mcculc@maui.net"><IMG SRC =
"http://ntweb1.imvi.com/carolm/images/btn_mail.gif"
   ALT="e-mail button" WIDTH=100 HEIGHT=100 BORDER=0 ></A>
<A HREF="http://ntweb1.imvi.com/carolm/home.htm"><IMG SRC =
"http://ntweb1.imvi.com/carolm/images/btn_home.gif"
   ALT="home button" WIDTH=100 HEIGHT=100 BORDER=0 ></A>
<P>
</CENTER>
<P>Copyright 1996 by <A
HREF="http://www.maui.net/~mcculc">Carol McCullough</A>
</html>
```

The Order document

This document can be printed, filled in, and mailed to the artist to order the artwork. It also gives the artist's phone number and other data, which enables the visitor to contact the artist directly. Refer to Figure 22-8 to see the appearance of this document.

When a user clicks the Order button on the Artwork Detail document, the ARTWORK_ID goes to the SQL statement in order.idc and the query is executed. Here is the SQL code:

```
Datasource: fubar
Username: system
Password: manager1
Template: order.htx
SQLStatement:
+ select
+ b.title, b.work_id, nvl(to_char(b.price,'$990.00'),'Not
For Sale!') price,
+ a.first_name, a.middle_name, a.last_name,
+ a.firm_name, a.address, a.city, a.state, a.zip,
a.specialty,
+ nvl(a.phone,'NONE') phone, nvl(a.fax,'NONE') fax,
nvl(a.email,'NONE') email
+ from artist a, artwork b
+ where a.artist_id = b.artist_id
+ and b.work_id = '%work_id%'
```

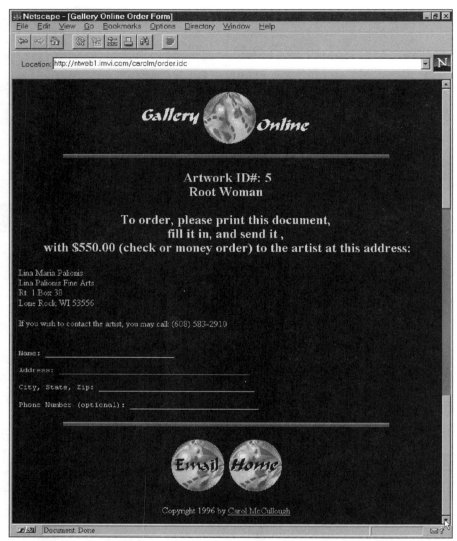

Figure 22-8: The Order document displays facts about the artwork and the artist.

This document also contains logic to handle cases where the artwork is not for sale. Look in the HTML markups for `<%if price EQ "Not For Sale!" %>` in the HTML markups shown in Listing 22-6. The only time the price column has the phrase "Not For Sale!" in it is when the price in the database is null, indicating it is not for sale. An appropriate message is placed on the Order document. For items that are for sale, the price and instructions on how to order are there instead.

This document contains logic to format the e-mail, phone, and fax numbers as well. This is simply to illustrate how you customize the look of the document, based on values from the database.

Listing 22-6   **HTML markups for Order document (order.htx)**

```
<HTML>
<HEAD>
<TITLE>Gallery Online Order Form</TITLE>
</HEAD>
<BODY>
<! Background is Black, text is yellow Link is neon blue,
Visited link is Green,
Active link is light blue>
<BODY BGCOLOR="000000" TEXT="#FFFF00" LINK="#3399FF"
      VLINK="#00FF00" ALINK="#33FFFF">
<TITLE>Online Gallery Order Form</TITLE>
<CENTER>
<IMG SRC = "http://ntweb1.imvi.com/carolm/images/head_sm.gif"
  ALT="[gallery online logo]" WIDTH=323 HEIGHT=110 >
<IMG SRC =
"http://ntweb1.imvi.com/carolm/images/lineredb.gif"
ALT="[line]" WIDTH=587 HEIGHT=7>
<%begindetail%>
<P>
<H2>
<%title%> <P>
</H2>
</CENTER>
<%if  price EQ "Not For Sale!" %>
   <CENTER>
   <H2>Sorry, this work of art is not for sale. You may
contact the artist by writing:</H2>
   </CENTER>
<%else%>
   <CENTER>
   <H2>
   To order, please print this document, <BR>
        fill it in, and send it , <BR>
   with <%price%> (check or money order) to the artist at
this address:<P>
```

(continued)

Listing 22-6 *(continued)*

```
) </CENTER>
   </H2><P>
<%endif%>
<%first_name%> <%middle_name%> <%last_name%><BR>
<%firm_name%><BR>
<%address%><BR>
<%city%> <%state%> <%zip%><P>
<%if   phone EQ "NONE" %>
   <BR>
<%else%>
   If you wish to contact the artist, you may call:
   <%phone%><BR>
<%endif%>
<%if   fax EQ "NONE" %>
   <P>
<%else%>
   Fax the artist at:
   <%fax%><BR>
<%endif%>
<%if   email EQ "NONE" %>
   <BR>
<%else%>
   E-mail: <%email%><BR>
<%endif%>
<P>
<PRE>
Name: _____
Address: _____
City, State, Zip: _____
Phone Number (optional): _____
</PRE>
<%enddetail%>
<%if CurrentRecord EQ 0 %>
<I><B>Sorry, no Details Available for this Artwork.
<P>
<%else%>
<%endif%>
<CENTER>
<IMG SRC =
"http://ntweb1.imvi.com/carolm/images/lineredb.gif"
ALT="[lline]" WIDTH=587 HEIGHT=7 >
<P>
<A HREF="mailto:mcculc@maui.net"><IMG SRC =
"http://ntweb1.imvi.com/carolm/images/btn_mail.gif"
   ALT="e-mail button" WIDTH=100 HEIGHT=100 BORDER=0 ></A>
<A HREF="http://ntweb1.imvi.com/carolm/home.htm"><IMG SRC =
```

```
"http://ntweb1.imvi.com/carolm/images/btn_home.gif"
  ALT="home button" WIDTH=100 HEIGHT=100 BORDER=0 ></A>
<P>
<P>Copyright 1996 by <A
HREF="http://www.maui.net/~mcculc">Carol McCullough</A>
</html>
```

Method 2: NetDynamics

You can go to the Spider Technologies Web site and try out the Art Gallery on the UNIX platform at: `http://www.netdynamics.com/action`. Go there and click on the link called Gallery Online. This project was developed in Windows 95 and ported to UNIX. The entire application, called NetDynamics project, appears on the CD-ROM in this book. (A "thank you" goes to Pramod Gopinath of Spider Technologies for technical assistance in bringing this project to successful completion.)

Creating a new project

The first step for using NetDynamics creates an environment for your entire set of Web documents. It establishes the most important pages, and then additional pages are built in later. The connection to the database tables is defined here.

Start the Oracle 7 database. Then start NetDynamics Studio. The studio has a Wizard that you use to create three pages right away. Choose Create New Project in the Startup window (see Figure 22-9).

Type in **Artgallery** as the project name and click on Create. Later, you open this project to make changes and additions to it. The next screen gives you several choices of things to do with the Wizards. Click on Search Page, Main Page(s), and a Drill Down Results Page and click on Next.

Create a data source for the project. Type **artgallery** in the Dataobject name. This is the name for the group of tables and columns that you may use in the project. Click on the Create Data Source button on the right side of the screen. This brings up the Data Source Window. Type **artgallery** in the Data Source Name field on the next window and click Next. Now, select the database name that you created when you installed the Intersol ODBC driver. Type **gallery** for the user ID and **gallery** for the password to get access to the tables you created for the online gallery in Oracle. Click on Finish to complete the data source. You now click on Next, as shown in Figure 22-10, to continue to the table selection screen.

Figure 22-9: Start up NetDynamics Studio and create a new project.

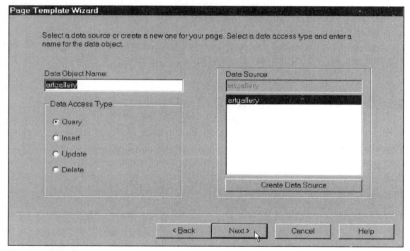

Figure 22-10: Use the Data Source for querying the tables.

Select the two tables for the art gallery, ARTIST and ARTWORK. Move each to the right (selected) window by highlighting and then clicking on the button with the greater than (>) sign. Your window looks like Figure 22-11 when you are ready to continue. Click Next and move to the Joins screen. Here, simply click on the Auto Join button and let the Wizard define the table join for you. Because the tables share the ARTIST_ID column, the Wizard has no trouble correctly linking the two tables. Click on the Next button for working on the Search Page.

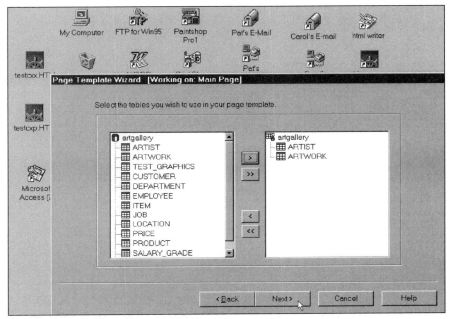

Figure 22-11: Select ARTIST and ARTWORK tables for this project.

The Query form

Looking at your specifications, select all the columns from the two tables that you've chosen for searching. Move each column to the right window by using the "greater than" button. Click them in the same order you want to see them on the screen, and you'll save some time. Figure 22-12 shows the list you create.

This document will need some work later, adding customized HTML to make it easier to use. The default document works, but does not include selection lists, which make the document easier to use for your visitor. Now, click on the Next button to prepare the Query Results document. The Wizard calls this the Main Page.

The Query Results document

Now it's time to put together the first cut on the Query Results document. Like the Query document, (that is, before we modify it with the editor), when we place the columns on the page is just the beginning. The final arrangement and the look of the document come later. Select Single Page for the layout type and click on the Next button to proceed with the design.

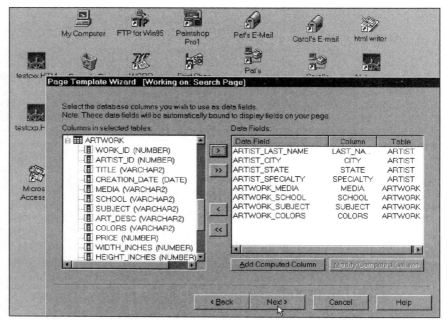

Figure 22-12: The Search Page window enables you to select all the columns to search in all tables.

Choose Report in the Style box and Table in the Layout box on the following screen. Click the Next button to move to the screen where all the columns are placed on the page is just the beginning. Here, using the specifications for this document, select all the columns to be displayed on the results page. Once again, move the selected items into the window on the right, as shown in Figure 22-13. Click on the Next button.

On the database actions screen, you need only select the navigational commands, leaving out the commands that allow changes to the data. The query results page is only for viewing the database, not changing it. So, select the First, Last, Next, and Prev commands, moving them to the right window. Click on the Next button to move on.

Choose ARTWORK_TITLE as the field where a hyperlink will send you to the drilldown results page, a.k.a. the Artwork Details document. Click on the Next button.

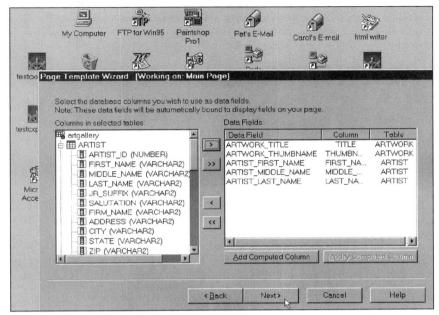

Figure 22-13: All columns that are selected become assigned to the document and bound to display fields.

Artwork Details document

The first thing to define on the Drilldown results page are the tables needed to display the details. You need the ARTIST table for the artist's name and the ARTWORK table for the title, description, and the rest of the details about the artwork itself. Choose the two tables here, and click on the Next button. Click the Auto Join button to enable the Wizard to connect the two tables for you. Then click the Next button. You are now at the layout screen.

Choose Report in the Style Box and Freeform in the Layout box for this one. Click the Next button. You've now reached the column selection screen. Referring again to the specifications, select all the columns needed for the Details document as displayed in Figure 22-14. The FILENAME column will be customized into an image HTML tag along with the PIXEL_WIDTH and PIXEL_HEIGHT columns.

The complete list of selected columns (using the names that the Wizard assigned) is as follows:

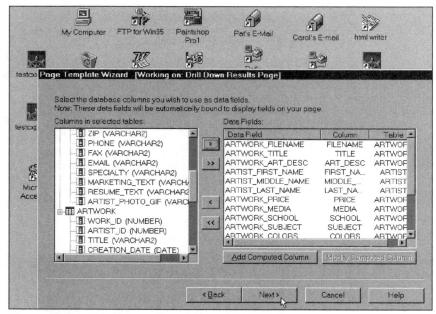

Figure 22-14: The Artwork Details document needs columns, as shown here.

➡ ARTWORK_FILENAME

➡ ARTWORK_PIXEL_WIDTH

☛ ARTWORK_PIXEL_HEIGHT

➡ ARTWORK_TITLE

➡ ARTIST_FIRST_NAME

➡ ARTIST_MIDDLE_NAME

➡ ARTIST_LAST_NAME

➡ ARTWORK_PRICE

➡ ARTWORK_MEDIA

➡ ARTWORK_WIDTH_INCHES

➡ ARTWORK_HEIGHT_INCHES

➡ ARTWORK_DEPTH_INCHES

➡ ARTWORK_COLORS

➡ ARTWORK_ART_DESC

➡ ARTWORK_SCHOOL

➡ ARTWORK_SUBJECT

Click on the Next button to reach the database action screen. Here, no actions are needed, because we see only a single row of data on the Artwork Details document. Click on the Next button and move to the hyperlink definition screen. Simply click on the right to get a menu of all the fields. Connect the ARTWORK_TITLE link on the Query Results document with the same column on the Artwork Details document. Click on the Next button. Click on the Finish button, and you have finished creating three functioning Web pages that access the database. This returns you to the NetDynamics Studio.

Compile and test by clicking on the menu items. Figures 22-15 through 22-17 show the Web documents as they were created by the NetDynamics Wizard. Although they are a bit awkward, they all work. We add the finishing details in the next section.

Use the Main Page Wizard to create the final two database documents, the Artist Profile and the Order document. You create the Home document by using traditional HTML editing. The steps to link them all together are covered later. Now, you'll see how these first three pages are edited for a better look and to display the graphics in place of the filenames for the artworks.

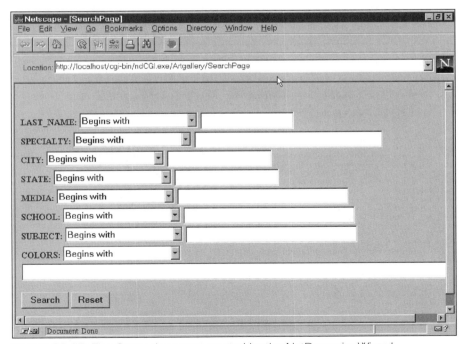

Figure 22-15: The Query document created by the NetDynamics Wizard.

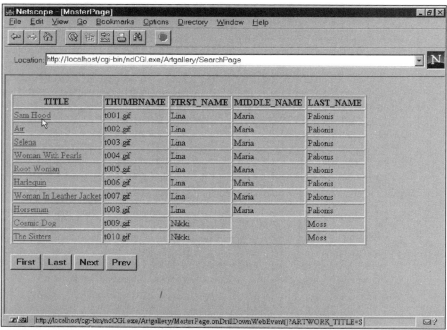

Figure 22-16: The Query Results document has a table layout.

Attention to details pays off when using NetDynamics

To test drive your new application, be careful to follow these steps in the exact order listed here. This order is very important, because you might get unexpected results and errors when in fact the documents are valid — if you fail to execute these in the correct order.

1. Start the Oracle database.

2. Start Web server.

3. Start NetDynamics Resident.

4. Start NetDynamics Controller.

5. Start Netscape.

6. Type the URL shown here in the location box, except replace *localhost* with your PC's name:
   ```
   http://localhost/cgi-bin/ndCGI.exe/Gallery/SearchPage
   ```

The Resident and Controller steps will start automatically for the newer releases of the product, so check your documentation.

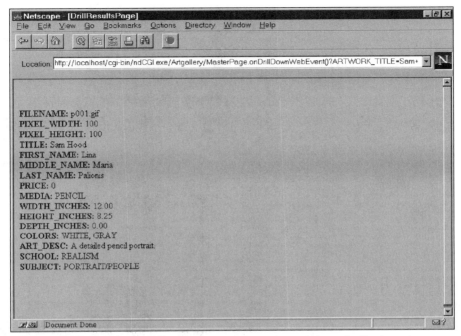

Figure 22-17: The Artwork Details document needs work to make the layout more attractive.

Adding images

Adding images in NetDynamics means adding a new object. The toolbar has an image button for this. You want to add a logo on top of each page, a horizontal line on the bottom, and two buttons (Home and Email) under the horizontal line. This section describes how to add one graphic image to the Query Form document (SearchPage). You add all the others in the same way.

To do this, go to NetDynamics Studio, open the Artgallery project, and highlight the SearchPage page. Now click on the Image icon on the left vertical toolbar. This adds a new image to this document, whose properties are listed in the right window. Refer to Figure 22-18, and modify the image properties as follows:

➡ **DefaultValue: graphic filename.** Connect the image object with a graphic file by typing the name of the file here. Precede the filename with a slash. Place the graphics files in the Document directory of your Server. For Windows 95, using Microsoft Front Page Personal Server, this is the C:\FrontPage Webs\Content directory.

➡ **Label: short description.** This description appears in the HTML Editor as a NetDynamics variable. Make the description short but descriptive enough to identify the image.

➡ **Name: short description.** Use the same description here as you put into Label.

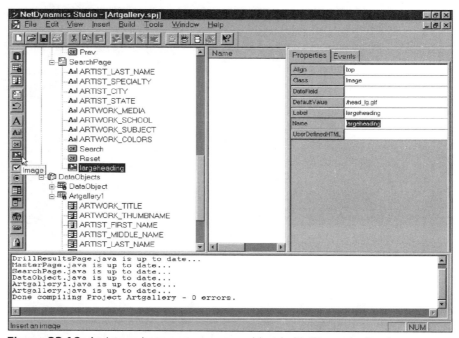

Figure 22-18: An image becomes one more object in NetDynamics Studio.

Edit the page in HTML Editor. You will see the image only as the label with two asterisks on either side, like all the other NetDynamics objects. Use Cut and Paste to move the image label to the location you prefer. Save the file and close the HTML Editor.

User-defined HTML

This project requires some HTML programming within the NetDynamics Studio. Following are the HTML markups that you place into the UserDefinedHTML property window for the Thumbnail column. This is the column that contains the filename for the small version of the artwork. This graphic is listed in a table on the Results document. Figure 22-19 shows the User-Defined HTML window where the following HTML markups reside.

```
<IMG SRC="/**ARTWORK_THUMBNAME**" width=100 height=100>
```

Figure 22-19: User-defined HTML changes the way a data field is displayed.

Markups for pop-up selection menus go into the User-Defined HTML window for several of the search parameter fields on the Search document. Here are the markups for the Specialty field:

```
Specialty (choose one):

<select name="specialty" size=1>

<OPTION VALUE="">ANY</option>

<OPTION VALUE=ACRYLIC>ACRYLIC</option>

<OPTION VALUE=CHARCOAL>CHARCOAL</option>

<OPTION VALUE=DIGITAL>DIGITAL</option>

<OPTION VALUE=PENCIL>PENCIL</option>

<OPTION VALUE=OIL>OIL</option>

<OPTION VALUE=WATERCOLOR>WATERCOLOR</option>

<OPTION VALUE=WOOD>WOOD</option>

</select>
```

Editing documents

You select your favorite HTML editor and NetDynamics starts it so that you can edit any of the Web documents it has created.

You add font sizes, centering, tables, and frames to the document as you want. Adjusting the font size of the NetDynamics object (such as the Artist Name) makes the resulting document display the artist's name in the font size selected. *You must be cautious while editing so that you do not alter the beginning and ending Spider commands, which are shown in square brackets.* These commands control the flow of the entire document.

Linking more pages

There are two more pages that link from the Artwork Details document (DrillDownPage) and these are created first and then linked to the page. Create them one at a time by using the NetDynamics Page Wizard. In the NetDynamics Studio, with the Artgallery project open, click on the Insert Page and then menu selections, then select Main as the page type. Use the specifications to complete the pages. *Be sure to include the ARTIST_ID in the Artist Profile document and the ARTWORK_ID in the Order document!* These link up the pages.

You accomplish the link by creating a Link object, assigning it to a data field, and linking it to a data field in the Artist Profile document. The procedure to do this is complex, and you may need assistance from Spider's capable technical support staff. Not only is the linking process complex, but it is doubly complex because there are two drill-down events on one page. This requires small modifications to the Java code that NetDynamics generates. With telephone support from Spider, you can successfully make the small modifications needed.

Using the CD-ROM

Summary

All the markups found here are also contained in the CD-ROM accompanying this book. By studying the markups and examples here and by reviewing the workings of the actual database examples on the Internet, you are now well equipped to start your own project. See the instructions found on the CD-ROM to install the software. After installing it, you have a working version of the project developed in this chapter. You can also follow the instructions here and create your own version of this project, using the data included on the CD-ROM, or you can create a whole new project, referring to the finished product included on the CD-ROM as a guide.

Creating the Access Database Tables

In This Chapter

Creating tables

Table relationships

Queries

Reports

Microsoft Access, like its competitors Paradox, Approach, and others, provides desktop computer users with an easy way to create powerful database applications. Why? Because these database engines come with development tools built in. In fact, the development tools are so well integrated that it is inconceivable to most PC users that they might be separated; and the development capability features help market these database engines. Thus, if you create the Art Gallery by using Access, it's a relatively simple chore. Unfortunately, you must program a good portion of the database application for an intranet or the Internet by using Web-database development tools. You cannot do Web programming with Access yet. Nonetheless, you can get off to a flying start by setting up the tables in Access — and even performing a query "trick" by using Access. For straightforward conversions of Access database tables, queries, and reports to static HTML documents, you can use Access Internet Assistant (see Chapter 11).

The authors chose Access as an example because a significant portion of the PC market uses it as a database. To create this example, you need Access (not provided). To run the ARTGAL demo on the CD-ROM you don't need Access, just the Access database file provided on the CD-ROM. If you don't have Access, you can create the Art Gallery database tables by using another database engine, and then import the comma-delimited data on the CD-ROM. That gives you database tables to use with Cold Fusion, the Web-database development tool covered in the next chapter.

Tables

In most cases, tables are straightforward to create. You will probably find constructing tables to be the easiest task you do in building your Web-database application.

ARTIS

Start a new database in Access (Version 7.0) and call it ARTGAL. Select the Tables tab and click on the New button. You get the New Table panel. Select Design View and click on the OK button. You get a form for creating a table. Refer to the Art Gallery database design in Chapter 20, "Art Gallery Database Project." That gives you the column names and sizes. Enter the first column (field) name **artist_id** and then tab to the data type, where you select Number. (Tab to Description if you would like to add a description phrase to remind you what artist_id stands for.) Take your cursor and go down to Field Size and click on the downward-pointing arrow. Select Integer, which will accommodate a number up to 32,000. You have now completed your first column (see Figure 23-1).

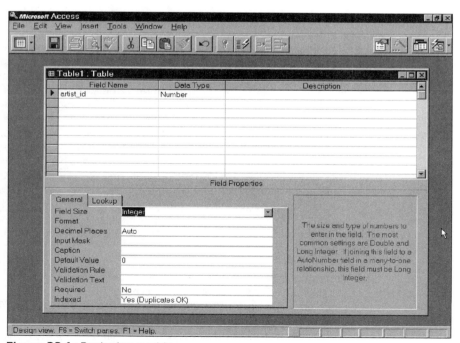

Figure 23-1: Beginning a table.

Move your cursor to the second line at the top and type the next column, **first_name.** Complete that column and the remaining columns according to the database design. When you get to the second- and third-from-last columns, marketing_text and resume_text, select Memo for the data type (see Figure 23-2).

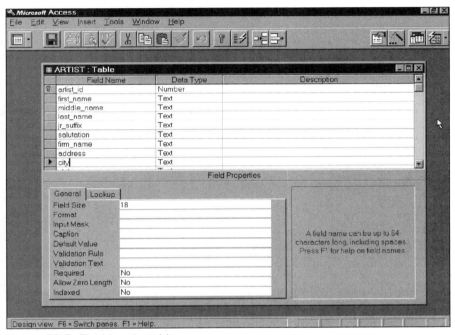

Figure 23-2: Finishing the table.

When you finish, double-click in the upper left-hand corner of the panel. Access asks whether you want to save Table 1; click on Yes. You then get a dialog box asking you to name the table; type **ARTIST** and click on OK (see Figure 23-3).

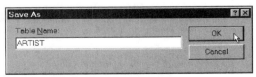

Figure 23-3: Naming the table.

Now, click on the Datasheet View icon in the upper left-hand corner of the window, just under File. You should see the table you have created. You can now fill in the table with data (see Figure 23-4).

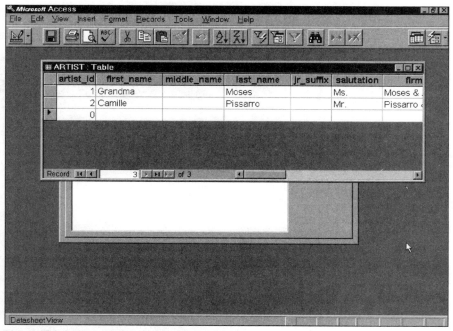

Figure 23-4: The ARTIST table (Datasheet View) with some trial data.

Creating tables is a straightforward process, and you can do the second one as easily as the first.

ARTWORK

Return to the database design in Chapter 20, "Art Gallery Database Project," and use it to create the second table: ARTWORK. For creation_date, select Date/Time and Short Date; for art_desc, select Text and Memo; for price, select Currency in dollars; and for inches and pixel measurements and copyright_year, select Number and Integer. The remainder of the columns are text (see Figures 23-5 and 23-6).

Notice in the Datasheet View that the ARTWORK table has the column artist_id in common with the ARTIST table. Make sure that the data types are the same for each of these common columns. Now that you have completed the tables, you can create the relationship between the tables.

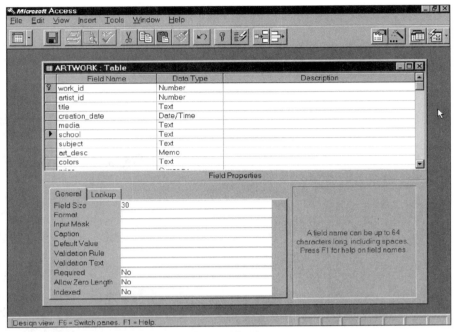

Figure 23-5: The ARTWORK table (Design View).

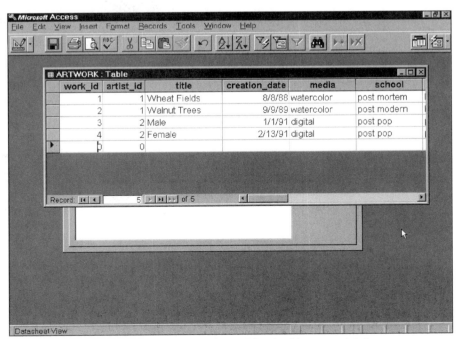

Figure 23-6: The ARTWORK table (Datasheet View) with some trial data.

Relationship

Next, you relate the tables by relating the common column (field) artist_id. Start from a freshly opened database view and click on the Relationships button (see Figure 23-7).

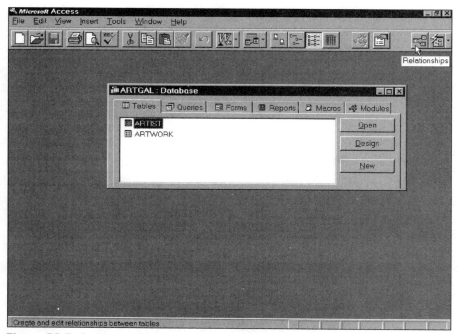

Figure 23-7: Start creating the relationship between tables.

A blank window appears (see Figure 23-8).

Size and place the Relationships window and the ARTGAL database window so that you can see them both at once for dragging and dropping (see Figure 23-9).

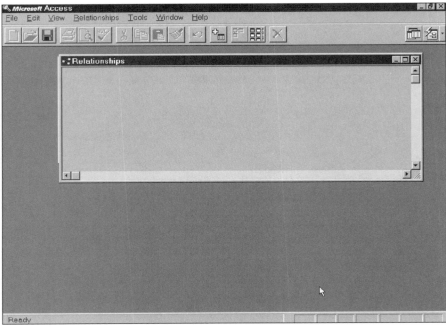

Figure 23-8: Use a blank window to create relationships.

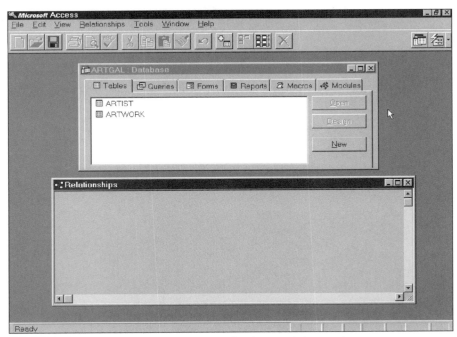

Figure 23-9: Size and place the windows for drag-and-drop action.

Drag the ARTIST table into the Relationships window by putting the cursor on the ARTIST table, holding down the left button, and dragging (see Figures 23-10 and 23-11).

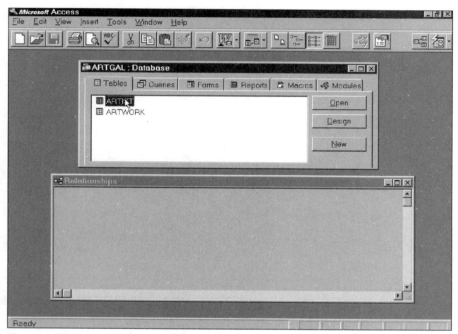

Figure 23-10: Drag the ARTIST table.

Do the same with the ARTWORK table so that both tables appear in the Relationships window (see Figure 23-12).

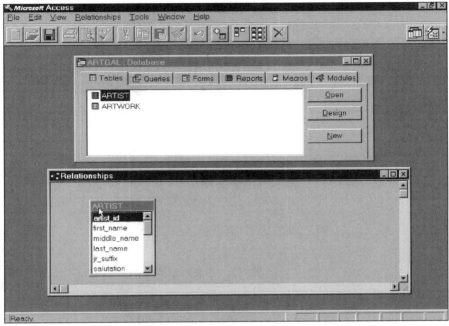

Figure 23-11: The ARTIST table in the Relationships window.

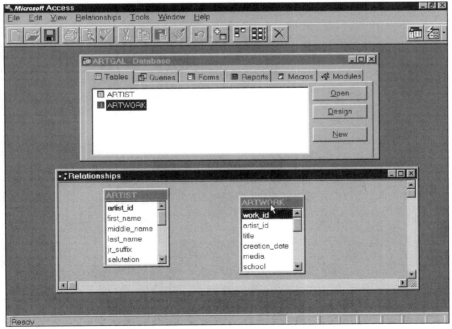

Figure 23-12: Both tables in the Relationships window.

Next, drag artist_id in the ARTIST table (in the Relationships window) to artist_id in the ARTWORK table. A Relationships dialog box pops up. Click on the Create button (see Figure 23-13).

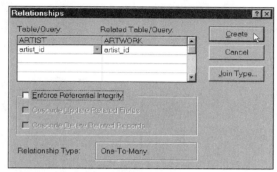

Figure 23-13: The Relationships panel.

As a result of clicking on Create, Access shows a relationship between the two tables. A line connects artist_id in each table (see Figure 23-14).

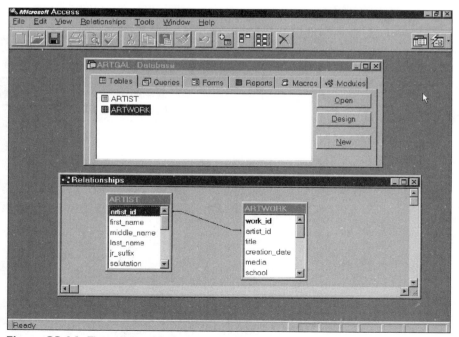

Figure 23-14: The relationship is shown graphically.

ARTGAL is now a relational database that includes two tables with the common column artist_id. Save the graphical presentation of the relationship when exiting the Relationships panel.

Queries

The database design from Chapter 20, "Art Gallery Database Project," is the basis for creating the following queries. Click on the Queries tab in the Database window and then click on the New button. You're ready to construct a query.

Why bother?

Except with an HTML conversion tool such as Access Internet Assistant, you cannot complete the database application for an intranet or the Internet in Access, so why bother doing the queries in Access? One reason is quick testing with some test data to determine whether the tables are well conceived. Perhaps the most practical reason is to generate the SQL code. You can do the queries quickly and easily in Access. Then you can have Access list the SQL code for the queries. Thus, you will have the code in hand. If you are using a Web-database development tool that requires you to provide SQL code, the Access code listing will help you with your Web-database application work.

Unfortunately, the Access SQL is not standard. Thus, if you *do* need to generate SQL code, Access does not do the job 100 percent for you. A better approach is to use MS Query, which is mentioned in Chapter 24. It is very similar to Access and comes with Windows 95.

Nonetheless, the SQL code you can generate with Access can be used with Cold Fusion's Access ODBC driver without any changes; thus strictly for the purposes of this project, Access is used to help create the SQL queries.

Create the queries

In Access, you create queries in a graphical user interface rather than by using a database language. Although using a GUI seems to be a natural process for creating tables, it is a little less natural for creating queries. To test what you do each step of the way, you should enter some test data in the tables you have created (see Listings 23-1 and 23-2).

Listing 23-1   Test data for the ARTIST table

```
1,"Grandma",,"Moses",,"Ms.","Moses & Associates","133 Moses
Lane","Mosesville","AK","24451","219-345-6789",,"gram@isp.com",
"oil","More with Moses.","yyyyyyyyy","moses.gif"
2,"Camille",,"Pissarro",,"Mr.","Pissarro & Company","122
Pissarro Rd.","Pissarroville","AZ","34410","429-456-7890",
,"cam@isp.com","oil","For your viewing pleasure with
Pissarro.","zzzzzzzzzz","pissarro.gif"
```

Listing 23-2   Test data for the ARTWORK table

```
1,1,"Wheat Fields",8/8/88 0:00:00,"watercolor","post mortem",
"landscape","Fields","green",$295.00,24,30,1,234,278,"field
.gif","t-field.gif",1988,"Moses"
2,1,"Walnut Trees",9/9/89 0:00:00,"watercolor","post modern",
"landscape","Trees","red",$235.00,25,29,1,270,310,"trees.gif",
"t-trees.gif",1989,"Moses"
3,2,"Male",1/1/91 0:00:00,"digital","post pop","portrait",
"Man","yellow",$275.00,26,30,2,278,337,"male.gif","t-male.gif",
1992,"Pissarro"
4,2,"Female",2/13/91 0:00:00,"digital","post pop","portrait",
"Woman","white",$250.00,18,32,1,134,260,"female.gif",
"t-female.gif",1992,"Pissarro"
```

The first query discussed here seeks artworks selected by the artist's name; in other words, all the artworks in the Art Gallery made by the individual artist chosen (see Chapter 20, Figure 20-3). These artworks go into the second HTML document (Chapter 20, Figure 20-4), a catalog of art. The database application generates this catalog on the fly based on a visitor's input.

Test data

Test data consists of a few records (as many as you need) to test your tables and queries in a number of different ways. You can use real data, or you can make up phony test data, as done in this chapter. Give some thought to structuring your test data so that it tests numerous features of your database.

Artist's works by artist's name

Click on the Queries tab and then click on Create. Select Design View on the New Query panel and click OK (see Figure 23-15).

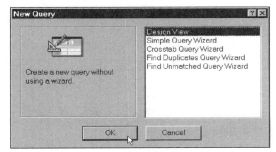

Figure 23-15: Starting construction of a query.

The first query selects artworks by an artist's name, last_name. It is specified in Chapter 20, Figure 20-4. It uses the columns first_name, middle_name, last_name, and jr_suffix from the ARTIST table, and thumbname and title from the ARTWORK table. Therefore, you must include both tables in the query. You first add the ARTIST table to the Query window by highlighting ARTIST and clicking on Add; then hightlight ARTWORK and click on Add. Both tables will appear in the Query window (see Figure 23-16).

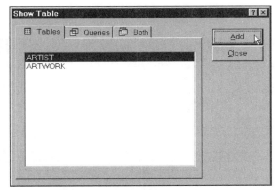

Figure 23-16: Add both tables to the Query window.

The query shows the tables with the relationship between them, just as in the Relationships window (see Figure 23-17).

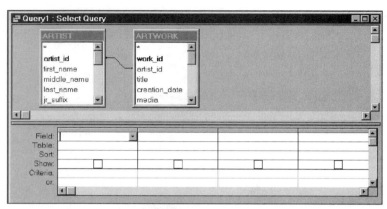

Figure 23-17: Both tables in the Query window.

Save the query; name it Artist by Name; and reopen it. By double-clicking on the specific columns you need in each table, you can add them to the query. For the column last_name, type in **Pissarro** on the Criteria line to do a selection based on the test data. Because your test data will be different, of course, you use a different word, one that tests the data for the last_name column (see Figure 23-18).

When you're finished, switch to Datasheet View by clicking on the Datasheet View icon in the upper left corner. You see that the query has returned the two works of art by the artist Pissarro from the test data (see Figure 23-19).

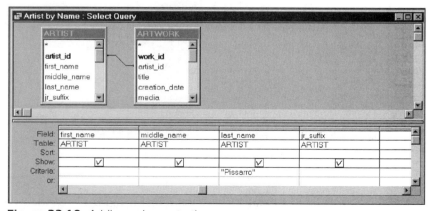

Figure 23-18: Adding columns to the query.

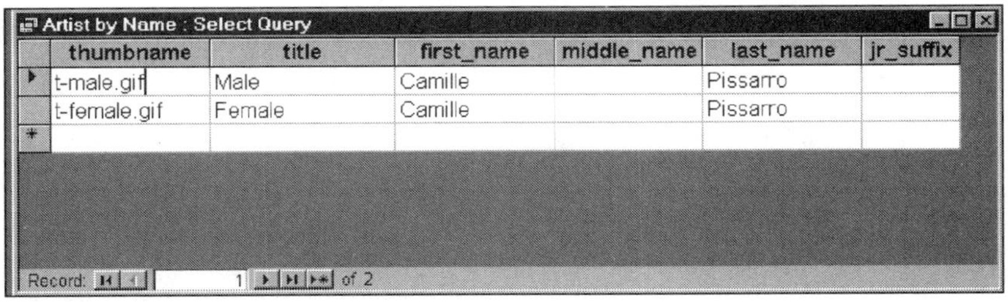

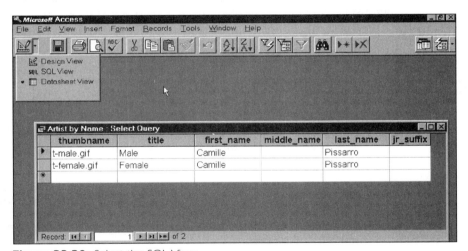

Figure 23-19: The query returns the data sought.

Next, click on the downward-pointing arrow by the Design View icon in the upper left corner. On the short menu, you have a choice of Design View, SQL View, and Datasheet View. Select SQL View (see Figure 23-20).

Figure 23-20: Select the SQL View.

The SQL window pops up with the SQL code in it for the query you have just constructed (see Figure 23-21).

Note that you can copy and paste this code to another program where you may need it. The code is included here for a more readable version:

```
SELECT DISTINCTROW ARTWORK.thumbname, ARTWORK.title,
ARTIST.first_name, ARTIST.middle_name, ARTIST.last_name,
ARTIST.jr_suffix
FROM ARTWORK INNER JOIN ARTIST ON ARTWORK.artist_id =
ARTIST.artist_id
WHERE (((ARTIST.last_name)="Pissarro"));
```

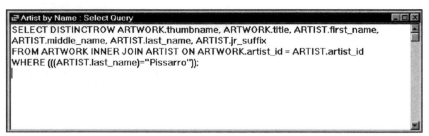

```
Artist by Name : Select Query                                          _ □ ×
SELECT DISTINCTROW ARTWORK.thumbname, ARTWORK.title, ARTIST.first_name,
ARTIST.middle_name, ARTIST.last_name, ARTIST.jr_suffix
FROM ARTWORK INNER JOIN ARTIST ON ARTWORK.artist_id = ARTIST.artist_id
WHERE (((ARTIST.last_name)="Pissarro"));
```

Figure 23-21: The SQL code.

Remaining queries

The remaining queries differ from the preceding in that they seek artworks generally rather than one artist's works. The variable is the quality or characteristic, which is the basis of the search. The variables are the following:

- Artworks by specialty (of the artists)
- Artworks by city (of the artists)
- Artworks by state (of the artists)
- Artworks by media (of the work)
- Artworks by school of art (of the work)
- Artworks by subject matter (of the work)
- Artworks by colors (in the work)

Each of these queries is identical to the Artist by Name query except that an additional column will be added. For example, for the Artworks by City search, add the column City to the query specifying a test data entry on the Criteria line (see Figure 23-22).

```
Art Works by City : Select Query                                       _ □ ×
  ┌─ARTIST──────┐      ┌─ARTWORK─────┐
  │ jr_suffix    │──────│ title        │
  │ salutation   │      │ creation_date│
  │ firm_name    │      │ media        │
  │ address      │      │ school       │
  │ city         │      │ subject      │
  │ state        │      │ art_desc     │
  └──────────────┘      └──────────────┘

Field:  last_name     jr_suffix      city
Table:  ARTIST        ARTIST         ARTIST
Sort:
Show:     ☑             ☑              ☐            ☐
Criteria:                            "Pissarroville"
or:
```

Figure 23-22: *Artworks by City* query.

The SQL code is almost identical to Artists by Name, as follows:

```
SELECT DISTINCTROW ARTWORK.thumbname, ARTWORK.title,
ARTIST.first_name, ARTIST.middle_name, ARTIST.last_name,
ARTIST.jr_suffix
FROM ARTIST INNER JOIN ARTWORK ON ARTIST.artist_id =
ARTWORK.artist_id
WHERE (((ARTIST.city)="Pissarroville"));
```

The remainder of this section shows the SQL code for each query, in the event that you need them to understand how to complete the Art Gallery project using the Web-database development tools of your choice (see Listings 23-3 through 23-8).

Listing 23-3   Artwork by specialty

```
SELECT DISTINCTROW ARTWORK.thumbname, ARTWORK.title,
ARTIST.first_name, ARTIST.middle_name, ARTIST.last_name,
ARTIST.jr_suffix
FROM ARTIST INNER JOIN ARTWORK ON ARTIST.artist_id =
ARTWORK.artist_id
WHERE (((ARTIST.specialty)="oil"));
```

Listing 23-4   Artwork by state

```
SELECT DISTINCTROW ARTWORK.thumbname, ARTWORK.title,
ARTIST.first_name, ARTIST.middle_name, ARTIST.last_name,
ARTIST.jr_suffix
FROM ARTIST INNER JOIN ARTWORK ON ARTIST.artist_id =
ARTWORK.artist_id
WHERE (((ARTIST.state)="AK"));
```

Listing 23-5   Artwork by media

```
SELECT DISTINCTROW ARTWORK.thumbname, ARTWORK.title,
ARTIST.first_name, ARTIST.middle_name, ARTIST.last_name,
ARTIST.jr_suffix
FROM ARTIST INNER JOIN ARTWORK ON ARTIST.artist_id =
ARTWORK.artist_id
WHERE (((ARTWORK.media)="watercolor"));
```

Listing 23-6   Artwork by school of art

```
SELECT DISTINCTROW ARTWORK.thumbname, ARTWORK.title,
ARTIST.first_name, ARTIST.middle_name, ARTIST.last_name,
ARTIST.jr_suffix
FROM ARTIST INNER JOIN ARTWORK ON ARTIST.artist_id =
ARTWORK.artist_id
WHERE (((ARTWORK.school)="post modern"));
```

Listing 23-7   Artwork by subject matter

```
SELECT DISTINCTROW ARTWORK.thumbname, ARTWORK.title,
ARTIST.first_name, ARTIST.middle_name, ARTIST.last_name,
ARTIST.jr_suffix
FROM ARTIST INNER JOIN ARTWORK ON ARTIST.artist_id =
ARTWORK.artist_id
WHERE (((ARTWORK.subject)="portrait"));
```

Listing 23-8   Artwork by colors

```
SELECT DISTINCTROW ARTWORK.thumbname, ARTWORK.title,
ARTIST.first_name, ARTIST.middle_name, ARTIST.last_name,
ARTIST.jr_suffix
FROM ARTIST INNER JOIN ARTWORK ON ARTIST.artist_id =
ARTWORK.artist_id
WHERE (((ARTWORK.colors)="yellow"));
```

As you may have noted, the only difference between all of these code listings is the last line.

Reports

Normally, you create database reports to print the information that a database application generates. In this case, your reports resulting from the queries will be HTML documents created on the fly using a template, as is discussed in Chapter 24, "Connecting the Access Database Application to the Web." (You therefore cannot use Version 7.0 of Access for the report portion of the project, although you can use Access Internet Assistant to create static HTML reports that can serve as the basis for template design in certain cases.) A visitor queries the database application by entering input into the HTML form in the first HTML document (see Chapter 20, Figure 20-3). The query returns the information required to create the second HTML document, which is a catalog (see Chapter 20, Figure 20-4), along with an HTML template for the catalog. Together, the information resulting from the query and the HTML template generate the catalog on the fly. The catalog contains thumbnail graphics representing the artworks together with the titles of the artworks and the artists' names.

From the catalog, visitors can elect to see the full digital version of an individual artwork together with more comprehensive information (the individual work). A visitor can also elect to see a resume of the artist (the professional profile). Because these visitor elections require further queries to generate the information for the individual work (third HTML document, Chapter 20, Figure 20-5) and the professional profile (fourth HTML document, Chapter 20, Figure 20-6), you must determine the additional information needed for these queries.

The easiest way to make a query to generate the information for the individual work is directly by work_id. The easiest way to generate the information for the professional profile is directly by artist_id. Because these two columns were not needed for display in the catalog, however, they were not included in the catalog design (Chapter 20, Figure 20-4). Nonetheless, these columns are needed in the catalog for the queries that return the individual work and the professional profile, even though they *will not be visible* to visitors. Add them to the columns that are returned by the original query (Chapter 20, Figure 20-3). To adjust all the queries just constructed, simply add the following after SELECT DISTINCTROW:

```
ARTWORK.work_id, ARTIST.artist_id,
```

Loading data

If you can get your data in digital form, you can load it more easily into a database application. For example, if the data exists in another database application, it can be exported in delimited form (that is, comma delimited) from that database and imported into your database. This is a simple procedure that you can learn easily by referring to your database engine software documentation.

For manual input, transferring data from a digital source, such as a word processing document, an e-mail message, or another digital text file, is preferable to typing the text. You simply highlight what you want to transfer, copy it to the Clipboard, and paste it into the appropriate row and column in your database table.

This change returns work_id and artist_id, which are needed for constructing the subsequent queries for the individual work document and the professional profile document. For example, the query Artist by Name changes as follows:

```
SELECT DISTINCTROW ARTWORK.work_id, ARTIST.artist_id,
ARTWORK.thumbname, ARTWORK.title, ARTIST.first_name,
ARTIST.middle_name, ARTIST.last_name, ARTIST.jr_suffix
FROM ARTWORK INNER JOIN ARTIST ON ARTWORK.artist_id =
ARTIST.artist_id
WHERE (((ARTIST.last_name)="Pissarro"));
```

It is smart to create and test prototype Web documents to be used in the Art Gallery. You then modify such Web documents to create the templates you need for generating documents on the fly with input from the database application. For a small number of documents that differ from each other, an HTML editor is all you need to do this. For a large number of similar documents, you might want to try a Web-publishing program such as HTML Transit, to generate your prototype Web documents.

Summary

The purpose of this chapter was to set up the Art Gallery tables in Access in which to store the Art Gallery data. To do the queries for a Web database application and to generate Web documents on the fly, you learn to use a Web-database development tool, Cold Fusion, in the next chapter. In the meanwhile, this chapter digressed by using Access to create the queries, primarily for the purpose of learning to generate the SQL code. This is a trick for non-programmers well worth acquiring that may come in handy for Web-database development.

Connecting the Access Database Application to the Web

For convenience, you can envision the database application as being connected to the Web site. In reality, the connections themselves — the connections between the HTML forms, the Web server, and the database engine — make up a major portion of the database application, and it doesn't make much sense to talk about the connections as if they were something separate or trivial. As you have seen in earlier chapters, you can make the connections with CGI scripts — if you're a programmer. If you're not, you need something like an authoring program to make the connection for you. Cold Fusion is a program that nonprogrammers can use easily and effectively to create Web-database applications without programming.

This chapter demonstrates how to use the Access tables created in the preceding chapter (and filled with data), HTML templates that you can easily create yourself, and Cold Fusion to create the Web-database application outlined in Chapter 20. Cold Fusion does not solve all things for you. You do have to know something about database applications to use it. The Art Gallery (ARTGAL) is a simple application that Cold Fusion can easily handle. In fact, Cold Fusion is a serious tool adequate to handle complex database development well beyond the capability of most nonprogrammers. Cold Fusion does its work with a database markup language that is, in effect, an extension to HTML.

Cold Fusion

Chapter 14, "Data Cataloging", is an important one, even if you never use the data cataloging technique. It demonstrates the idea of creating a complex document with mail merging. It might be appropriate for you to go back and review it now before reading this chapter, because it will help you understand this chapter better.

What is needed is a way to do a mail merge on the fly in response to a query. A visitor initiates the query by using a form in an HTML document. The query causes certain data to be selected from tables and merged into an HTML template. The Web server generates (publishes) the template filled with the selected data on the fly. If you were to invent a system to make this happen, what would it look like?

First, you need variables. The HTML template document must include variables. Each variable represents a piece of data from a column in a table. The convenient thing to do is to name the variable after the column. Thus, the variable for an artist's last name in the template is last_name, the same as the column. After the "mail-merge," the variable last_name in the HTML template will display "Smith" in the HTML document created on the fly, based on data from the row for Harriet Smith, an artist. Second, you need HTML markup-like instructions to create the queries and other database processes as easily as if you were using HTML. Third, you need a program that handles all this behind the scenes for you. Essentially, this is what Cold Fusion does.

Cold Fusion (Version 1.5) has plenty of competition as a Web-database application *authoring* program. It was chosen for the Art Gallery project because it runs on Windows NT; you can create Cold Fusion applications using Windows 95; it was one of the first such programs available; and it has a wide range of capabilities that will satisfy experienced database programmers as well as novices. You may want to try some of its competitors, too (see Chapter 16). For the Art Gallery, Cold Fusion works just fine, and you will find it easy to use.

Perhaps the best way to describe Cold Fusion is to say that it works a little like a spreadsheet (such as Lotus 123). You don't have to be a programmer to use a spreadsheet, but you do need to learn spreadsheet commands. Cold Fusion's database language is like spreadsheet commands. To be more specific, it's like a set of special extensions to HTML — which is exactly what it is.

Database Markup Language

Cold Fusion calls its HTML markup-like instructions Database Markup Language (DBML). Why not? Makes sense, particularly because it's easy — like HTML. Here are a few of the markups:

➥ DBQUERY: Sends an SQL query to the database application. You supply the SQL query.

➥ DBOUTPUT: Shows the results of a query with HTML markups and result set fields.

➥ DBTABLE: Displays the result set fields in a preformatted table.

➥ DBCOL: Shows the result set fields in a preformatted table.

➥ DBINSERT: Inserts data into a table.

➥ DBIF: Creates IF...ELSE statements.

The attributes of the markups are important, too. The next several sections list these attributes.

DBQUERY attributes

➥ NAME: The name that you give the query.

➥ DATASOURCE: The name of the data source (database application).

➥ SQL: SQL statement.

DBOUTPUT attributes

➥ QUERY: The name of the query for which the output is furnished.

DBTABLE attributes

➥ QUERY: The name of the query for which the output in table form is furnished.

➥ MAXROWS: Maximum number of rows to be displayed.

➥ COLSPACING: Number of spaces between columns.

DBCOL attributes

➥ WIDTH: Width of column.

➥ ALIGN: Column alignment (RIGHT, LEFT, CENTER).

➥ TEXT: Double-quote delimited text.

DBINSERT Attributes

➥ DATASOURCE: Name of data source (database application).

➥ TABLENAME: Name of table into which you insert data.

DBIF Syntax

➥ is: Compares two values and returns true if they are identical.

➥ is not: Opposite of is.

➥ greater than: Determines whether a value is greater than a second value.

➥ less than: Determines whether a value is less than a second value.

WebSite

The ARTGAL demo uses O'Reilly & Associates WebSite Web server (Version 1.1). WebSite runs in Windows 95. Because Windows 95 is a multitasking operating system, a Web server can run with other programs simultaneously. Thus, you can use a Web browser to access WebSite at the same time WebSite is running. Likewise, you can make a query through a Web browser to a Cold Fusion database application at the same time WebSite and the application are running. Therefore, you can do development and testing on one PC even though it's a client-server application. A WebSite trial version is available for download on the O'Reilly & Associates Web site (www.ora.com).

WebSite Pro

This package comes with some extras, such as the Hot Dog HTML editor and a scaled-down version of Cold Fusion. Besides an attractive price, the advantage of this special package is that Cold Fusion can link to the WebSite server through the WebSite API as well as via CGI. The WebSite API is a faster connection. The full-featured version of Cold Fusion, however, is not included, and you may need it if your Web-database applications are complex. This book uses the full version of Cold Fusion and the CGI script to do the demonstration Art Gallery, but the ARTGAL demo can be done exactly the same with the WebSite Pro package.

Installation

Installation of Access, WebSite, and Cold Fusion are beyond the scope of this book, but all are quite easy. For Access, you need to install the software using the Microsoft Office installation process if you bought Access as a part of Microsoft Office.

OBDC driver

If you plan to use Access for Web-database applications, it might be a good idea to load the 32-bit ODBC driver onto your hard drive. You may need it for something sooner or later.

To use the Art Gallery demo from the CD-ROM, you do not need Access. The Access ARTGAL database file is provided on the CD-ROM. That's all you need to run the demo. If you will be doing some experimenting or developing yourself (using this chapter as a guide), however, you need Access.

For WebSite, you have to plug in an IP address. So long as you don't go on an intranet or the Internet, you can make up the IP address you use (if you don't have a real IP address). Make sure that WebSite doesn't boot with your computer. It takes up system resources, and you won't want it running except when you're using it. To configure WebSite, use the right mouse button and click on the icon in the lower right-hand corner and select WebSite Server Properties. You can get started easily, however, without doing any configuring, except entering the IP number.

Cold Fusion installs nicely. For the Art Gallery demo, you must have the Access OBDC driver (supplied by Cold Fusion) installed. When the Cold Fusion installation program provides you with the opportunity to choose an OBDC driver, be sure to include that one.

Both Cold Fusion and WebSite offer you instructions and tutorial materials in HTML for you to read via your Web browser. Be sure to take advantage of this convenience. As easy to install as these programs are — and they are easy — if you have never installed a Web server or a database middleware program before, you may need a little help.

Getting Started

An easy place to start the Art Gallery project is by doing what you already know how to do: the HTML documents. Simply create the HTML documents you want to use. Use sample data for one artist to create the documents. Tune them. Make them look good. To turn them into templates, simply substitute the column names for the sample data that you used. Thus, if you have a sentence that includes the name Harriet Smith, then Harriet Smith becomes first_name last_name. That's easy enough.

Next, you create the query input HTML document by using HTML forms markups. Then you apply Cold Fusion DBML markups to all the HTML documents you have done.

Generating SQL statements

For SQL statements, you must use SQL code prefaced by the DBML markup *DBSQL*. If you are not a programmer, this is where Access comes in handy. You can use Access to make the queries visually and then have Access generate the SQL code. Normally, you would be out of luck with Access, because it doesn't generate true SQL. You would have to make some adjustments, which isn't an attractive proposition if you're not a programmer. Tuning SQL statements is tedious enough without additional problems. Fortunately, you're in luck, because the Cold Fusion's Access OBDC driver enables the native Access SQL statements to flow through as if they were real SQL.

Microsoft Query

You can also use Microsoft Query, a visual SQL query tool that comes with Windows 95 and other Microsoft software, to create a query and to generate the SQL code (see Figure 24-1). This creates the real thing, and if you do a lot of Web-database applications, you will want to use this for your queries instead of Access. It's quite similar to Access, and real SQL code will run in Access as well as the Access native SQL.

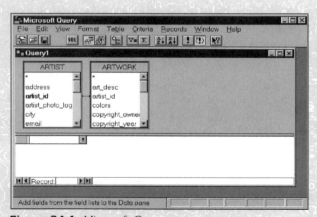

Figure 24-1: Microsoft Query.

Using SQL code can be tedious. Although it is not difficult and is well within a nonprogrammer's capability, like any code, it must be *exactly* correct to work. You are probably better off using MS Query, Access, or another database engine or tool to generate SQL code than attempting to write it by yourself. It will still take some trial and error to get it right. Some SQL queries cannot be done using Access, as you will see, and you have to construct the queries after generating portions using Access.

Template descriptions

For the ARTGAL project (see Figure 24-2), there are five HTML templates and one normal HTML document. These templates are described in the following sections.

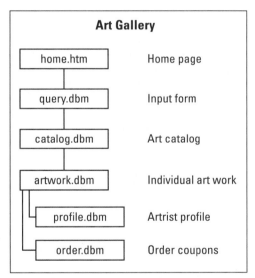

Figure 24-2: ARTGAL Web documents.

home.html (normal HTML document)

This is the home page (first HTML document). If you want a visitor's browser to load this automatically and do not want to have to include it in a Web address, name it index.html. (This first document could be created by a database, if desired.)

query.dbm (template — generates an HTML document on the fly)

This is the first template, and it generates the document that contains the visitor fill-in forms. Visitors provide their input here. This could just as easily be a second normal HTML document hyperlinked to home.html. It is presented as a template to illustrate how a document can be generated on the fly with a simple button-click CGI action. After all, Cold Fusion uses CGI scripts to do its serious work. Why not take advantage of its CGI capability to do simple work too? This is particularly true where it is convenient to make every HTML document at your Web site one delivered from a database.

catalog.dbm (template — generates an HTML document on the fly)

This is the HTML document delivered on the fly in response to a visitor's input (query). It is a custom-generated art catalog. Only the artworks selected based on a visitor's input are included in this document. Although the ARTGAL project is a simple one, with this document, it illustrates the potential power of Web-database technology to provide custom-generated multimedia information to people in response to their choices.

artwork.dbm (template — generates an HTML document on the fly)

When a visitor looks through the catalog and chooses an artwork to inspect more closely, this document is delivered on the fly with a large presentation of one artwork.

profile.dbm (template — generates an HTML document on the fly)

If a visitor wants to know more about the artist who created the artwork in artwork.dbm, this artist's profile is the resulting document delivered on the fly. This is one of two documents that a visitor can choose in artwork.dbm.

order.dbm (template — generates an HTML document on the fly)

This is the other document a visitor can choose in artwork.dbm. This document is an order form and is generated on the fly.

As you will see, these templates are mostly like normal HTML documents. If you're proficient in HTML, you'll understand these templates immediately.

The Web documents are presented in their natural sequence. Note, however, that from the document artwork.dbm, you can go via hyperlink to either profile.dbm or order.dbm.

Templates

To make analyzing the templates, constructing the queries, and testing the results realistic, you can add appropriate test data to the ARTGAL database application. To avoid confusion, the test data used for this chapter is different from the test data used for the preceding chapter (see Listings 24-1 and 24-2). The test data is as follows:

Listing 24-1   **Test data for the ARTIST table**

```
1,"Priscilla",,"Paint",,"Ms.","Paint Associates","144 Paint
Lane","Paintville","PA","91967","890-123-4567",,,"pris
@artformoney.com","oil","A painting on the wall by Pris,
is a room to remember.","A well-established oil painter of
renown, Priscilla Paint is a graduate of the Yankton
Academy of Art and an occasional instructor at
Transylvania State University where she teaches drawing
and oil painting. She has exhibited in various art
festivals and galleries in Pusan, Budapest, Hyderabad,
Pretoria, New York, and other cities. She has won many
awards, and her paintings are in the permanent collections
of six American and four foreign art museums.","pris.gif"
2,"Bo","Lo","Photo","Jr.","Mr.","Photo Company","122 Photo
Road","Photoville","FL","12518","123-456-7890",,,"bo@photos
forless.com","photography","For fine photographs of
buildings, contact Bo today.","Acclaimed as a leading
photographer of buildings world-wide, Bo Photo continues
to be a front-runner as is evidenced by his numerous cover
photos for real estate, construction, and architecture
magazines. Over a eighteen-year period he has had his
photos featured in museum exhibits while at the same time
has enjoyed substantial commercial success as well. He has
been on assignment to photograph buildings in major
European cities such as St. Petersburg and Madrid as well
as almost every major American city.","bo.gif"
```

Listing 24-2   **Test data for the ARTWORK table**

```
1,1,"Fruits",9/5/88 0:00:00,"oil","post-mortem","still",
"Lots of fruit.","yellow",$165.00,32,23,2,384,256,
"fruits.gif","tfruit.gif",1988,"P. Paint"
2,1,"Flowers",9/3/89 0:00:00,"oil","post-mortem","still",
```

(continued)

Listing 24-2 (continued)

```
"flowers.gif","tflower.gif",1989,"P. Paint"
3,2,"Office 32",9/11/91 0:00:00,"photography","real-pics",
"building","Peaceful place.","green",
$235.00,33,19,1,384,256,"office32.gif","toff32.gif",1991,"B.
Photo"
4,2,"Office 79",9/17/91 0:00:00,"photography","real-pics",
"building","Building with blue.","blue",
$50.00,27,21,1,384,256,"office79.gif","toff79.gif",1992,"B.
Photo"
```

This test includes references to four digital graphics and to an additional four thumbnail graphics.

home.htm

Look for the reference to Cold Fusion's CGI script generator (dbml.exe) toward the bottom of the document:

```
<FORM METHOD="POST" ACTION="../../cgi-shl/dbml.exe?
template=query.dbm">
<INPUT TYPE="SUBMIT" VALUE="Query the Gallery"></FORM>
```

This HTML form uses the template query.dbm to generate an HTML document on the fly. Following is the code for the template:

```
<HTML><HEAD><TITLE>Gallery Online — Access DB
Demonstration</TITLE></HEAD><BODY>

<BODY BGCOLOR="000000" TEXT="#FFFF00" LINK="#3399FF"
VLINK="#00FF00" ALINK="#33FFFF">

<A NAME="TopOfForm">

<CENTER><IMG SRC="head_lg.gif" ALT="[gallery online logo]"
WIDTH=442 HEIGHT=238></CENTER>

<H1>This site is a demonstration of an Access database
connected to the
World Wide Web.</H1>
```

```
A Web Page with Database has these great advantages:
<UL>
<LI>More interactive site.
<LI>Pages customized to each person.
<LI>Easier navigation within your site.
<LI>Easier maintenance with less programming.
<LI>Better flexibility for changes.
</UL>

Database is especially useful for you if your Web site (or
your ideal Web site)  meets any one of these criteria:
<UL>
<LI>Needs frequent updates.
<LI>Has more than ten pages.
<LI>Contains so much data it's hard to find anything.
<LI>Needs search capabilities.
<LI>Collects any information, such as a purchase order,
from visitors.
<LI>Needs to track hits.
</UL>

<CENTER>
<FORM METHOD="POST" ACTION="../../cgi-shl/dbml.exe?tem
plate=query.dbm">
<INPUT TYPE="SUBMIT" VALUE="Query the Gallery">
</FORM>
<P>
<IMG SRC = "lineredb.gif" ALT="[lline]" WIDTH=587
HEIGHT=7>
<P>
&#169 1996 by Carol McCullough and Joseph T. Sinclair
</CENTER>
</BODY></HTML>
```

As you can see, except for the form markups, this is a normal HTML dcou-
ment. It results in a page that looks like the one shown in Figure 24-3.

Note the button labeled Query the Gallery. When a visitor clicks on that
button, an HTML document based on query.dbm is generated.

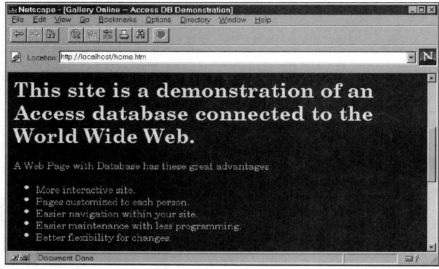

Figure 24-3: The home page (first HTML document).

query.dbm

In this template, each input is an HTML form. Here's a sample:

```
<FORM METHOD="POST" ACTION="dbml.exe?template=catalog.dbm">
.
.
Specialty (choose one): <SELECT NAME="specialty" SIZE=1>
<OPTION VALUE=ANY>ANY</OPTION>
<OPTION VALUE=ACRYLIC>ACRYLIC</OPTION>
<OPTION VALUE=CHARCOAL>CHARCOAL</OPTION>
<OPTION VALUE=DIGITAL>DIGITAL</OPTION>
<OPTION VALUE=PENCIL>PENCIL</OPTION>
<OPTION VALUE=PHOTOGRAPHY>PHOTOGRAPHY</OPTION>
<OPTION VALUE=OIL>OIL</OPTION>
<OPTION VALUE=WATERCOLOR>WATERCOLOR</OPTION>
<OPTION VALUE=WOOD>WOOD</OPTION>
</SELECT></P>
```

This results in an input box that looks like the one in Figure 24-4.

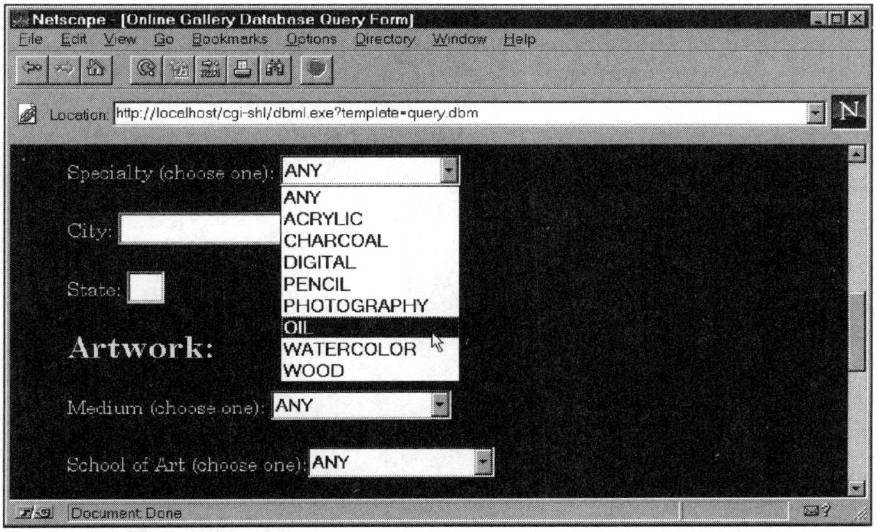

Figure 24-4: A query box.

The entire template looks like normal HTML. The HTML forms also look normal in the following document:

```
<HTML><HEAD><TITLE>Online Gallery Database Query
Form</TITLE></HEAD><BODY>

<BODY BGCOLOR="000000" TEXT="#FFFF00" LINK="#3399FF"
    VLINK="#00FF00" ALINK="#33FFFF">

<CENTER><IMG SRC="../head_sm.gif" ALT="[Gallery Online
Logo]" WIDTH=323 HEIGHT=110></CENTER>
<PRE>

</PRE>
<H1>Art Gallery Online</H1>
<H2>Please enter a query:</H2>

Use the form below to search our gallery database.
You can fill in any of the lines that you wish to use to
narrow down your search. Press the Search button
when you are ready.
</P>
<FORM METHOD="POST" ACTION="dbml.exe?template=catalog.dbm">
<DL>
<DD><H2>Artist:</H2>
```

(continued)

```
(continued)
Last Name (starts with):
<INPUT NAME = "last_name"><BR>
Case Sensitive!<P>

<P>Specialty (choose one): <SELECT NAME="specialty"
SIZE=1>
<OPTION VALUE=ANY>ANY</OPTION>
<OPTION VALUE=ACRYLIC>ACRYLIC</OPTION>
<OPTION VALUE=CHARCOAL>CHARCOAL</OPTION>
<OPTION VALUE=DIGITAL>DIGITAL</OPTION>
<OPTION VALUE=PENCIL>PENCIL</OPTION>
<OPTION VALUE=PHOTOGRAPHY>PHOTOGRAPHY</OPTION>
<OPTION VALUE=OIL>OIL</OPTION>
<OPTION VALUE=WATERCOLOR>WATERCOLOR</OPTION>
<OPTION VALUE=WOOD>WOOD</OPTION>
</SELECT></P>
<P>
City: <INPUT TYPE=text SIZE=18 MAXLENGTH=18
NAME="city"></P>
<P>
State: <INPUT TYPE=text SIZE=2 MAXLENGTH=2
NAME="state"></P>
<H2>Artwork:</H2>
<P>Medium (choose one): <SELECT NAME="media" SIZE=1>
<OPTION VALUE=ANY>ANY</option>
<OPTION VALUE=ACRYLIC>ACRYLIC</option>
<OPTION VALUE=DIGITAL>DIGITAL</option>
<OPTION VALUE=PASTEL>PASTEL</option>
<OPTION VALUE=PENCIL>PENCIL</option>
<OPTION VALUE=PHOTOGRAPHY>PHOTOGRAPHY</OPTION>
<OPTION VALUE=OIL>OIL</option>
<OPTION VALUE=WATERCOLOR>WATERCOLOR</option>
</SELECT></P>
<P>School of Art (choose one):<SELECT NAME="school"
SIZE=1>
<OPTION VALUE=ANY>ANY</option>
<OPTION VALUE=EXPRESSIONISM>EXPRESSIONISM</OPTION>
<OPTION VALUE=IMPRESSIONISM>IMPRESSIONISM</OPTION>
<OPTION VALUE=MODERN>MODERN</OPTION>
<OPTION VALUE=POST-MODERN>POST-MODERN</OPTION>
<OPTION VALUE=POST-MORTEM>POST-MORTEM</OPTION>
<OPTION VALUE=REALISM>REALISM</OPTION>
<OPTION VALUE=REAL-PICS>REAL-PICS</OPTION>
<OPTION VALUE=SURREALISM>SURREALISM</OPTION>
<OPTION VALUE=WHIMSY>WHIMSY</OPTION>
</SELECT></P>
<P>Subject Matter (choose one):<SELECT NAME="subject"
```

```
SIXE=1>
<OPTION VALUE=ANY>ANY</OPTION>
<OPTION VALUE=ANIMALS/WILDLIFE>ANIMALS/WILDLIFE</OPTION>
<OPTION VALUE=BUILDING>BUILDING</OPTION>
<OPTION VALUE=FANTASY>FANTASY</OPTION>
<OPTION VALUE=FLORAL>FLORAL</OPTION>
<OPTION VALUE=LANDSCAPE>LANDSCAPE</OPTION>
<OPTION VALUE=PORTRAIT/PEOPLE>PORTRAIT/PEOPLE</OPTION>
<OPTION VALUE=STILL>STILL LIFE</OPTION>
</SELECT></P>
<p>Colors (choose one):<select name="colors" size=1>
<OPTION VALUE=ANY>ANY</OPTION>
<OPTION VALUE=AMBER>AMBER</OPTION>
<OPTION VALUE=BLACK>BLACK</OPTION>
<OPTION VALUE=BLUE>BLUE</OPTION>
<OPTION VALUE=GRAY>GRAY</OPTION>
<OPTION VALUE=GREEN>GREEN</OPTION>
<OPTION VALUE=LAVENDER>LAVENDER</OPTION>
<OPTION VALUE=NAVY>NAVY</OPTION>
<OPTION VALUE=OLIVE>OLIVE</OPTION>
<OPTION VALUE=ORANGE>ORANGE</OPTION>
<OPTION VALUE=PINK>PINK</OPTION>
<OPTION VALUE=PURPLE>PURPLE</OPTION>
<OPTION VALUE=RED>RED</OPTION>
<OPTION VALUE=TAN>TAN</OPTION>
<OPTION VALUE=WHITE>WHITE</OPTION>
<OPTION VALUE=YELLOW>YELLOW</OPTION>
</SELECT></P>
<PRE>

</PRE>
<INPUT TYPE="SUBMIT" VALUE="  Search    "> <INPUT
TYPE="RESET" VALUE=" Reset   ">
</FORM><CENTER></DL>
<PRE>

</PRE>
<IMG SRC="../lineredb.gif" ALT="[Line]" WIDTH=587 HEIGHT=7>
<P>
<A HREF="../cmmar1.htm"><IMG SRC = "../btn_home.gif"
ALT="home button" WIDTH=100 HEIGHT=100 BORDER=0 ></A>
<P>
<P>&#169 1996 Carol McCullough and Joseph T. Sinclair
</CENTER>
</BODY></HTML>
```

So far, you probably haven't seen much that's different from what you've been doing with HTML (see Figure 24-5).

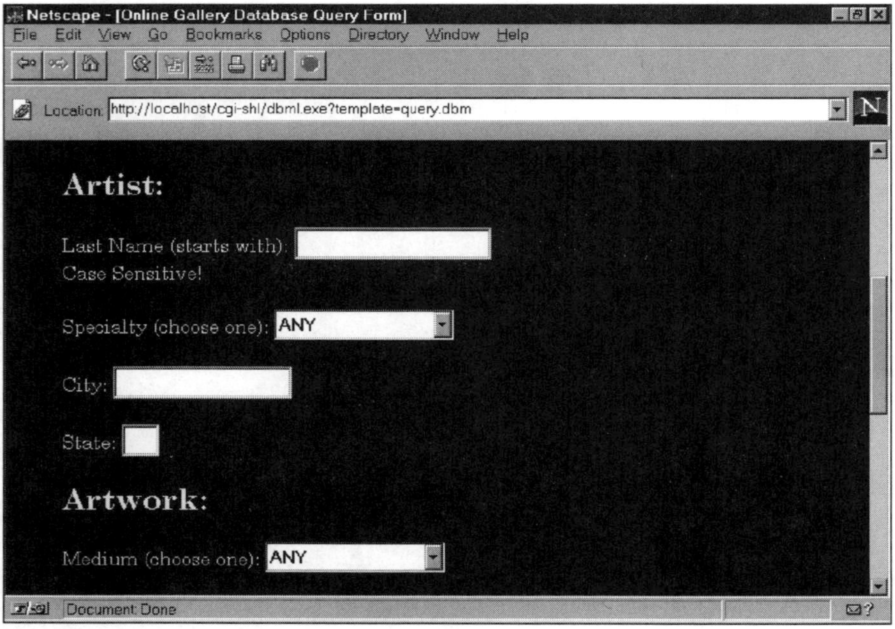

Figure 24-5: This is clearly a visitor input document.

catalog.dbm

This is the first template containing an SQL statement. Note that in cata-log.dbm, described here, that the SQL statement is surrounded by

```
<DBQUERY NAME="" SQL="">
```

and followed by

```
<DBOUTPUT>…</DBOUTPUT>
```

The SQL query is as follows:

```
SELECT DISTINCTROW ARTWORK.thumbname, ARTWORK.title,
ARTWORK.work_id, ARTIST.first_name, ARTIST.middle_name,
ARTIST.last_name, ARTIST.jr_suffix, ARTIST.city,
ARTIST.state, ARTIST.specialty, ARTWORK.media,
ARTWORK.school, ARTWORK.subject, ARTWORK.colors
FROM ARTIST INNER JOIN ARTWORK ON ARTIST.artist_id=
ARTWORK.artist_id
WHERE (((ARTIST.last_name)='#last_name#' OR
'#last_name#'='') AND ((ARTIST.city)='#city#' OR
```

```
'#city#'='') AND ((ARTIST.state)='#state#' OR
'#state#'='') AND ((ARTIST.specialty)='#specialty#' OR
'#specialty#'='ANY') AND ((ARTWORK.media)='#media#' OR
'#media#'='ANY') AND ((ARTWORK.school)='#school#' OR
'#school#'='ANY') AND ((ARTWORK.subject)='#subject#' OR
'#subject#'='ANY') AND ((ARTWORK.colors)='#colors#' OR
'#colors#'='ANY'));
```

This SQL statement is somewhat complex, but, except for the SQL statement, the HTML document (template) shown here looks normal:

```
<HTML><HEAD><TITLE>Gallery Online — Query Results Summary
List</TITLE></HEAD>
<BODY>

<BODY BGCOLOR="000000" TEXT="#FFFF00" LINK="#3399FF"
VLINK="#00FF00" ALINK="#33FFFF">

<CENTER>
<IMG SRC="../head_sm.gif" ALT="[Gallery Online Logo]"
WIDTH=323 HEIGHT=110>
<PRE>

</PRE>
<H2>Here is the result of your query:</H2>

<IMG SRC="../lineredb.gif" ALT="[Line]" WIDTH=587 HEIGHT=7>
<PRE>

</PRE>
<FORM METHOD="POST" ACTION="../../cgi-shl/dbml.exe?tem
plate=artwork.dbm">
<B>
<TABLE BORDER=5 CELLPADDING=2 CELLSPACING=5>
<TR>
<TD><CENTER>To select Work, click here,<BR>
then go to bottom and click "Details"</CENTER></TD>
<TD><CENTER><H3>TITLE</H3></CENTER></TD>
<TD><CENTER><H3>ARTIST</H3></CENTER></TD>
</TR>
<DBQUERY NAME="smallart" DATASOURCE="ARTGAL"
SQL="SELECT DISTINCTROW ARTWORK.thumbname, ARTWORK.title,
ARTWORK.work_id, ARTIST.first_name, ARTIST.middle_name,
ARTIST.last_name, ARTIST.jr_suffix, ARTIST.city,
ARTIST.state, ARTIST.specialty, ARTWORK.media,
ARTWORK.school, ARTWORK.subject, ARTWORK.colors
FROM ARTIST INNER JOIN ARTWORK ON ARTIST.artist_id=
```

(continued)

```
(continued)
ARTWORK.artist_id
WHERE (((ARTIST.last_name)='#last_name#' OR
'#last_name#'='') AND ((ARTIST.city)='#city#' OR
'#city#'='') AND ((ARTIST.state)='#state#' OR '#state#'='')
AND ((ARTIST.specialty)='#specialty#' OR
'#specialty#'='ANY') AND ((ARTWORK.media)='#media#' OR
'#media#'='ANY') AND ((ARTWORK.school)='#school#' OR
'#school#'='ANY') AND ((ARTWORK.subject)='#subject#' OR
'#subject#'='ANY') AND ((ARTWORK.colors)='#colors#' OR
'#colors#'='ANY'));
">

<DBOUTPUT QUERY="smallart">
<TR>
<TD><INPUT TYPE="RADIO" NAME="work_id" VALUE=#work_id#>
<IMG SRC='../#thumbname#' ALT="Picture of Art"></TD>
<TD>#title#</TD>
<TD>#first_name# #middle_name# #last_name# #jr_suffix#</TD>
</TR>
</DBOUTPUT></TABLE></B>
<P>
If you do not make a selection, you will get an error
message.
<PRE>

</PRE>
<DBIF #smallart.RecordCount# is 0>
<I><B>Sorry, no Works Available for this criteria.</B>
<P>
<DBELSE>
<CENTER><H2>Click here to see a larger picture and more
details.</H2>
<P>
<INPUT TYPE="SUBMIT" VALUE="  Details  "></CENTER>
</DBIF><CENTER>
<PRE>

</PRE>
<IMG SRC="../lineredb.gif" ALT="[Line]" WIDTH=587 HEIGHT=7>
<P>
<A HREF="../home.htm"><IMG SRC="../btn_home.gif" ALT="home
button" WIDTH=100 HEIGHT=100 BORDER=0></A>
<P>
&#169 1996 Carol McCullough and Joseph T. Sinclair
</B></CENTER>

</BODY></HTML>
```

Note that the database output (that is, `<DBOUTPUT>...</DBOUTPUT>`) is stated once in the template. Of course, the database application generates as many outputs as satisfy the query. Thus, a number of artworks are likely to appear in this custom-generated catalog (see Figure 24-6).

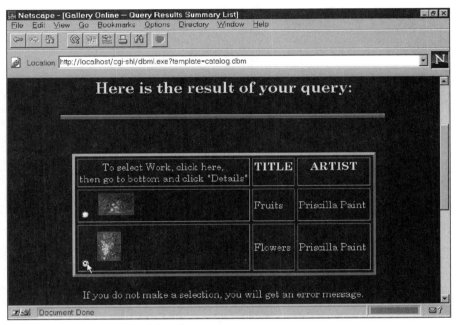

Figure 24-6: The Art Gallery catalog.

artwork.dbm

A visitor can choose to look at a larger version of each artwork in the catalog together with information on each artwork. Again, there is a substantial SQL statement:

```
SELECT DISTINCTROW ARTWORK.work_id, ARTIST.artist_id,
ARTWORK.thumbname, ARTWORK.title, ARTWORK.filename,
ARTWORK.pixel_height, ARTWORK.pixel_width,
ARTWORK.art_desc, ARTWORK.price, ARTWORK.media,
ARTWORK.creation_date, ARTWORK.height_inches,
ARTWORK.width_inches, ARTWORK.depth_inches, ARTWORK.school,
ARTWORK.subject, ARTWORK.colors, ARTIST.first_name,
ARTIST.middle_name, ARTIST.last_name, ARTIST.jr_suffix
FROM ARTWORK INNER JOIN ARTIST ON ARTWORK.artist_id =
ARTIST.artist_id
WHERE (((ARTWORK.work_id)=#work_id#));
```

Note that the query clearly is directed to finding an artwork:

```
WHERE (((ARTWORK.work_id)=#work_id#));
```

The entire template, as seen in the following, otherwise looks normal:

```
<HTML><HEAD><TITLE>Online Gallery Artwork
Detail</TITLE></HEAD><BODY>

<BODY BGCOLOR="000000" TEXT="#FFFF00" LINK="#3399FF"
VLINK="#00FF00" ALINK="#33FFFF">

<CENTER>
<IMG SRC="../head_sm.gif" ALT="[Gallery Online Logo]"
WIDTH=323 HEIGHT=110>

<H2>Artwork Details</H2>

<IMG SRC="../lineredb.gif" ALT="[Line]" WIDTH=587 HEIGHT=7>
<PRE>

</PRE>
<DBQUERY NAME="bigart" DATASOURCE="ARTGAL"
SQL="SELECT DISTINCTROW ARTWORK.work_id, ARTIST.artist_id,
ARTWORK.thumbname, ARTWORK.title, ARTWORK.filename,
ARTWORK.pixel_height, ARTWORK.pixel_width,
ARTWORK.art_desc, ARTWORK.price, ARTWORK.media,
ARTWORK.creation_date, ARTWORK.height_inches,
ARTWORK.width_inches, ARTWORK.depth_inches, ARTWORK.school,
ARTWORK.subject, ARTWORK.colors, ARTIST.first_name,
ARTIST.middle_name, ARTIST.last_name, ARTIST.jr_suffix
FROM ARTWORK INNER JOIN ARTIST ON ARTWORK.artist_id =
ARTIST.artist_id
WHERE (((ARTWORK.work_id)=#work_id#));">

<DBOUTPUT QUERY="bigart">

<IMG SRC="../#filename#" ALT="Picture of Art"
HEIGHT=#pixel_height# WIDTH=#pixel_width# ALIGN="TOP">
<P>
<H2>#title#</H2>
<H3>#art_desc#</H3>
<PRE>

</PRE>
<TABLE BORDER=5 CELLPADDING=2 CELLSPACING=5>
<TR>
<TD><H2>Artist: #first_name# #middle_name# #last_name#
#jr_suffix#</H2></TD>
```

```
<TD></TD>
</TR>
<TR>
<TD><H2>Price: #DollarFormat(price)#</H2></TD>
<TD></TD>
</TR>
<TR>
<TD><H2>Media: #media#</H2></TD>
<TD><H2>Creation: #DateFormat(creation_date)#</H2></TD>
</TR>
<TR>
<TD><H2>Size (inches): #height_inches# x #width_inches# x
#depth_inches#</H2></TD>
<TD><H2>School: #school#</H2></TD>
</TR>
<TR>
<TD><H2>Subject: #subject#</H2></TD>
<TD><H2>Colors: #colors#</H2></TD>
</TR>
</TABLE>
<PRE>

</PRE>
<FORM METHOD="POST" ACTION="../cgi-shl/dbml.exe?
template=profile.dbm">
<H2><INPUT TYPE="HIDDEN" NAME="artist_id"
VALUE=#artist_id#>
See details about the <INPUT TYPE="SUBMIT" VALUE="  Artist
"></H2>
</FORM>
<FORM METHOD="POST" ACTION="../cgi-shl/dbml.exe?
template=order.dbm">
<H2><INPUT TYPE="HIDDEN" NAME="work_id" VALUE=#work_id#>
Fill in our <INPUT TYPE="SUBMIT" VALUE=" Order Form
"></H2>
</FORM>
</DBOUTPUT>
<PRE>

</PRE>
<IMG SRC = "../lineredb.gif" ALT="[Line]" WIDTH=587
HEIGHT=7>
<P>
<A HREF="../home.htm"><IMG SRC="../btn_home.gif" ALT="home
button" WIDTH=100 HEIGHT=100 BORDER=0></A>
<P>
&#169 1996 Carol McCullough and Joseph T. Sinclair
</CENTER>
</BODY></HTML>
```

An attractive document emerges out of all these HTML markups (see Figure 24-7).

Figure 24-7: The artwork document shows one artwork.

Note that two buttons give you two choices for additional documents. First is the Artist button, which gives you more information on the artist. Second is the Order button, which takes you to a form to order the artwork.

profile.dbm

This document is at the end of the chain, along with the Order document. The important part of the SQL statement is this:

```
WHERE (((ARTIST.artist_id)=#artist_id#));
```

This statement ties the artwork in ARTWORK to the artist's profile information in ARTIST. Here's the entire query:

```
SELECT DISTINCTROW ARTIST.artist_id,
ARTIST.artist_photo_logo, ARTIST.firm_name, ARTIST.address,
ARTIST.city, ARTIST.state, ARTIST.zip, ARTIST.phone,
ARTIST.fax, ARTIST.email, ARTIST.specialty, ARTIST.
marketing_text, ARTIST.resume_text, ARTIST.first_name,
```

```
ARTIST.middle_name, ARTIST.last_name, ARTIST.jr_suffix
FROM ARTWORK INNER JOIN ARTIST ON
ARTWORK.artist_id=ARTIST.artist_id
WHERE (((ARTIST.artist_id)=#artist_id#));
```

The profile simply provides information on the artist along with the artist's photograph or other artistic likeness, as in the following:

```
<HTML><HEAD><TITLE>Online Gallery Artist
Profile</TITLE></HEAD><BODY>

<BODY BGCOLOR="000000" TEXT="#FFFF00" LINK="#3399FF"
     VLINK="#00FF00" ALINK="#33FFFF">

<H2>Online Gallery Artist Profile</H2>
<PRE>

</PRE>
<CENTER><IMG SRC="../head_sm.gif" ALT="[gallery online
logo]" WIDTH=323 HEIGHT=110>
<P>
<IMG SRC = "../lineredb.gif" ALT="[line]" WIDTH=587
HEIGHT=7></CENTER>
<PRE>

</PRE>
<DBQUERY NAME="artistpro" DATASOURCE="ARTGAL"
SQL="SELECT DISTINCTROW ARTIST.artist_id,
ARTIST.artist_photo_logo, ARTIST.firm_name, ARTIST.address,
ARTIST.city, ARTIST.state, ARTIST.zip, ARTIST.phone,
ARTIST.fax, ARTIST.email, ARTIST.specialty, ARTIST.
marketing_text, ARTIST.resume_text, ARTIST.first_name,
ARTIST.middle_name, ARTIST.last_name, ARTIST.jr_suffix
FROM ARTWORK INNER JOIN ARTIST ON
ARTWORK.artist_id=ARTIST.artist_id
WHERE (((ARTIST.artist_id)=#artist_id#));">

<DBOUTPUT QUERY="artistpro">

<CENTER>
<IMG SRC="../#artist_photo_logo#" ALT="[Picture of Artist]"
ALIGN="TOP">
</CENTER>
<PRE>

</PRE>
<H3>Name: #first_name# #middle_name# #last_name#
```

(continued)

```
(continued)
#jr_suffix#<BR>
Company: #firm_name#<BR>
Address: #address#<BR>
#city#, #state# #zip#
<P>
Phone: #phone#<BR>
Fax: #fax#<BR>
E-mail: #email#
<P>
Specialty: #specialty#
<P>
</H3>
<PRE>

</PRE>
<CENTER>
#marketing_text#
<PRE>

</PRE>
<H3><B>Profile</B></H3>
#resume_text#
</DBOUTPUT>
<PRE>

</PRE>
<IMG SRC="../lineredb.gif" ALT="[line]" WIDTH=587 HEIGHT=7>
<P>
<A HREF=../home.htm"><IMG SRC="../btn_home.gif" ALT="home
button" WIDTH=100 HEIGHT=100 BORDER=0></A>
<P>
&#169 1996 Carol McCullough and Joseph T. Sinclair
</CENTER>

</BODY></HTML>
```

The profile document makes an attractive place to get information about the artist (see Figure 24-8).

This is the end of the line; or, more accurately, the end of the line is a fork with two prongs. The profile is at the end of one prong, and the order coupon is at the end of the other prong.

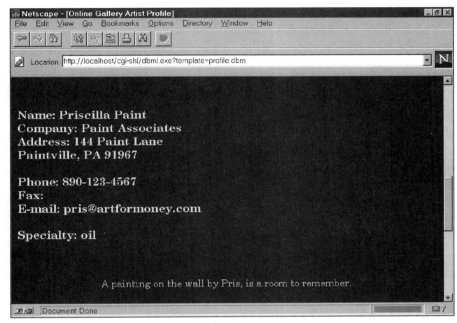

Figure 24-8: Information about the artist.

order.dbm

Should a visitor want to buy an artwork, you have to make it easy for him or her. One simple way to do it is to provide an order coupon. The order document with the coupon is specific to the artwork that the visitor has accessed. The important part of this query is:

```
WHERE (((ARTWORK.work_id)=#work_id#));
```

This queries the artwork row, where it gets the price that is stated in the order document. Here is the full query:

```
SELECT DISTINCTROW ARTIST.artist_id, ARTIST.firm_name,
ARTIST.address, ARTIST.city, ARTIST.state, ARTIST.zip,
ARTIST.first_name, ARTIST.middle_name, ARTIST.last_name,
ARTIST.jr_suffix, ARTWORK.work_id, ARTWORK.title,
ARTWORK.price
FROM ARTWORK INNER JOIN ARTIST ON
ARTWORK.artist_id=ARTIST.artist_id
WHERE (((ARTWORK.work_id)=#work_id#));
```

The document is simple. As the following shows, it contains the price, the artist's address, and a coupon:

```
<HTML><HEAD><TITLE>Gallery Online Order
Form</TITLE></HEAD><BODY>

<BODY BGCOLOR="000000" TEXT="#FFFF00" LINK="#3399FF"
VLINK="#00FF00" ALINK="#33FFFF">

<H2>Online Gallery Order Form</H2>
<PRE>


</PRE>
<CENTER><IMG SRC="../head_sm.gif" ALT="[gallery online
logo]" WIDTH=323 HEIGHT=110>
<P>
<IMG SRC="../lineredb.gif" ALT="[line]" WIDTH=587 HEIGHT=7>
<PRE>


</PRE>
<DBQUERY NAME="order" DATASOURCE="ARTGAL"
SQL="SELECT DISTINCTROW ARTIST.artist_id, ARTIST.firm_name,
ARTIST.address, ARTIST.city, ARTIST.state, ARTIST.zip,
ARTIST.first_name, ARTIST.middle_name, ARTIST.last_name,
ARTIST.jr_suffix, ARTWORK.work_id, ARTWORK.title,
ARTWORK.price
FROM ARTWORK INNER JOIN ARTIST ON
ARTWORK.artist_id=ARTIST.artist_id
WHERE (((ARTWORK.work_id)=#work_id#));">

<DBOUTPUT QUERY="order">

<H2>#title#</H2></CENTER>
<PRE>


</PRE>
<DBIF #price# is 0>
<CENTER><H2>Sorry, this work of art is not for sale.<BR>
You may contact the artist by writing:</H2>
<DBELSE>
<CENTER><H2>To order, please print this document,<BR>
fill it in, and send it with #DollarFormat(price)# (check
or money order)<BR>
to the artist at this address:</H2>
```

```
</DBIF>
<PRE>

</PRE>
<H3>#first_name# #middle_name# #last_name# #jr_suffix#<BR>
#firm_name#<BR>
#address#<BR>
#city#, #state# #zip#</CENTER>
</DBOUTPUT>
<PRE>


Name: _____

Address: _____

City, State, Zip: _____

Phone Number (optional): _____


</PRE>
<CENTER><IMG SRC="../lineredb.gif" ALT="[Line]" WIDTH=587
HEIGHT=7>
<P>
<A HREF="../home.htm"><IMG SRC="../btn_home.gif" ALT="home
button" WIDTH=100 HEIGHT=100 BORDER=0></A>
</B>
<P>
&#169 1996 Carol McCullough and Joseph T.
Sinclair</CENTER>

</BODY></HTML>
```

Again, this document is at the end of the line; that is, at the end of one prong of the fork at the end of the line (see Figure 24-9).

By now, you should feel comfortable with the HTML programming for the templates. The details of constructing the SQL statements follow. First, however, it's useful to go over some particulars of organization.

Figure 24-9: The order form.

The Directories

For your convenience, use two subdirectories off the directory Internet (or some other name) for Cold Fusion and WebSite:

➡ Website

➡ Cfusion

Install WebSite into the Website directory. The WebSite directory tree is shown in Figure 24-10.

The subdirectory htdocs is the WebSite default root directory for documents in the free trial version. If it isn't present in the version you have, create it. Create a subdirectory to htdocs named artgal. Place all ARTGAL files (including GIFs) there, except for the templates. Also place the Access database application artgal.mdb there. Notice the cgi-shl subdirectory created by the WebSite installation. That's WebSite's equivalent of the cgi-bin where the CGI scripts go.

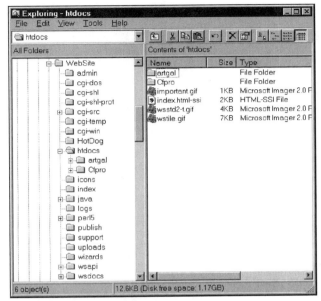

Figure 24-10: The WebSite directory tree.

Install Cold Fusion in the Cfusion subdirectory. The Cold Fusion directory tree is shown in Figure 24-11.

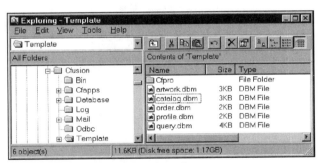

Figure 24-11: The Cold Fusion directory tree.

Place all the templates in the Template directory. Keep in mind that there are a few setup procedures for WebSite and Cold Fusion that are beyond the scope of this book. This chapter instructs you only in additional procedures required for the ARTGAL project.

Next, right-click on the WebSite icon and select WebSite Server Properties. Select the Mapping tab (see Figure 24-12).

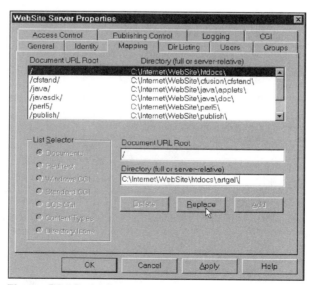

Figure 24-12: Select the Mapping tab.

In the Document URL Root, select internet\website\htdocs. In the Directory (Full or Server-Relative) input, add **\artgal.** The result should be \Internet\WebSite\htdocs\artgal. Click on OK (see Figure 24-13).

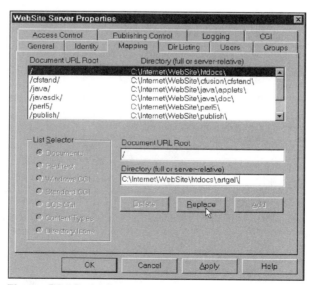

Figure 24-13: Adding artgal.

This action makes artgal the document root directory for WebSite for the purposes of the ARTGAL project. This just makes your work more convenient. Now you're set to proceed to constructing the queries.

Constructing the SQL Queries

To construct the SQL queries, go to Access and open the artgal.mdb database application. The queries constructed for practice in the preceding chapter are not applicable here. The task is to construct queries that enable the HTML documents that make up the Art Gallery. Thus, you need to construct SQL queries for the five templates. When you finish, you take the SQL queries, add the DBML markups, and paste the queries into the templates. Start with the query for catalog.dbm. This is the first SQL query.

Designing the catalog.dbm query

Here's the idea. You want to give visitors maximum freedom to enter input without requiring them to understand Boolean searches. In other words, you want to construct some fixed and easy queries. There are several ways to do this well. Here's one (see Figure 24-14):

last_name	input OR null
AND	
city	input OR null
AND	
state	input OR null
AND	
specialty	selection OR *ANY*
AND	
media	selection OR *ANY*
AND	
school	selection OR *ANY*
AND	
subject	selection OR *ANY*
AND	
colors	selection OR *ANY*

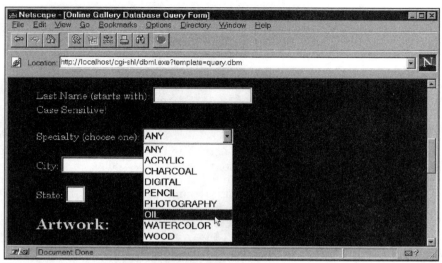

Figure 24-14: An input box and a selection box.

As you can see, you have to satisfy all the queries, because they are linked by AND operators. But each query has an easy out. For example, you can enter a name in the first input for last_name, but if you don't enter anything, it's null (no entry); and a null satisfies the query. For the selection queries, the default is ANY. Thus, if you make no selection, the query is satisfied. All this query needs is one input or one selection, and it can do its work. Anything additional narrows the scope of the query (that is, makes it more precise). Now that the query is designed, you can use the visual query process in Access to construct the query.

First, you open a new query and add the two tables ARTIST and ART-WORK. Next, from the tables, add the columns just specified (that is, last_name, city, state, and so forth) to the query (see Figure 24-15).

For each column that's part of the query, you add the query statement in proper SQL to create a kind of subquery. For example, the SQL statement for last_name is:

```
((ARTIST.last_name)='#last_name#' OR '#last_name#'='')
```

When a visitor enters a name in the last_name entry box, Cold Fusion transmits that to the ARTIST table. In the catalog.dbm template, #last_name# is the variable where the entry will appear if in the table. Thus, #last_name# appears as part of the SQL query. Use two double quotation marks ("") to indicate a null when #last_name# is not in the table.

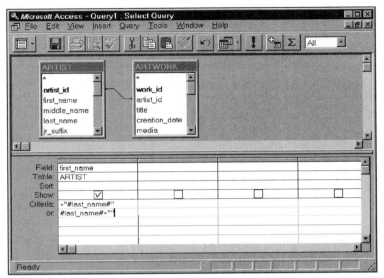

Figure 24-15: Creating a column subquery.

The SQL statement for *specialty* is:

```
((ARTIST.specialty)='#specialty#' OR '#specialty#'='ANY')
```

When a visitor selects a specialty in the selection box, Cold Fusion transmits that selection to the ARTWORK table. In the catalog.dbm template, #specialty# is the variable where the selection will appear if it's in the table. Therefore, #specialty# appears as part of the SQL query (see Figure 24-16). The default entry or null is indicated by ANY.

Unfortunately, you cannot easily string all these subqueries together in the Access Design View to construct this complex query. Thus, you have to improvise. You can create each subquery individually. So, have Access create each individual SQL subquery by using the SQL View; copy and paste the subqueries into the catalog.dbm template; and then connect the SQL subqueries together independently of Access using ANDs. Do that right in the catalog.dbm HTML template.

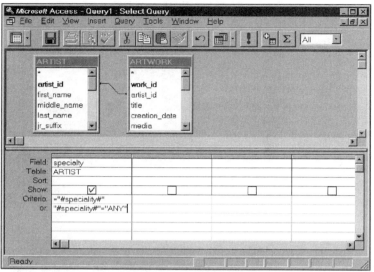

Figure 24-16: Creating another column subquery.

After you have completed the SQL subqueries and have finished connecting them together using ANDs, the SQL query is as shown previously, under the subheading catalog.dbm. After you add the add DBML markups (at the beginning and end), it looks like the following:

```
<DBQUERY NAME="smallart" DATASOURCE="ARTGAL"
SQL="SELECT DISTINCTROW ARTWORK.thumbname, ARTWORK.title,
ARTWORK.work_id, ARTIST.first_name, ARTIST.middle_name,
ARTIST.last_name, ARTIST.jr_suffix, ARTIST.city,
ARTIST.state, ARTIST.specialty, ARTWORK.media,
ARTWORK.school, ARTWORK.subject, ARTWORK.colors
FROM ARTIST INNER JOIN ARTWORK ON ARTIST.artist_id=
ARTWORK.artist_id
WHERE (((ARTIST.last_name)='#last_name#' OR
'#last_name#'='') AND ((ARTIST.city)='#city#' OR
'#city#'='') AND ((ARTIST.state)='#state#' Or '#state#'='')
AND ((ARTIST.specialty)='#specialty#' OR
'#specialty#'='ANY') AND ((ARTWORK.media)='#media#' OR
'#media#'='ANY') AND ((ARTWORK.school)='#school#' OR
'#school#'='ANY') AND ((ARTWORK.subject)='#subject#' OR
'#subject#'='ANY') AND ((ARTWORK.colors)='#colors#' OR
'#colors#'='ANY')):
">
```

Give the query the name *smallart*. To use the output from the database tables, you use the output markups. You place the opening output markup first:

```
<DBOUTPUT QUERY="smallart">
```

Note that the name smallart links the DBQUERY markup to the BDOUTPUT markup. Next, you create your HTML document just as you would normally. Remember, you are creating a template. Therefore, use the variables instead of actual data. In other words, instead of $165 use #price#. After you finish the section of the document that contains all the variables, you close the output with the following markup:

```
</DBOUTPUT>
```

It's that easy to do a template. Review the entire Web document under the subheading catalog.dbm for the details. The toughest part is the query.

IF...ELSE

This template has a markup like the IF...THEN statement covered in Chapter 14, "Data Cataloging". It's an IF...ELSE statement. The markups are:

> *<DBIF value operator value>*   Two values compared.
>
> HTML and DBML
>
> *<DBELSE>*
>
> HTML and DBML
>
> *</DBIF>*

Stated in English, it says, "If the variable equals X, a certain section of the Web document appears; if not (or else), an alternative section of the Web document appears." For example, if the entries in the query document result in no artwork being selected, the IF...ELSE statement in this template displays the sentence: "Sorry, no works available for these criteria." Otherwise, it displays the sentence, "If you do not make a selection, you will get an error message," and the sentence, "Click here to see a larger picture and more details." Here's what the actual IF...ELSE markups for this template look like (see Figures 24-17 and 24-18):

```
<DBIF #smallart.RecordCount# is 0>
<H3><B>Sorry, no works available for these criteria.</B></H3>
<DBELSE>
<P>
If you do not make a selection, you will get an error
message.
<PRE>
```

(continued)

```
(continued)
</PRE>
<H2>Click here to see a larger picture and more
details.</H2>
<P>
<INPUT TYPE="SUBMIT" VALUE="  Details  ">
</DBIF>
```

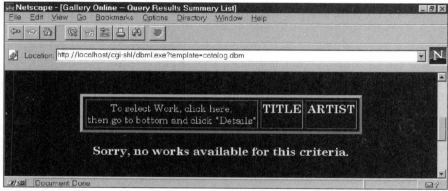

Figure 24-17: An IF alternative.

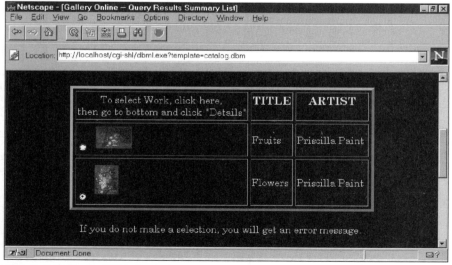

Figure 24-18: An ELSE alternative.

As you can see, the IF...ELSE markups provide you with extra flexibility for creating dynamic Web documents.

Designing the artwork.dbm query

This query is straightforward. You just have to make sure to include all the necessary variables that you want to publish. Here they are:

- thumbname
- title
- filename
- pixel_height
- pixel_width
- art_desc
- price
- media
- creation_date
- height_inches
- width_inches
- depth_inches
- school
- subject
- first_name
- middle_name
- last_name
- jr_suffix

The specific data you seek is for a certain artwork. That artwork is identified by an ID number: *#work_id#*. Thus, the query lists all the variables and the following:

```
WHERE (((ARTWORK.work_id)=#work_id#))
```

Add the database markups, and the query looks like this:

```
<DBQUERY NAME="bigart" DATASOURCE="ARTGAL"
SQL="SELECT DISTINCTROW ARTWORK.work_id, ARTIST.artist_id,
ARTWORK.thumbname, ARTWORK.title, ARTWORK.filename,
ARTWORK.pixel_height, ARTWORK.pixel_width,
ARTWORK.art_desc, ARTWORK.price, ARTWORK.media,
ARTWORK.creation_date, ARTWORK.height_inches,
ARTWORK.width_inches, ARTWORK.depth_inches, ARTWORK.school,
```

(continued)

```
(continued)
ARTWORK.subject, ARTWORK.colors, ARTIST.first_name,
ARTIST.middle_name, ARTIST.last_name, ARTIST.jr_suffix
FROM ARTWORK INNER JOIN ARTIST ON ARTWORK.artist_id =
ARTIST.artist_id
WHERE (((ARTWORK.work_id)=#work_id#));">
```

Don't forget the database output markups. Review the entire template in the section about artwork.dbm. Notice that the links to the last two documents are simple CGI statements similar to the one in home.htm. See an explanation of these CGI statements in the later section on CGI scripts.

Designing the profile.dbm query

The query for the profile template is similar to artwork.dbm. You are simply publishing specific data (SELECT variables) for a specific artist (WHERE artist=variable). After you add the database markups, the query is:

```
<DBQUERY NAME="artistpro" DATASOURCE="ARTGAL"
SQL="SELECT DISTINCTROW ARTIST.artist_id,
ARTIST.artist_photo_logo, ARTIST.firm_name, ARTIST.address,
ARTIST.city, ARTIST.state, ARTIST.zip, ARTIST.phone,
ARTIST.fax, ARTIST.email, ARTIST.specialty,
ARTIST.marketing_text, ARTIST.resume_text,
ARTIST.first_name, ARTIST.middle_name, ARTIST.last_name,
ARTIST.jr_suffix
FROM ARTWORK INNER JOIN ARTIST ON
ARTWORK.artist_id=ARTIST.artist_id
WHERE (((ARTIST.artist_id)=#artist_id#));">
```

Not much to this query. It's long, but it's simple.

Designing the order.dbm query

Just as for profile.dbm, the query for the order document is simple. You are simply publishing specific data (SELECT variables) for a specific artwork (WHERE artwork=variable). After you add the database markups, the query is:

```
<DBQUERY NAME="order" DATASOURCE="ARTGAL"
SQL="SELECT DISTINCTROW ARTIST.artist_id, ARTIST.firm_name,
ARTIST.address, ARTIST.city, ARTIST.state, ARTIST.zip,
ARTIST.first_name, ARTIST.middle_name, ARTIST.last_name,
```

```
ARTIST.jr_suffix, ARTWORK.work_id, ARTWORK.title,
ARTWORK.price
FROM ARTWORK INNER JOIN ARTIST ON
ARTWORK.artist_id=ARTIST.artist_id
WHERE (((ARTWORK.work_id)=#work_id#));">
```

This template also has an IF...ELSE statement, which returns a specific message if the artwork is not for sale (that is, #price#=0):

```
<DBIF #price# is 0>
<CENTER><H2>Sorry, this work of art is not for sale.<BR>
You may contact the artist by writing:</H2>
<DBELSE>
<CENTER><H2>To order, please print this document,<BR>
fill it in, and send it with #DollarFormat(price)# (check
or money order)<BR>
to the artist at this address:</H2>
</DBIF>
```

This document is the last one, and you have finished designing the SQL queries. As you can see, designing a query logically is sometimes a tough task. After it's designed, constructing the query statement is usually just busy work. There's one remaining task that needs to be covered. For that, go back to the first template.

Invoking the Cold Fusion CGI Script

The template query.dbm serves as a good example for the CGI script, because it uses the CGI script a great deal. The CGI script is a file named dbml.exe that is located in the WebSite cgi-shl subdirectory, but it's a Cold Fusion file. The first input in query.dbm is an input for the last name of an artist:

```
<FORM METHOD="POST" ACTION="dbml.exe?template=catalog.dbm">
<DL>
<DD><H2>Artist:</H2>

Last Name (starts with):
<INPUT NAME = "last_name"><BR>
Case Sensitive!
```

It looks like Figure 24-19.

Figure 24-19: Input for the last name of the artist.

Note that the ACTION is using the dbml.exe to take the input #last_name# and put it in the catalog.dbm template. This is not a query, but Cold Fusion enables this ACTION to save you from having to write CGI scripts. Note, however, that you can use this ACTION without an input. Look at the template artword.dbm. It uses this CGI script to give visitors a choice of links to the profile and order documents. By clicking on the screen button, a visitor can choose either. Here's how it looks (see Figure 24-20):

```
<FORM METHOD="POST" ACTION="../cgi-
shl/dbml.exe?template=profile.dbm">
<H2><INPUT TYPE="HIDDEN" NAME="artist_id"
VALUE=#artist_id#>
See details about the <INPUT TYPE="SUBMIT" VALUE="  Artist
"></H2>
</FORM>
<FORM METHOD="POST" ACTION="../cgi-
shl/dbml.exe?template=order.dbm">
<H2><INPUT TYPE="HIDDEN" NAME="work_id" VALUE=#work_id#>
Fill in our <INPUT TYPE="SUBMIT" VALUE=" Order Form
"></H2>
</FORM>
```

Figure 24-20: A CGI script provides choice.

Thus, a click on a screen button can initiate a CGI script preprogrammed with a variable from a database. This technique gives you another building block with which to work in constructing a flexible and functional Web site with a Web-database application.

Cookies

Although using cookies is beyond the scope of the Art Gallery project, it is worth mentioning, should you desire to do a more ambitious Web-database project. Cold Fusion will create a cookie and subsequently receive it. What's a cookie? A *cookie* is a small packet of information that a Web server or database application stores in a visitor's browser (see Figure 24-21).

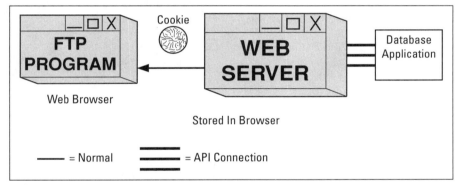

Figure 24-21: From server to browser.

The cookie is URL specific; that is, it is only transmitted by a browser to the Web site from which it came. After the database application stores the cookie in a visitor's browser, each time the visitor's browser requests a document from that Web site, it transmits the cookie to the Web server (see Figure 24-22).

For Cold Fusion, the cookie contains the following:

    <DBCOOKIE NAME VALUE EXPIRES>

NAME	Name of cookie
VALUE	Assigned value
EXPIRES	Expiration of cookie (date or days)

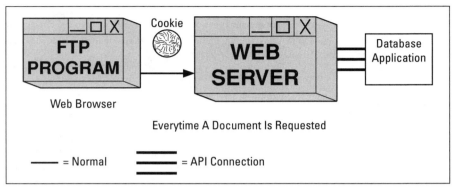

Figure 24-22: From browser to server.

Thus, the following statement gives you a way to track a visitor at your Web site (see Figure 24-23):

```
<DBCOOKIE NAME=visitorid Value=1437 EXPIRES=50>
```

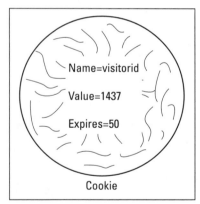

Figure 24-23: A small packet of information.

The visitor's ID number, 1437, enables the database application to track the visitor as he or she navigates through the Web site. The cookie is stored in the visitor's Web browser for 50 days. Thus, whenever the visitor returns to the Web site during the 50 days, the Web server recognizes the visitor as number 1437.

You can use cookies to track a visitor at a Web site, to create a shopping cart application, to make sure that visitors don't see the same advertisement twice, to give visitors a preference regarding content or Web-site document organization, and to otherwise use in situations where you desire to keep track of or accommodate a visitor.

For Cold Fusion, you retrieve cookies with the DBOUTPUT commmand, as follows:

```
<DBOUTPUT>
#Cookie.visitorid#
</DBOUTPUT>
```

Who is keeping track of you?

To see who is keeping track of you, look in the cookies.txt file among the files with your Netscape browser. Might be interesting. Although many characters are garbled, some phrases are readable. To see the specifications for cookies, go to http://www.netscape.com/newref/std/cookie_spec.html (see Figure 24-24)

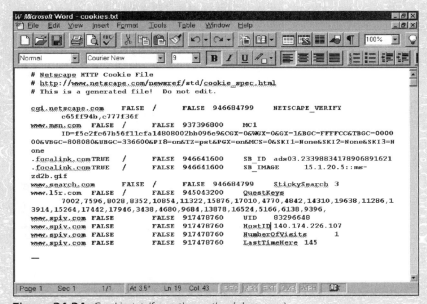

Figure 24-24: Cookie.txt (from the author's browser).

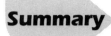

Summary

For this chapter, you must develop your tables and fill them with data in Access. After it's completed, however, you no longer need Access to make ARTGAL run. You need only a Web server, Cold Fusion, and the ARTGAL database application file. In other words, you can develop tables on Windows 95, upload the resulting Access database application file to a Windows NT server, develop the queries in Cold Fusion on Windows 95, upload the queries to the Windows NT server running with Cold Fusion, connect a Web server, and you're in business with advanced Web-database technology.

What's the advantage of using a client-server database engine like Oracle or SQL Server? When an SQL query goes to an Access database application file to get data, the ODBC driver that Cold Fusion uses processes the query and does the work. This slows down performance. When an SQL query goes to a client-server database engine, the ODBC driver passes the query through to the database engine, which processes the query and does the work. This runs faster, because client-server database engines are designed to handle multiple queries quickly. Thus, an Access database application file works fine up to a certain level of traffic. For high traffic, you need a client-server database engine to maintain high performance.

You can use Cold Fusion with a variety of database engines. For a high-traffic Web site, you might want to have a client-server database engine at the Web site. After you have absorbed the information in this chapter, you might want to graduate to the prior chapters that show you how to create this same Web-database application using Oracle 7 and NetDynamics.

This is a long chapter with plenty of HTML and DBML markups. Don't let it overwhelm you. Take it one piece at a time and digest it. You really don't have to be a programmer to use Cold Fusion and basic SQL. You must, however, have a good grasp of HTML, and you must have a reasonable understanding of relational databases

Visitor-Tracking Database Applications

Web servers record the number of visits (hits) to each HTML document in every directory (folder) in a Web site. The Web server does not record how many hits result from a visitor revisiting a directory or who the visitor is. Anyone interested in acquiring marketing statistics seeks a more definitive compilation of these statistics. Additionally, those persons interested in on-site marketing and customer service seek more effective ways to accommodate visitors. *Visitor-tracking* database applications can accumulate meaningful statistics that provide the basis for custom HTML documents — even entire custom document systems — for a visitor, generated simultaneously and based a visitor's visiting pattern at the Web site.

Statistics

Visitor-tracking software detects and records the hits a visitor makes within a Web site. These hits go into a personal database row for the visitor, where they accumulate for analysis. The database can also accommodate other means of obtaining information about a visitor, such as input from a visitor questionnaire.

Custom Documents

Using a person's visiting patterns to generate a custom-made Web presentation offers possibilities for many approaches. A simple way of doing this is to accumulate information about an individual's visiting patterns during the first visiting session and then store such information in the database. The next time the visitor returns to the Web site, he or she receives a custom-made Web site generated right then, based on the prior information. You need not, however, wait for a visitor to return. Based on a visitor's visiting patterns, you can almost immediately (as soon as a pattern is established) begin to provide the visitor with custom-made HTML documents — during his or her first visit.

Why would you want to do this? Marketing is one reason. If you sell sporting goods on the Web, a visitor who comes in and noses around the tennis equipment makes a good prospect to buy tennis equipment, accessories, and clothing. All these tennis items may not necessarily be in the same place in the Web catalog. But a visitor-tracking database application can make it seem to the visitor as if the catalog is really a tennis catalog instead of a general sporting goods catalog.

The goal for that example is to get the visitor to the merchandise he or she is seeking as quickly as possible and as easily as possible. But marketing presents just one example. In the tennis example, the visitor doesn't really get to the tennis merchandise. He or she gets to the information *about* the tennis merchandise, and the sporting goods vendor hopes that such information will sell the product. You can use the same approach for any situation where a visitor seeks information about something. The goal is to get the visitor to the information sought as quickly as possible and as easily as possible.

Getting a visitor to the information as soon as possible materializes in three ways:

➥ You can provide the visitor with custom HTML documents generated on the spot.

➥ Custom information (different multimedia elements) can be inserted automatically for each visitor into an otherwise-identical HTML document.

➥ A custom e-mail message can be sent to the visitor.

Keep in mind that visitor-tracking software does not necessarily *limit* you to visitor-tracking. You can also provide a questionnaire for visitors, which, if submitted, will potentially give you additional valuable information to use in the generation of custom-made documents on the fly. Thus, instead of broadcasting your Web site, you can *narrowcast* it to meet the needs of every visitor. Through the vehicle of follow-up e-mail, the customized experience can even continue after the visitor leaves the Web site.

Making It Work

The following sections discuss how a visitor to a Web site might give revealing clues about himself or herself.

Active accommodation

Most tracking software requires a visitor to register by filling out a questionnaire. That information goes into a database row for the visitor. The database row receives an ID number, too. As the visitor navigates through the Web site, the tracking program records every hit. When a pattern finally emerges, the tracking program starts providing custom documents.

An alternative requires judgment on the part of the site administrator. The administrator reviews the visitor's row of data and makes a judgment as to which of several tracks the visitor should be on. When the visitor returns, the program provides the visitor with a custom Web site preordained for that visitor and other visitors with similar interests.

Passive queues

A *passive* system works by using a visitor's Internet address without the visitor filling in a questionnaire. An ID number identifies the proper row to input data each time the visitor returns. Indeed, each time a visitor with the same address returns, it is just as if the visitor had given his or her name in a questionnaire. Of course, it is preferable to have the visitor's name and other information.

Innocuous questions that gather information are *passive queues*. Passive queues can be subtle. For example, they can seem to accommodate the visitor. Given a choice, if a visitor elects to see the *text-only* Web presentation, you can assume with a reasonable degree of accuracy that the visitor does not have a computer capable of surfing the Web in multimedia. Some people still access the Web with a text-only browser. That fact by itself may tell you something about the visitor. Any time a visitor makes a choice to answer even the most innocuous request, you can accumulate the information in the visitor's database row, and you will learn more about the visitor (see Figure 25-1).

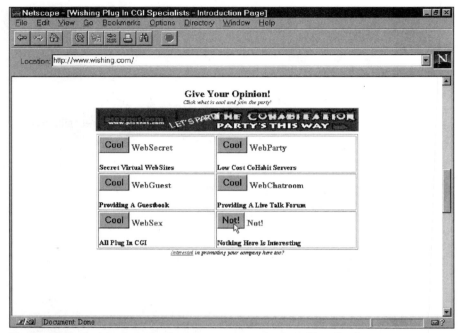

Figure 25-1: A visitor's choice becomes an entry in a tracking database.

Accumulation

The visitor-tracking program does not have to react immediately or on the next visit. For example, the program can wait for a visitor to visit the same HTML document ten times, or ten visiting sessions, before it begins providing custom HTML documents. You don't have to collect all the information at one time or in one questionnaire. You can present numerous questionnaires in one session or in numerous sessions. You can make the questionnaire short and innocuous or long and to the point. Whatever the information-gathering scheme, all information goes into the visitor's row in the database, where it accumulates for analysis by the visitor-tracking program itself or by the Web-site administrator.

Custom-generated HTML documents

As this book discusses elsewhere, a *query* can provide the trigger for a custom-made Web document generated on the fly. Likewise, visitor activity at a Web site with visitor-tracking software can create input to a database application that triggers a custom Web document generated simultaneously.

E-mail

Generating custom Web documents on the spot is not the only possible response. Suppose that your auto dealership has a Web site. Your experience indicates that about the fifth time someone revisits a particular Web document featuring a particular model auto, such a visitor becomes a hot prospect. Your visitor-tracking software might automatically send such a visitor a special e-mail message inducing him or her to take some action toward a purchase. You could even automatically send along some additional information from your database in the e-mail message to the visitor, such as a current inventory of the requisite model listing colors and accessory equipment. Or perhaps the visitor-tracking program doesn't send e-mail to the visitor at all but to a salesperson instead. The possibilities abound.

Shopping cart

This type of software application works well for creating "shopping carts" at Web sites that sell goods at retail (such as an online catalog). The software records where a visitor goes in the catalog and what buying decisions the visitor makes (see Figure 25-2). Finally, the software puts the purchase choices into an order form.

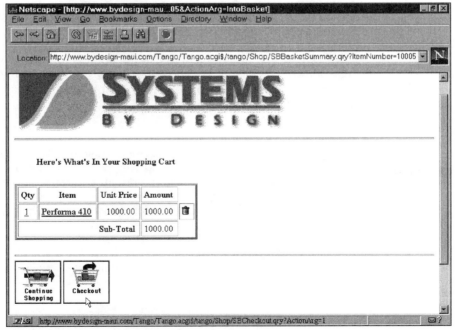

Figure 25-2: A shopping cart tracks a visitor as she fills her cart with purchases.

Software

Creating comprehensive visitor-tracking software can be a substantial programming task. Fortunately, interest runs high in this area, and several vendors offer visitor-tracking software. W3.COM, for example, offers Personal Web Site, which does many of the things discussed in this chapter — without any programming required. See the following Internet address:

```
http://w3.com
```

Another affordable answer is the WebSex service — which has nothing to do with sex. Rather, WebSex offers guest books and visitor hit counts, and gathers visitor e-mail addresses and tells where they came from, all for $36 per year and with no coding required. See the site at

```
http://www.wishing.com
```

Unless your Web site is large and well funded, your best approach may be to purchase and use such software in place of programming visitor-tracking applications yourself.

You can look at this software two ways. First, because visitor-tracking software provides for HTML document generation in response to input from questionnaires as well as from visitor-tracking, it is perfectly suitable for database application uses beyond visitor-tracking (such as for custom documents created simultaneously based on questionnaire input). Second — and conversely — you do not have to use the document-on-the-fly generating capabilities of such software; you can use the software simply to accumulate statistics about the use of your Web site by visitors and later use such statistics for marketing analysis.

Summary

Visitor-tracking software is useful for giving visitors what they want; that is, customizing Web documents for them based on information accumulated about them. This software works best when it uses a database application to store information on each visitor. As a visitor returns to the Web site, more information accumulates about him or her. The system can be made to work well. What you do with the information accumulated, however, is beyond the scope of this book and is left to marketing analysts.

Unique Web-Database Software

26

Some Web-database software is unique enough that it deserves special mention. This chapter introduces five software packages that stand out. The first, GNNserver, is a complete Internet-intranet development platform in addition to being a competent multimedia Web-database system. The second, Oracle PowerBrowser, is a special intranet development system as well as a Web-database system. The third, Microsoft SQL Server, is an example of a database server with built-in Web-database development capability. The fourth is the WebSite server bundled with Cold Fusion, the system used for the Art Gallery demonstration. The fifth, NetScheme, provides a new way of using databases on TCP/IP networks.

GNNpress and GNNserver

GNN, a subsidiary of America Online, offers a set of tools for browsing, authoring, and Web publishing (formerly Navisoft NaviPress and NaviServer). The browser works in combination with the authoring tool. Together, they make up GNNpress. GNNpress, in turn, works with GNNserver to create a Web-database development system; the system includes a database engine. You can download them free at from this URL:

```
http://www.tools.gnn.com/download.html
```

Browser

GNNpress is a Web browser that offers the usual features and works with all Web servers. In addition, it is a WYSIWYG Web-document editor, which enables you to edit Web documents without knowing HTML and without looking at the Web document *source*. More than that, it is also a Web-site management tool. The GNNpress includes a MiniWeb feature, showing you a graphical map of your Web site's HTML documents and how they relate to one another (see Figure 26-1). The only catch: These additional features work only with GNNserver. With GNNpress and GNN server, you can create and maintain a Web site remotely without knowing much about HTML.

Why is this system important? You can provide a service over the Internet to subscribers. Either at their own domain name or under a blanket domain name, each subscriber can have his or her own Web site. Each subscriber creates a personal Web site by using GNNpress. They can even see their own Web sites diagrammed on their PC screens (see Figure 26-1). To enable this service, you operate GNNserver just as you do any other Web server.

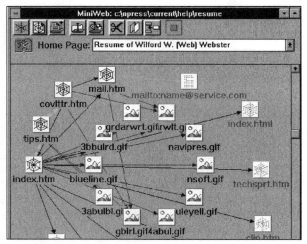

Figure 26-1: GNNpress features the MiniWeb map showing all Web documents.

Beyond the Internet, this system furnishes an intranet with an easy way to provide a Web server but at the same time offer each employee the opportunity to become a Web publisher, too. All an employee needs to create a Web site remotely is the GNNpress browser. Because the rise of intranets has been a grass roots movement, this Web system is ideal. It enables departments, groups, and individuals within an organization to easily publish online.

Some other features that GNNpress offers are the following:

➠ Interactive HTML table creation using a table menu and dialog boxes. It supports table, row, cell, caption alignment, border sizing, cell spacing, cell padding, and more.

➠ A pop-up window to define page body attributes, such as background image (wallpaper), text color, and link color. Choose colors with a window of colors rather than using those RGB color numbers.

➠ Direct access to HTML code using the HTML editing window within GNNpress. You can return easily to the WYSIWYG view.

➠ Error messages for incorrect markups.

GNNhost

GNN offers a service called *GNNhost*. It hosts Web sites (Web documents) for its subscribers. Using GNNhost, you can create and maintain your Web site directly. And, of course, it uses GNNpress and GNNserver. Here's how it works:

➠ Subscribe to the service and install GNNpress on your computer.

➠ Create your Web documents and upload them. You can use GNNpress to assist you.

➠ Click on the Edit button to open a Web document in the GNNpress editor. Edit and update the document in WYSIWYG.

➠ Click on the Save button, and save the changes directly to the GNNserver.

There are plenty of buttons or pull-down menus for formatting text, lists, tables, headings, and so on. The built-in image editor creates clickable image maps. By combining the editor and the browser, GNNpress enables you to create a hyperlink in a document you're editing by browsing to the URL to be linked and clicking the Copy URL button. Presto! The hyperlink appears in your document. The great thing about this GNNhost service is that you can easily duplicate it yourself for your Internet subscribers or intranet employees — simply by using GNNserver.

Server

The server side of the GNN package runs on Windows NT and UNIX. Download GNNserver free from this URL:

```
http://www.tools.gnn.com/download.html
```

The server is a full-featured server that provides all the normal Web server functions, as well as enables the special capabilities mentioned previously. But why does this deserve mention in a Web-database book? GNNserver has Web-database development capability and comes bundled with an Illustra database engine.

Illustra

Illustra is worthy of mention in this chapter by itself; but, because it is bundled with GNNserver, it is included here rather than separately. Illustra is a hybrid object-oriented relational database engine. As such, it is superior for handling multimedia publishing and is ideal for the Web. A privately held company, Illustra merged with Informix in 1996, and you can expect the Illustra technology to continue to be at the forefront of enabling high-powered multimedia publishing and multimedia object management. An Illustra database engine also includes provisions for plug-in modules called *DataBlades,* which extend its already robust multimedia capability to esoteric technologies at the leading edge. Informix has embraced Illustra technology and has incorporated it into Universal Server.

One third-party DataBlade example is the capability to do image searches based not on text meta-information but on the image color and pattern characteristics themselves. For example, suppose that you have a photograph of a brown cow grazing in a green field on a clear sunny day. The colors are brown (cow), green (grass), and blue (sky). The search will search through all the digital photographs in the Illustra database and find the ones that have the three colors in a pattern that resembles a cow grazing in a field. No text is used to do the search.

Illustra is remarkable software at any price, and it's even more remarkable that it's bundled with GNNserver for a free download. Don't miss the Illustra Web site:

```
http://www.illustra.com.
```

Web-database capability

GNNsever has its own Web-database development capability, a module called *nsdb*. It works with any database server that has an ODBC driver. Naturally, it works with the bundled Illustra database engine. The nsdb module has built-in HTML forms based on an ad-hoc query system. It is written in TCL, a simple scripting language similar to Perl. The entire GNNserver software package is specifically tuned to run quickly and efficiently with TCL, presumably enjoying a substantial speed advantage over Perl CGI scripts. You *can* use other languages, too, however, such as C, to do custom programming.

The ad-hoc system has prebuilt HTML forms for the following:

➡ Creating new tables

➡ Modifying the columns of existing tables

➡ Adding and changing data in tables

➡ Querying tables using HTML forms (generated for you)

After you create them, you can edit these database connection forms with GNNpress's forms menu and without any HTML markups or CGI script writing.

The GNNServer checks hyperlinks and repairs them as needed. It also works with firewall security. Another feature called, *Autolinking*, looks promising. Autolinking searches for related text phrases and suggests hyperlinks for you. For example, if one of your Web documents discusses gemstones and there is a geologist Web document also, Autolinking suggests adding a link from key phrases such as *diamonds* in your gemstones document to the geologist document.

Multiuser system

Every Web-database software system is potentially a multiuser system. For example, should you obtain an Oracle database engine, link it to your Web server by using NetDynamics or a comparable tool, and use it for your Web site, the Oracle database engine will likely be underused. Several or perhaps even hundreds more users might share the same database system with you for their Web sites. Although this is clearly a benefit to all, each user would have to obtain a copy of NetDynamics and do their own custom development from scratch.

On the other hand, GNNserver was designed for multiple Web sites with database use. Moreover, it provides database programming integration and requires only the GNNpress enhanced browser for developing. Thus, it provides special but powerful benefits, particularly for multiple Web sites of small to medium size.

Text-search engine

If the foregoing is not enough for you, this software package *also* includes a text-search engine. The engine can search all the documents that the Web server hosts.

Development platform

Clearly, this browser-server system is more than just a Web browser or a Web server. It's a development platform, and one that does not use strictly proprietary standards. TCL, for example, is a widely available scripting language. You can take advantage of Illustra's third-party DataBlades. The nsdb module provides you with a way to do Web-database applications without programming.

Oracle PowerBrowser

The Oracle PowerBrowser tool contains several interesting features that make it unique among Web-database tools. Intended mostly for intranet applications, but capable of more, this tool works well as a supplement to other database Web-development tools. Download it for free from this URL:

```
http://www.oracle.com/products/websystem/powerbrowser/html/
index.html
```

Oracle PowerBrowser handles access to the Internet, intranet, your local PC, and databases that reside in any of those three places.

The Oracle PowerBrowser offers database power on the desktop for PCs. It includes a Web server designed to serve several clients (a small LAN); the browser itself doubles as a Web browser and an HTML authoring program; and the system also includes a "lite" scaled down database engine (see Figure 26-2). Although you can imagine that this Web-database system might be handy in many different situations, it is *not* simple to use.

Figure 26-2: Oracle PowerBrowser has a built-in database with a sample Clothing Catalog Web site.

To make a database application, you must use PL/SQL, Oracle's extension language for SQL. It is similar to BASIC and is easy to program. Oracle provides HTML extensions for PL/SQL to accommodate HTML programming. Although database applications are easy to program within the PowerBrowser system, programming is still programming. If you're not a programmer, you will have to hire someone to create Web presentations using this software. Perhaps in the future Oracle will incorporate an easy-to-use Web-database development tool similar to PowerObjects, making the PowerBrowser more usable by nonprogrammers. Until then, its potential will be limited for nonprogrammers.

The HTML extensions for Oracle's PL/SQL are in the Appendixes as an example of HTML language extensions. Although such HTML extensions may seem simple, you have to write other programming as well to make workable Web documents.

Although from an ease-of-use point of view, PowerBrowser is marginal for nonprogrammers, overall the PowerBrowser is an interesting Web system and development tool for small networks. Presumably, it will eventually become easier to use. When it does, it will enjoy a wider popularity

The Web browser

Oracle's PowerBrowser Web browser has a look similar to Netscape. It supports the HTML 2.0 standard, plus many of the 3.0 standards, such as tables and GIF animations. You can use a bookmark file on a shared server, so that you and your coworkers can keep each other up to date with bookmarks that are relevant to the group. You can toggle easily between your personal bookmark file and the shared one.

Perhaps the most important aspect of the PowerBrowser is the capability to use Network Loadable Objects (covered shortly in this chapter). This gives the PowerBrowser the flexibility to address itself to special intranet situations that require special programming.

The Web server

This server enables you to serve files to others on an intranet. This is a good way to share a document without needing to copy it to a separate shared area first. Your coworkers can simply go to your PC, using their own browsers, and retrieve the file for themselves, or simply view it as any other Web document. Two of its more interesting features are:

➡ **Database Wizard.** This gives you a nice graphical layout of all the tables you can access on a database. By simply double-clicking on one, you can open it in a spreadsheet format and edit the data. It uses database drivers to reach Oracle databases and ODBC databases. Both local databases and remote databases are available by using this tool. You can create Web documents that contain the results of a query you write. You choose the fields you want in the query and in the results listing. PowerBrowser automatically generates a Web document and displays the query results.

➡ **Web Page Wizard.** The Wizard guides you through the creation of a simple home page for yourself. Anyone with HTML experience will not need this, but for novices, it's convenient.

Special programming

One of the primary benefits of PowerBrowser is the capability to do special programming to create special Web-database applications. You can program modular programs or obtain them from others to use. You can also use scripting.

Network Loadable Objects

A Network Loadable Object (NLO) can be any kind of third-party software, such as a video player or a document reader. It can also be something you have programmed yourself. After it's connected to PowerBrowser, you can use the additional capabilities of an NLO right in the browser, and you can adapt Web pages to use it as well. An NLO is compatible with the Netscape 2.0 plug-in standards. NLOs can really jazz up your presentation on the Web. They can perform essential functions, too. For example, a mortgage company that has an intranet can create an NLO that is a financial program, which enables managers to use the PowerBrowser to make financial computations right in a Web document. NLOs are true executables. This means that, unlike Java, an NLO written for UNIX must be rewritten for Windows NT or other platforms.

Oracle BASIC scripting

PowerBrowser integrates the familiar BASIC language. This enables you to create your own scripts that execute within the browser environment. You can add programming to your Web documents.

Microsoft SQL Server

SQL Server 6.5 is a relational database with client-server capabilities similar to comparable Oracle, IBM, Informix, and Sybase database engines. In fact, it's a sister of the Sybase SQL Server 11, having originated in a joint development effort between Microsoft and Sybase. It runs in only Windows NT. SQL Server 6.5 is part of the suite of Microsoft programs called the Back Office. The Windows NT platform is becoming a popular one for hosting intranet servers, and demand is growing for database integration with Internet and intranet servers. Microsoft has developed some additional tools that make it more efficient to retrieve data from the database for use on the Web.

Internet Information Server (IIS)

IIS stands for *Internet Information Server*. This is a program that's part of the Windows NT Server. It interprets requests for database access in two ways.

The first way is the most dynamic and allows on-the-fly queries and database updates. It uses the *Internet Database Connector* (IDC) tool. This tool takes any SQL statement and sends it to the SQL Server database. The database executes the statement, and the results return to IDC, which applies an HTML template and sends the resulting HTML document to the Web server. For example, to start the ball rolling, a visitor goes to an address book Web site. He fills in *Smith* in the Name field of a search form and clicks the Submit button. IIS sends *Smith* to IDC. IDC plugs *Smith* into its SQL statement so that the query now searches for the address of *Smith* in the database. IDC sends this customized query to the SQL Server database and retrieves Smith's address. IDC plugs Smith's address into an HTML template that places Smith's address in a nice blocked-out format similar to an address label. IIS takes the resulting HTML document and sends it to the NT Server, which passes it to the visitor as if it were a normal HTML document (see Figure 26-3).

Web Assistant

The second way to get information from the database uses a different tool, called the HTML Web Assistant, a wizard-like tool (see Figure 26-4). This tool becomes a part of the SQL Server database and is triggered by database events, such as updating a row in the database. HTML documents are generated periodically, and they reside on the NT Server as static Web documents. Using the same Address Book database, here's how it works with HTML Web Assistant. A trigger is designed in the SQL Server database that fires whenever an address in the Address Book database changes, is added, or is removed. This trigger starts the HTML Web assistant. The Web Assistant runs a query that retrieves all the addresses. It sends this set of data to IIS. IIS merges the data with an HTML template. IIS has now created an HTML document that looks like an alphabetical listing of address labels. IIS sends this new Web document to the NT Server, where it replaces the existing address label document. A visitor to the site browses the address label document and is able to scroll through all the addresses.

All this is done with very straightforward programming and HTML markups. Using IIS avoids the need for using CGI scripts, which are more difficult to program and tend to run more slowly than the IIS tool. The IIS works with other databases using the ODBC drivers.

SQL Server is a major database engine with easily used Web-database development tools built in. Although this will no doubt become commonplace, it is still somewhat unique.

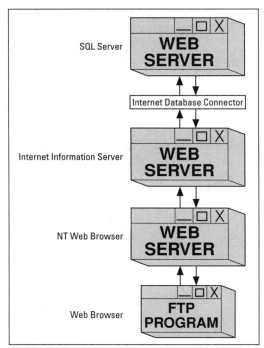

Figure 26-3: Your Web Browser gets an HTML document that was built on the NT by IIS and IDC.

WebSite — Cold Fusion

The WebSite Web server is a popular and solid server and is easy to use, too. And you can download it free from the O'Reilly & Associates Web site (http://www.website.ora.com). It's unique in that it will run on Windows 95 as well as on Windows NT. WebSite Pro is bundled with Cold Fusion, an easy-to-use Web-database development tool for nonprogrammers as well as programmers. In Windows 95, you can run WebSite, Cold Fusion, and a

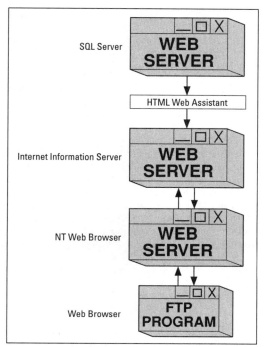

Figure 26-4: The HTML Web Assistant sends data to IIS, which generates new documents to replace existing ones on the NT server.

Web browser at the same time but in different threads (that is, a multi-tasking operating system runs seperate programs simultaneously in different threads). This enables you to develop easily on Windows 95 and test your applications. Because this combination is used for the Art Gallery demonstration in this book, this review is short. Nonetheless, this is a package you will want to consider.

The temporary Web site

All Web sites run 24 hours per day, right? Not necessarily. Are there times when you might want to run a Web site for an hour? Four hours? Just long enough to provide someone access to a database application? Here's how you do it. First, you need an IP number (IP address). You don't need a domain name. For your Internet access account, your ISP normally provides you with a dynamically assigned IP number, which means that it's a different number each time you dial in. This won't work. You need a specific IP number you can use. You can get this number in three ways:

(continued)

(continued)

1. Some ISPs assign you a permanent IP number. Therefore, you may already have one.

2. You almost always get a permanent IP number with an ISDN Internet access account.

3. You can ask your ISP to assign a specific IP number to you temporarily.

The key is to run WebSite on Windows 95 using a specific IP number (IP address), which you can announce before going online. You simply go on the Internet as you normally do when using your consumer Internet access account. (It must be a SLIP/PPP account.) Make sure that WebSite is running. While you're online, anyone knowing your IP number can access your temporary Web site just by plugging your IP number into their Web browser as a URL. As soon as you get offline, your temporary Web site disappears to everyone on the Web. If you develop a Web-database application using Cold Fusion and a database engine such as Access, you can make that application available whenever your temporary Web site is online. Remember, this is possible because WebSite runs in Windows 95. Of course, if your operating system is Windows NT, you can do this with any Web server that runs on Windows NT.

Data Navigation on the Web

This section features NetScheme, which has much potential for both intranets and the Internet. Programmers and nonprogrammers can employ it to use the data in existing database applications with less effort and in new ways. NetScheme uses object-oriented technology to make productive database activities easier.

Datamarts

Many large organizations currently make their various database applications accessible over a network by all employees who need it. This is called *data warehousing*. A variation is the smaller *datamart*. Whereas a data warehouse is an enterprise-wide project, a datamart may serve only a portion of the organization's employees activities.

It is becoming popular to use an intranet to access the data in a data warehouse or a datamart through a Web browser. The Web browser gateway (HTML forms, CGI scripts, and Web-database applications) becomes the standard and easy-to-use way employees access the data they need. The Web also provides means of navigating by using hyperlinks.

There is inevitably an assortment of legacy database applications in most organizations. It is important to maintain the integrity of such database applications. But the datamart must make the data easily available to all employees who need it. Netscheme is an inexpensive and easy-to-employ means of using the data without disturbing the underlying database applications.

Modeler

The NetScheme program starts by making a model of your database application. The model allows you to experiment with your database application without changing the original application. If changes are warranted, you can make the changes to your database application.

The model is object-oriented. By manipulating the objects, you can prune, change, reorganize, and add to your database application, all without making any changes to the original application. Your revised application will run just as if you had made changes to the original application. This enables users to do the following:

- Experiment without affecting the original application.
- Make new applications that run without affecting the original.
- Make subapplications (limited applications) that run via NetScheme and can be used by special groups of users (visitors, for example).
- Test prototypes without affecting the original. The resulting revised applications or new applications can be reverse-engineered to change the original application by using the method you would normally use to change it.
- Provide the tables and columns with user-friendly names.

Nonprogrammers who are familiar with database applications can do this. The NetScheme Modeler presents information to users that they can understand without being database experts. The Modeler runs in Windows 95.

Navigation

NetScheme also automatically creates a set of HTML templates and forms, which enable you to navigate through the data. For example, NetScheme renders a database table into an HTML table in an HTML document. If there is a foreign key column in the table (a column in common with another table), the key column data entries automatically become hyperlinks to their corresponding table. Thus, if a customer database application has a table of names, addresses, and telephone numbers and is related to a second table of billing data by a common column *customer number*, the customer number in each table becomes a hyperlink to the other table. It's an alternative to using queries, an alternative that nonexperts can use.

NetScheme also automatically changes templates and forms to correspond to changes you make in the model. You can also provide custom-made templates to be used by NetScheme. This gives you considerable flexibility in creating useful HTML documents on the fly.

NetScheme's Navigation Server uses the model to process requests from a Web browser into queries against the original database application that underlies the model. Although this is a simple concept, it runs into many practical problems. The NetScheme program has the functions to handle many of these problems. For example, a Web browser could make a request that would deliver a huge amount of data to the user. NetScheme has a *data governor* built in to prevent this from occurring. NetScheme also keeps a record of a visitor's session for later reference, if needed. Don't forget that you can alter the model before you make it available on a network. The Navigation Server runs in Windows NT.

Visitors

What capability can you provide to Internet or intranet visitors?

➡ The ability to work with relational database applications without training.

➡ Navigation through data by using hyperlinks.

➡ Flexible use of data without changing the underlying database applications.

➡ Access to a session record.

Developers

As a developer, you will find NetScheme does the work for you automatically. You don't have to be a programmer. You can change database applications or limit access to database applications without changing the underlying original database application, and you can do it by dragging and dropping objects. You can change an existing database application into a Web catalog almost automatically.

NetScheme provides rapid application development. involving end-users more productively in the design process. If end-users can drag and drop, they can design. With ODBC connectivity, you can use NetScheme with other development tools, too.

Summary

The four software packages presented here indicate that database applications bring a new dimension to publishing on the Web. They are flexible and within the grasp of nonprogrammers. NetScheme also shows that the Web brings a new dimension to using databases as well.

Text
Search
Technology

In This Chapter

Text searchs

Boolean searches

Natural language

Text-search engines

Data also resides outside the structured world of databases. It's called *information,* and it manifests itself in text documents. The sheer enormity of the volume of text documents in business, industry, academia, and other activities has given rise to entire industries of physical indexing, cataloging, keying, and similar techniques. Now, as such information is digitized or as it originates in digital form, it is susceptible to treatment with digital technology. Because the Web is a collection of digital documents, the Web itself is especially susceptible to such treatment.

Text Searches

Text searches provide a useful way to find information in a large repository of documents. Such searches go through every document to identify the information sought.

Key word searches

You can facilitate a text search by choosing and indexing the key words yourself; that is, you decide what words will appear in the index. You would do this for a printed book, for example. This approach provides results similar to a book. If the searcher's key words match the indexer's key words in a book, the searcher can find what he or she seeks. A substantial book with a short index provides very limited searching capability. Even a long index in a printed book leaves much to be desired. A digital system can do a better job, because in a digital system, every word in the text can be in the index. In other words, key words need not be chosen for inclusion in the index; the digital index includes *every* word.

Full-text searches

If you look at a collection of digital text documents as a type of database, then it makes sense to apply the database idea of searching through such data to find what you need. Because the text documents are not neatly structured like data in flat-file, relational, object-oriented, and universal databases, normal relational database queries will not work. What *does* work is a full-text search; that is, the text-search engine goes through all the documents, looking at all the words, to match them to key words or word phrases supplied by the person searching. The key words or phrases help identify documents that contain the information the searcher seeks.

For example, suppose that you try to determine what type of coal was used for fuel in the locomotives of the late nineteenth century. You might scan through books and periodical articles of that era regarding trains, looking for such words as *fuel*, *coal*, *anthracite*, *bituminous*, and *locomotives*. If the information exists in digital form, a digital-text-search engine can do the same thing much more quickly than you can.

Digitizing printed text

How do you digitize printed text that did not originate in digital form? First, you scan the text on an image scanner. Then you use an optical character recognition program (OCR) to translate the scanned image of the text document into a text file (that is, a word processing file). The translation will not be 100 percent accurate, but it may be close enough to reach almost 100 percent accuracy by applying additional techniques, such as spell checking. After the printed text is in digital text form, you can use a full-text-search engine to find what you are looking for.

Full text

A full-text search means that the text-search engine searches every word in every document in the system. A system can be small, with just a few dozen documents, or it can be large — with millions of documents. The documents can be business correspondence, magazine articles, or state statutes. The first thing a text-search engine does is index all the words in the system (that is, it maps all the words in the text into a digital index). You index your document system by using the search engine before someone can use the search engine to run a search. The indexing takes a considerable amount of time compared to other computer operations, but such prior indexing enables a person doing a search to use the text-search engine to search the entire repository of documents completely and quickly.

Results

What are the results of a full-text-search? Unlike a normal database query that results in a report of a row or rows that matches the query, a text search results in the identification of a document or documents that may, *or may not*, include the information sought. In other words, you may find information that fits the key words but is nonetheless not the information you're seeking.

Boolean Searches

Boolean searches compare all words to the key words that a person uses for the search. It's black and white: Either it's the same or it isn't. Matches must be exact.

Boolean operators are *AND*, *OR*, *NOT*, *NEAR*, *WITHIN*, and parentheses. They can help you better define a search. For example, *roses AND tulips* yields only text that includes *both* "roses" and "tulips." *Roses OR tulips,* however, yields text that includes *either* "roses" or "tulips." Using parentheses, you can expand the search. For example, *(roses AND tulips) OR (violets OR daffodils)* yields text that includes either roses and tulips together, or violets alone, or daffodils alone.

Even with complex Boolean queries, many matches will be missed because a word was a slightly different version or because you didn't think of a synonym that you could have used. Although Boolean searches can be valuable techniques, they have limitations.

Natural Language Queries

With a *natural language query,* you use a conversational syntax rather than complex Boolean operators. For example, you might say, "Tell me about the coal used as fuel in locomotives." This is more intuitive than a complex Boolean query. For the untrained person, it is certainly easier; not many computer novices have mastered the proper syntax for Boolean logic.

The quoted sentence in the preceding paragraph offers key words on which a computer can search. In processing the natural language statement, the search engine implies *ANDs* and *ORs*. In a large group of documents, the natural language query may return too many documents as being potential matches. You must use methods for narrowing the results. Additionally, key words always have their limitations. If you can use methods to expand the number of key words, you are likely to get more potentially matching documents that can then be processed with the methods for narrowing the results.

Relevancy

The general method for narrowing results is determining relevancy and creating a relevancy ranking. For example, if a text search indicates that 35 documents may contain the information you seek, a relevancy ranking might say that 3 of them show a 90 percent chance of being relevant, 12 of them show an 80 percent chance of being relevant, 14 of them show a 70 percent chance of being relevant, and so on.

You also can use relevancy to expand the search, as you see in the sections "Stemming," "Thesaurus expansion," and "Statistical Query Expansion." For example, a text search can be used to identify additional key words that are not necessarily synonyms but that can be used productively.

You can do part of the relevancy processing during the indexing. You can do the remainder during the text search itself. For example, during the indexing of the previous example, the occurrences of the word *locomotive* can be counted. Later, when someone does a search, the word-occurrence count for *locomotive* need not be calculated and can be used directly in further calculations.

When?

If the text-search software expands the number of key words based on a person's query and then narrows the results somehow, it's interesting to know when it does its expansion and narrowing. If the text-search engine does all this work during the indexing, the speed of the search will be very fast. Unfortunately, in such a case, the index will be impracticably huge and will take a long time to create. Thus, the text-search engine does part of its work during the indexing and part of its work during the search. The design of the text-search software determines how the text-search engine divides the expansion and narrowing processes between the indexing and the searching. In other words, some of the expansion and narrowing is done during the indexing, and later the text-search software does additional expansion and narrowing during the search process.

Statistical relevancy

The computer can count the occurrences of key words in documents to determine relevancy. The more occurrences there are, the more relevant the document is. This makes sense so long as the key words themselves narrow the search adequately. If not, statistical relevancy begs the question.

Proximity

The proximity of key words to each other can be an important indicator. For example, if *coal* and *locomotive* are always close together in a document, that may indicate a greater likelihood of finding the information sought than if *coal* and *locomotive* are usually far apart. The computer can measure this in a text search.

Position

If the position of the key words in the documents is determined, presumably the documents where the key words appear near the beginning of the document are more relevant documents than ones where they appear toward the end.

Comparative length

A longer document is likely to have more occurrences of key words. Therefore, an adjustment must be made for the length of the document to make a statistical analysis more meaningful.

Frequency

Words that appear very frequently in a group of documents lose their value for doing productive searches. The computer can generate a list of such frequent words for you and then automatically ignore some or all of them.

Normalization

The computer can measure the occurrences of key words in a document and compare that frequency to the occurrences of the key words in the entire document system. If the frequency is comparatively higher, it indicates greater relevancy.

Stop list

Many words are distributed evenly across documents and do not distinguish one document from another. The words *the* and *but* are examples. Such words go on a stop list and are ignored.

Stemming

If key words are truncated to their stems and expanded to their plurals and other forms, the searches on such words and their variations will yield a greater number of potentially relevant documents.

Thesaurus expansion

An automatic thesaurus can expand a text search. The synonyms of the key words are added to the search as additional key words. The synonyms are not necessarily limited to *Roget's Thesaurus* synonyms. In addition, synonyms can be generated by the text-search engine based on relevancy processing.

Statistical Query Expansion

Statistical Query Expansion (SQE) provides a method of expanding a search before subjecting it to the relevancy process. This technique generates a word list of related words in the document system. These words are not synonyms of the key words and do not have a predefined relationship to the key words. They are terms that occur together at a frequency threshold above coincidence and therefore may indicate that a notable relationship exists. Information changes rapidly each year, and the SQE technique transcends prior inclinations about definitions (synonyms) and related words.

This technique also has a psychological element. People *recognize* better than they *remember*. It is more difficult and time-consuming to remember key words regarding the information sought than to recognize key words that are useful in a search. Thus, the SQE technique generates a list of associated words from which a person can choose appropriate additional key words for use in a search.

The SQE technique points out, however, why it is sometimes difficult to classify how relevancy techniques work. In this case, text-search software can also use the SQE technique to narrow the search as well as to enlarge it.

The SQE technique can sort the documents into clusters according to their degree of association with the terms being searched. Then the text-search engine examines the vocabulary in each cluster for relevancy, as though each cluster were unrelated to the remainder of the document system. Presumably, some clusters will be more relevant than others. This approach provides a different analysis and yields a dissimilar set of documents, which are — it is hoped — more relevant.

Relevancy process

After the text-search engine expands the search by using relevancy techniques, the search will most likely yield more documents. Then the text-search engine must apply relevancy processing to narrow the results. Not every text-search program uses all the relevancy techniques included in this chapter. Each text-search software package is a unique mix of the various techniques applied at various times and in various phases of the text-search process.

Boolean versus Other Techniques

Experts argue about whether Boolean and the other text-search techniques covered should be used together. They yield different lists of resulting documents. To conduct the widest possible search, logic dictates the use of both but, in some cases, Boolean searches may not be worth the time and trouble used to perform them and then to evaluate their results. In other cases, Boolean searches can be effective. Only search experience can tell you when Boolean searches can be an effective part of your search scheme. The non-Boolean techniques represent the state-of-the-art effort to get away from the Boolean approach and conduct more effective searching for the information needed.

Access

What's the purpose of all these text-search techniques? It's all about access to information. They help you find:

➥ Information you know exists

➥ Information you think exists

➥ Information you don't know exists

Within large Web sites, or considering the Web itself as one huge document system, text-search engines provide access to information on the Web that you need to find.

Text-Search Engines

Until just recently, text-search engines were primarily programs for corporations and institutions and were comparatively expensive. Even today, the industrial-strength programs remain expensive, although they have come down in price considerably. Some scaled-down text-search engines are free or inexpensive. See Architext Software's Excite (`http://www.excite.com`) and Tippecanoe Systems' Tecumseh Scout (`http://www.tippecanoe.com`). Some desktop text-search engines are priced within the consumer range. But you have to make a substantial purchase to get many of the techniques covered in this chapter featured in a text-search engine for network use. Nonetheless, because of the nature and popularity of the Web, text-search engines have become popular.

All text-search engines are not created equal. You must assess their features and their capacity. You will find that text-search software that can easily and quickly search ten million documents tends to be more expensive than similar software that can handle only five thousand documents.

Text searches are not new to PC owners. Software products such as Lotus Magellan for the PC have been available for many years. They are designed to work on your PC and search through the text files on your hard disk to find the information or file you seek.

Try your text-search engine

Windows 95 has a built-in text search. (Try it: Start ➪ Find ➪ Files or Folders ➪ Advanced, and plug in a word to search). This word-search engine is something you can use on your own PC to search through your files, and it can give you an idea of how handy a search engine might be for visitors at a Web site — even a small Web site. The Windows search engine is simple. It merely names the file in which a key word is located. It does not identify the place in the document. It's useful nonetheless, and it's easy to see why text-search engines are becoming popular on the Internet and on intranets.

Can text-search techniques be used in a structured database? Many database engines include bits and pieces of text-search techniques. There's no reason they cannot go further. Searching the text while it is still in the database makes sense.

Installing a text-search engine

Installing a text-search engine may be the most difficult task in using one. Many use Perl scripts, and you may have to install a Perl interpreter first. You can download a Perl interpreter from the Internet, and you need to follow the instructions carefully to install one properly. If you type **perl -v** on the command line in a DOS window (followed by pressing Enter) and get back a paragraph of information, you will know that Perl is probably installed properly.

Text-search engines seem to take a huge amount of system resources to get set up and to index a document system. You may find it difficult or impossible to do without plenty of RAM. Even 32MB is not too much and is a minimal requirement for setting up some text engines. A text-search engine indexes most of the words in the document system. This takes time, and, of course, the larger the document system, the more time it takes, and the larger the resulting index file is. This is not your game if your server is tight on RAM or hard disk space.

After the initial setup and indexing is complete, the text-search engine runs easily and is easy to use. You can configure a text-search engine for different purposes and different situations. You can include all or part of your document system. After you set up the search engine, your job is finished for a while. As you add new documents to your document system, or as your documents otherwise change, you need to do an update indexing or a complete reindexing, as the situation warrants.

Specific installation steps

First, you use the text-search engine to index the documents you want to include in your search system. On your own computer or on your server computer where you have access to the file system, the search engine can search all the text files on a directory (folder) or on numerous directories. At a Web site that does not belong to you, you have to access each Web document in the entire Web site manually to index the documents, unless you can gain access to that Web site's file directories (unlikely). It is possible to send out robots to index other Web sites automatically. Robots, however, may be irritating to Webmasters as they hit on every Web document. At a Web site with a hundred documents, that's a hundred hits just from your robot.

Second, you must set up the search mechanism so that a visitor can do a search easily and effectively. This entails providing the actual mechanism for doing the search using an HTML form. Along with the setup goes the responsibility to train your visitors to use the text-search engine. Don't forget to include some easily accessible instructions. The instructions should be progressively more difficult. A visitor wanting to do a quick search should have something easy to read. A visitor wanting to do an exhaustive search should have something comprehensive to read about the various techniques for improving a search.

Custom installations

Vendors often sell text-search engines bare bones, because there so many applications. Almost every installation is a custom installation that requires programming expertise. Setting up a text-search engine to search your Web site, however, is straightforward and does not necessarily have to be difficult.

Updating

To keep a text-search service current, you must use some method of indexing new text files and reindexing old text files that have changed. With some text-search engines, the only way you can update is to completely reindex. Because indexing takes so much time for numerous files, reindexing is a significant task.

Reindexing

Some search engines use database techniques to store the indexes they compile. They create multiple indexes in a database application: one to start and one for each update. They can add to or make changes in the original index by creating another new index for new information. Text-search engines that do not have this capability must reindex the entire text-document system to update.

Create a database?

Can you create a document system that appears and functions as if it were a structured database? With text-search engines, this idea has taken root on the Web. A catalog approach to storing information may be an alternative in some cases to a structured database approach. Rather than a row with various items of information in columns, you create a catalog entry (document) of unstructured information. You then use a text-search engine for your queries. Thus, you can provide to your visitors the use of natural language queries.

Although text-search engines are designed primarily to search preexisting document systems, there is no reason that you can't use a text-search engine in a carefully chosen situation to search a system of unstructured documents created to build a database system. For example, the following paragraph might be used instead of a row with many columns of data:

Petro Petroleum Company, 501 E. 23rd St., Poughkeepsie, New York, 01234, 601-123-4567, President: Richard D. Mahn, Executive Vice President: Judith R. Towns, Treasurer: Stanton C. Lensworth. Petro is primarily a manufacturer and marketer of derivative petroleum products for the trucking industry. Gold Valley Oil & Gas, Ltd., Kitchener, Ontario, is the parent corporation of Petro with a 65 percent ownership, and Petro acts as Gold Valley's distributor for petroleum products in the New England region. Petro had gross sales of over 11 million dollars for petroleum products in 1995 and, in addition, had sales of over two million dollars for related services to trucking companies. Founded in 1964 by Richard D. Mahn and incorporated in 1977 in New Jersey, Petro has a manufacturing facility in Wichita Falls, Texas, and does business in the states of New York, New Jersey, Connecticut, and Massachusetts.

Imagine the preceding paragraph with hundreds, thousands, or tens of thousands of others like it, each one a document. With a text-search engine, you can search on key words to find information. A search on *derivative petroleum products* would turn up the Petro Petroleum Company.

Because the Web is essentially a document system, it lends itself well to text searches. Thus, it is entirely feasible to use a system of paragraphs (each a document), or even longer text blocks (each a document), together with a text-search engine, as a data-retrieval system.

How does such a system compare with a relational database application? The information in a text-search system is essentially unstructured and does not provide the precision and efficiency that a relational database application does. Searches are likely to be unwieldy compared to an SQL query. Your search on *derivative petroleum products* may turn up dozens or hundreds of possibilities. Even with relevancy ratings the results may be unwieldy. When you do research or you attempt to find relevant documents, this approach may be acceptable or even a benefit. When you are using database technology in your business to gain instant access to business data, a text search is not likely to be precise enough to get the job done efficiently. Therefore, you need to evaluate your situation carefully before installing such a system in a Web site or anywhere else. Nonetheless, even with its disadvantages, this system will work as a data-retrieval system in some situations.

Sparco sells computer components on the Web. Each component has its own descriptive paragraph in Sparco's catalog. If you are looking for an ISDN modem and search on the acronym *ISDN*, the search will yield not only the ISDN modems of the various vendors but also other ISDN communications equipment, such as network routers. For Sparco's customers this makes a practical system that simulates browsing through a printed catalog.

Text-Search Applications and the Web

A text-search application can provide your Web visitors with an easy means of finding information. This is particularly important for Web systems where large numbers of text documents are included.

You can direct your search engine to go out on the Web to predesignated sites to search for information for your visitors. The search engine does this for specific URLs during the indexing process. As a service to your visitors, horse lovers, you can use a search engine to index all the other Web sites that feature thoroughbred horses. Thus, a visitor using the text search at your Web site can cover your Web site and other similar Web sites in one search.

Searching the Web for information or excitement

How about a text search of the entire Web? Most search engines send out robots to gather information on Web sites. Some robots index the HTML title and header from each Web site. Others summarize the text at a Web site and then index the summaries. Some even index the entire text in each document at every Web site.

Some search engines create a database from descriptive paragraphs written by staff or submitted by Webmasters. The paragraphs are indexed. The search engine then searches the paragraphs. Yahoo takes such an approach and uses an Open Text search engine. This is the same search engine as is used in the Open Text Livelink Search system, which includes a Netscape Commerce Server.

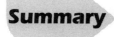

Summary

Full-text searches have emerged as a useful information search technique in the new network computing environments of the Internet, intranets, and the Web. Text searching may be more widely implemented within other database applications as a supplementary query technique, especially where text is an important multimedia element. Text-search engines are not a substitute for other database engines where precise, unambiguous, and direct access to specific data is needed.

Ideas for Using Web-Database Technology

The UNIX Conundrum

UNIX is the operating system of ISPs. Many use Berkeley UNIX. Unfortunately, UNIX versions of the scalable database engines, such as Oracle, are developed for SCO UNIX or other versions popular with corporations. Berkeley UNIX has been overlooked. The various versions of UNIX are not compatible with each other. That means that one of the premises of this book — that most readers will use a UNIX database engine through an ISP — may not be a viable one. Most ISPs are not going to give up Berkeley UNIX. So, what's the answer to this conundrum? One answer is for ISPs to start running Windows NT servers for their Web-site customers who need a database engine. (See the following section, "ODBC/Win NT Work-Around for the UNIX Conundrum.")

ODBC/Win NT Work-Around for the UNIX Conundrum

One answer to the UNIX conundrum is to run the scalable database engine on a Windows NT server. Connect the Windows NT database engine to the UNIX Web server, via ODBC, over the local network. Thus, without using Windows NT as an Internet server, you can still use Windows NT, a scaleable database engine, and Berkeley UNIX to enable database operations in a Web site (see Figure 28-1).

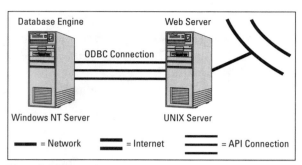

Figure 28-1: A Windows NT database engine on the Web.

This is not a terribly expensive solution, although it does require the addition of a PC and the Windows NT operating system. You also have the maintenance of operating the server PC. If you and enough other customers request it, your ISP might provide database services this way. Alternatively, you can obtain and put the PC (including Windows NT) on your ISP's premises and pay a monthly fee to have it maintained. This is a *cohost* and saves the cost of a dedicated line. Perhaps you can trade database timesharing to the ISP for maintenance.

Don't confuse this solution with using Windows NT in place of UNIX as the network operating system. This solution works through the UNIX computer of your ISP. At press time, Microsoft had disabled Windows NT Workstation — digitially through software changes and then legally through licensing — so that it is unsuitable for use at an Internet Web site. For the work-around suggested here, you have to use the full Windows NT Server (considerably more expensive) or OS/2 Warp (considerably less expensive).

ODBC

Open Database Connectivity (ODBC) is Microsoft's database Application Programming Interface (API). It has become the industry standard for database engines, other database programs, and nondatabase programs to use to connect to (communicate with) each other. Other database APIs exist, but ODBC is the most widely used, particularly in PC systems. ODBC eliminates the need for a software developer to write a communications interface for every probable program to which its database software might be connected. One size fits all: ODBC.

ODBC client

A front-end program, or client, that is used to access data in a separate database application, must connect somehow with that application. The connection is made through ODBC. Thus, the client is an ODBC client. (At a Web site that uses a database engine, the Web server is the ODBC client.)

DBMS server

A DBMS server (database engine) must communicate somehow with clients that will access and use the data within. ODBC makes the connection and enables the communication.

ODBC driver

A DBMS server needs an ODBC driver to enable the use of ODBC. The driver is specifically written for the DBMS server. An ODBC client can access any DBMS server for which there is an ODBC driver. Thus, the ODBC driver is the intermediary between the client and the server and is part of the DBMS server software.

For a database engine used with a Web server, the database engine is the ODBC server, and the Web server is the ODBC client. This assumes that the database engine has an ODBC driver and that the Web server is ODBC compliant. Any nondatabase program that is ODBC compliant can be an ODBC client for any database engine with an ODBC driver.

ODBC Summary

ODBC saves developers a lot of work and makes things easier for users by setting a widely used standard for database connectivity.

JDBC

Java Database Connectivity (JDBC) has been established recently as a standard for using Java with database applications. For use on the Web, this seems likely to grow in importance. See Chapter 29, "Advanced Web-Database Technology," for more information.

Work-Around for a Database Engine that Does Not Store Binary Files

Few database engines have caught up with the multimedia times. They don't store nontext data well, if at all. Clearly, the hybrid object-oriented/relational database engines will gain in popularity, particularly for data systems that handle multimedia data. (Keep an eye on Illustra.) Until then, however, you may have to work around this deficiency. A work-around is especially important for the Web, which is a text-based multimedia publishing system. What are you going to do with all those GIFs? What about Java applets? Real Audio files?

One way to handle these multimedia objects is simply to reference them in a column instead of storing them in the database. Store them in directories (folders), and place their filenames (and relative paths, if required) as text entries in columns in appropriate tables. This is a simple but adequate solution.

Exporting and Importing with ASCII Delimited

One thing to keep in mind is that raw data is easy to transfer from one database application to another.

ASCII delimited

Every database engine has an import and an export function, which facilitates transfers of raw data. This can be done with an ASCII file. The columns are delimited with punctuation, spaces, or character counts (fixed-width columns). Perhaps the most popular method is the *comma-delimited* ASCII file. Each column is separated by a comma. Nonetheless, text columns can include commas within, because the contents of each column are set off with quotation marks (for example, "data","data","data"). Unfortunately, this means you cannot use quotation marks within columns. The following is an example of a comma-delimited database row:

```
1,"Priscilla",,"Paint",,"Ms.","Paint Associates","144 Paint
Lane","Paintville","PA","91967","890-123-4567",,"pris@art
formoney.com","oil","A painting on the wall by Pris, is a room
to remember.","A well-established oil painter of renown,
Priscilla Paint is a graduate of the Yankton Academy of Art
and an occasional instructor at Transylvania State University
where she teaches drawing and oil painting. She has exhibited
in various art festivals and galleries in Pusan, Budapest,
Hyderabad, Pretoria, New York, and other cities. She has
won many awards, and her paintings are in the permanent
collections of six American and four foreign art museums.",
"pris.gif"
```

These delimited transfers are cross-platform. Any database engine on any operating system can export or import a delimited ASCII file.

Remember, however, that the transfer of the raw data does not transfer any of the programming of the database application itself. You can have a wonderful database application, but when you export the raw data, none of the wonderfulness goes with the data. The data is simply rows and columns of data, nothing more. When you import such data, your first task is to set up tables to accommodate the data received (unless the tables have been set up previously).

Database applications

You can export and import database applications, too. The raw data usually goes with these transfers. Such transfers are not necessarily cross-platform, however, and are usually limited to same-brand database software. Attempts at setting standards for database applications to facilitate universal transfers have not realized success. Many database engines, however, have filters for importing database application files from other brands of database engines.

Oracle's Export and Import

Moving data from one Oracle database to another works most efficiently by using Oracle's Export and Import utilities. Any part of the database, from a single table to the entire database, can be exported and imported. Tables are created automatically if they do not exist on the import side. Indexes, security, referential integrity, even database triggers and procedures, are all available for export and import. If you develop a Web-database system using Oracle's PL/SQL procedures, you can export the entire application by exporting the appropriate portions of the database.

Oracle and ASCII files

Oracle has a utility called SQL*Loader that enables you to bring in ASCII files that contain table data. Data can be appended, or can be used to replace a table. The utility can create the table, or you can have the utility give you an error message if the table already exists, or, if the table does not already exist, you can have it do whichever makes sense in your situation.

Unfortunately, pulling data out of Oracle into a comma-delimited file is overly difficult. Your best bet is to write a report that arranges the data into columns and rows, plug in quotation marks around the data, and write it to a file. For example, here is the SQL code to pull out a few columns of the ARTIST table and place them into the typical comma-delimited format:

```
select artist_id,
   ',"' || first_name || '","' .
   '"' || middle_name || '","' ,
   '"' || last_name || '"'
from artist
```

Basically, the quotation marks and commas are added by concatenating them onto each column's data in the select statement. Number fields usually do not need quotation marks, so they are not included in the example.

Cross-Platform Madness

Everyone agrees that cross-platform development is a great thing. Why develop separately for Windows, Macintosh, and UNIX? If you can develop once and have your software (database application) run on multiple operating systems, you will save time, money, and effort. It's not quite that simple, however, because you have to keep several things in mind at once. Look for answers to the following questions.

Database engine

Is the database engine cross-platform? Will it run on UNIX, Macintosh, and Windows NT (or another operating system that's important to you)? For example, you may run a database application in-house for employees on your intranet today, using Windows NT. Tomorrow, fate may dictate that you set it up for customers at XYZ Internet Provider. Very likely, XYZ Internet Provider will be using another operating system (such as UNIX).

Database development tools

Take a simple task such as setting up the tables. Suppose that the database engine is to run on a UNIX system. You are using a Macintosh. Are there tools available for the Mac that will enable you make the database tables? If so, will they work for the UNIX database engine? If not, will you have to borrow someone's UNIX computer to do the tables?

Web-database development tools

Beyond the tables, you will have to create the remainder of the database application. Again, suppose that the database is to run on a UNIX system. You are using Windows 95. Are tools available for Windows 95 that will enable you to construct the database application? After the application is finished, will it run on UNIX?

What do you have to buy (or license)?

What's it going to cost to develop and operate a Web-database application? When you're working with cross-platform tools and programs, you need to consider the cost of software carefully.

Worst case

What's the worst case? Suppose that the database application is to go on a UNIX system. You work on a PC. For some reason, it's not feasible for you to access the UNIX database engine for the purposes of development and testing. The solution is that you buy and install *two database engines*. One runs on the UNIX system and supports the final application. The other runs on your PC or intranet, and it is to be used strictly for development and testing.

The Web-database application must run in UNIX, but you will do the development on a PC. Although the tool you use is cross-platform, a run-time copy of the tool must be present to enable the database application. You must buy and install *two tools*. One runs on the UNIX system and makes your database application work. The other runs on your PC and enables you to develop and test the database application you are constructing.

Thus, the worst case requires the purchase (or licensing) of *four programs*, even though all the programs are cross-platform.

Best case

What's the best case? You buy (or license) an integrated Web-server/database engine complete with integrated development tools. This software will run on UNIX, Windows, or the Macintosh. One license agreement covers the use of one copy for general use and another copy on another computer for development; or all development work is done through the browser.

In between

Most cases will fall in between the best case and the worst case. Thus, it pays to evaluate very carefully each bit of software you buy prior to purchase. Take advantage of the Web, and download the timed trial versions for evaluation.

UNIX rule

A general rule (unscientifically estimated) is that a Windows program costs three to four times as much in the UNIX version. This is the financial side of cross-platformness.

It's not where you're going, it's how you get there

After you have your database application up and running on an intranet or the Internet, anyone with a Web browser can access it. Does it matter whether they are using Windows, Macintosh, or UNIX to access your database application? No. Over a TCP/IP network, an individual's operating system is irrelevant. Thus, from the visitor's point of view, the Web is completely cross-platform. As demonstrated earlier, however, the fact that it's cross-platform for visitors doesn't mean that it's cross-platform for developers.

Copy and Paste

Copy and paste is a convenient but underused technique. It will become more important as data originates more and more in digital form. There is no reason to type data when you can highlight text, copy it to the Clipboard, and paste it into a column in a database table.

Validation

Validation, the act of checking your data before placing it into your database, gives you much better data to work with. A database engine can do some validation for you, such as verifying that only numeric data goes into certain columns. Another very important validation is called *referential integrity*. This means that the keys in related tables are all valid. For example, suppose that you have a video rental database. You have a price_code in the VIDEO table that indicates the price of the video. The actual price stays in a PRICE_LOOKUP table. A good validation system would not allow you to update that video row with an invalid price_code.

The sooner you catch an error, the easier it is to fix. For example, if your screen popped up an error message the moment you typed an invalid price_code and then gave you a chance to fix it, you would never get an invalid price_code in the table. Better yet, suppose that your screen pops up with a selection list of valid price_codes, and you use your mouse to pick one? This last technique is easy to use, of course, with HTML forms.

If your front-end forms do not validate your data, it's a good idea to run validation queries to flush out bad data. For example, you can run a query that finds duplicates in key fields where no duplicates should occur.

Cookies

How can a Web server keep track of a specific browser? It can use a *cookie*. A Web server can deposit a small packet of information in a Web browser for future reference. Thereafter, each time the browser accesses a document at the Web site, the browser transmits the cookie to the Web server.

Web server

To keep track of specific browsers, a Web server must use unique information for each cookie. A unique ID number or unique name are two straightforward ways. If a server deposits a cookie with a unique identifier in a browser, it can recognize that browser on subsequent accesses during the same visit or on subsequent visits. A cookie that has generic information (non-unique information) might be useful, too, but cannot be used to track individual browsers.

Web browser

The cookie deposited in the browser is URL specific. In other words, the information in the cookie will be transmitted to only the Web server that deposited it, not to all Web servers.

Cookie file

The cookie file is cookie.txt, which is found in a Netscape directory (folder). Other Web systems (servers and browsers) can use cookies, too. For the specification on cookies, see the following URL:

```
http://www.netscape.com/newref/std/cookie_spec.html
```

See Chapter 24, "Connecting the Access Database Application to the Web", for a brief explanation of how to use cookies with Cold Fusion.

Visitor tracking

CGI scripts can report a specific browser's accesses to Web documents to track a visitor. What you get is a list of accesses. The cookie and a Web-database application enable more useful visitor tracking. Accumulating a record of accesses in a database application is an orderly method of tracking. A database application also allows generation of Web documents on the fly in response to a visitor's accesses.

Network Computers (NCs)

NCs are here already. Network Computing Devices (NCD) by the end of the first half of 1996 had already sold over 60,000 NCs. The NCD Xplora is the archetypical NC device. It runs on a TCP/IP network (that is, an intranet or the Internet) and can use Windows programs (Windows NT), X-Windows programs (UNIX), or act as a mainframe terminal. It's fast and has great graphics capability. It comes in a small box about the size of an external modem. Moreover, it is truly an NC. It has no floppy drive, no hard drive, no Zip drive, no CD-ROM, and only enough RAM to operate on a network (about 4MB). It depends on the network for its programming and digital storage resources. NCD has signed an agreement with IBM regarding NCs, and IBM itself will be selling several NC models by the beginning of 1997.

The NC offers an organization the opportunity to extend its informational resources to additional employees at a minimal cost in training, hardware, and maintenance. With an NC, the Web browser becomes the gateway to all information, both inside the organization and outside. Web browsers are easy to use, and, as you now know, they can provide straightforward access to both legacy and new database applications.

Oracle is committed to making NCs work, although it will not manufacture NCs. Along with IBM, Sun, Apple, Netscape, and other partners, it has set an NC standard and is licensing an N/C logo to those NCs that meet the standard (This book uses "NC" in the generic sense.). Oracle is also selling NC software, including an operating system.

The question is, What limitations do NCs have that you need to take into consideration in designing Web-database applications? Certainly the small amount of RAM is one limitation. Although a digression on NCs is beyond the scope of this book, you need to keep up to date on NCs to do a competent database development job. The fact that your organization does not have NCs now is not relevant. It will have NCs someday, and now is the time to plan for them.

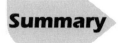

Summary

This chapter covered some ideas that stand out and are perhaps not covered adequately elsewhere in the book. Although this book takes many nonprogrammers into new territory, the authors' intent is to avoid crossing over the line into areas where nonprogrammers do not want to go. This chapter is designed to help you feel comfortable in the new territory.

Advanced Web-Database Technology

The use of databases with multimedia technology (that is, the Web) is advanced technology by itself. With the proliferation of digital information, you need a database to store and keep track of such information. Because information is increasingly multimedia information, databases have a big job. For example, a document is no longer just text. A document can include graphics, audio, video, animation, or even executables (programs) — all binary files. Before long, a normal document might consist of four or five binary files as well as a text file.

The Web is a multimedia medium. Today, it is easy to see that a Web document often fits the preceding description, one text file with several binary files. Tomorrow, many kinds of routine documents, from e-mail messages to letters or reports, will be multimedia documents. A database application is the most rational and efficient way to organize these documents, whether on the Web or off.

Database Technology

E-mail clients already use databases to store your e-mail messages. The features of e-mail clients will grow more powerful as more database features are built in. This is one example of the use of a database in an ordinary program. Other programs have built-in databases, too.

The idea of using databases for multimedia publishing did not originate with the Web. It originated back in the eighties, when several different people used the idea. Compton tried to patent the idea based on its use of a database application to store information in the *Compton's Multimedia Encyclopedia* on a CD-ROM, but its patent was eventually invalidated based on prior existing usage. Thus, using databases for the Web, a multimedia medium, is not revolutionary. It's just a natural extension of the prior use of databases to organize and store multimedia information. Anyone who has ever torn their hair out trying to keep track of all the multimedia files in a multimedia title or for a substantial Web site understands the problem.

As has been mentioned already, however, storage and management are not the only reasons to use a database for the Web. Some things can be done *only* by using a database.

The authors hope that this book gives you a good start in using databases for the Web. Web-database development tools will proliferate. Many will be easy enough for nonprogrammers to use; many are already. ISPs will start offering database services; some already do. Many new intranets will use databases right from the beginning to avoid the shortcomings of building a large, cumbersome file structure for a Web site. Using a database to organize, store, and manage a substantial Web site will become commonplace. But that's not the end of the story.

Object-Oriented Technology

Object technology is the technology of object-oriented programming, object-oriented database applications, and distributed objects. Object technology is well beyond the scope of this book, but it bears mentioning, because it is already extending its reach over the Web. What is an object? One way to think of an object is as a small program that performs a function. String a few objects together and you have a full-fledged program. In this view, an object is a program module. A full-fledged program is a modular construction. It's not quite that simple, however, and a more enlightening look at an object is to see it as a process with its own data.

For example, the shortcut icon in Windows 95 for Word for Windows (WinWord) might be thought of as an object. You click on it, and WinWord quickly loads:

Word

However, the icon is really nothing more than a shortcut to starting the program, and you have to look a little further to find an object. You can create a shortcut in Windows 95 to a WinWord document. When you click on the document shortcut (document icon), WinWord loads itself and its data, the WinWord document. Thus, WinWord appears on the screen, ready to go, with the document showing. Following is what that icon looks like:

Research.doc

This is more like a object, because it includes a program and its data. WinWord, of course, is not a small program, but it illustrates the idea.

An object is actually even more complex than the preceding illustration. An object has a standard way of interfacing with other objects. Thus, regardless of who creates a program in an object-oriented system, it works with all other objects that have been created using the object-oriented programming language. Objects, therefore, may be thought of as building blocks that can be used individually or in a larger structure too; that is, they can perform their own function with their own data or be part of something larger that performs more functions and includes more data. Moreover, the objects can be distributed (for example, over a network) and even assembled on the fly. Envision a dozen objects flying over the Internet into your PC and assembling themselves into a spreadsheet program (see Figure 29-1 for an example from Applix at `http://www.applix.com`). The object technology for the Web is Java, which is an object-oriented programming language.

Netscape - [GIF image 851x566 pixels]
File Edit View Go Bookmarks Options Directory Window Help

Netsite: http://www.applix.com/anyware/demo/WebShtSS.gif

NAME	LAST	NET CHG	PCT CHG	LOW	HIGH	VOL/1000	BID	ASK	TRADES THROUGH
PEOPLE BK PR	129 1/2	+ 6	4.86%	129 1/2	129 1/2	0.1	129 1/2	134	01:04 PM Jun 14, 1996
IOT GROUP INC	21 3/4	+ 5 3/4	35.94%	19	22 3/4	2,411.0	21 3/4	22 1/4	01:38 PM Jun 14, 1996
ANDRX OP	15 3/8	+ 3 3/8	28.13%	12	16	1,836.0	15 1/4	15 3/4	01:39 PM Jun 14, 1996
COMMET CORP	13 1/2	+ 3 3/8	33.33%	13 1/2	13 1/2	0.2	10	13 1/2	11:54 AM Jun 14, 1996
CORPORATE EXP	45 1/4	+ 3 9/16	8.55%	41 5/8	45 1/4	865.8	45	45 1/4	01:39 PM Jun 14, 1996
UNIFY CORP	15	+ 3	25.00%	14 1/2	16	2,286.3	14 7/8	15 1/4	01:39 PM Jun 14, 1996
ASPECT TELECOM	53 1/4	+ 3	5.97%	49 1/2	53 1/4	111.5	52 1/2	53 1/4	01:36 PM Jun 14, 1996
DUPONT PHOTOMSK	20	+ 3	17.65%	19 1/2	23 1/2	3,469.2	20	20 1/4	01:39 PM Jun 14, 1996
ADTRAN INC	72 3/4	+ 2 7/8	4.11%	69 1/4	73 1/2	249.5	72 3/4	73 1/2	01:31 PM Jun 14, 1996
MIORION OP	23 1/2	+ 2 3/4	13.25%	21	24 1/2	523.2	23 1/2	24	01:36 PM Jun 14, 1996

	NASDAQ MARKET DIGEST --->	VOL/1000	Advanced:	121,058.26	ISSUES	Advanced:	1654	New Highs:	116
NAS/NMS COMPSITE	1213.20	-6.45		Declined:	177,711.96		Declined:	2025	New Lows:	48
DJ INDUSTRIAL	5656.10	-1.85		Unchanged:	32,704.30		Unchanged:	919		
S&P 500 INDEX	667.51	-0.41		TOTAL:	331,484.52		TOTAL:	4608	Updated @	01:39 PM

Figure 29-1: The Applix Java spreadsheet program.

Java

Java is a new language adapted specifically for the Internet, combining the best of several programming languages. The unique architecture behind Java allows for some very sophisticated applications.

Java enables a programmer to create small applications, or applets, which are stored on the Web server and downloaded to the browser automatically. When a visitor goes to an HTML document that calls the applet, the server sends the entire applet to the browser. This means that the applet now resides on the visitor's computer (the client) without ever requiring the visitor to specifically download anything. It's done automatically. The applet (on the client) runs whenever the visitor goes to that HTML document. This makes applets run faster than server-side programs.

Many browsers already support Java (such as Netscape 2.0). The HTML markup that tells the browser to run a Java applet is the following:

```
<applet code="applet class" width=10 height=140></applet>
```

Java enhances a Web-database site when used at the interface between the visitor's browser and the database. One example of Java working with a database appears on the Avitec WebContact Web site (http://www.avitek.com/demos/contact/demo.html), where a visitor can search for Web designers. This is a demonstration site that illustrates how to use Java to search a database. Figure 29-2 shows the architecture of the site. Here's how it works:

1. **A visitor clicks on the Start button (see Figure 29-3).** The server loads the Java applet into the visitor's computer (the client).

2. **The visitor now begins a search for all contacts whose first names begin with the letter A.** The search commences when the visitor clicks on the Search button.

3. **The Java applet sends the search parameter (the letter A) to the Web server.**

4. **The Web server sends it to the Internet Information Server (IIS).**

5. **The IIS sends it to the Internet Database Connection (IDC), which converts it into a query and sends it to the database.**

6. **The database processes the query and returns the results to the IDC.**

7. **The IDC passes this result on to the IIS, where it is combined with an HTML template and returned as an HTML document to the Web server.**

8. **The Web server sends the HTML document to the browser.**

9. Java intercepts it before it gets to the browser, pulls the query results from the document, formats them into a Java window, and updates the current Web document with the results.

Figure 29-2: Java controls the data flow to and from the client-side browser.

Figure 29-3: The Java applet runs inside a window within this Web document.

There are several good reasons to go to all the trouble of making a Java applet. Without Java, the Web-database interface must always return an HTML document. The context of the visitor's query, update, or other transaction is lost. The Java applet, on the other hand, keeps the visitor's current context. Other features that can be used in a Java-to-database applet are

➡ Pop-up message boxes. Because Java traps the responses from the Web server before the browser gets them, Java can handle them more appropriately. An error message can pop up in a small window with an OK button. The user reads the message and clicks OK to continue.

➡ Field validation. Validation of fields, using either some validation routine within the applet, or using a call to the database to look up values, can be done seamlessly. This validation can be done when the visitor moves from one field to the next, rather than when the visitor clicks on a button.

➡ Floating windows. Java can define a special class of object that creates a desktop window. This means that the familiar methods of manipulating windows, including Maximize, Minimize, and using Tab to toggle from one window to another, are all available within the browser document.

➡ Multiuser, multithread tasks. Most client-server databases handle multiple users by prioritizing them and switching from one to the other according to an algorithm that minimizes turnaround time for all users. Java can be programmed to carry out a similar process. For example, a single Java applet can retrieve data from the database and start up and run an animation at the same time.

Java's client-side execution reduces the traffic across the network. This helps speed up the performance of applications like VRML, 3D graphics, and mathematical calculations. A 3D charting program uses Java to present three-dimensional graphs from database data. The graphs can be rotated, resized, and recalculated using this client-side Java applet. Infospace loads a Java applet that creates 3D charts in several formats, including VRML. The Web site (http://www.infospace-inc.com) offers a free trial download of the software and a demonstration (see Figure 29-4).

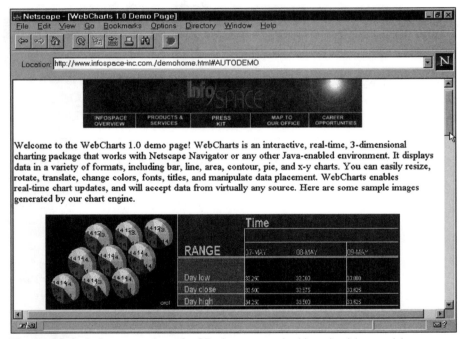

Figure 29-4: A demonstration of a 3D chart created with a database and Java.

Many of the first Java applets available seem to be graphical presentations. Any type of program, however, can be written in Java, even programs so long that they become something more than applets (that is, full-fledged applications).

JDBC

Java Database Connectivity (JDBC) is an Application Programming Interface for connecting Java directly to a database. It is similar to Microsoft's ODBC standard. With JDBC, it is possible to program fully distributed database applications that work on any hardware and software supports Java. The data source can be from any ODBC-compliant data-base. The database can be on the Internet or an intranet, and the person accessing the data can use any Internet-connected computer with Netscape or another Java-capable browser.

JDBC has two pieces, the Manager and the Driver. The Manager is the client-side communicator that transmits Java commands from the Java applet to the server-side JDBC Driver. The Driver handles communication to and from the database. To make this work, the database must have a JDBC Driver in place. Oracle, Sybase, IBM, and some other major data-base vendors are already working on their JDBC drivers. If no JDBC Driver exists for the particular database you are using, a third piece, the JDBC-ODBC Bridge, converts the JDBC commands into ODBC commands and passes them to the ODBC Driver. JDBC and ODBC are very similar, so this is a fairly simple bridge.

JDBC even connects remote databases across the Internet. It uses the Universal Resource Locator (URL) standard to assign unique names to each database instance on the Internet. It uses the prefix *jdbc* or *jdbc-odbc* to tell the server which API to use like this:

```
jdbc://host.mydomain.com/jdbc_db_file
```

If your database uses the JDBC-ODBC bridge, your URL might look like this:

```
jdbc:odbc//host.mydomain.com/odbc_db_file
```

The JDBC protocol is new. The first standard was published in March of 1996; its future depends on what competing protocols appear and which ones become the most popular.

A JDBC Driver for Oracle was announced in June 1996 by Weblogic, Inc, dbKona version 2.0. Weblogic declared it will have a version for SQL Server and Sybase soon. The dbKona software was originally a proprietary driver for the Java-to-database interface. Version 2.0 was revised to be JDBC compliant. See the company's Web site for the latest news:

```
http://www.weblogic.com/index_noframe.html
```

Summary

If object-oriented programming is onthe Web, there will be plenty of objects zooming around the Internet or your intranet. Objects are binary files. To control objects and multimedia information, you need an object-oriented database engine and application.

Object-oriented database applications are great for constructing complex procedures out of objects in the database. For such work, they operate faster and with greater agility than relational databases. One simple "query" can launch a complex procedure. Relational databases are faster for simple queries involving data from a few tables. The longer and more complex the query, the more poorly relational databases perform. Thus, a hybrid object-oriented-relational database engine offers some of the best features of both types of databases. That's why the Illustra database engine is mentioned often in this book. Illustra is the database technology of the future.

Until Illustra matures, keep an eye on Java and its database capabilities. Java is more than a programming language for applets. You can create full-fledged applications, such as word processors, spreadsheets, browsers, and servers.

On the practical side, you can use Java to do queries. In other words, you can use Java to create database applications using available database engines, even though they are not object-oriented database engines. Nonprogrammers need not be excluded from using Java. In the second half of 1996, a number of Java authoring programs will be available that will give nonprogrammers the capability to do Java programming. Jamba, WebGalaxy, and JDesigner Pro are examples.

As the database connectivity standards for Java fall into place, Java authoring programs will offer more competent database-application development capability. Just how far you can go with an authoring program as a nonprogrammer is always a question, but straightforward database applications using Java should prove relatively easy for you. And where are you going to store all your Java objects? In your Illustra (or comparable) database, of course.

Java may not be something you want to digest right now, and it will take some time to mature as a development environment. It is something to keep your eye on if you are interested in using Web-database applications on the Web.

Symbols and Numbers

T

The Fun & Easy Way™ to learn about computers and more!

Here's a complete listing of IDG Books' ...For Dummies® titles

Title	Author	ISBN	Price
DATABASE			
Access 2 For Dummies®	by Scott Palmer	ISBN: 1-56884-090-X	$19.95 USA/$26.95 Canada
Access Programming For Dummies®	by Rob Krumm	ISBN: 1-56884-091-8	$19.95 USA/$26.95 Canada
Approach 3 For Windows® For Dummies®	by Doug Lowe	ISBN: 1-56884-233-3	$19.99 USA/$26.99 Canada
dBASE For DOS For Dummies®	by Scott Palmer & Michael Stabler	ISBN: 1-56884-188-4	$19.95 USA/$26.95 Canada
dBASE For Windows® For Dummies®	by Scott Palmer	ISBN: 1-56884-179-5	$19.95 USA/$26.95 Canada
dBASE 5 For Windows® Programming For Dummies®	by Ted Coombs & Jason Coombs	ISBN: 1-56884-215-5	$19.99 USA/$26.99 Canada
FoxPro 2.6 For Windows® For Dummies®	by John Kaufeld	ISBN: 1-56884-187-6	$19.95 USA/$26.95 Canada
Paradox 5 For Windows® For Dummies®	by John Kaufeld	ISBN: 1-56884-185-X	$19.95 USA/$26.95 Canada
DESKTOP PUBLISHING/ILLUSTRATION/GRAPHICS			
CorelDRAW! 5 For Dummies®	by Deke McClelland	ISBN: 1-56884-157-4	$19.95 USA/$26.95 Canada
CorelDRAW! For Dummies®	by Deke McClelland	ISBN: 1-56884-042-X	$19.95 USA/$26.95 Canada
Desktop Publishing & Design For Dummies®	by Roger C. Parker	ISBN: 1-56884-234-1	$19.99 USA/$26.99 Canada
Harvard Graphics 2 For Windows® For Dummies®	by Roger C. Parker	ISBN: 1-56884-092-6	$19.95 USA/$26.95 Canada
PageMaker 5 For Macs® For Dummies®	by Galen Gruman & Deke McClelland	ISBN: 1-56884-178-7	$19.95 USA/$26.95 Canada
PageMaker 5 For Windows® For Dummies®	by Deke McClelland & Galen Gruman	ISBN: 1-56884-160-4	$19.95 USA/$26.95 Canada
Photoshop 3 For Macs® For Dummies®	by Deke McClelland	ISBN: 1-56884-208-2	$19.99 USA/$26.99 Canada
QuarkXPress 3.3 For Dummies®	by Galen Gruman & Barbara Assadi	ISBN: 1-56884-217-1	$19.99 USA/$26.99 Canada
FINANCE/PERSONAL FINANCE/TEST TAKING REFERENCE			
Everyday Math For Dummies™	by Charles Seiter	ISBN: 1-56884-248-1	$14.99 USA/$22.99 Canada
Personal Finance For Dummies™ For Canadians	by Eric Tyson & Tony Martin	ISBN: 1-56884-378-X	$18.99 USA/$24.99 Canada
QuickBooks 3 For Dummies®	by Stephen L. Nelson	ISBN: 1-56884-227-9	$19.99 USA/$26.99 Canada
Quicken 8 For DOS For Dummies, 2nd Edition	by Stephen L. Nelson	ISBN: 1-56884-210-4	$19.95 USA/$26.95 Canada
Quicken 5 For Macs® For Dummies®	by Stephen L. Nelson	ISBN: 1-56884-211-2	$19.95 USA/$26.95 Canada
Quicken 4 For Windows® For Dummies, 2nd Edition	by Stephen L. Nelson	ISBN: 1-56884-209-0	$19.95 USA/$26.95 Canada
Taxes For Dummies, 1995 Edition	by Eric Tyson & David J. Silverman	ISBN: 1-56884-220-1	$14.99 USA/$20.99 Canada
The GMAT® For Dummies™	by Suzee Vlk, Series Editor	ISBN: 1-56884-376-3	$14.99 USA/$20.99 Canada
The GRE® For Dummies™	by Suzee Vlk, Series Editor	ISBN: 1-56884-375-5	$14.99 USA/$20.99 Canada
Time Management For Dummies™	by Jeffrey J. Mayer	ISBN: 1-56884-360-7	$16.99 USA/$22.99 Canada
TurboTax For Windows® For Dummies®	by Gail A. Helsel, CPA	ISBN: 1-56884-228-7	$19.99 USA/$26.99 Canada
GROUPWARE/INTEGRATED			
ClarisWorks For Macs® For Dummies®	by Frank Higgins	ISBN: 1-56884-363-1	$19.99 USA/$26.99 Canada
Lotus Notes For Dummies®	by Pat Freeland & Stephen Londergan	ISBN: 1-56884-212-0	$19.95 USA/$26.95 Canada
Microsoft® Office 4 For Windows® For Dummies®	by Roger C. Parker	ISBN: 1-56884-183-3	$19.95 USA/$26.95 Canada
Microsoft® Works 3 For Windows® For Dummies®	by David C. Kay	ISBN: 1-56884-214-7	$19.99 USA/$26.99 Canada
SmartSuite 3 For Dummies®	by Jan Weingarten & John Weingarten	ISBN: 1-56884-367-4	$19.99 USA/$26.99 Canada
INTERNET/COMMUNICATIONS/NETWORKING			
America Online® For Dummies, 2nd Edition	by John Kaufeld	ISBN: 1-56884-933-8	$19.99 USA/$26.99 Canada
CompuServe For Dummies, 2nd Edition	by Wallace Wang	ISBN: 1-56884-937-0	$19.99 USA/$26.99 Canada
Modems For Dummies, 2nd Edition	by Tina Rathbone	ISBN: 1-56884-223-6	$19.99 USA/$26.99 Canada
MORE Internet For Dummies®	by John R. Levine & Margaret Levine Young	ISBN: 1-56884-164-7	$19.95 USA/$26.95 Canada
MORE Modems & On-line Services For Dummies®	by Tina Rathbone	ISBN: 1-56884-365-8	$19.99 USA/$26.99 Canada
Mosaic For Dummies, Windows Edition	by David Angell & Brent Heslop	ISBN: 1-56884-242-2	$19.99 USA/$26.99 Canada
NetWare For Dummies, 2nd Edition	by Ed Tittel, Deni Connor & Earl Follis	ISBN: 1-56884-369-0	$19.99 USA/$26.99 Canada
Networking For Dummies®	by Doug Lowe	ISBN: 1-56884-079-9	$19.95 USA/$26.95 Canada
PROCOMM PLUS 2 For Windows® For Dummies®	by Wallace Wang	ISBN: 1-56884-219-8	$19.99 USA/$26.99 Canada
TCP/IP For Dummies®	by Marshall Wilensky & Candace Leiden	ISBN: 1-56884-241-4	$19.99 USA/$26.99 Canada

For scholastic requests & educational orders please call Educational Sales at 1. 800. 434. 2086

FOR MORE INFO OR TO ORDER, PLEASE CALL ▶ 800. 762. 2974

For volume discounts & special orders please call Tony Real, Special Sales, at 415. 655. 3048

The Internet For Macs® For Dummies® 2nd Edition	by Charles Seiter	ISBN: 1-56884-371-2	$19.99 USA/$26.99 Canada
The Internet For Macs® For Dummies® Starter Kit	by Charles Seiter	ISBN: 1-56884-244-9	$29.99 USA/$39.99 Canada
The Internet For Macs® For Dummies® Starter Kit Bestseller Edition	by Charles Seiter	ISBN: 1-56884-245-7	$39.99 USA/$54.99 Canada
The Internet For Windows® For Dummies® Starter Kit	by John R. Levine & Margaret Levine Young	ISBN: 1-56884-237-6	$34.99 USA/$44.99 Canada
The Internet For Windows® For Dummies® Starter Kit, Bestseller Edition	by John R. Levine & Margaret Levine Young	ISBN: 1-56884-246-5	$39.99 USA/$54.99 Canada

MACINTOSH

Mac® Programming For Dummies®	by Dan Parks Sydow	ISBN: 1-56884-173-6	$19.95 USA/$26.95 Canada
Macintosh® System 7.5 For Dummies®	by Bob LeVitus	ISBN: 1-56884-197-3	$19.95 USA/$26.95 Canada
MORE Macs® For Dummies®	by David Pogue	ISBN: 1-56884-087-X	$19.95 USA/$26.95 Canada
PageMaker 5 For Macs® For Dummies®	by Galen Gruman & Deke McClelland	ISBN: 1-56884-178-7	$19.95 USA/$26.95 Canada
QuarkXPress 3.3 For Dummies®	by Galen Gruman & Barbara Assadi	ISBN: 1-56884-217-1	$19.99 USA/$26.99 Canada
Upgrading and Fixing Macs® For Dummies®	by Kearney Rietmann & Frank Higgins	ISBN: 1-56884-189-2	$19.95 USA/$26.95 Canada

MULTIMEDIA

Multimedia & CD-ROMs For Dummies® 2nd Edition	by Andy Rathbone	ISBN: 1-56884-907-9	$19.99 USA/$26.99 Canada
Multimedia & CD-ROMs For Dummies® Interactive Multimedia Value Pack, 2nd Edition	by Andy Rathbone	ISBN: 1-56884-909-5	$29.99 USA/$39.99 Canada

OPERATING SYSTEMS:

DOS

MORE DOS For Dummies®	by Dan Gookin	ISBN: 1-56884-046-2	$19.95 USA/$26.95 Canada
OS/2® Warp For Dummies® 2nd Edition	by Andy Rathbone	ISBN: 1-56884-205-8	$19.99 USA/$26.99 Canada

UNIX

MORE UNIX® For Dummies®	by John R. Levine & Margaret Levine Young	ISBN: 1-56884-361-5	$19.99 USA/$26.99 Canada
UNIX® For Dummies®	by John R. Levine & Margaret Levine Young	ISBN: 1-878058-58-4	$19.95 USA/$26.95 Canada

WINDOWS

MORE Windows® For Dummies® 2nd Edition	by Andy Rathbone	ISBN: 1-56884-048-9	$19.95 USA/$26.95 Canada
Windows® 95 For Dummies®	by Andy Rathbone	ISBN: 1-56884-240-6	$19.99 USA/$26.99 Canada

PCS/HARDWARE

Illustrated Computer Dictionary For Dummies® 2nd Edition	by Dan Gookin & Wallace Wang	ISBN: 1-56884-218-X	$12.95 USA/$16.95 Canada
Upgrading and Fixing PCs For Dummies® 2nd Edition	by Andy Rathbone	ISBN: 1-56884-903-6	$19.99 USA/$26.99 Canada

PRESENTATION/AUTOCAD

AutoCAD For Dummies®	by Bud Smith	ISBN: 1-56884-191-4	$19.95 USA/$26.95 Canada
PowerPoint 4 For Windows® For Dummies®	by Doug Lowe	ISBN: 1-56884-161-2	$16.99 USA/$22.99 Canada

PROGRAMMING

Borland C++ For Dummies®	by Michael Hyman	ISBN: 1-56884-162-0	$19.95 USA/$26.95 Canada
C For Dummies® Volume 1	by Dan Gookin	ISBN: 1-878058-78-9	$19.95 USA/$26.95 Canada
C++ For Dummies®	by Stephen R. Davis	ISBN: 1-56884-163-9	$19.95 USA/$26.95 Canada
Delphi Programming For Dummies®	by Neil Rubenking	ISBN: 1-56884-200-7	$19.99 USA/$26.99 Canada
Mac® Programming For Dummies®	by Dan Parks Sydow	ISBN: 1-56884-173-6	$19.95 USA/$26.95 Canada
PowerBuilder 4 Programming For Dummies®	by Ted Coombs & Jason Coombs	ISBN: 1-56884-325-9	$19.99 USA/$26.99 Canada
QBasic Programming For Dummies®	by Douglas Hergert	ISBN: 1-56884-093-4	$19.95 USA/$26.95 Canada
Visual Basic 3 For Dummies®	by Wallace Wang	ISBN: 1-56884-076-4	$19.95 USA/$26.95 Canada
Visual Basic "X" For Dummies®	by Wallace Wang	ISBN: 1-56884-230-9	$19.99 USA/$26.99 Canada
Visual C++ 2 For Dummies®	by Michael Hyman & Bob Arnson	ISBN: 1-56884-328-3	$19.99 USA/$26.99 Canada
Windows® 95 Programming For Dummies®	by S. Randy Davis	ISBN: 1-56884-327-5	$19.99 USA/$26.99 Canada

SPREADSHEET

1-2-3 For Dummies®	by Greg Harvey	ISBN: 1-878058-60-6	$16.95 USA/$22.95 Canada
1-2-3 For Windows® 5 For Dummies® 2nd Edition	by John Walkenbach	ISBN: 1-56884-216-3	$16.95 USA/$22.95 Canada
Excel 5 For Macs® For Dummies®	by Greg Harvey	ISBN: 1-56884-186-8	$19.95 USA/$26.95 Canada
Excel For Dummies® 2nd Edition	by Greg Harvey	ISBN: 1-56884-050-0	$16.95 USA/$22.95 Canada
MORE 1-2-3 For DOS For Dummies®	by John Weingarten	ISBN: 1-56884-224-4	$19.99 USA/$26.99 Canada
MORE Excel 5 For Windows® For Dummies®	by Greg Harvey	ISBN: 1-56884-207-4	$19.95 USA/$26.95 Canada
Quattro Pro 6 For Windows® For Dummies®	by John Walkenbach	ISBN: 1-56884-174-4	$19.95 USA/$26.95 Canada
Quattro Pro For DOS For Dummies®	by John Walkenbach	ISBN: 1-56884-023-3	$16.95 USA/$22.95 Canada

UTILITIES

Norton Utilities 8 For Dummies®	by Beth Slick	ISBN: 1-56884-166-3	$19.95 USA/$26.95 Canada

VCRS/CAMCORDERS

VCRs & Camcorders For Dummies™	by Gordon McComb & Andy Rathbone	ISBN: 1-56884-229-5	$14.99 USA/$20.99 Canada

WORD PROCESSING

Ami Pro For Dummies®	by Jim Meade	ISBN: 1-56884-049-7	$19.95 USA/$26.95 Canada
MORE Word For Windows® 6 For Dummies®	by Doug Lowe	ISBN: 1-56884-165-5	$19.95 USA/$26.95 Canada
MORE WordPerfect® 6 For Windows® For Dummies®	by Margaret Levine Young & David C. Kay	ISBN: 1-56884-206-6	$19.95 USA/$26.95 Canada
MORE WordPerfect® 6 For DOS For Dummies®	by Wallace Wang, edited by Dan Gookin	ISBN: 1-56884-047-0	$19.95 USA/$26.95 Canada
Word 6 For Macs® For Dummies®	by Dan Gookin	ISBN: 1-56884-190-6	$19.95 USA/$26.95 Canada
Word For Windows® 6 For Dummies®	by Dan Gookin	ISBN: 1-56884-075-6	$16.95 USA/$22.95 Canada
Word For Windows® For Dummies®	by Dan Gookin & Ray Werner	ISBN: 1-878058-86-X	$16.95 USA/$22.95 Canada
WordPerfect® 6 For DOS For Dummies®	by Dan Gookin	ISBN: 1-878058-77-0	$16.95 USA/$22.95 Canada
WordPerfect® 6.1 For Windows® For Dummies® 2nd Edition	by Margaret Levine Young & David Kay	ISBN: 1-56884-243-0	$16.95 USA/$22.95 Canada
WordPerfect® For Dummies®	by Dan Gookin	ISBN: 1-878058-52-5	$16.95 USA/$22.95 Canada

Fun, Fast, & Cheap!™

The Internet For Macs® For Dummies® Quick Reference
by Charles Seiter

ISBN:1-56884-967-2
$9.99 USA/$12.99 Canada

Windows® 95 For Dummies® Quick Reference
by Greg Harvey

ISBN: 1-56884-964-8
$9.99 USA/$12.99 Canada

Photoshop 3 For Macs® For Dummies® Quick Reference
by Deke McClelland

ISBN: 1-56884-968-0
$9.99 USA/$12.99 Canada

WordPerfect® For DOS For Dummies® Quick Reference
by Greg Harvey

ISBN: 1-56884-009-8
$8.95 USA/$12.95 Canada

Title	Author	ISBN	Price
DATABASE			
Access 2 For Dummies® Quick Reference	by Stuart J. Stuple	ISBN: 1-56884-167-1	$8.95 USA/$11.95 Canada
dBASE 5 For DOS For Dummies® Quick Reference	by Barrie Sosinsky	ISBN: 1-56884-954-0	$9.99 USA/$12.99 Canada
dBASE 5 For Windows® For Dummies® Quick Reference	by Stuart J. Stuple	ISBN: 1-56884-953-2	$9.99 USA/$12.99 Canada
Paradox 5 For Windows® For Dummies® Quick Reference	by Scott Palmer	ISBN: 1-56884-960-5	$9.99 USA/$12.99 Canada
DESKTOP PUBLISHING/ILLUSTRATION/GRAPHICS			
CorelDRAW! 5 For Dummies® Quick Reference	by Raymond E. Werner	ISBN: 1-56884-952-4	$9.99 USA/$12.99 Canada
Harvard Graphics For Windows® For Dummies® Quick Reference	by Raymond E. Werner	ISBN: 1-56884-962-1	$9.99 USA/$12.99 Canada
Photoshop 3 For Macs® For Dummies® Quick Reference	by Deke McClelland	ISBN: 1-56884-968-0	$9.99 USA/$12.99 Canada
FINANCE/PERSONAL FINANCE			
Quicken 4 For Windows® For Dummies® Quick Reference	by Stephen L. Nelson	ISBN: 1-56884-950-8	$9.95 USA/$12.95 Canada
GROUPWARE/INTEGRATED			
Microsoft® Office 4 For Windows® For Dummies® Quick Reference	by Doug Lowe	ISBN: 1-56884-958-3	$9.99 USA/$12.99 Canada
Microsoft® Works 3 For Windows® For Dummies® Quick Reference	by Michael Partington	ISBN: 1-56884-959-1	$9.99 USA/$12.99 Canada
INTERNET/COMMUNICATIONS/NETWORKING			
The Internet For Dummies® Quick Reference	by John R. Levine & Margaret Levine Young	ISBN: 1-56884-168-X	$8.95 USA/$11.95 Canada
MACINTOSH			
Macintosh® System 7.5 For Dummies® Quick Reference	by Stuart J. Stuple	ISBN: 1-56884-956-7	$9.99 USA/$12.99 Canada
OPERATING SYSTEMS:			
DOS			
DOS For Dummies® Quick Reference	by Greg Harvey	ISBN: 1-56884-007-1	$8.95 USA/$11.95 Canada
UNIX			
UNIX® For Dummies® Quick Reference	by John R. Levine & Margaret Levine Young	ISBN: 1-56884-094-2	$8.95 USA/$11.95 Canada
WINDOWS			
Windows® 3.1 For Dummies® Quick Reference, 2nd Edition	by Greg Harvey	ISBN: 1-56884-951-6	$8.95 USA/$11.95 Canada
PCs/HARDWARE			
Memory Management For Dummies® Quick Reference	by Doug Lowe	ISBN: 1-56884-362-3	$9.99 USA/$12.99 Canada
PRESENTATION/AUTOCAD			
AutoCAD For Dummies® Quick Reference	by Ellen Finkelstein	ISBN: 1-56884-198-1	$9.95 USA/$12.95 Canada
SPREADSHEET			
1-2-3 For Dummies® Quick Reference	by John Walkenbach	ISBN: 1-56884-027-6	$8.95 USA/$11.95 Canada
1-2-3 For Windows® 5 For Dummies® Quick Reference	by John Walkenbach	ISBN: 1-56884-957-5	$9.95 USA/$12.95 Canada
Excel For Windows® For Dummies® Quick Reference, 2nd Edition	by John Walkenbach	ISBN: 1-56884-096-9	$8.95 USA/$11.95 Canada
Quattro Pro 6 For Windows® For Dummies® Quick Reference	by Stuart J. Stuple	ISBN: 1-56884-172-8	$9.95 USA/$12.95 Canada
WORD PROCESSING			
Word For Windows® 6 For Dummies® Quick Reference	by George Lynch	ISBN: 1-56884-095-0	$8.95 USA/$11.95 Canada
Word For Windows® For Dummies® Quick Reference	by George Lynch	ISBN: 1-56884-029-2	$8.95 USA/$11.95 Canada
WordPerfect® 6.1 For Windows® For Dummies® Quick Reference, 2nd Edition	by Greg Harvey	ISBN: 1-56884-966-4	$9.99 USA/$12.99/Canada

Macworld® Mac® & Power Mac SECRETS™, 2nd Edition

by David Pogue & Joseph Schorr

HOT!

This is the definitive Mac reference for those who want to become power users! Includes three disks with 9MB of software!

WINNERS 1994-95 TECHNICAL PUBLICATIONS AND ART COMPETITIONS OF THE SOCIETY FOR TECHNICAL COMMUNICATION

ISBN: 1-56884-175-2
$39.95 USA/$54.95 Canada

Includes 3 disks chock full of software.

NEWBRIDGE BOOK CLUB SELECTION

Macworld® Mac® FAQs™

by David Pogue

HOT!

Written by the hottest Macintosh author around, David Pogue, *Macworld Mac FAQs* gives users the ultimate Mac reference. Hundreds of Mac questions and answers side-by-side, right at your fingertips, and organized into six easy-to-reference sections with lots of sidebars and diagrams.

ISBN: 1-56884-480-8
$19.99 USA/$26.99 Canada

Macworld® System 7.5 Bible, 3rd Edition

by Lon Poole

ISBN: 1-56884-098-5
$29.95 USA/$39.95 Canada

NATIONAL BESTSELLER!

Macworld® ClarisWorks 3.0 Companion, 3rd Edition

by Steven A. Schwartz

ISBN: 1-56884-481-6
$24.99 USA/$34.99 Canada

NATIONAL BESTSELLER!

Macworld® Complete Mac® Handbook Plus Interactive CD, 3rd Edition

by Jim Heid

BMUG SPRING 1995 CHOICE PRODUCT

ISBN: 1-56884-192-2
$39.95 USA/$54.95 Canada

Includes an interactive CD-ROM.

NEWBRIDGE BOOK CLUB SELECTION

Macworld® Ultimate Mac® CD-ROM

by Jim Heid

ISBN: 1-56884-477-8
$19.99 USA/$26.99 Canada

CD-ROM includes version 2.0 of QuickTime, and over 65 MB of the best shareware, freeware, fonts, sounds, and more!

Macworld® Networking Bible, 2nd Edition

by Dave Kosiur & Joel M. Snyder

ISBN: 1-56884-194-9
$29.95 USA/$39.95 Canada

Macworld® Photoshop 3 Bible, 2nd Edition

by Deke McClelland

ISBN: 1-56884-158-2
$39.95 USA/$54.95 Canada

Includes stunning CD-ROM with add-ons, digitized photos and more.

WINNERS 1994-95 TECHNICAL PUBLICATIONS AND ART COMPETITIONS OF THE SOCIETY FOR TECHNICAL COMMUNICATION

NEW!

Macworld® Photoshop 2.5 Bible

by Deke McClelland

ISBN: 1-56884-022-5
$29.95 USA/$39.95 Canada

NATIONAL BESTSELLER!

Macworld® FreeHand 4 Bible

by Deke McClelland

ISBN: 1-56884-170-1
$29.95 USA/$39.95 Canada

Macworld® Illustrator 5.0/5.5 Bible

by Ted Alspach

ISBN: 1-56884-097-7
$39.95 USA/$54.95 Canada

Includes CD-ROM with QuickTime tutorials.

For scholastic requests & educational orders please call Educational Sales, at 1. 800. 434. 2086

FOR MORE INFO OR TO ORDER, PLEASE CALL ▶ 800 762 2974

For volume discounts & special orders please call Tony Real, Special Sales, at 415. 655. 3048

"Macworld Complete Mac Handbook Plus CD covered everything I could think of and more!"

Peter Tsakiris, New York, NY

"Very useful for PageMaker beginners and veterans alike— contains a wealth of tips and tricks to make you a faster, more powerful PageMaker user."

Paul Brainerd, President and founder, Aldus Corporation

"Thanks for the best computer book I've ever read—*Photoshop 2.5 Bible*. Best $30 I ever spent. I *love* the detailed index....Yours blows them all out of the water. This is a great book. We must enlighten the masses!"

Kevin Lisankie, Chicago, Illinois

"Macworld Guide to ClarisWorks 2 is the easiest computer book to read that I have ever found!"

Steven Hanson, Lutz, FL

"...thanks to the *Macworld Excel 5 Companion*, 2nd Edition occupying a permanent position next to my computer, I'll be able to tap more of Excel's power."

Lauren Black, Lab Director, *Macworld* Magazine

Macworld® QuarkXPress 3.2/3.3 Bible
by Barbara Assadi & Galen Gruman
ISBN: 1-878058-85-1
$39.95 USA/$52.95 Canada
Includes disk with QuarkXPress XTensions and scripts.

Macworld® PageMaker 5 Bible
by Craig Danuloff
ISBN: 1-878058-84-3
$39.95 USA/$52.95 Canada
Includes 2 disks with PageMaker utilities, clip art, and more.

Macworld® FileMaker Pro 2.0/2.1 Bible
by Steven A. Schwartz
ISBN: 1-56884-201-5
$34.95 USA/$46.95 Canada
Includes disk with ready-to-run data bases.

Macworld® Word 6 Companion, 2nd Edition
by Jim Heid
ISBN: 1-56884-082-9
$24.95 USA/$34.95 Canada

NEWBRIDGE BOOK CLUB SELECTION

Macworld® Guide To Microsoft® Word 5/5.1
by Jim Heid
ISBN: 1-878058-39-8
$22.95 USA/$29.95 Canada

Macworld® ClarisWorks 2.0/2.1 Companion, 2nd Edition
by Steven A. Schwartz
ISBN: 1-56884-180-9
$24.95 USA/$34.95 Canada

Macworld® Guide To Microsoft® Works 3
by Barrie Sosinsky
ISBN: 1-878058-42-8
$22.95 USA/$29.95 Canada

Macworld® Excel 5 Companion, 2nd Edition
by Chris Van Buren & David Maguiness
ISBN: 1-56884-081-0
$24.95 USA/$34.95 Canada

NEWBRIDGE BOOK CLUB SELECTION

Macworld® Guide To Microsoft® Excel 4
by David Maguiness
ISBN: 1-878058-40-1
$22.95 USA/$29.95 Canada

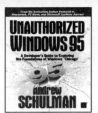

Unauthorized Windows® 95: A Developer's Guide to Exploring the Foundations of Windows "Chicago"
by Andrew Schulman

ISBN: 1-56884-169-8
$29.99 USA/$39.99 Canada

Unauthorized Windows® 95 Developer's Resource Kit
by Andrew Schulman

ISBN: 1-56884-305-4
$39.99 USA/$54.99 Canada

Best of the Net
by Seth Godin

ISBN: 1-56884-313-5
$22.99 USA/$32.99 Canada

Detour: The Truth About the Information Superhighway
by Michael Sullivan-Trainor

ISBN: 1-56884-307-0
$22.99 USA/$32.99 Canada

PowerPC Programming For Intel Programmers
by Kip McClanahan

ISBN: 1-56884-306-2
$49.99 USA/$64.99 Canada

Foundations™ of Visual C++ Programming For Windows® 95
by Paul Yao & Joseph Yao

ISBN: 1-56884-321-6
$39.99 USA/$54.99 Canada

Heavy Metal™ Visual C++ Programming
by Steve Holzner

ISBN: 1-56884-196-5
$39.95 USA/$54.95 Canada

Heavy Metal™ OLE 2.0 Programming
by Steve Holzner

ISBN: 1-56884-301-1
$39.95 USA/$54.95 Canada

Lotus Notes Application Development Handbook
by Erica Kerwien

ISBN: 1-56884-308-9
$39.99 USA/$54.99 Canada

The Internet Direct Connect Kit
by Peter John Harrison

ISBN: 1-56884-135-3
$29.95 USA/$39.95 Canada

Macworld® Ultimate Mac® Programming
by Dave Mark

ISBN: 1-56884-195-7
$39.95 USA/$54.95 Canada

The UNIX®-Haters Handbook
by Simson Garfinkel, Daniel Weise, & Steven Strassmann

ISBN: 1-56884-203-1
$16.95 USA/$22.95 Canada

Learn C++ Today!
by Martin Rinehart

ISBN: 1-56884-310-0
34.99 USA/$44.99 Canada

Type & Learn™ C
by Tom Swan

ISBN: 1-56884-073-X
34.95 USA/$44.95 Canada

Type & Learn™ Windows® Programming
by Tom Swan

ISBN: 1-56884-071-3
34.95 USA/$44.95 Canada

IBM™

IBM PRESS

IDG BOOKS WORLDWIDE

இப் புத்தகங்கள் மிகவும் நல்லவை

(way cool)

OS/2® Warp Internet Connection: Your Key to Cruising the Internet and the World Wide Web

by Deborah Morrison

OS/2 users can get warped on the Internet using the OS/2 Warp tips, techniques, and helpful directories found in *OS/2 Warp Internet Connection*. This reference covers OS/2 Warp Internet basics, such as e-mail use and how to access other computers, plus much more! The Internet gets more complex every day, but for OS/2 Warp users it just got a whole lot easier! Your value-packed disk includes 10 of the best internet utilities to help you explore the Net and save money while you're on-line!

EXPERT AUTHOR PROFILE
Deborah Morrison (Raleigh, NC) is an award-winning IBM writer who specializes in TCP/IP and the Internet. She is currently the editor-in-chief of IBM's *TCP/IP Connection* quarterly magazine.

ISBN: 1-56884-465-4
$24.99 USA/$34.99 Canada
Includes one 3.5" disk

Available: Now

Official Guide to Using OS/2® Warp

by Karla Stagray & Linda S. Rogers

IDG Books and IBM have come together to produce the most comprehensive user's guide to OS/2 Warp available today. From installation to using OS/2 Warp's BonusPak programs, this book delivers valuable help to the reader who needs to get up and running fast. Loaded with working examples, easy tips, and operating system concepts, *Official Guide to Using OS/2 Warp* is the only official user's guide authorized by IBM.

EXPERT AUTHOR PROFILE
Karla Stagray and Linda Rogers (Boca Raton, FL) both have a unique understanding of computer software and hardware. As award-winning IBM writers, Stagray and Rogers have received Society of Technical Communicators awards for various endeavors.

ISBN: 1-56884-466-2
$29.99 USA/$39.99 Canada

Available: Now

OS/2® Warp Uncensored

by Peter G. Magid & Ira H. Schneider

Exploit the power of OS/2 Warp and learn the secrets of object technology for the Workplace Shell. This all new book/CD-ROM bundle, for power users and intermediate users alike, provides the real inside story—not just the "what," but the "how" and "why" — from the folks who designed and developed the Workplace Shell. Packed with tips and techniques for using IBM's REXX programming language, and the bonus CD includes new bitmaps, icons, mouse pointers, REXX scripts, and an Object Tool!

EXPERT AUTHOR PROFILE
Peter G. Magid (Boca Raton, FL) is the User Interface Design Lead for the Workplace Shell and has over 12 years of programming experience at IBM. He is a graduate of Tulane University, and holds a B.S. degree in Computer Science.

Ira H. Schneider (Boca Raton, FL) has focused on enhancements to the Workplace Shell and has over 25 years of experience with IBM. He has held numerous lead programming positions within IBM and graduated from Northeastern University with a B.S. degree in Electrical Engineering.

ISBN: 1-56884-474-3
$39.99 USA/$54.99 Canada
Includes one CD-ROM

Available: Now

OS/2® Warp FAQs™

by Mike Kaply & Timothy F. Sipples

At last, the ultimate answer book for every OS/2 Warp user. Direct from IBM's Service Hotline, *OS/2 Warp FAQs* is a comprehensive question-and-answer guide that helps you optimize your system and save time by putting the answers to all your questions right at your fingertips. CD includes FAQs from the book in an easy-to-search format, plus hard-to-find device drivers for connecting to peripherals, such as printers.

EXPERT AUTHOR PROFILE
Mike Kaply (Boca Raton, FL) is currently on the OS/2 Help Manager Development Team at IBM in Boca Raton, Florida. He holds a B.S. degree in Mathematics and Computer Science from Southern Methodist University.

Timothy F. Sipples (Chicago, IL) is an OS/2 Warp specialist from IBM. He has written for *OS/2 Magazine* and was named "Team OS/2er of the Year" by *OS/2 Professional*.

ISBN: 1-56884-472-7
$29.99 USA/$42.99 Canada
Includes one CD-ROM

Available: Now

OS/2® Warp and PowerPC: Operating in the New Frontier

by Ken Christopher, Scott Winters & Mary Pollack Wright

The software makers at IBM unwrap the IBM and OS/2 mystique to share insights and strategies that will take business computing into the 21st century. Readers get a long, hard look at the next generation of OS/2 Warp for PowerPC.

EXPERT AUTHOR PROFILE
Ken Christopher (Boca Raton, FL) is Program Director of Development for OS/2 for Power PC. He has been a key player in the development on OS/2 Warp.

Scott Winters (Boca Raton, FL) is lead architect of OS/2 for the PowerPC. He has been instrumental in the development on OS/2 Warp on the PowerPC platform.

Mary Pollack Wright (Boca Raton, FL) is currently the technical editor for the OS/2 Techinical Library. She has been part of the OS/2 team since 1985. Her technical articles on OS/2 have been published in the *OS/2 Developer* magazine and *OS/2 Notebooks*.

ISBN: 1-56884-458-1
$29.99 USA/$39.99 Canada

Available: Now

Order Center: **(800) 762-2974** *(8 a.m.–6 p.m., EST, weekdays)*

3/26/96

Quantity	ISBN	Title	Price	Total

Shipping & Handling Charges

	Description	First book	Each additional book	Total
Domestic	Normal	$4.50	$1.50	$
	Two Day Air	$8.50	$2.50	$
	Overnight	$18.00	$3.00	$
International	Surface	$8.00	$8.00	$
	Airmail	$16.00	$16.00	$
	DHL Air	$17.00	$17.00	$

*For large quantities call for shipping & handling charges.
**Prices are subject to change without notice.

Ship to:

Name _____

Company _____

Address _____

City/State/Zip _____

Daytime Phone _____

Payment: ☐ Check to IDG Books Worldwide (US Funds Only)

☐ VISA   ☐ MasterCard   ☐ American Express

Card # _____ Expires _____

Signature _____

Subtotal _____

CA residents add
applicable sales tax _____

IN, MA, and MD
residents add
5% sales tax _____

IL residents add
6.25% sales tax _____

RI residents add
7% sales tax _____

TX residents add
8.25% sales tax _____

Shipping _____

Total _____

Please send this order form to:
IDG Books Worldwide, Inc.
Attn: Order Entry Dept.
7260 Shadeland Station, Suite 100
Indianapolis, IN 46256

Allow up to 3 weeks for delivery.
Thank you!

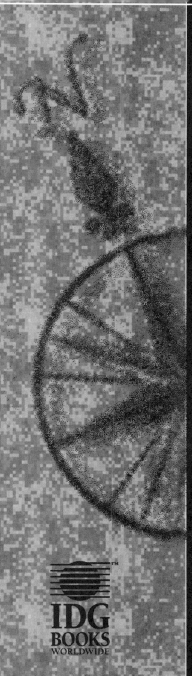

IDG BOOKS WORLDWIDE, INC.
END-USER LICENSE AGREEMENT

Read This. You should carefully read these terms and conditions before opening the software packet(s) included with this book ("Book"). This is a license agreement ("Agreement") between you and IDG Books Worldwide, Inc. ("IDGB"). By opening the accompanying software packet(s), you acknowledge that you have read and accept the following terms and conditions. If you do not agree and do not want to be bound by such terms and conditions, promptly return the Book and the unopened software packet(s) to the place you obtained them for a full refund.

1. **License Grant**. IDGB grants to you (either an individual or entity) a nonexclusive license to use one copy of the enclosed software program(s) (collectively, the "Software") solely for your own personal or business purposes on a single computer (whether a standard computer or a workstation component of a multi-user network). The Software is in use on a computer when it is loaded into temporary memory (i.e., RAM) or installed into permanent memory (e.g., hard disk, CD-ROM or other storage device). IDGB reserves all rights not expressly granted herein.

2. **Ownership**. IDGB is the owner of all rights, title and interests, including copyright, in and to the compilation of the Software recorded on the CD-ROM. Copyright to the individual programs on the CD-ROM is owned by the author or other authorized copyright owner of each program. Ownership of the Software and all proprietary rights relating thereto remain with IDGB and its licensors.

3. **Restrictions On Use and Transfer**.

   You may only (i) make one copy of the Software for backup or archival purposes, or (ii) transfer the Software to a single hard disk, provided that you keep the original for backup or archival purposes. You may not (i) rent or lease the Software, (ii) copy or reproduce the Software through a LAN or other network system or through any computer subscriber system or bulletin-board system, or (iii) modify, adapt or create derivative works based on the Software.

   You may not reverse engineer, decompile, or disassemble the Software. You may transfer the Software and user documentation on a permanent basis, provided that the transferee agrees to accept the terms and conditions of this Agreement and you retain no copies. If the Software is an update or has been updated, any transfer must include the most recent update and all prior versions.

4. **Restrictions on Use of Individual Programs**. You must follow the individual requirements and restrictions detailed for each individual program in the CD-ROM of this Book. These limitations are contained in the individual license agreements recorded on the CD-ROM. These restrictions include a requirement that after using the program for the period of time specified in its text, the user must pay a registration fee or discontinue use. By opening the Software packet(s), you will be agreeing to abide by the licenses and restrictions for these individual programs. None of the material on this disk(s) or listed in this Book may ever be distributed, in original or modified form, for commercial purposes.

5. **Limited Warranty**.

   (a) IDGB warrants that the Software and CD-ROM are free from defects in materials and workmanship under normal use for a period of sixty (60) days from the date of purchase of this Book. If IDGB receives notification within the warranty period of defects in materials or workmanship, IDGB will replace the defective CD-ROM.

   (b) IDGB AND THE AUTHOR OF THE BOOK DISCLAIM ALL OTHER WARRANTIES, EXPRESS OR IMPLIED, INCLUDING WITHOUT LIMITATION IMPLIED WARRANTIES OF MERCHANTABILITY AND FITNESS FOR A PARTICULAR PURPOSE, WITH RESPECT TO THE SOFTWARE, THE PROGRAMS, THE SOURCE CODE CONTAINED THEREIN, AND/OR THE TECHNIQUES DESCRIBED IN THIS BOOK. IDGB DOES NOT WARRANT THAT THE FUNCTIONS CONTAINED IN THE SOFTWARE WILL MEET YOUR REQUIREMENTS OR THAT THE OPERATION OF THE SOFTWARE WILL BE ERROR FREE.

   This limited warranty gives you specific legal rights, and you may have other rights which vary from jurisdiction to jurisdiction.

6. **Remedies**.

   (a) IDGB's entire liability and your exclusive remedy for defects in materials and workmanship shall be limited to replacement of the Software, which is returned to IDGB at the address set forth below with a copy of your receipt. This Limited Warranty is void if failure of the Software has resulted from accident, abuse, or misapplication. Any replacement Software will be warranted for the remainder of the original warranty period or thirty (30) days, whichever is longer.

(b) In no event shall IDGB or the author be liable for any damages whatsoever (including without limitation damages for loss of business profits, business interruption, loss of business information, or any other pecuniary loss) arising out of the use of or inability to use the Book or the Software, even if IDGB has been advised of the possibility of such damages.

(c) Because some jurisdictions do not allow the exclusion or limitation of liability for consequential or incidental damages, the above limitation or exclusion may not apply to you.

7. **U.S. Government Restricted Rights**. Use, duplication, or disclosure of the Software by the U.S. Government is subject to restrictions stated in paragraph (c) (1) (ii) of the Rights in Technical Data and Computer Software clause of DFARS 252.227-7013, and in subparagraphs (a) through (d) of the Commercial Computer—Restricted Rights clause at FAR 52.227-19, and in similar clauses in the NASA FAR supplement, when applicable.

8. **General**. This Agreement constitutes the entire understanding of the parties, and revokes and supersedes all prior agreements, oral or written, between them and may not be modified or amended except in a writing signed by both parties hereto which specifically refers to this Agreement. This Agreement shall take precedence over any other documents that may be in conflict herewith. If any one or more provisions contained in this Agreement are held by any court or tribunal to be invalid, illegal or otherwise unenforceable, each and every other provision shall remain in full force and effect.